THE INHUMANS

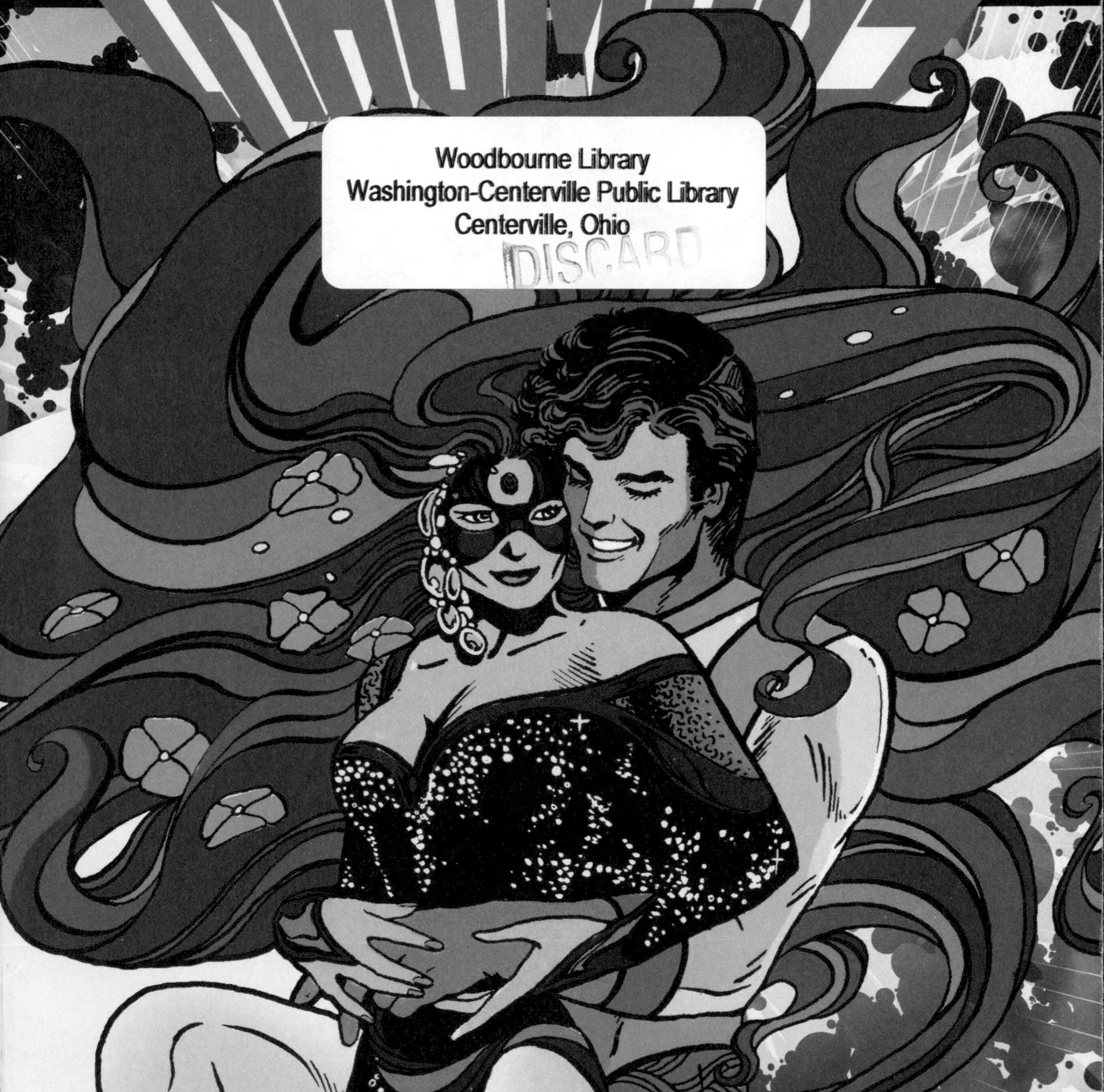

BY RIGHT OF BIRTH

BY

ANN NOCENTI, LOU MOUGIN,
BRET BLEVINS & RICHARD HOWELL

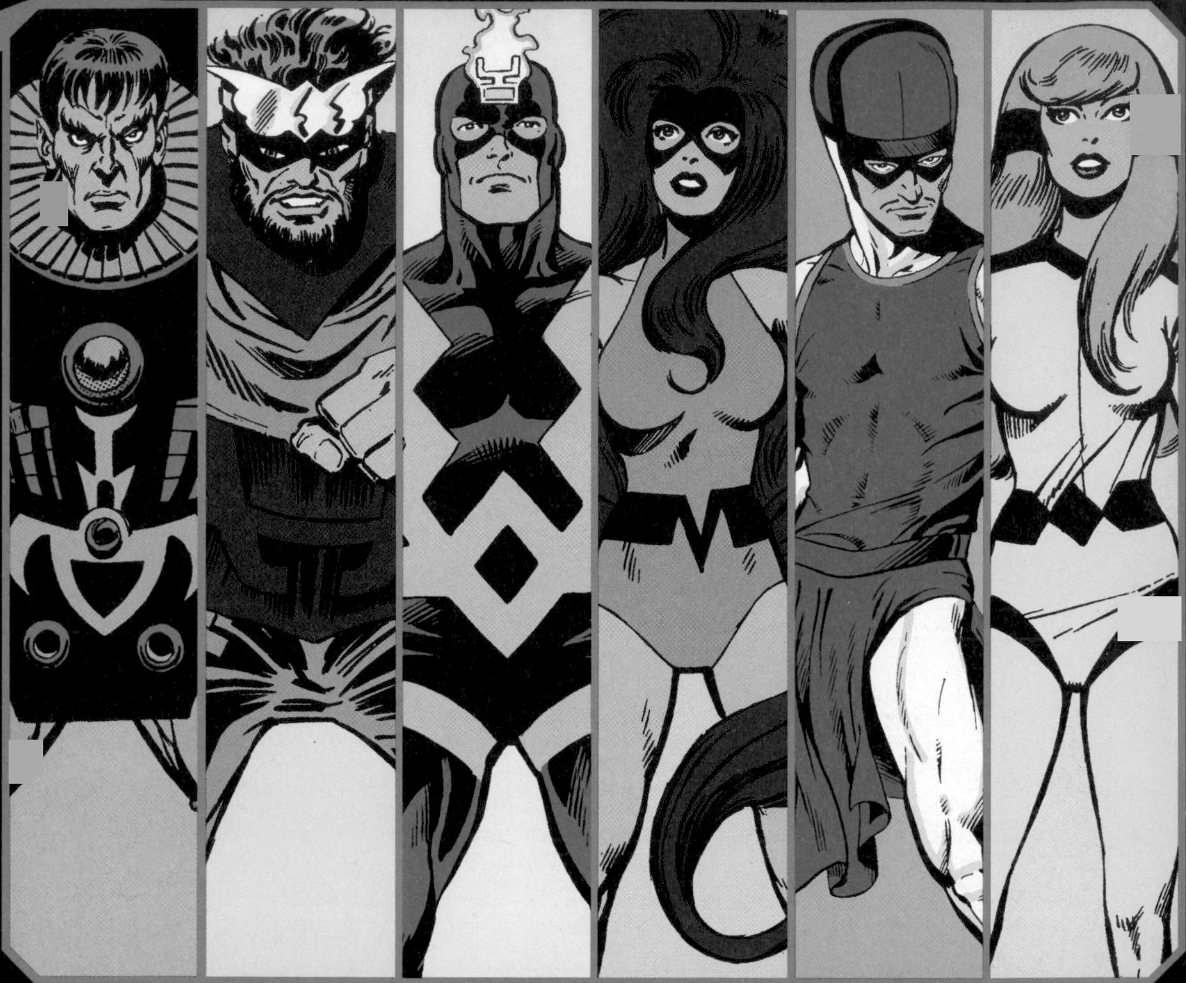

COLLECTION EDITOR: **MARK D. BEAZLEY**
ASSISTANT EDITORS: **ALEX STARBUCK** & **NELSON RIBEIRO**
EDITOR, SPECIAL PROJECTS: **JENNIFER GRÜNWALD**
SENIOR EDITOR, SPECIAL PROJECTS: **JEFF YOUNGQUIST**
RESEARCH: **STUART VANDAL**
LAYOUT: **JEPH YORK**
PRODUCTION: **COLORTEK**
BOOK DESIGNER: **RODOLFO MURAGUCHI**
SVP OF PRINT & DIGITAL PUBLISHING SALES: **DAVID GABRIEL**

EDITOR IN CHIEF: **AXEL ALONSO**
CHIEF CREATIVE OFFICER: **JOE QUESADA**
PUBLISHER: **DAN BUCKLEY**
EXECUTIVE PRODUCER: **ALAN FINE**

INHUMANS: BY RIGHT OF BIRTH. Contains material originally published in magazine form as MARVEL GRAPHIC NOVEL: THE INHUMANS and INHUMANS: THE UNTOLD SAGA. First printing 2013. ISBN# 978-0-7851-8504-8. Published by MARVEL WORLDWIDE, INC., a subsidiary of MARVEL ENTERTAINMENT, LLC. OFFICE OF PUBLICATION: 135 West 50th Street, New York, NY 10020.

Printed in the U.S.A. ALAN FINE, EVP - Office of the President, Marvel Worldwide, Inc. and EVP & CMO Marvel Characters B.V.; DAN BUCKLEY, Publisher & President - Print, Animation & Digital Divisions; JOE QUESADA, Chief Creative Officer; TOM BREVOORT, SVP of Publishing; DAVID BOGART, SVP of Operations & Procurement, Publishing; C.B. CEBULSKI, SVP of Creator & Content Development; DAVID GABRIEL, SVP of Print & Digital Publishing Sales; JIM O'KEEFE, VP of Operations & Logistics; DAN CARR, Executive Director of Publishing Technology; SUSAN CRESPI, Editorial Operations Manager; ALEX MORALES, Publishing Operations Manager; STAN LEE, Chairman Emeritus. For information regarding advertising in Marvel Comics or on Marvel.com, please contact Niza Disla, Director of Marvel Partnerships, at ndisla@marvel.com. For Marvel subscription inquiries, please call 800-217-9158. **Manufactured between 9/6/2013 and 10/14/2013 by R.R. DONNELLEY, INC., SALEM, VA, USA.**

10 9 8 7 6 5 4 3 2 1

THE INHUMANS

BY RIGHT OF BIRTH

MARVEL GRAPHIC NOVEL: THE INHUMANS & INHUMANS: THE UNTOLD SAGA

WRITERS:

ANN NOCENTI & LOU MOUGIN

PENCILERS:

BRET BLEVINS & RICHARD HOWELL

INKERS:

AL WILLIAMSON & VINCE COLLETTA

COLORISTS:

MICHAEL HIGGINS & RICHARD HOWELL

LETTERERS:

JIM NOVAK, GASPAR SALADINO & DIANA ALBERS

ASSISTANT EDITOR:

DARYL EDELMAN

EDITORS:

BOB HARRAS & MARK GRUENWALD

FRONT COVER ARTISTS:

BRET BLEVINS & THOMAS MASON

BACK COVER ARTISTS:

RICHARD HOWELL & MATT MILLA

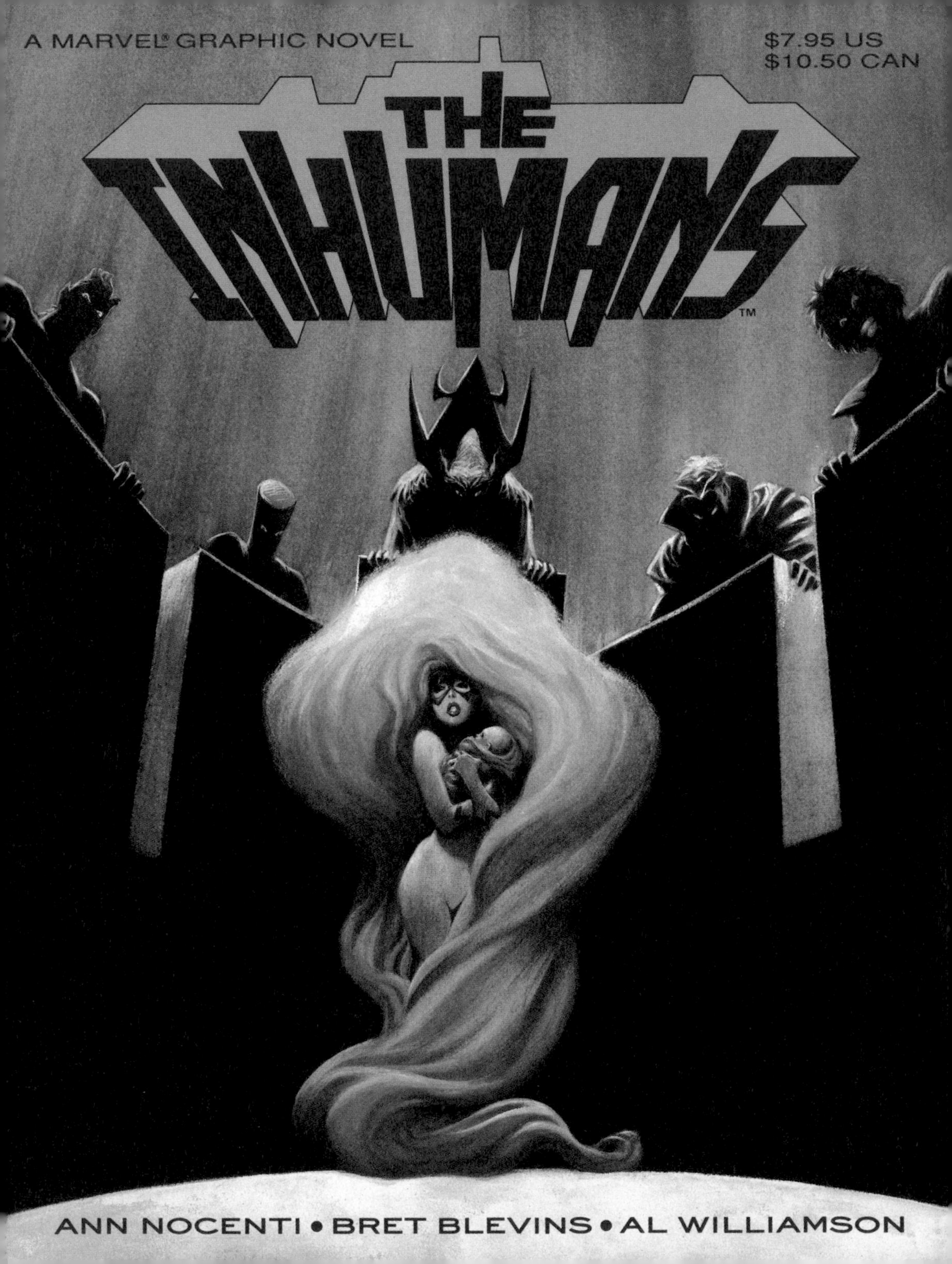
A MARVEL® GRAPHIC NOVEL
$7.95 US
$10.50 CAN
THE INHUMANS™
ANN NOCENTI • BRET BLEVINS • AL WILLIAMSON

A MARVEL® GRAPHIC NOVEL

the
INHUMANS

by

ANN NOCENTI
writer

BRET BLEVINS
penciler

AL WILLIAMSON
inker

JIM NOVAK

GASPAR SALADINO
letterers

MICHAEL HIGGINS
colorist

DARYL EDELMAN
assistant editor

BOB HARRAS
editor

TOM DeFALCO
editor in chief

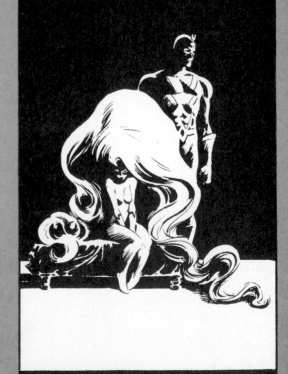

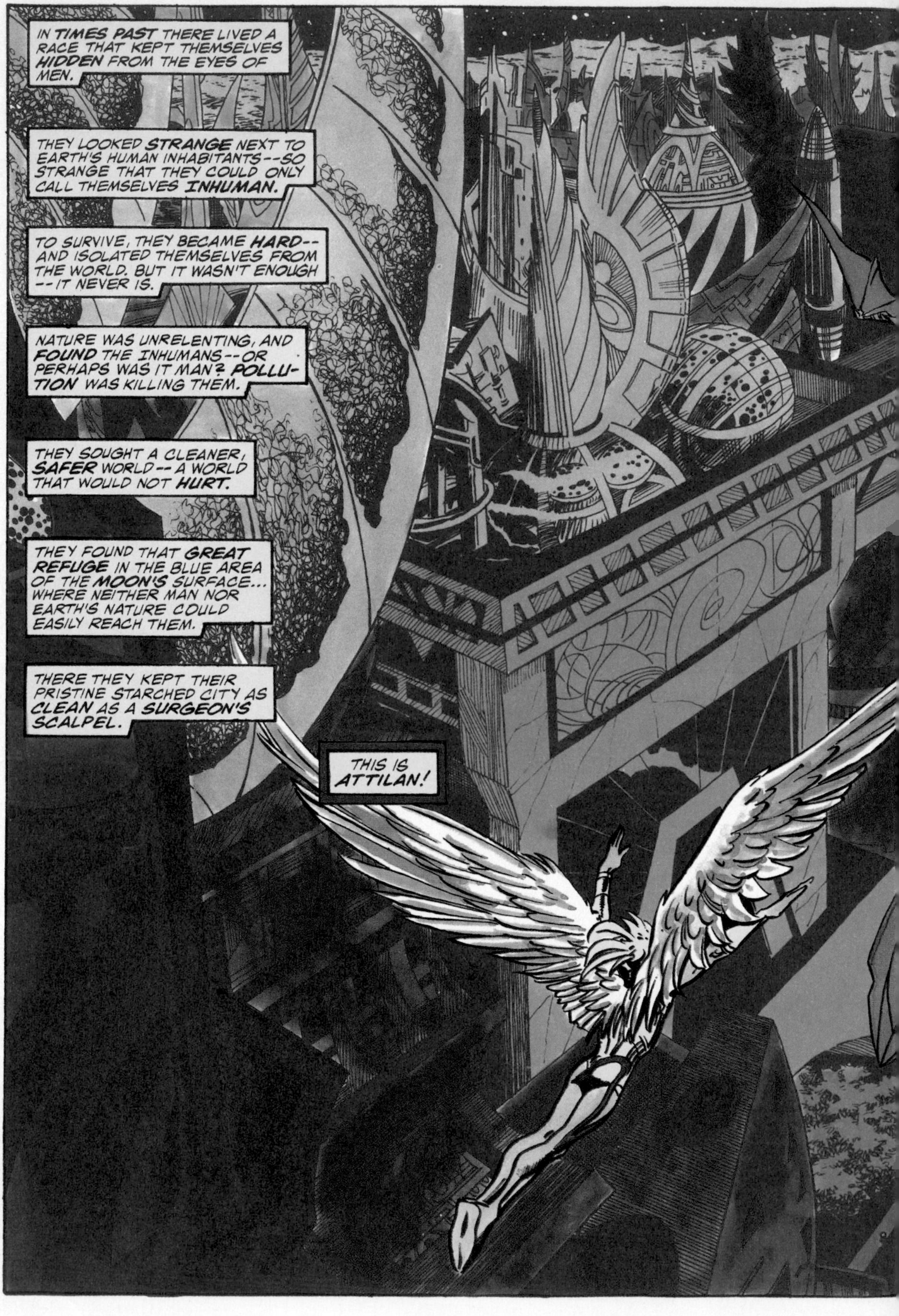
IN TIMES PAST THERE LIVED A RACE THAT KEPT THEMSELVES HIDDEN FROM THE EYES OF MEN.
THEY LOOKED STRANGE NEXT TO EARTH'S HUMAN INHABITANTS--SO STRANGE THAT THEY COULD ONLY CALL THEMSELVES INHUMAN.
TO SURVIVE, THEY BECAME HARD--AND ISOLATED THEMSELVES FROM THE WORLD. BUT IT WASN'T ENOUGH--IT NEVER IS.
NATURE WAS UNRELENTING, AND FOUND THE INHUMANS--OR PERHAPS WAS IT MAN? POLLUTION WAS KILLING THEM.
THEY SOUGHT A CLEANER, SAFER WORLD--A WORLD THAT WOULD NOT HURT.
THEY FOUND THAT GREAT REFUGE IN THE BLUE AREA OF THE MOON'S SURFACE... WHERE NEITHER MAN NOR EARTH'S NATURE COULD EASILY REACH THEM.
THERE THEY KEPT THEIR PRISTINE STARCHED CITY AS CLEAN AS A SURGEON'S SCALPEL.
THIS IS ATTILAN!

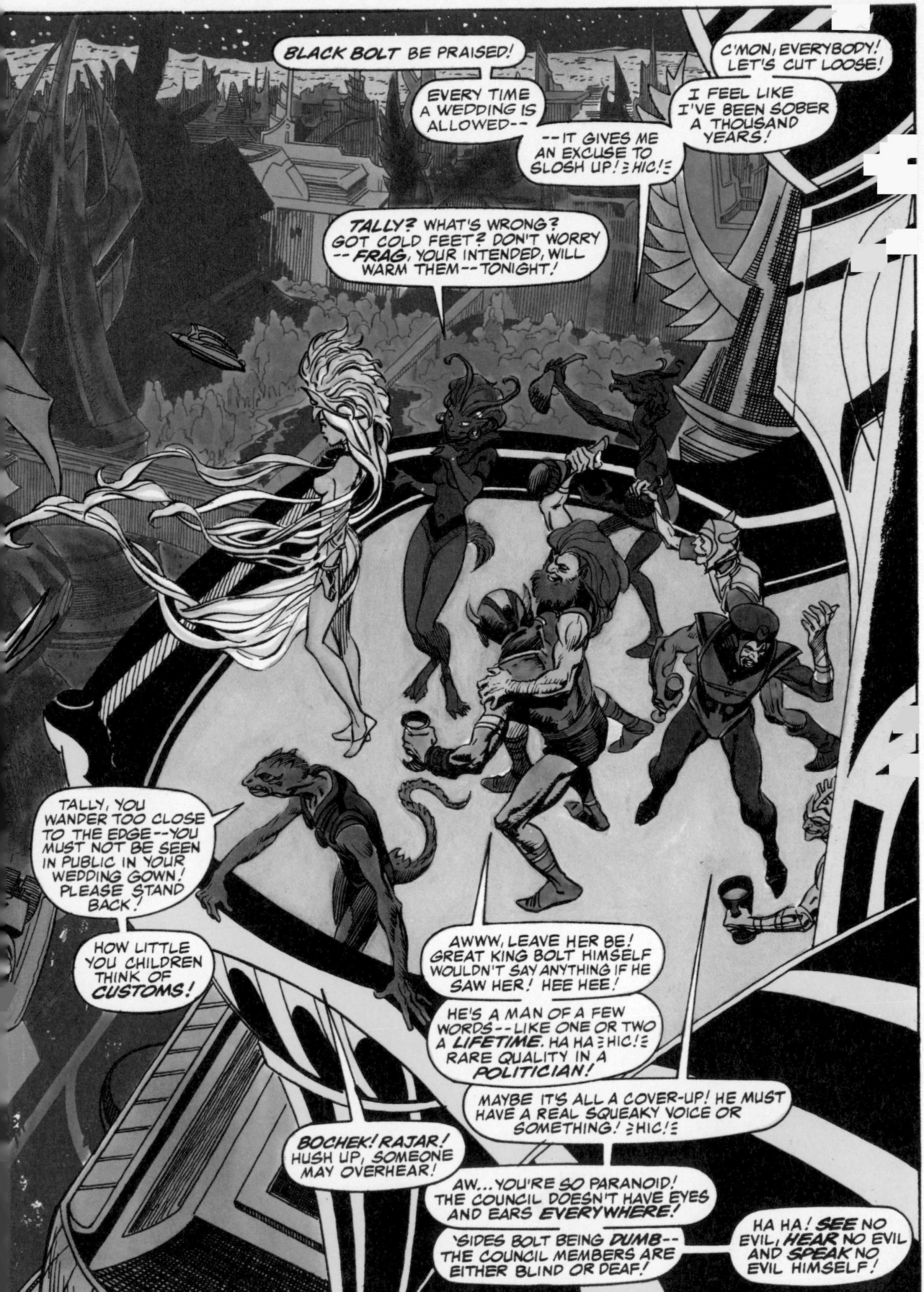
BLACK BOLT BE PRAISED!
EVERY TIME A WEDDING IS ALLOWED--
--IT GIVES ME AN EXCUSE TO SLOSH UP! ≡HIC!≡
C'MON, EVERYBODY! LET'S CUT LOOSE!
I FEEL LIKE I'VE BEEN SOBER A THOUSAND YEARS!
TALLY? WHAT'S WRONG? GOT COLD FEET? DON'T WORRY --FRAG, YOUR INTENDED, WILL WARM THEM--TONIGHT!
TALLY, YOU WANDER TOO CLOSE TO THE EDGE--YOU MUST NOT BE SEEN IN PUBLIC IN YOUR WEDDING GOWN! PLEASE STAND BACK!
HOW LITTLE YOU CHILDREN THINK OF CUSTOMS!
AWWW, LEAVE HER BE! GREAT KING BOLT HIMSELF WOULDN'T SAY ANYTHING IF HE SAW HER! HEE HEE!
HE'S A MAN OF A FEW WORDS--LIKE ONE OR TWO A LIFETIME. HA HA ≡HIC!≡ RARE QUALITY IN A POLITICIAN!
MAYBE IT'S ALL A COVER-UP! HE MUST HAVE A REAL SQUEAKY VOICE OR SOMETHING! ≡HIC!≡
BOCHEK! RAJAR! HUSH UP, SOMEONE MAY OVERHEAR!
AW... YOU'RE SO PARANOID! THE COUNCIL DOESN'T HAVE EYES AND EARS EVERYWHERE!
'SIDES BOLT BEING DUMB-- THE COUNCIL MEMBERS ARE EITHER BLIND OR DEAF!
HA HA! SEE NO EVIL, HEAR NO EVIL AND SPEAK NO EVIL HIMSELF!

BAH! YOU ALL COMPLAIN THE COUNCIL'S LAWS ARE SO STIFLING AND REPRESSIVE...

TALLY'S SO LUCKY--I HOPE THE COUNCIL PICKS ME A HUSBAND SOON!

HOW PRETTILY IT FLUTTERS... AS IF IT WERE ALIVE.

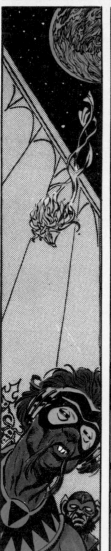

WHAT'S THAT WHITE THING FALLING TO-WARDS US?

IT'S A GIRL!

SHE'S FALLING!

WHO'S FALLING?

8

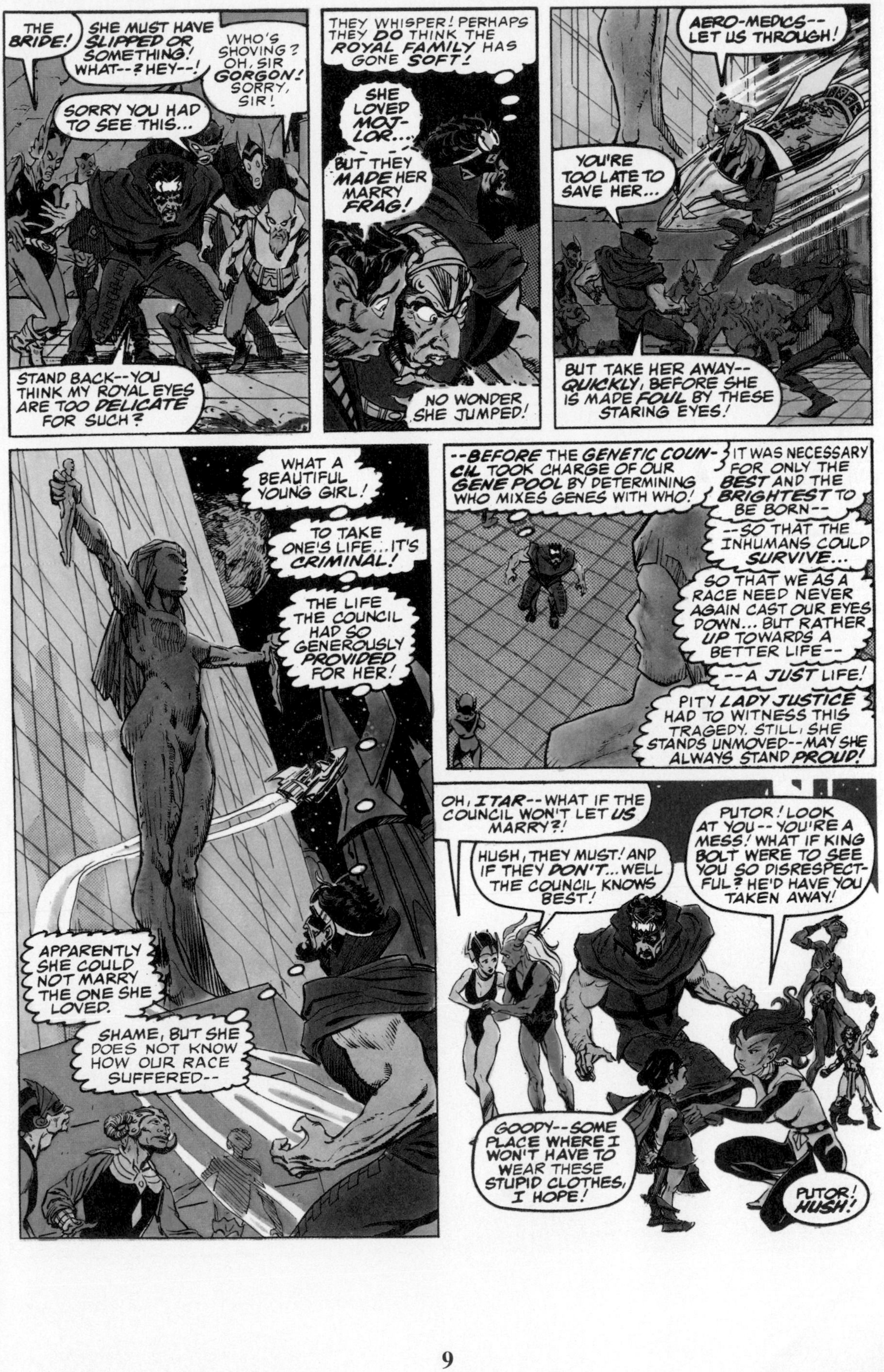
THE BRIDE!
SHE MUST HAVE SLIPPED OR SOMETHING! WHAT--? HEY--!
WHO'S SHOVING? OH, SIR GORGON! SORRY, SIR!
SORRY YOU HAD TO SEE THIS...
STAND BACK--YOU THINK MY ROYAL EYES ARE TOO DELICATE FOR SUCH?
THEY WHISPER! PERHAPS THEY DO THINK THE ROYAL FAMILY HAS GONE SOFT!
SHE LOVED MOJ-LOR....
BUT THEY MADE HER MARRY FRAG!
NO WONDER SHE JUMPED!
AERO-MEDICS--LET US THROUGH!
YOU'RE TOO LATE TO SAVE HER...
BUT TAKE HER AWAY--QUICKLY, BEFORE SHE IS MADE FOUL BY THESE STARING EYES!
WHAT A BEAUTIFUL YOUNG GIRL!
TO TAKE ONE'S LIFE... IT'S CRIMINAL!
THE LIFE THE COUNCIL HAD SO GENEROUSLY PROVIDED FOR HER!
APPARENTLY SHE COULD NOT MARRY THE ONE SHE LOVED.
SHAME, BUT SHE DOES NOT KNOW HOW OUR RACE SUFFERED--
--BEFORE THE GENETIC COUNCIL TOOK CHARGE OF OUR GENE POOL BY DETERMINING WHO MIXES GENES WITH WHO!
IT WAS NECESSARY FOR ONLY THE BEST AND THE BRIGHTEST TO BE BORN--
--SO THAT THE INHUMANS COULD SURVIVE...
SO THAT WE AS A RACE NEED NEVER AGAIN CAST OUR EYES DOWN... BUT RATHER UP TOWARDS A BETTER LIFE--
--A JUST LIFE!
PITY LADY JUSTICE HAD TO WITNESS THIS TRAGEDY. STILL, SHE STANDS UNMOVED--MAY SHE ALWAYS STAND PROUD!
OH, ITAR--WHAT IF THE COUNCIL WON'T LET US MARRY?!
HUSH, THEY MUST! AND IF THEY DON'T... WELL THE COUNCIL KNOWS BEST!
PUTOR! LOOK AT YOU--YOU'RE A MESS! WHAT IF KING BOLT WERE TO SEE YOU SO DISRESPECTFUL? HE'D HAVE YOU TAKEN AWAY!
GOODY--SOME PLACE WHERE I WON'T HAVE TO WEAR THESE STUPID CLOTHES, I HOPE!
PUTOR! HUSH!

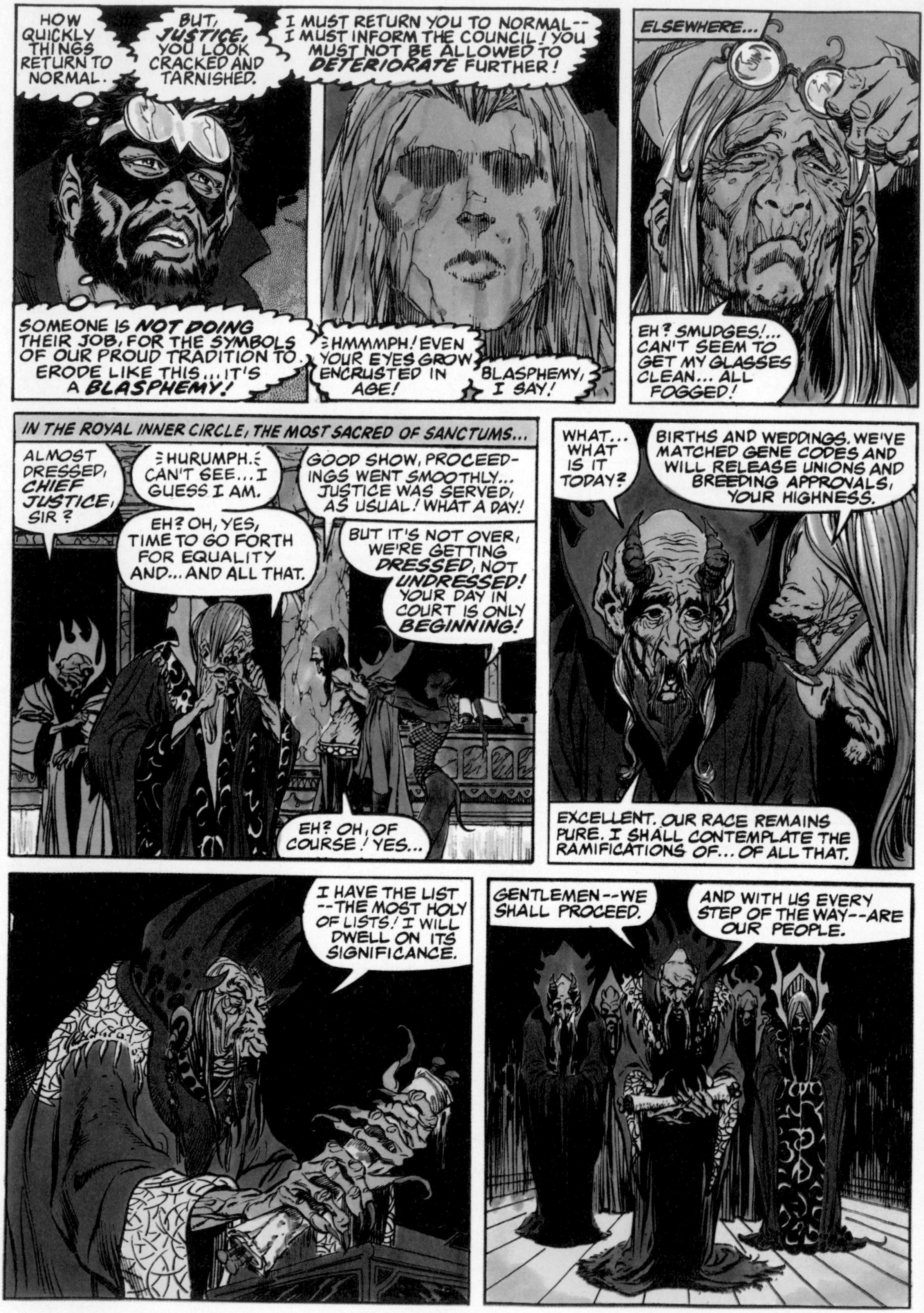
HOW QUICKLY THINGS RETURN TO NORMAL.
BUT, JUSTICE, YOU LOOK CRACKED AND TARNISHED.
I MUST RETURN YOU TO NORMAL-- I MUST INFORM THE COUNCIL! YOU MUST NOT BE ALLOWED TO DETERIORATE FURTHER!
SOMEONE IS NOT DOING THEIR JOB, FOR THE SYMBOLS OF OUR PROUD TRADITION TO ERODE LIKE THIS... IT'S A BLASPHEMY!
HMMMPH! EVEN YOUR EYES GROW ENCRUSTED IN AGE!
BLASPHEMY, I SAY!
ELSEWHERE...
EH? SMUDGES!... CAN'T SEEM TO GET MY GLASSES CLEAN... ALL FOGGED!
IN THE ROYAL INNER CIRCLE, THE MOST SACRED OF SANCTUMS...
ALMOST DRESSED, CHIEF JUSTICE, SIR?
HURUMPH. CAN'T SEE... I GUESS I AM.
GOOD SHOW, PROCEEDINGS WENT SMOOTHLY... JUSTICE WAS SERVED, AS USUAL! WHAT A DAY!
EH? OH, YES, TIME TO GO FORTH FOR EQUALITY AND... AND ALL THAT.
BUT IT'S NOT OVER, WE'RE GETTING DRESSED, NOT UNDRESSED! YOUR DAY IN COURT IS ONLY BEGINNING!
EH? OH, OF COURSE! YES...
WHAT... WHAT IS IT TODAY?
BIRTHS AND WEDDINGS. WE'VE MATCHED GENE CODES AND WILL RELEASE UNIONS AND BREEDING APPROVALS, YOUR HIGHNESS.
EXCELLENT. OUR RACE REMAINS PURE. I SHALL CONTEMPLATE THE RAMIFICATIONS OF... OF ALL THAT.
I HAVE THE LIST --THE MOST HOLY OF LISTS! I WILL DWELL ON ITS SIGNIFICANCE.
GENTLEMEN--WE SHALL PROCEED.
AND WITH US EVERY STEP OF THE WAY--ARE OUR PEOPLE.

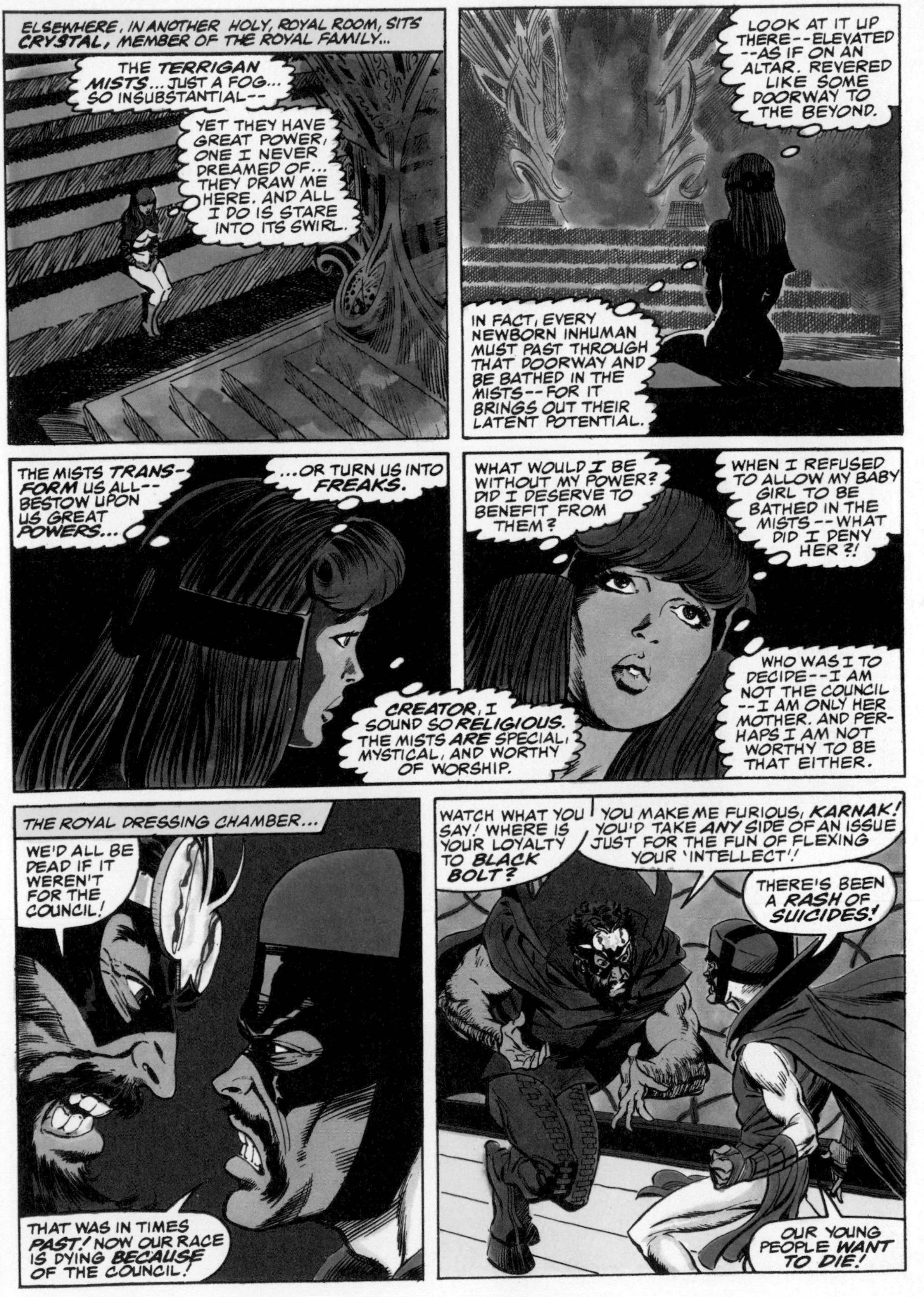
ELSEWHERE, IN ANOTHER HOLY, ROYAL ROOM, SITS CRYSTAL, MEMBER OF THE ROYAL FAMILY...
THE TERRIGAN MISTS... JUST A FOG... SO INSUBSTANTIAL--
YET THEY HAVE GREAT POWER, ONE I NEVER DREAMED OF... THEY DRAW ME HERE. AND ALL I DO IS STARE INTO ITS SWIRL.
LOOK AT IT UP THERE--ELEVATED --AS IF ON AN ALTAR. REVERED LIKE SOME DOORWAY TO THE BEYOND.
IN FACT, EVERY NEWBORN INHUMAN MUST PAST THROUGH THAT DOORWAY AND BE BATHED IN THE MISTS--FOR IT BRINGS OUT THEIR LATENT POTENTIAL.
THE MISTS TRANS-FORM US ALL-- BESTOW UPON US GREAT POWERS...
...OR TURN US INTO FREAKS.
CREATOR, I SOUND SO RELIGIOUS. THE MISTS ARE SPECIAL, MYSTICAL, AND WORTHY OF WORSHIP.
WHAT WOULD I BE WITHOUT MY POWER? DID I DESERVE TO BENEFIT FROM THEM?
WHEN I REFUSED TO ALLOW MY BABY GIRL TO BE BATHED IN THE MISTS--WHAT DID I DENY HER?!
WHO WAS I TO DECIDE--I AM NOT THE COUNCIL --I AM ONLY HER MOTHER. AND PER-HAPS I AM NOT WORTHY TO BE THAT EITHER.
THE ROYAL DRESSING CHAMBER...
WE'D ALL BE DEAD IF IT WEREN'T FOR THE COUNCIL!
THAT WAS IN TIMES PAST! NOW OUR RACE IS DYING BECAUSE OF THE COUNCIL!
WATCH WHAT YOU SAY! WHERE IS YOUR LOYALTY TO BLACK BOLT?
YOU MAKE ME FURIOUS, KARNAK! YOU'D TAKE ANY SIDE OF AN ISSUE JUST FOR THE FUN OF FLEXING YOUR 'INTELLECT'!
THERE'S BEEN A RASH OF SUICIDES!
OUR YOUNG PEOPLE WANT TO DIE!

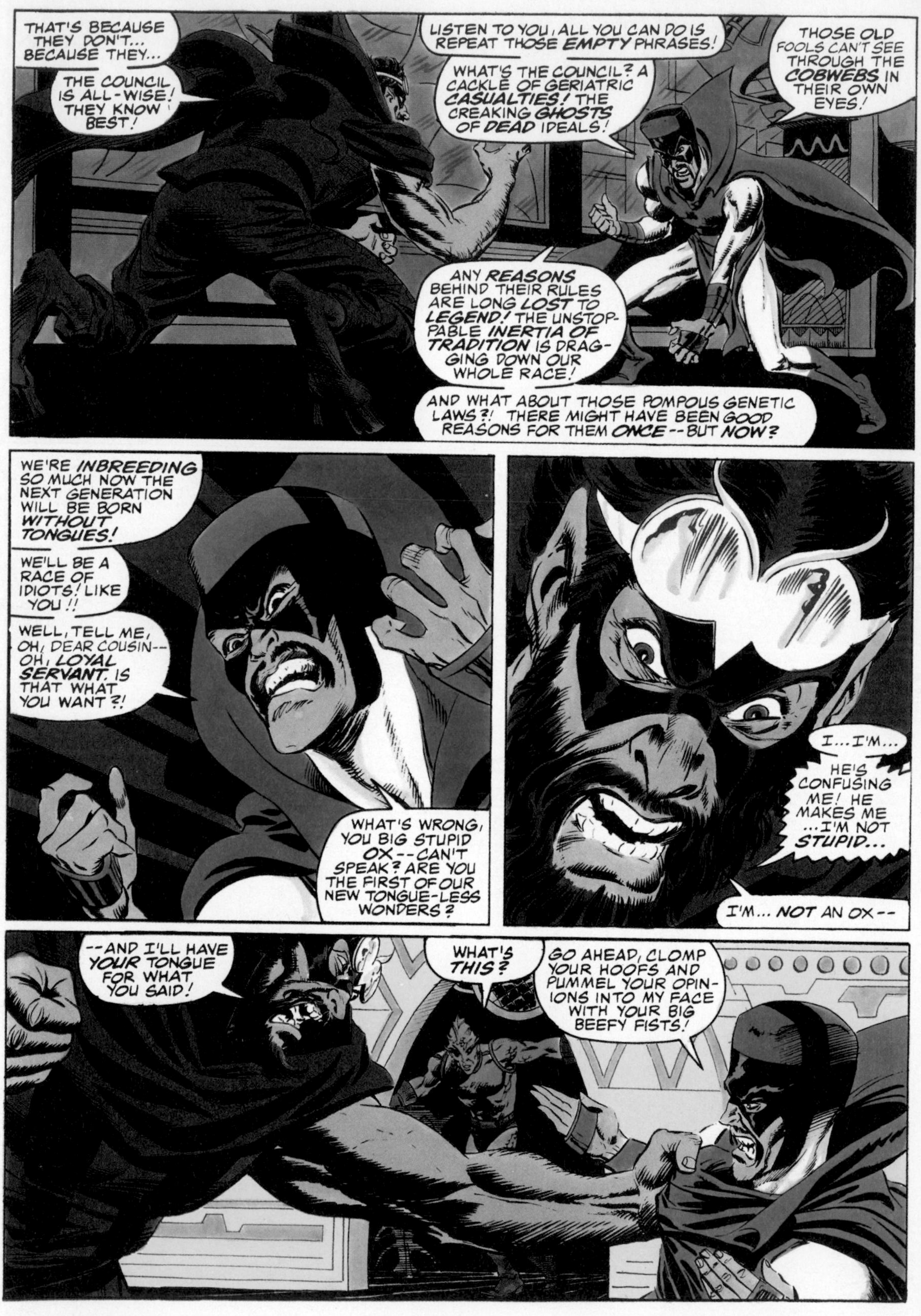
THAT'S BECAUSE THEY DON'T... BECAUSE THEY...
THE COUNCIL IS ALL-WISE! THEY KNOW BEST!
LISTEN TO YOU, ALL YOU CAN DO IS REPEAT THOSE EMPTY PHRASES!
WHAT'S THE COUNCIL? A CACKLE OF GERIATRIC CASUALTIES! THE CREAKING GHOSTS OF DEAD IDEALS!
THOSE OLD FOOLS CAN'T SEE THROUGH THE COBWEBS IN THEIR OWN EYES!
ANY REASONS BEHIND THEIR RULES ARE LONG LOST TO LEGEND! THE UNSTOPPABLE INERTIA OF TRADITION IS DRAGGING DOWN OUR WHOLE RACE!
AND WHAT ABOUT THOSE POMPOUS GENETIC LAWS?! THERE MIGHT HAVE BEEN GOOD REASONS FOR THEM ONCE -- BUT NOW?
WE'RE INBREEDING SO MUCH NOW THE NEXT GENERATION WILL BE BORN WITHOUT TONGUES!
WE'LL BE A RACE OF IDIOTS! LIKE YOU!!
WELL, TELL ME, OH, DEAR COUSIN-- OH, LOYAL SERVANT, IS THAT WHAT YOU WANT?!
WHAT'S WRONG, YOU BIG STUPID OX -- CAN'T SPEAK? ARE YOU THE FIRST OF OUR NEW TONGUE-LESS WONDERS?
I... I'M...
HE'S CONFUSING ME! HE MAKES ME ...I'M NOT STUPID...
I'M... NOT AN OX --
-- AND I'LL HAVE YOUR TONGUE FOR WHAT YOU SAID!
WHAT'S THIS?
GO AHEAD, CLOMP YOUR HOOFS AND PUMMEL YOUR OPINIONS INTO MY FACE WITH YOUR BIG BEEFY FISTS!

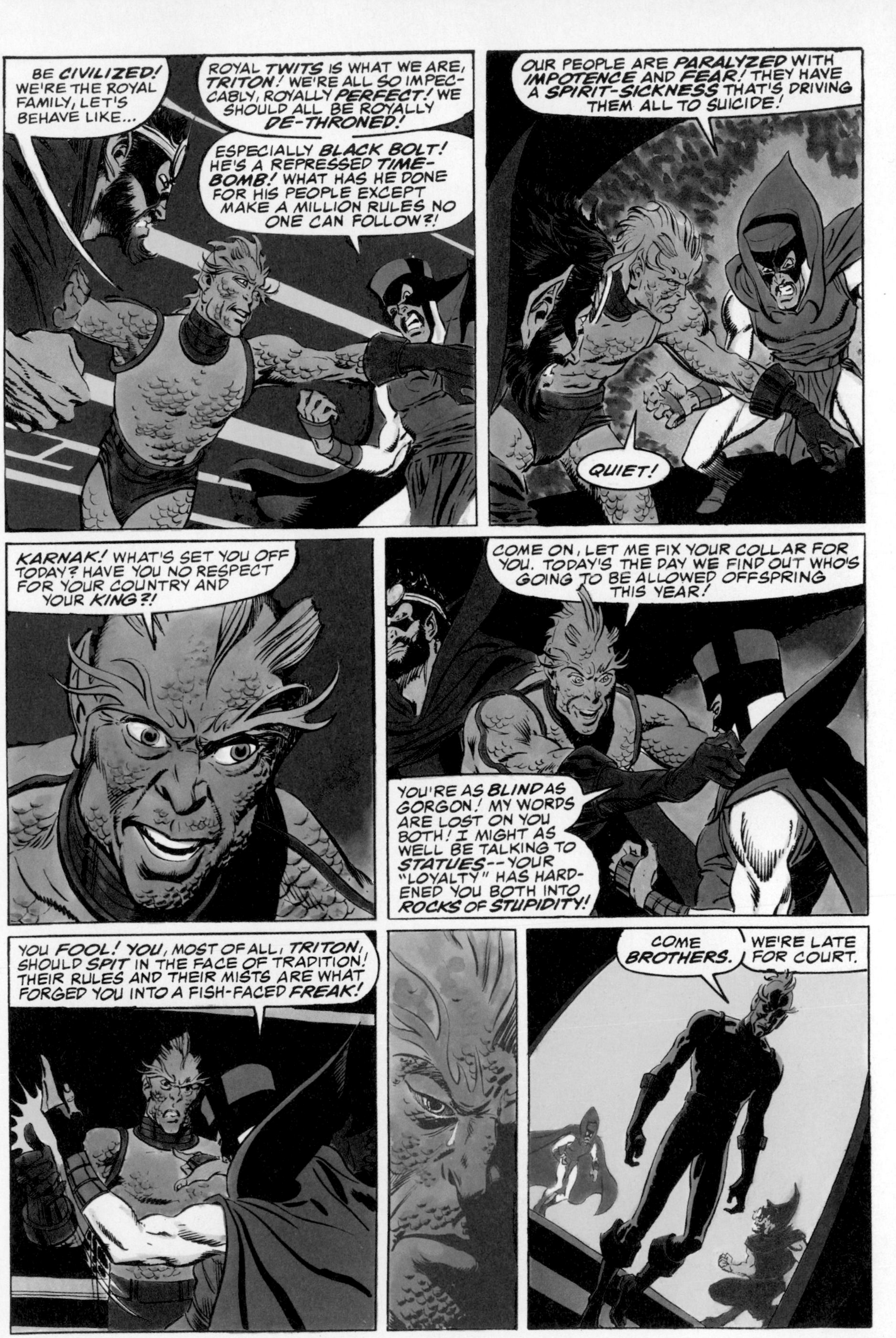
BE CIVILIZED! WE'RE THE ROYAL FAMILY, LET'S BEHAVE LIKE...
ROYAL TWITS IS WHAT WE ARE, TRITON! WE'RE ALL SO IMPECCABLY, ROYALLY PERFECT! WE SHOULD ALL BE ROYALLY DE-THRONED!
ESPECIALLY BLACK BOLT! HE'S A REPRESSED TIME-BOMB! WHAT HAS HE DONE FOR HIS PEOPLE EXCEPT MAKE A MILLION RULES NO ONE CAN FOLLOW?!
OUR PEOPLE ARE PARALYZED WITH IMPOTENCE AND FEAR! THEY HAVE A SPIRIT-SICKNESS THAT'S DRIVING THEM ALL TO SUICIDE!
QUIET!
KARNAK! WHAT'S SET YOU OFF TODAY? HAVE YOU NO RESPECT FOR YOUR COUNTRY AND YOUR KING?!
COME ON, LET ME FIX YOUR COLLAR FOR YOU. TODAY'S THE DAY WE FIND OUT WHO'S GOING TO BE ALLOWED OFFSPRING THIS YEAR!
YOU'RE AS BLIND AS GORGON! MY WORDS ARE LOST ON YOU BOTH! I MIGHT AS WELL BE TALKING TO STATUES--YOUR "LOYALTY" HAS HARDENED YOU BOTH INTO ROCKS OF STUPIDITY!
YOU FOOL! YOU, MOST OF ALL, TRITON, SHOULD SPIT IN THE FACE OF TRADITION! THEIR RULES AND THEIR MISTS ARE WHAT FORGED YOU INTO A FISH-FACED FREAK!
COME BROTHERS.
WE'RE LATE FOR COURT.

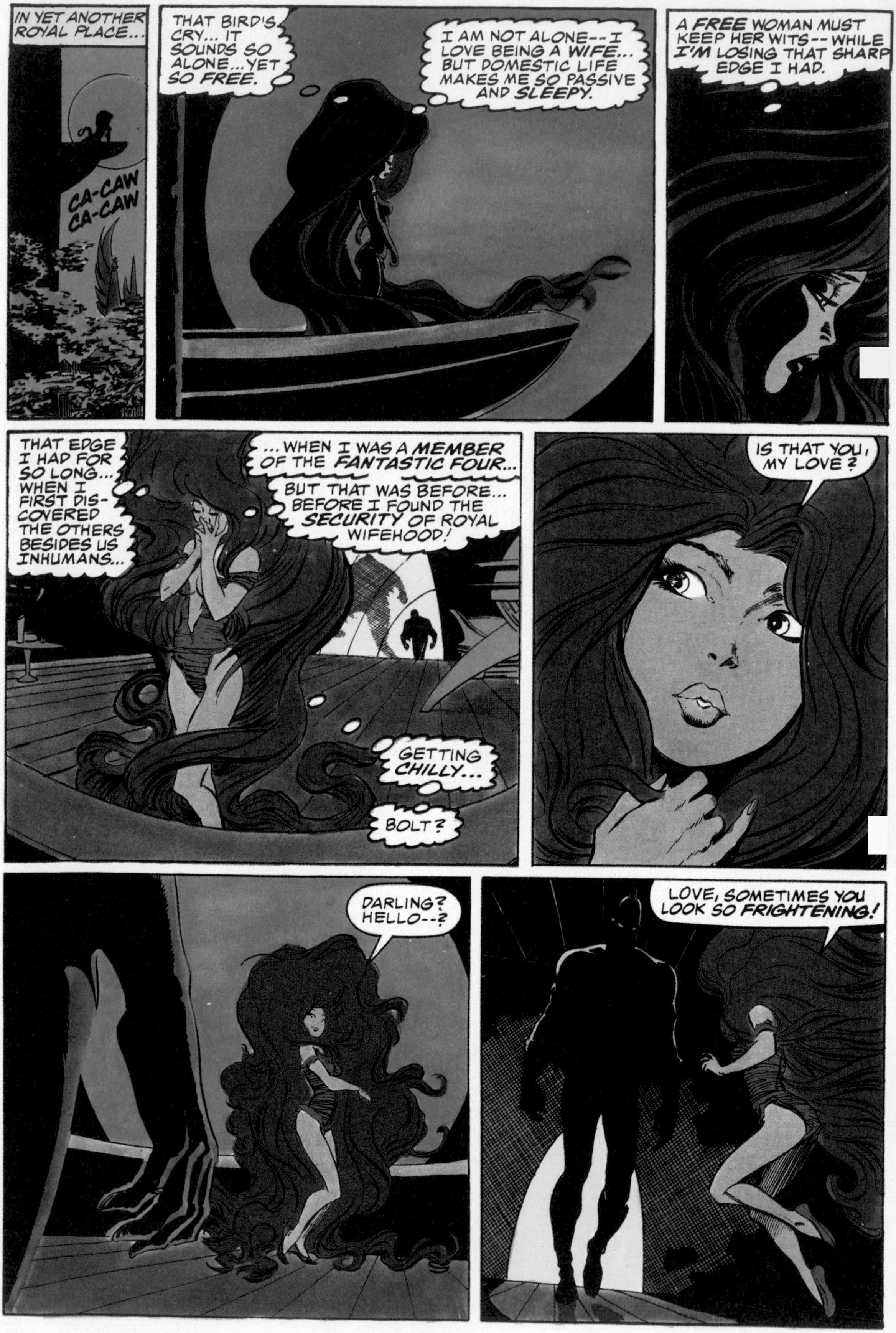
IN YET ANOTHER ROYAL PLACE...
CA-CAW CA-CAW
THAT BIRD'S CRY... IT SOUNDS SO ALONE... YET SO FREE.
I AM NOT ALONE-- I LOVE BEING A WIFE... BUT DOMESTIC LIFE MAKES ME SO PASSIVE AND SLEEPY.
A FREE WOMAN MUST KEEP HER WITS-- WHILE I'M LOSING THAT SHARP EDGE I HAD.
THAT EDGE I HAD FOR SO LONG... WHEN I FIRST DISCOVERED THE OTHERS BESIDES US INHUMANS...
...WHEN I WAS A MEMBER OF THE FANTASTIC FOUR...
BUT THAT WAS BEFORE... BEFORE I FOUND THE SECURITY OF ROYAL WIFEHOOD!
GETTING CHILLY...
BOLT?
IS THAT YOU, MY LOVE?
DARLING? HELLO--?
LOVE, SOMETIMES YOU LOOK SO FRIGHTENING!

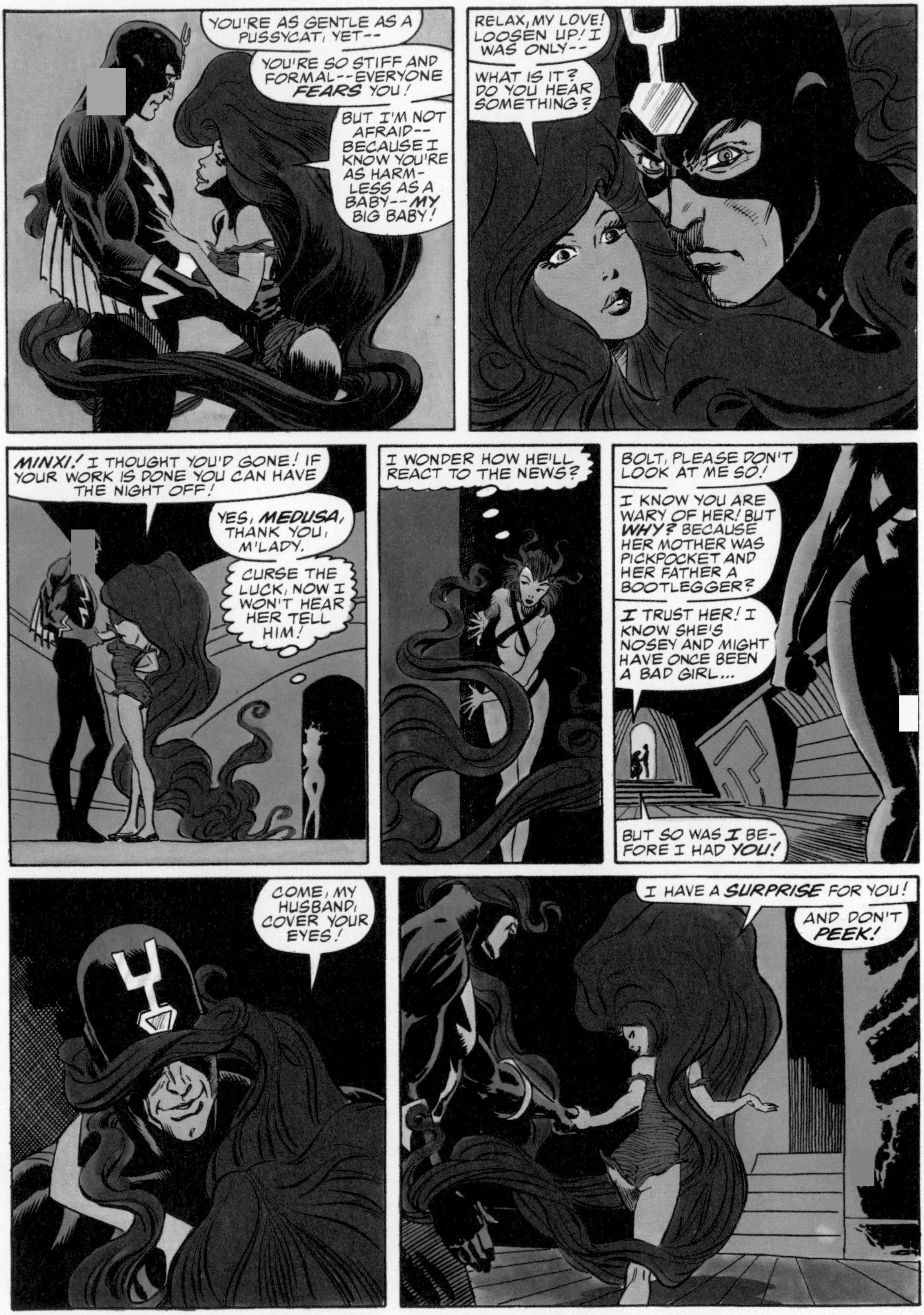
YOU'RE AS GENTLE AS A PUSSYCAT, YET--
YOU'RE SO STIFF AND FORMAL--EVERYONE FEARS YOU!
BUT I'M NOT AFRAID--BECAUSE I KNOW YOU'RE AS HARMLESS AS A BABY--MY BIG BABY!
RELAX, MY LOVE! LOOSEN UP! I WAS ONLY--
WHAT IS IT? DO YOU HEAR SOMETHING?
MINXI! I THOUGHT YOU'D GONE! IF YOUR WORK IS DONE YOU CAN HAVE THE NIGHT OFF!
YES, MEDUSA, THANK YOU, M'LADY.
CURSE THE LUCK, NOW I WON'T HEAR HER TELL HIM!
I WONDER HOW HE'LL REACT TO THE NEWS?
BOLT, PLEASE DON'T LOOK AT ME SO!
I KNOW YOU ARE WARY OF HER! BUT WHY? BECAUSE HER MOTHER WAS PICKPOCKET AND HER FATHER A BOOTLEGGER?
I TRUST HER! I KNOW SHE'S NOSEY AND MIGHT HAVE ONCE BEEN A BAD GIRL...
BUT SO WAS I BEFORE I HAD YOU!
COME, MY HUSBAND, COVER YOUR EYES!
I HAVE A SURPRISE FOR YOU!
AND DON'T PEEK!

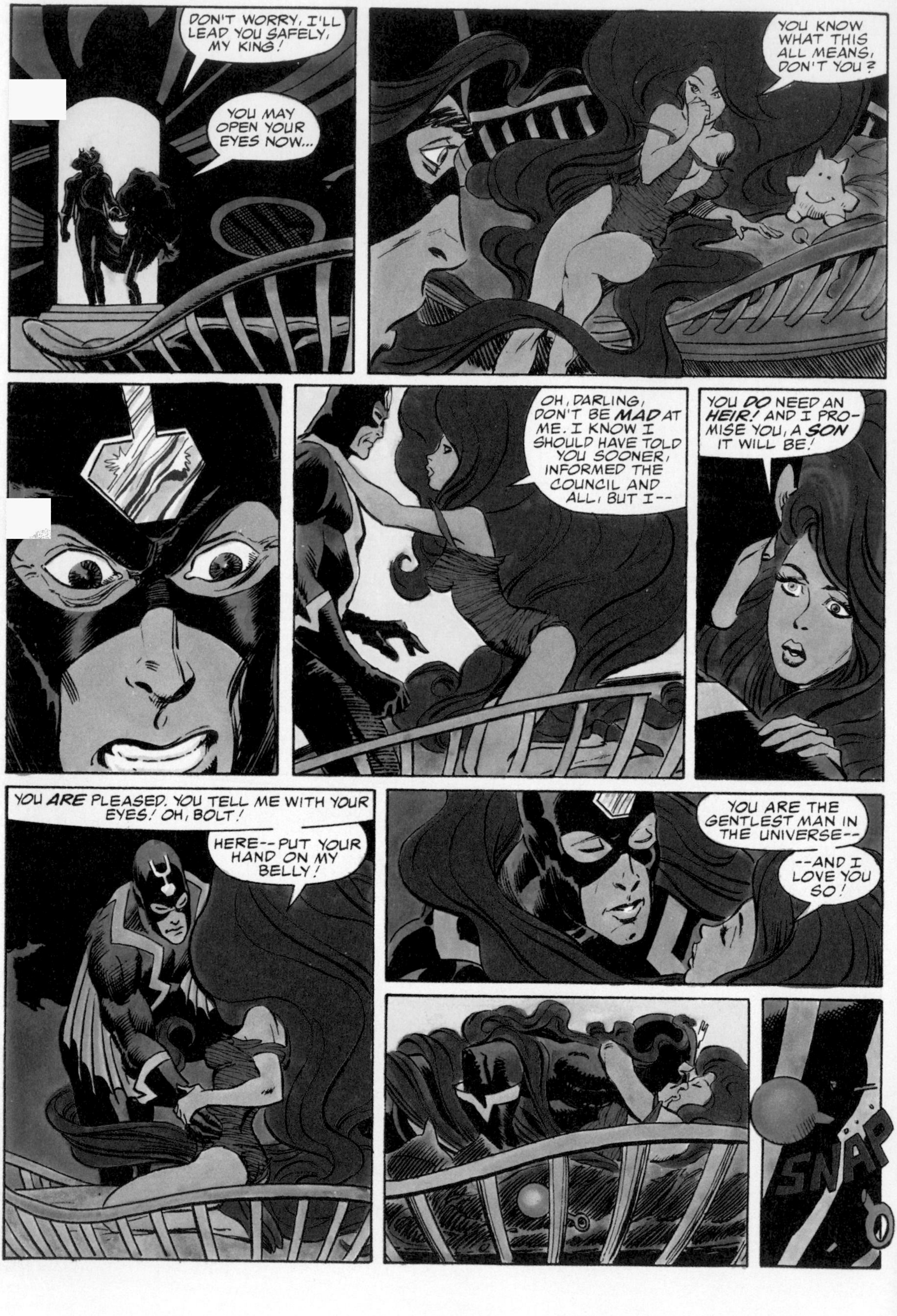
DON'T WORRY, I'LL LEAD YOU SAFELY, MY KING!
YOU MAY OPEN YOUR EYES NOW...
YOU KNOW WHAT THIS ALL MEANS, DON'T YOU?
OH, DARLING, DON'T BE MAD AT ME. I KNOW I SHOULD HAVE TOLD YOU SOONER, INFORMED THE COUNCIL AND ALL, BUT I--
YOU DO NEED AN HEIR! AND I PROMISE YOU, A SON IT WILL BE!
YOU ARE PLEASED. YOU TELL ME WITH YOUR EYES! OH, BOLT!
HERE--PUT YOUR HAND ON MY BELLY!
YOU ARE THE GENTLEST MAN IN THE UNIVERSE--
--AND I LOVE YOU SO!
SNAP

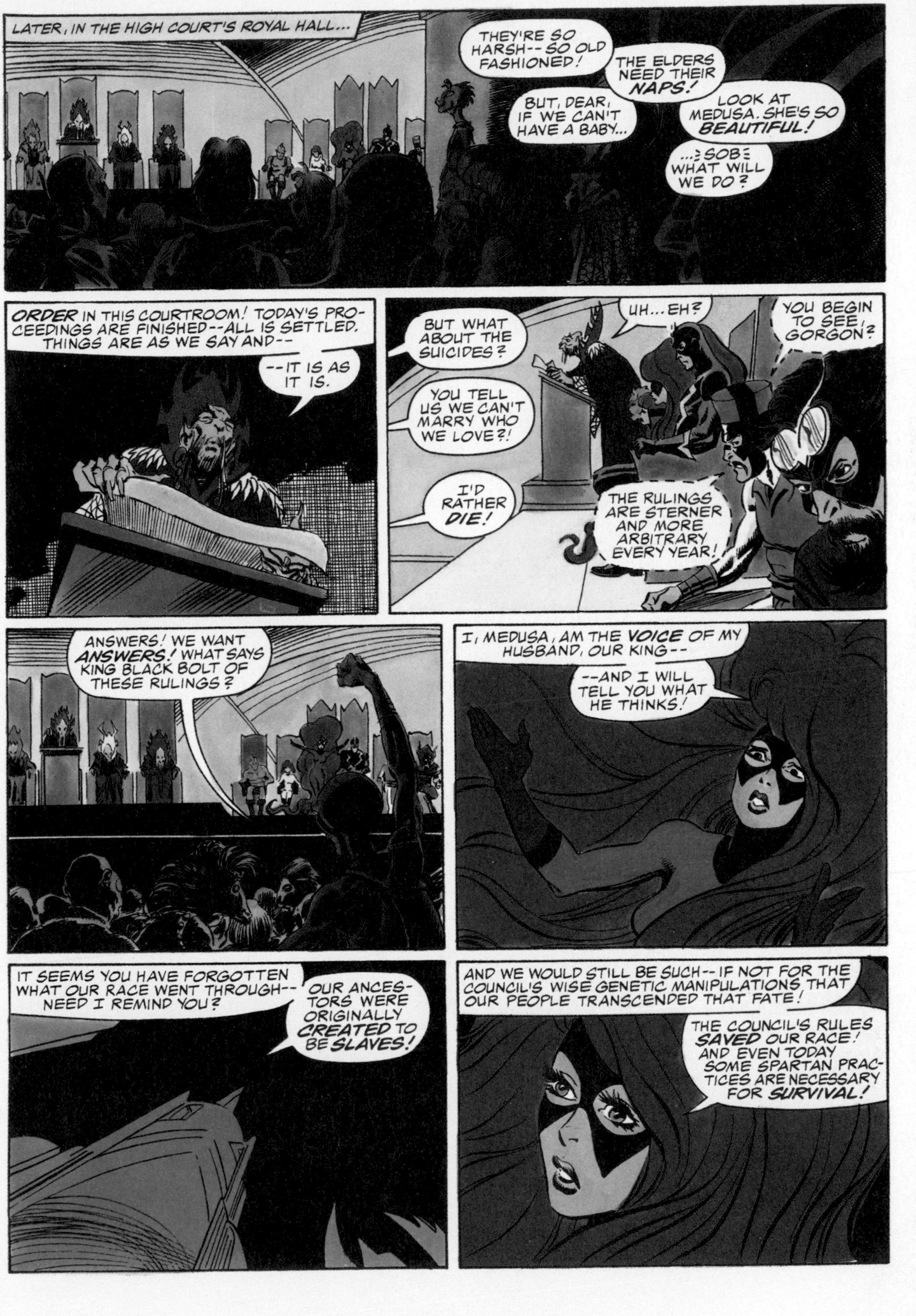
LATER, IN THE HIGH COURT'S ROYAL HALL...
THEY'RE SO HARSH-- SO OLD FASHIONED!
THE ELDERS NEED THEIR NAPS!
BUT, DEAR, IF WE CAN'T HAVE A BABY...
LOOK AT MEDUSA. SHE'S SO BEAUTIFUL!
...SOB WHAT WILL WE DO?
ORDER IN THIS COURTROOM! TODAY'S PROCEEDINGS ARE FINISHED--ALL IS SETTLED. THINGS ARE AS WE SAY AND--
--IT IS AS IT IS.
BUT WHAT ABOUT THE SUICIDES?
UH...EH?
YOU BEGIN TO SEE, GORGON?
YOU TELL US WE CAN'T MARRY WHO WE LOVE?!
I'D RATHER DIE!
THE RULINGS ARE STERNER AND MORE ARBITRARY EVERY YEAR!
ANSWERS! WE WANT ANSWERS! WHAT SAYS KING BLACK BOLT OF THESE RULINGS?
I, MEDUSA, AM THE VOICE OF MY HUSBAND, OUR KING--
--AND I WILL TELL YOU WHAT HE THINKS!
IT SEEMS YOU HAVE FORGOTTEN WHAT OUR RACE WENT THROUGH-- NEED I REMIND YOU?
OUR ANCESTORS WERE ORIGINALLY CREATED TO BE SLAVES!
AND WE WOULD STILL BE SUCH--IF NOT FOR THE COUNCIL'S WISE GENETIC MANIPULATIONS THAT OUR PEOPLE TRANSCENDED THAT FATE!
THE COUNCIL'S RULES SAVED OUR RACE! AND EVEN TODAY SOME SPARTAN PRACTICES ARE NECESSARY FOR SURVIVAL!

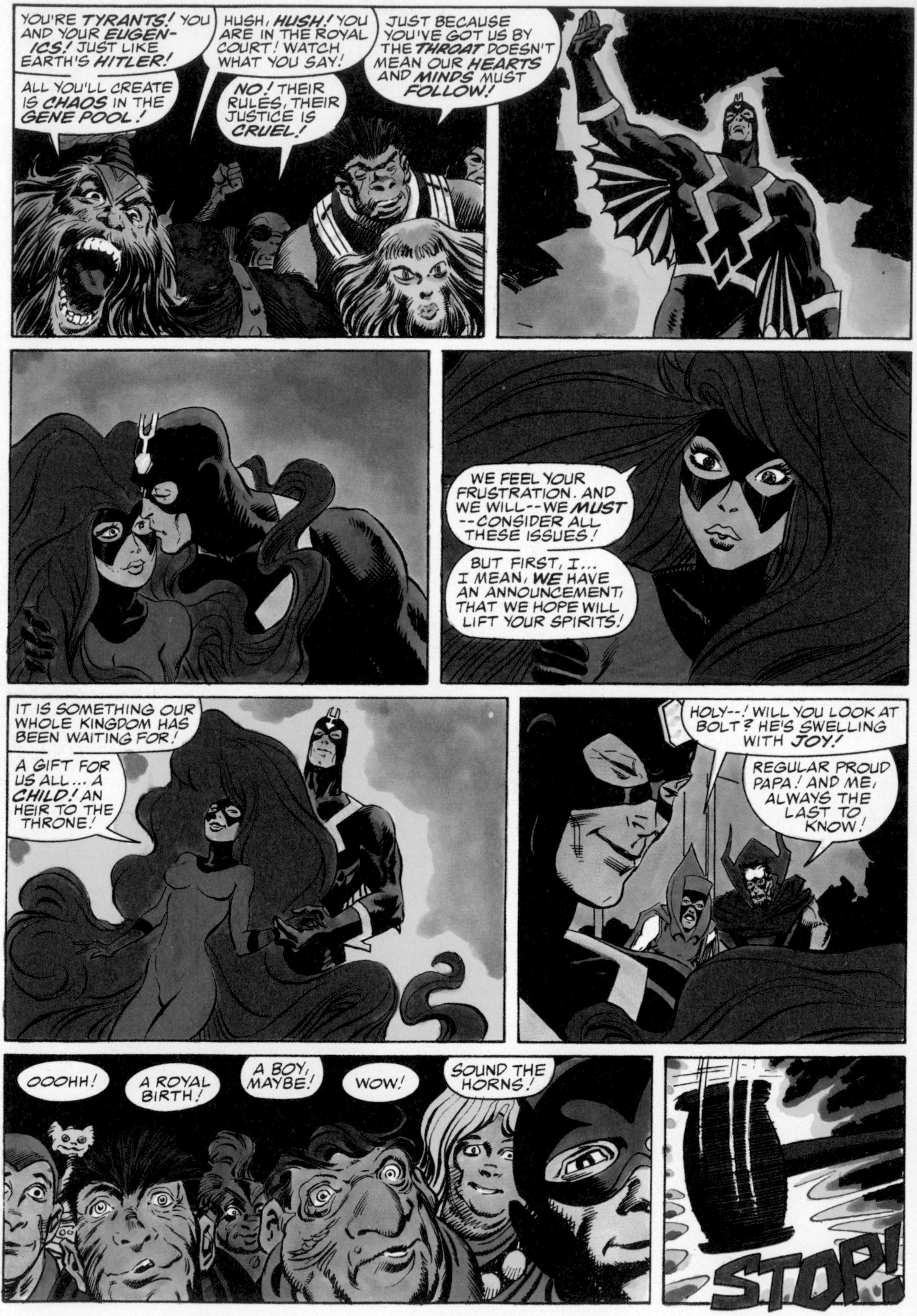
YOU'RE TYRANTS! YOU AND YOUR EUGENICS! JUST LIKE EARTH'S HITLER!
ALL YOU'LL CREATE IS CHAOS IN THE GENE POOL!
HUSH, HUSH! YOU ARE IN THE ROYAL COURT! WATCH WHAT YOU SAY!
NO! THEIR RULES, THEIR JUSTICE IS CRUEL!
JUST BECAUSE YOU'VE GOT US BY THE THROAT DOESN'T MEAN OUR HEARTS AND MINDS MUST FOLLOW!
WE FEEL YOUR FRUSTRATION. AND WE WILL--WE MUST--CONSIDER ALL THESE ISSUES!
BUT FIRST, I... I MEAN, WE HAVE AN ANNOUNCEMENT, THAT WE HOPE WILL LIFT YOUR SPIRITS!
IT IS SOMETHING OUR WHOLE KINGDOM HAS BEEN WAITING FOR!
A GIFT FOR US ALL... A CHILD! AN HEIR TO THE THRONE!
HOLY--! WILL YOU LOOK AT BOLT? HE'S SWELLING WITH JOY!
REGULAR PROUD PAPA! AND ME, ALWAYS THE LAST TO KNOW!
OOOHH!
A ROYAL BIRTH!
A BOY, MAYBE!
WOW!
SOUND THE HORNS!
STOP!

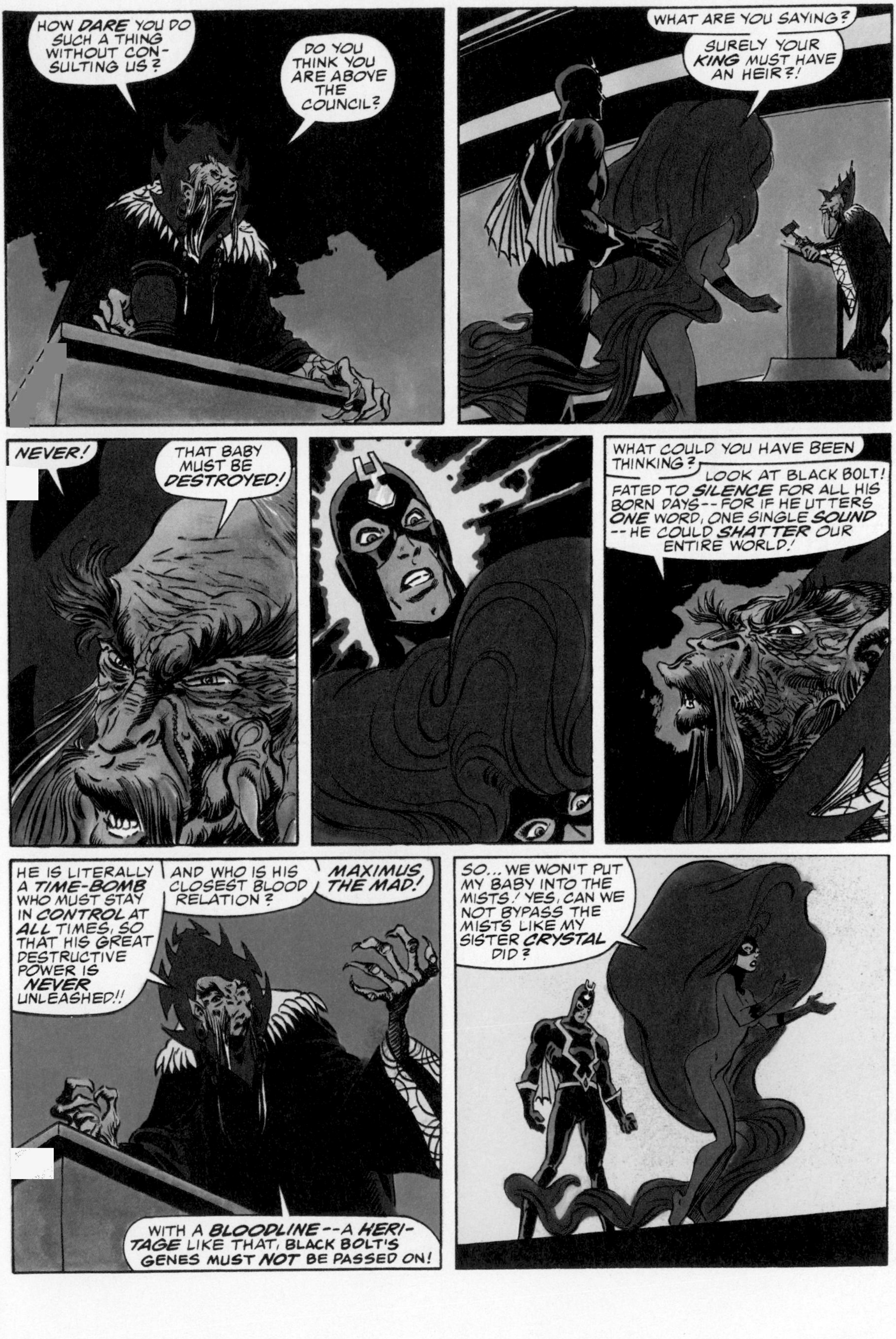
HOW DARE YOU DO SUCH A THING WITHOUT CON-SULTING US?
DO YOU THINK YOU ARE ABOVE THE COUNCIL?
WHAT ARE YOU SAYING?
SURELY YOUR KING MUST HAVE AN HEIR?!
NEVER!
THAT BABY MUST BE DESTROYED!
WHAT COULD YOU HAVE BEEN THINKING?
LOOK AT BLACK BOLT! FATED TO SILENCE FOR ALL HIS BORN DAYS--FOR IF HE UTTERS ONE WORD, ONE SINGLE SOUND --HE COULD SHATTER OUR ENTIRE WORLD!
HE IS LITERALLY A TIME-BOMB WHO MUST STAY IN CONTROL AT ALL TIMES, SO THAT HIS GREAT DESTRUCTIVE POWER IS NEVER UNLEASHED!!
AND WHO IS HIS CLOSEST BLOOD RELATION?
MAXIMUS THE MAD!
WITH A BLOODLINE--A HERI-TAGE LIKE THAT, BLACK BOLT'S GENES MUST NOT BE PASSED ON!
SO... WE WON'T PUT MY BABY INTO THE MISTS! YES, CAN WE NOT BYPASS THE MISTS LIKE MY SISTER CRYSTAL DID?

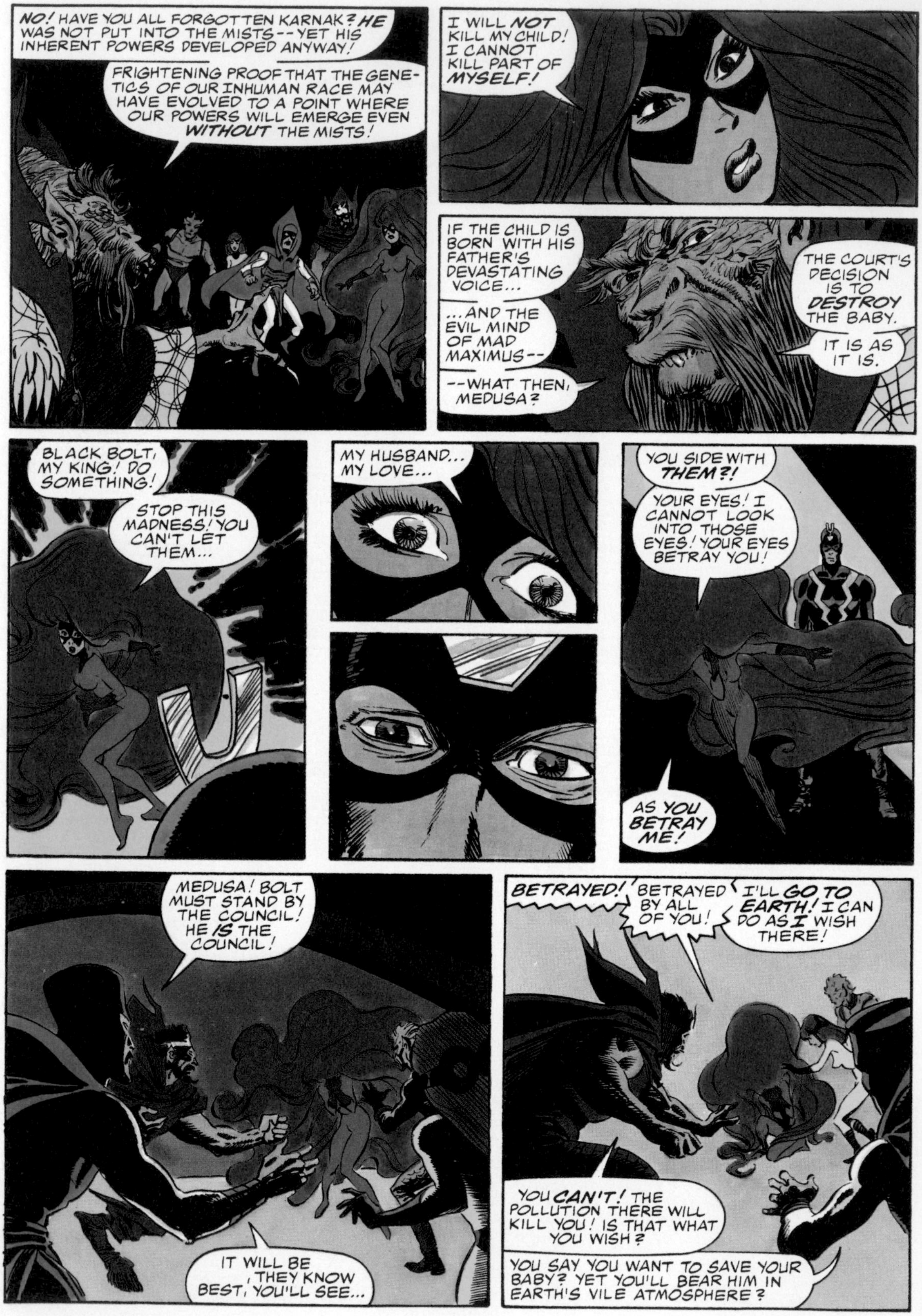
NO! HAVE YOU ALL FORGOTTEN KARNAK? HE WAS NOT PUT INTO THE MISTS--YET HIS INHERENT POWERS DEVELOPED ANYWAY!
FRIGHTENING PROOF THAT THE GENETICS OF OUR INHUMAN RACE MAY HAVE EVOLVED TO A POINT WHERE OUR POWERS WILL EMERGE EVEN WITHOUT THE MISTS!
I WILL NOT KILL MY CHILD! I CANNOT KILL PART OF MYSELF!
IF THE CHILD IS BORN WITH HIS FATHER'S DEVASTATING VOICE...
...AND THE EVIL MIND OF MAD MAXIMUS--
--WHAT THEN, MEDUSA?
THE COURT'S DECISION IS TO DESTROY THE BABY.
IT IS AS IT IS.
BLACK BOLT, MY KING! DO SOMETHING!
STOP THIS MADNESS! YOU CAN'T LET THEM...
MY HUSBAND... MY LOVE...
YOU SIDE WITH THEM?!
YOUR EYES! I CANNOT LOOK INTO THOSE EYES! YOUR EYES BETRAY YOU!
AS YOU BETRAY ME!
MEDUSA! BOLT MUST STAND BY THE COUNCIL! HE IS THE COUNCIL!
IT WILL BE, THEY KNOW BEST, YOU'LL SEE...
BETRAYED!
BETRAYED BY ALL OF YOU!
I'LL GO TO EARTH! I CAN DO AS I WISH THERE!
YOU CAN'T! THE POLLUTION THERE WILL KILL YOU! IS THAT WHAT YOU WISH?
YOU SAY YOU WANT TO SAVE YOUR BABY? YET YOU'LL BEAR HIM IN EARTH'S VILE ATMOSPHERE?

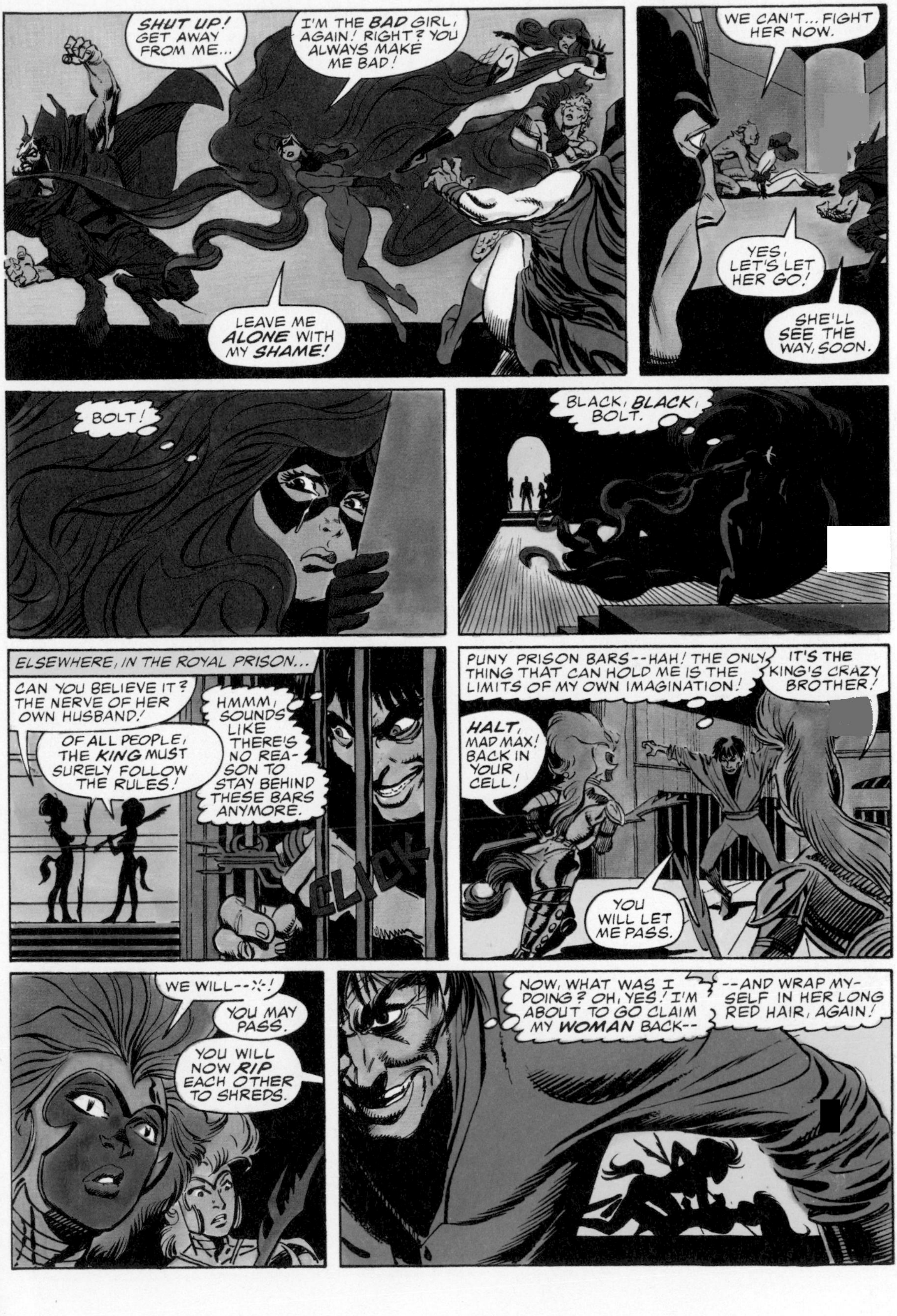
SHUT UP! GET AWAY FROM ME...
I'M THE BAD GIRL, AGAIN! RIGHT? YOU ALWAYS MAKE ME BAD!
LEAVE ME ALONE WITH MY SHAME!
WE CAN'T... FIGHT HER NOW.
YES, LET'S LET HER GO!
SHE'LL SEE THE WAY, SOON.
BOLT!
BLACK, BLACK, BOLT.
ELSEWHERE, IN THE ROYAL PRISON...
CAN YOU BELIEVE IT? THE NERVE OF HER OWN HUSBAND!
OF ALL PEOPLE, THE KING MUST SURELY FOLLOW THE RULES!
HMMM, SOUNDS LIKE THERE'S NO REASON TO STAY BEHIND THESE BARS ANYMORE.
CLICK
PUNY PRISON BARS--HAH! THE ONLY THING THAT CAN HOLD ME IS THE LIMITS OF MY OWN IMAGINATION!
IT'S THE KING'S CRAZY BROTHER!
HALT, MAD MAX! BACK IN YOUR CELL!
YOU WILL LET ME PASS.
WE WILL--*!
YOU MAY PASS.
YOU WILL NOW RIP EACH OTHER TO SHREDS.
NOW, WHAT WAS I DOING? OH, YES! I'M ABOUT TO GO CLAIM MY WOMAN BACK--
--AND WRAP MYSELF IN HER LONG RED HAIR, AGAIN!

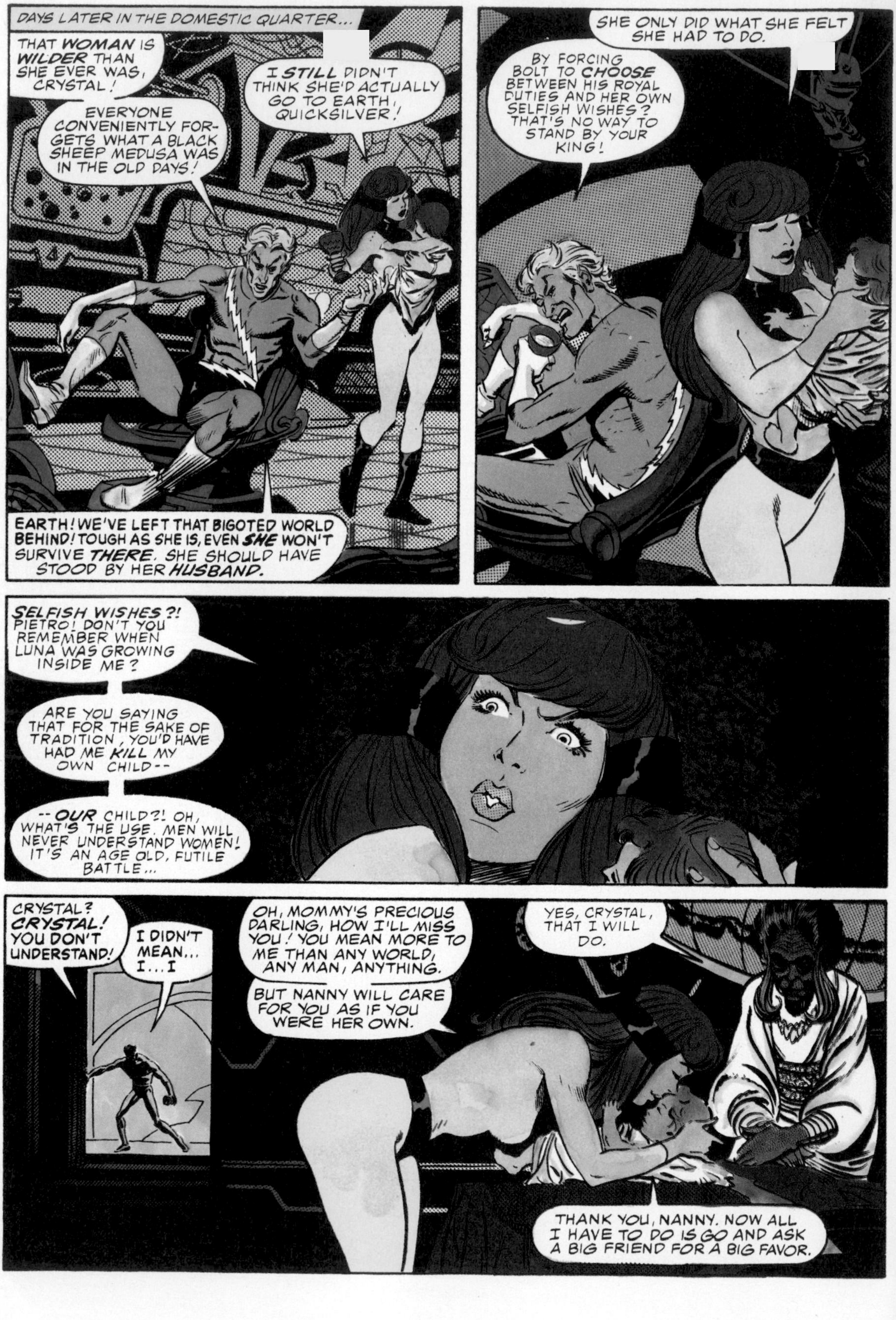
DAYS LATER IN THE DOMESTIC QUARTER...
THAT WOMAN IS WILDER THAN SHE EVER WAS, CRYSTAL!
EVERYONE CONVENIENTLY FORGETS WHAT A BLACK SHEEP MEDUSA WAS IN THE OLD DAYS!
I STILL DIDN'T THINK SHE'D ACTUALLY GO TO EARTH, QUICKSILVER!
EARTH! WE'VE LEFT THAT BIGOTED WORLD BEHIND! TOUGH AS SHE IS, EVEN SHE WON'T SURVIVE THERE. SHE SHOULD HAVE STOOD BY HER HUSBAND.
SHE ONLY DID WHAT SHE FELT SHE HAD TO DO.
BY FORCING BOLT TO CHOOSE BETWEEN HIS ROYAL DUTIES AND HER OWN SELFISH WISHES? THAT'S NO WAY TO STAND BY YOUR KING!
SELFISH WISHES?! PIETRO! DON'T YOU REMEMBER WHEN LUNA WAS GROWING INSIDE ME?
ARE YOU SAYING THAT FOR THE SAKE OF TRADITION, YOU'D HAVE HAD ME KILL MY OWN CHILD--
--OUR CHILD?! OH, WHAT'S THE USE. MEN WILL NEVER UNDERSTAND WOMEN! IT'S AN AGE OLD, FUTILE BATTLE...
CRYSTAL? CRYSTAL! YOU DON'T UNDERSTAND!
I DIDN'T MEAN... I...I
OH, MOMMY'S PRECIOUS DARLING, HOW I'LL MISS YOU! YOU MEAN MORE TO ME THAN ANY WORLD, ANY MAN, ANYTHING.
BUT NANNY WILL CARE FOR YOU AS IF YOU WERE HER OWN.
YES, CRYSTAL, THAT I WILL DO.
THANK YOU, NANNY. NOW ALL I HAVE TO DO IS GO AND ASK A BIG FRIEND FOR A BIG FAVOR.

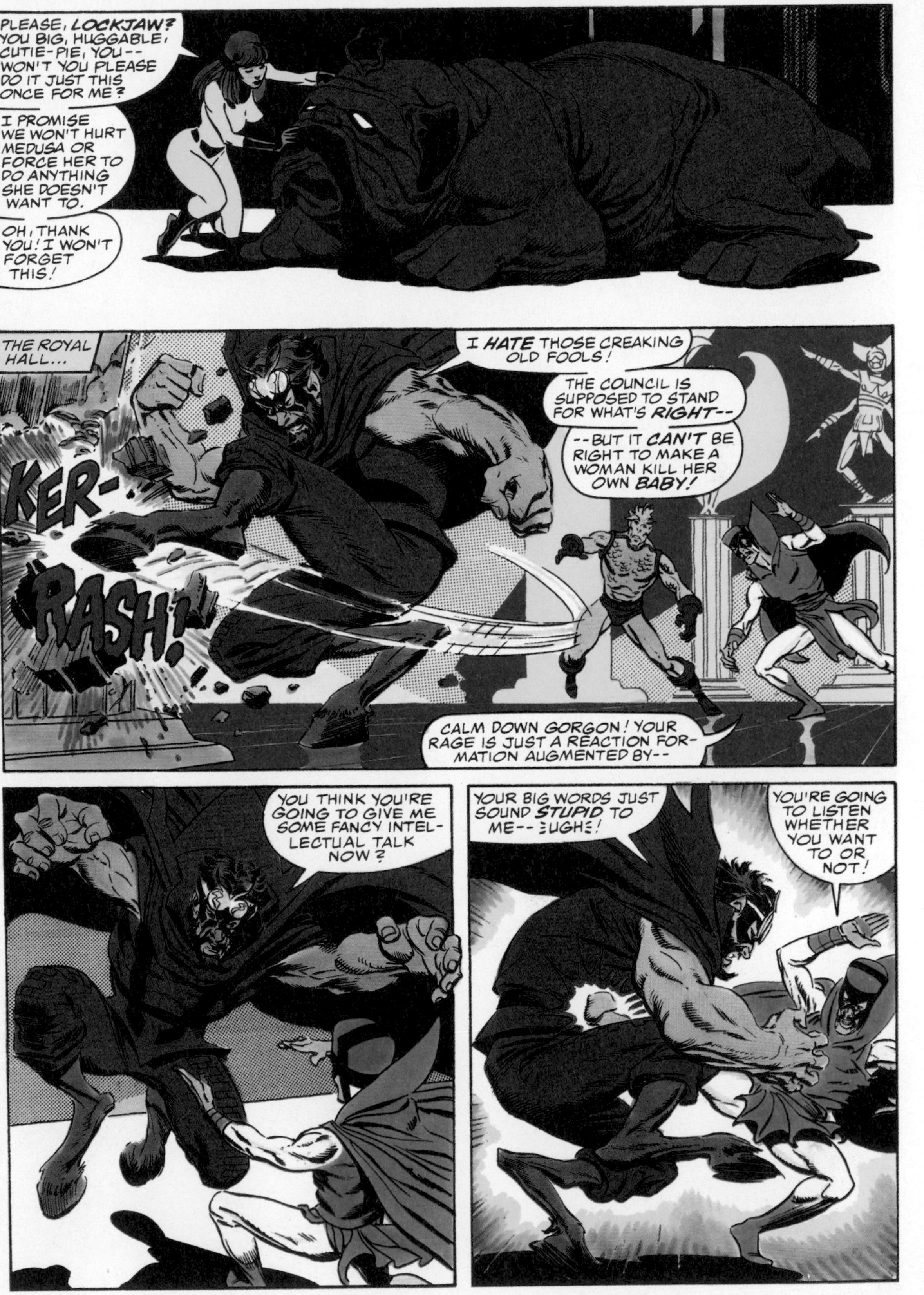
PLEASE, LOCKJAW? YOU BIG, HUGGABLE, CUTIE-PIE, YOU-- WON'T YOU PLEASE DO IT JUST THIS ONCE FOR ME?
I PROMISE WE WON'T HURT MEDUSA OR FORCE HER TO DO ANYTHING SHE DOESN'T WANT TO.
OH, THANK YOU! I WON'T FORGET THIS!
THE ROYAL HALL...
KER-RASH!
I HATE THOSE CREAKING OLD FOOLS!
THE COUNCIL IS SUPPOSED TO STAND FOR WHAT'S RIGHT--
--BUT IT CAN'T BE RIGHT TO MAKE A WOMAN KILL HER OWN BABY!
CALM DOWN GORGON! YOUR RAGE IS JUST A REACTION FORMATION AUGMENTED BY--
YOU THINK YOU'RE GOING TO GIVE ME SOME FANCY INTELLECTUAL TALK NOW?
YOUR BIG WORDS JUST SOUND STUPID TO ME-- UGH!
YOU'RE GOING TO LISTEN WHETHER YOU WANT TO OR NOT!

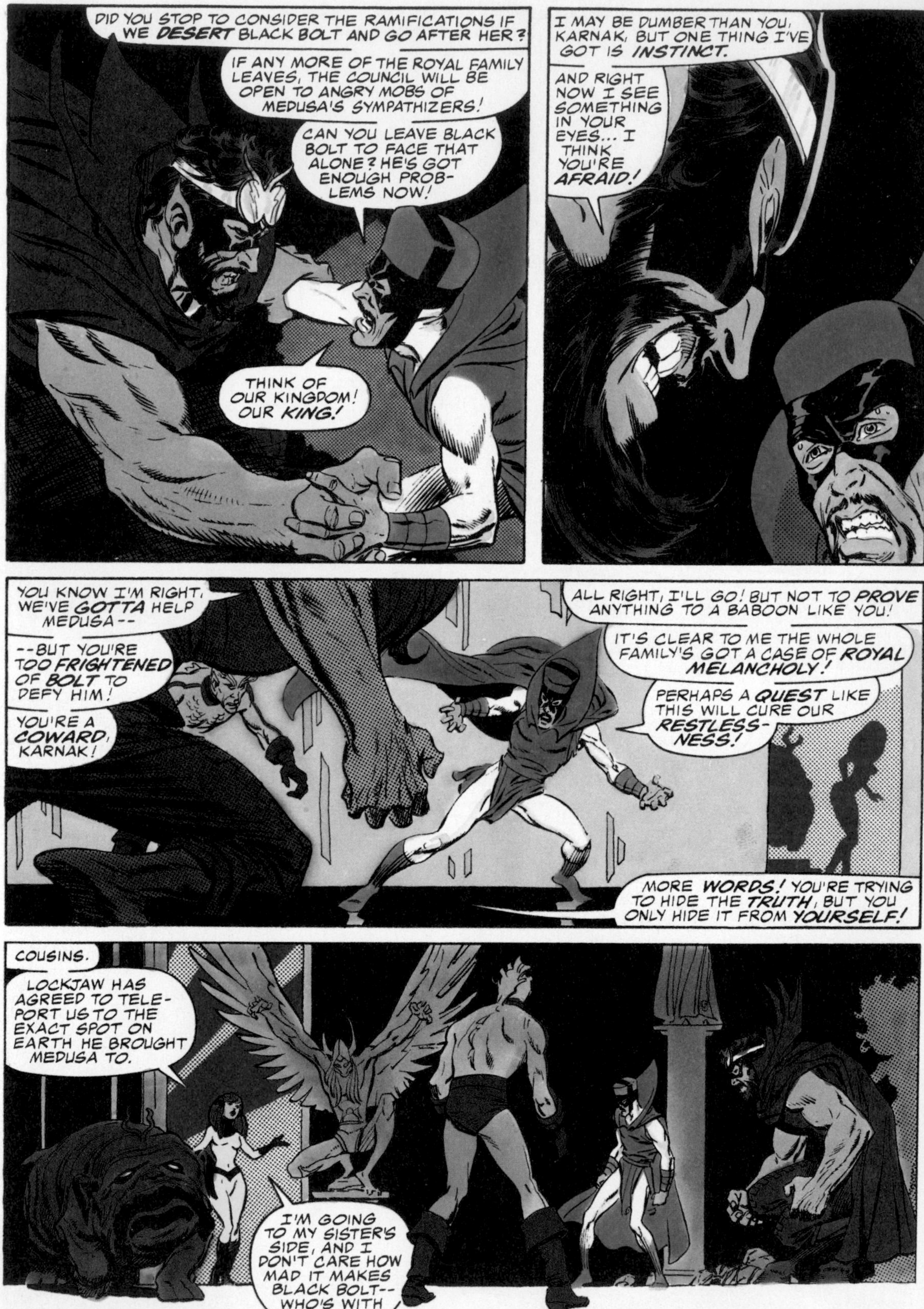
DID YOU STOP TO CONSIDER THE RAMIFICATIONS IF WE DESERT BLACK BOLT AND GO AFTER HER?
IF ANY MORE OF THE ROYAL FAMILY LEAVES, THE COUNCIL WILL BE OPEN TO ANGRY MOBS OF MEDUSA'S SYMPATHIZERS!
CAN YOU LEAVE BLACK BOLT TO FACE THAT ALONE? HE'S GOT ENOUGH PROB-LEMS NOW!
THINK OF OUR KINGDOM! OUR KING!
I MAY BE DUMBER THAN YOU, KARNAK, BUT ONE THING I'VE GOT IS INSTINCT.
AND RIGHT NOW I SEE SOMETHING IN YOUR EYES... I THINK YOU'RE AFRAID!
YOU KNOW I'M RIGHT. WE'VE GOTTA HELP MEDUSA--
--BUT YOU'RE TOO FRIGHTENED OF BOLT TO DEFY HIM!
YOU'RE A COWARD, KARNAK!
ALL RIGHT, I'LL GO! BUT NOT TO PROVE ANYTHING TO A BABOON LIKE YOU!
IT'S CLEAR TO ME THE WHOLE FAMILY'S GOT A CASE OF ROYAL MELANCHOLY!
PERHAPS A QUEST LIKE THIS WILL CURE OUR RESTLESS-NESS!
MORE WORDS! YOU'RE TRYING TO HIDE THE TRUTH, BUT YOU ONLY HIDE IT FROM YOURSELF!
COUSINS.
LOCKJAW HAS AGREED TO TELE-PORT US TO THE EXACT SPOT ON EARTH HE BROUGHT MEDUSA TO.
I'M GOING TO MY SISTER'S SIDE, AND I DON'T CARE HOW MAD IT MAKES BLACK BOLT-- WHO'S WITH ME?

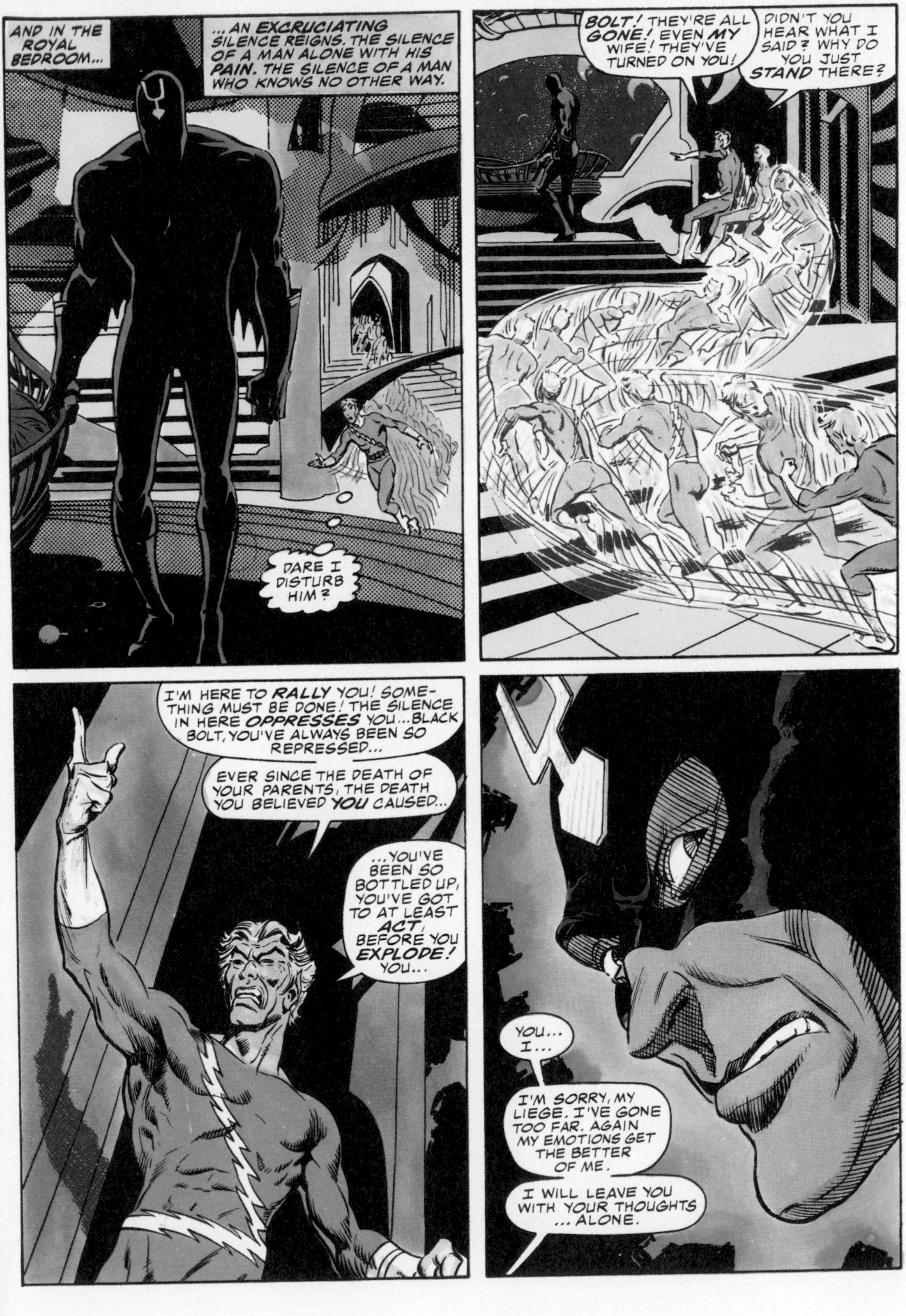
AND IN THE ROYAL BEDROOM...
...AN EXCRUCIATING SILENCE REIGNS. THE SILENCE OF A MAN ALONE WITH HIS PAIN. THE SILENCE OF A MAN WHO KNOWS NO OTHER WAY.
DARE I DISTURB HIM?
BOLT! THEY'RE ALL GONE! EVEN MY WIFE! THEY'VE TURNED ON YOU!
DIDN'T YOU HEAR WHAT I SAID? WHY DO YOU JUST STAND THERE?
I'M HERE TO RALLY YOU! SOMETHING MUST BE DONE! THE SILENCE IN HERE OPPRESSES YOU...BLACK BOLT, YOU'VE ALWAYS BEEN SO REPRESSED...
EVER SINCE THE DEATH OF YOUR PARENTS, THE DEATH YOU BELIEVED YOU CAUSED...
...YOU'VE BEEN SO BOTTLED UP, YOU'VE GOT TO AT LEAST ACT, BEFORE YOU EXPLODE! YOU...
YOU... I...
I'M SORRY, MY LIEGE. I'VE GONE TOO FAR. AGAIN MY EMOTIONS GET THE BETTER OF ME.
I WILL LEAVE YOU WITH YOUR THOUGHTS ...ALONE.

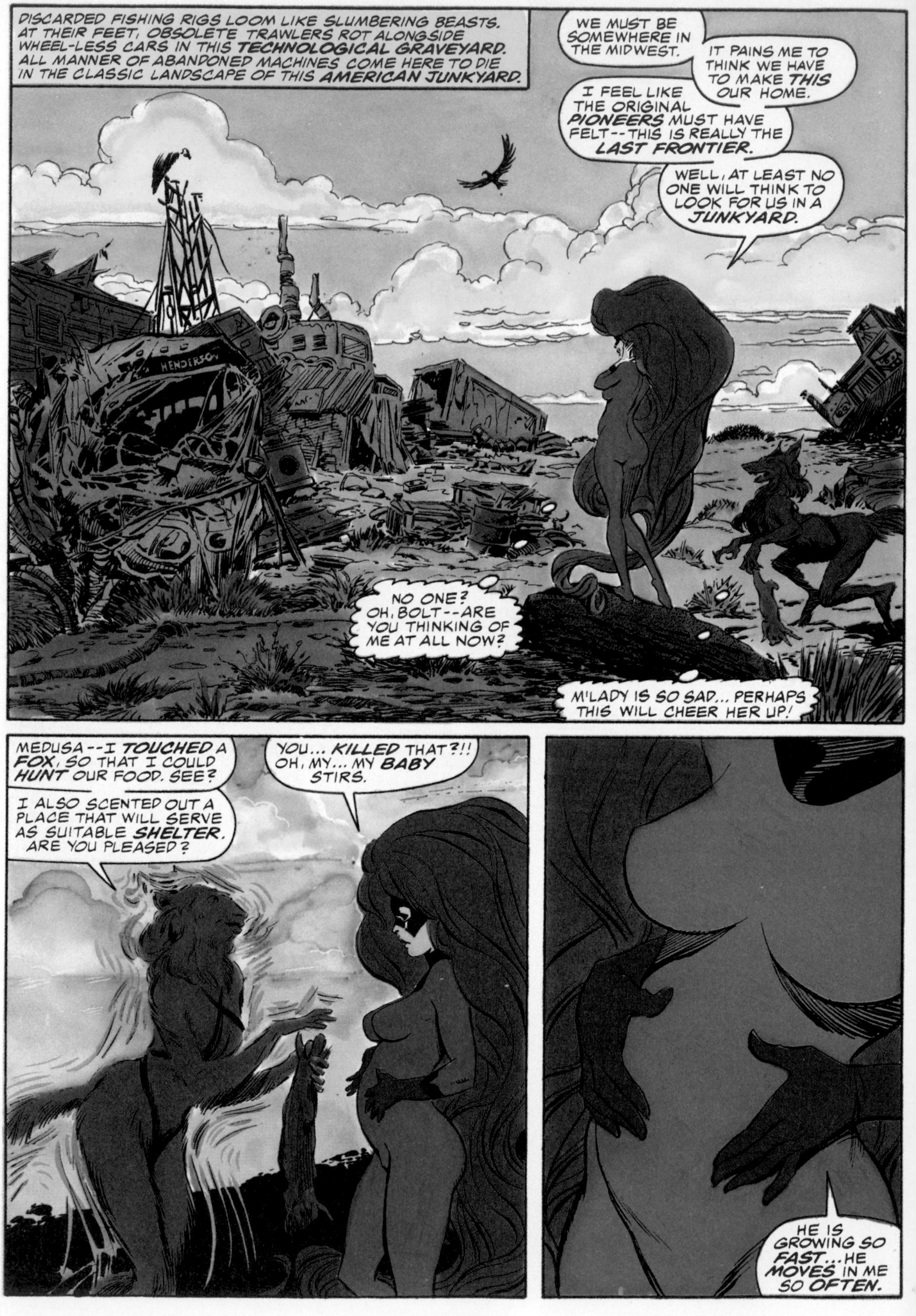
DISCARDED FISHING RIGS LOOM LIKE SLUMBERING BEASTS. AT THEIR FEET, OBSOLETE TRAWLERS ROT ALONGSIDE WHEEL-LESS CARS IN THIS TECHNOLOGICAL GRAVEYARD. ALL MANNER OF ABANDONED MACHINES COME HERE TO DIE IN THE CLASSIC LANDSCAPE OF THIS AMERICAN JUNKYARD.
WE MUST BE SOMEWHERE IN THE MIDWEST.
IT PAINS ME TO THINK WE HAVE TO MAKE THIS OUR HOME.
I FEEL LIKE THE ORIGINAL PIONEERS MUST HAVE FELT--THIS IS REALLY THE LAST FRONTIER.
WELL, AT LEAST NO ONE WILL THINK TO LOOK FOR US IN A JUNKYARD.
HENDERSON
NO ONE? OH, BOLT--ARE YOU THINKING OF ME AT ALL NOW?
M'LADY IS SO SAD... PERHAPS THIS WILL CHEER HER UP!
MEDUSA--I TOUCHED A FOX, SO THAT I COULD HUNT OUR FOOD. SEE?
I ALSO SCENTED OUT A PLACE THAT WILL SERVE AS SUITABLE SHELTER. ARE YOU PLEASED?
YOU... KILLED THAT?!! OH, MY... MY BABY STIRS.
HE IS GROWING SO FAST... HE MOVES IN ME SO OFTEN.

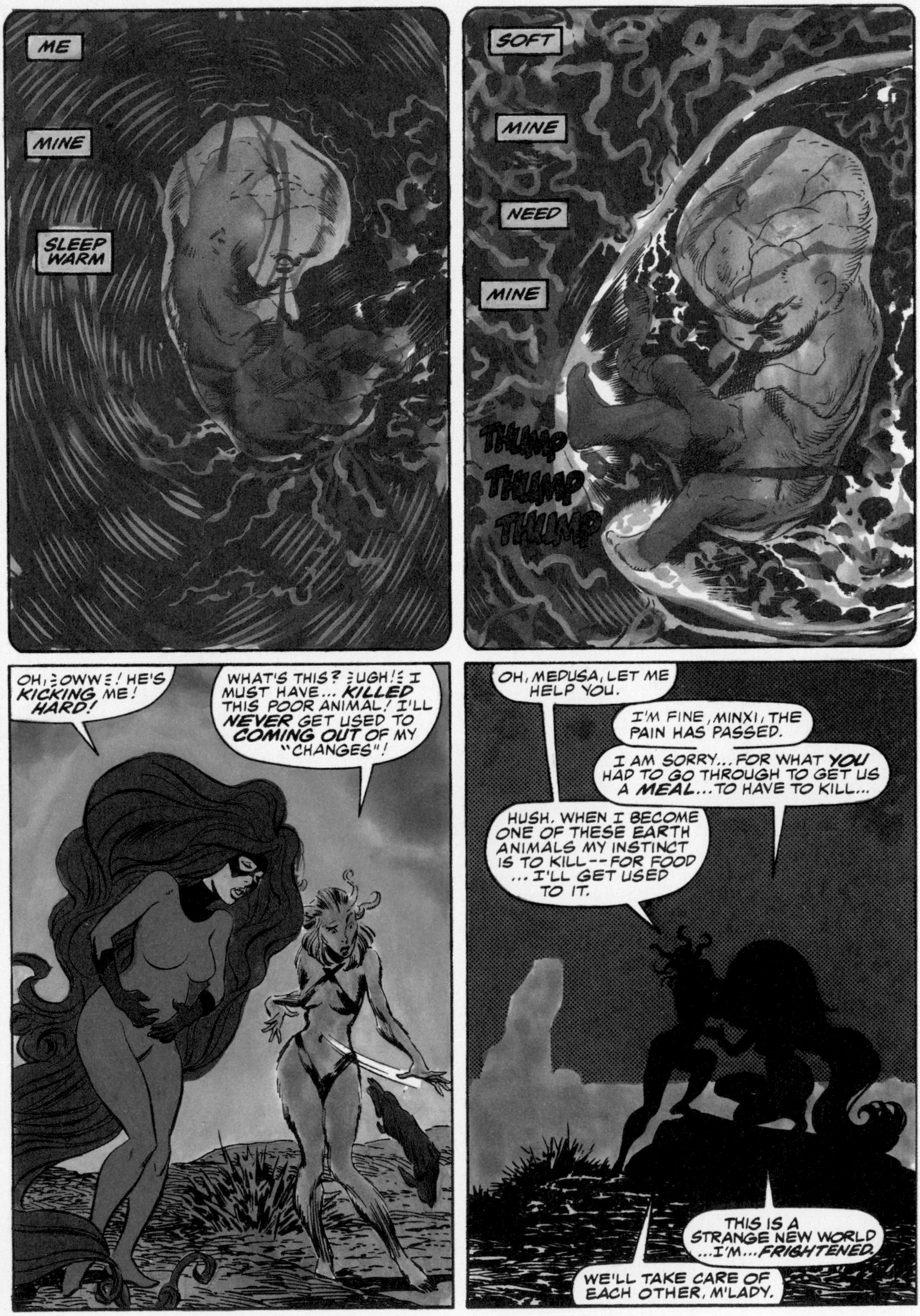
ME
MINE
SLEEP WARM
SOFT
MINE
NEED
MINE
THUMP THUMP THUMP
OH, OWW! HE'S KICKING ME! HARD!
WHAT'S THIS? UGH! I MUST HAVE... KILLED THIS POOR ANIMAL! I'LL NEVER GET USED TO COMING OUT OF MY "CHANGES"!
OH, MEDUSA, LET ME HELP YOU.
I'M FINE, MINXI, THE PAIN HAS PASSED.
I AM SORRY... FOR WHAT YOU HAD TO GO THROUGH TO GET US A MEAL... TO HAVE TO KILL...
HUSH. WHEN I BECOME ONE OF THESE EARTH ANIMALS MY INSTINCT IS TO KILL--FOR FOOD ... I'LL GET USED TO IT.
THIS IS A STRANGE NEW WORLD ...I'M... FRIGHTENED.
WE'LL TAKE CARE OF EACH OTHER, M'LADY.

IN ATTILAN...

YES!!

IT WORKS! A FEW MORE ADJUSTMENTS TO SOLIDIFY THE HOLOGRAM-- AND HE'LL LOOK LIKE THE REAL THING!

MY LIEGE, MY KING, MY BROTHER...

...HOW I HATE YOU!

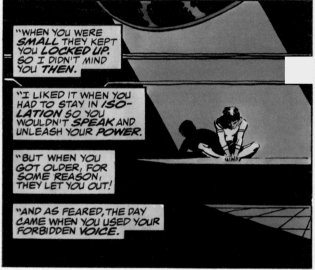

"WHEN YOU WERE SMALL THEY KEPT YOU LOCKED UP. SO I DIDN'T MIND YOU THEN.

"I LIKED IT WHEN YOU HAD TO STAY IN ISOLATION SO YOU WOULDN'T SPEAK AND UNLEASH YOUR POWER.

"BUT WHEN YOU GOT OLDER, FOR SOME REASON, THEY LET YOU OUT!

"AND AS FEARED, THE DAY CAME WHEN YOU USED YOUR FORBIDDEN VOICE.

"THE DAY BLACK BOLT SCREAMED!

EEEEEE EEEEEEE

"AND THAT SCREAM DROVE ME MAD!

"BUT THAT WAS NOTHING-- COMPARED TO WHAT YOUR SCREAM DID TO OUR PARENTS!

EEEEEEE EE

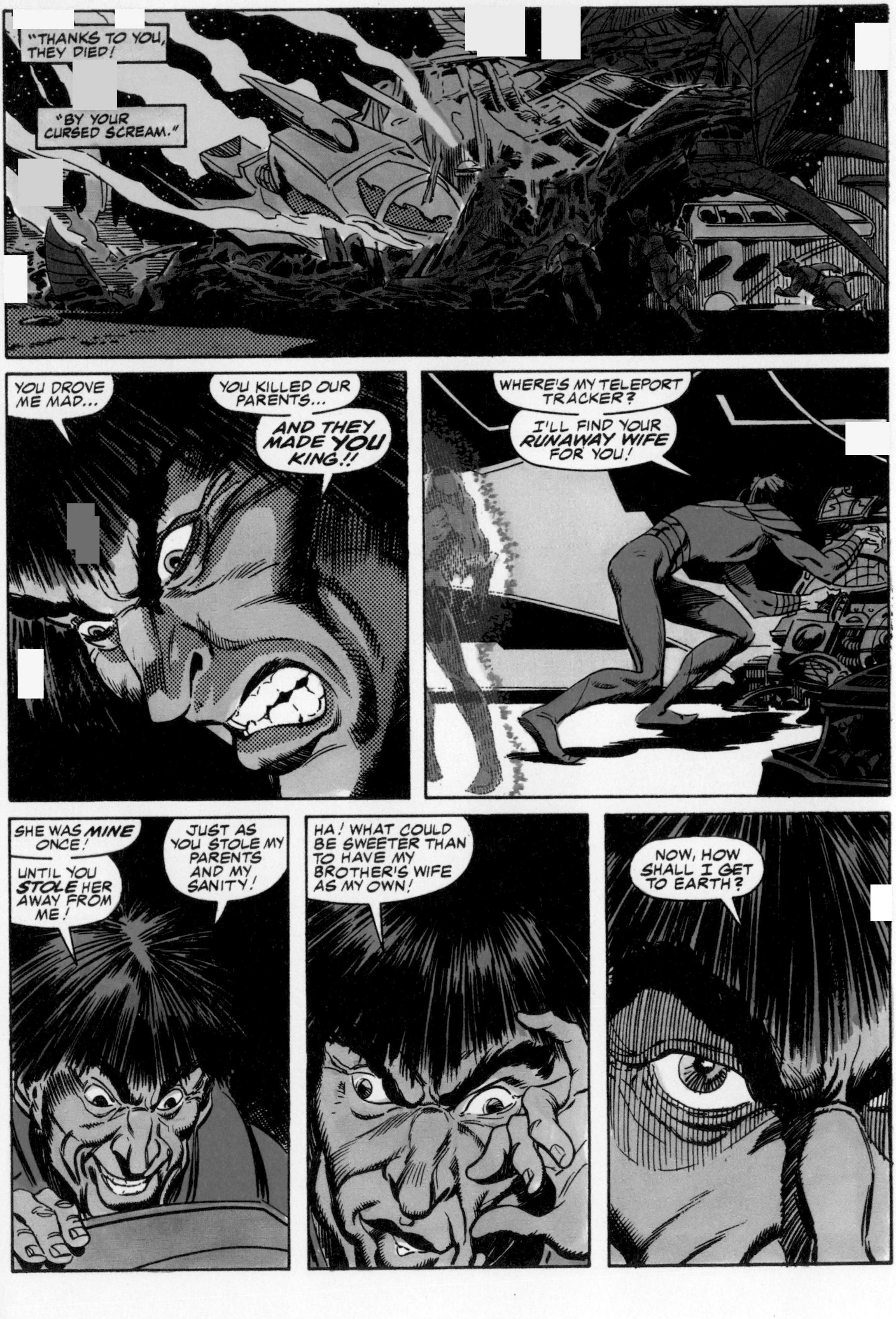
"THANKS TO YOU, THEY DIED!
"BY YOUR CURSED SCREAM."
YOU DROVE ME MAD...
YOU KILLED OUR PARENTS...
AND THEY MADE YOU KING!!
WHERE'S MY TELEPORT TRACKER?
I'LL FIND YOUR RUNAWAY WIFE FOR YOU!
SHE WAS MINE ONCE!
UNTIL YOU STOLE HER AWAY FROM ME!
JUST AS YOU STOLE MY PARENTS AND MY SANITY!
HA! WHAT COULD BE SWEETER THAN TO HAVE MY BROTHER'S WIFE AS MY OWN!
NOW, HOW SHALL I GET TO EARTH?

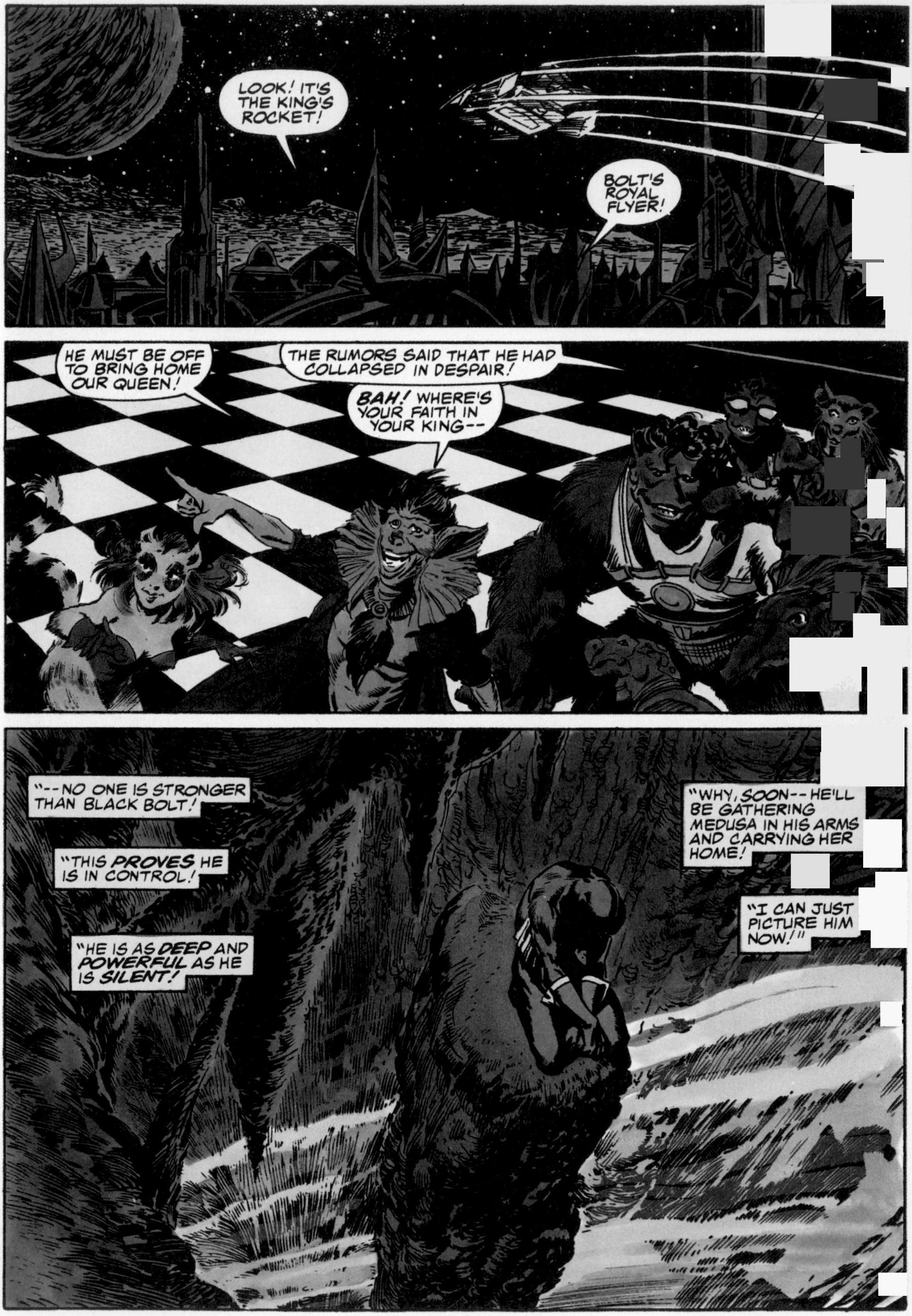
LOOK! IT'S THE KING'S ROCKET!
BOLT'S ROYAL FLYER!
HE MUST BE OFF TO BRING HOME OUR QUEEN!
THE RUMORS SAID THAT HE HAD COLLAPSED IN DESPAIR!
BAH! WHERE'S YOUR FAITH IN YOUR KING--
"--NO ONE IS STRONGER THAN BLACK BOLT!
"THIS PROVES HE IS IN CONTROL!
"HE IS AS DEEP AND POWERFUL AS HE IS SILENT!
"WHY, SOON--HE'LL BE GATHERING MEDUSA IN HIS ARMS AND CARRYING HER HOME!
"I CAN JUST PICTURE HIM NOW!"

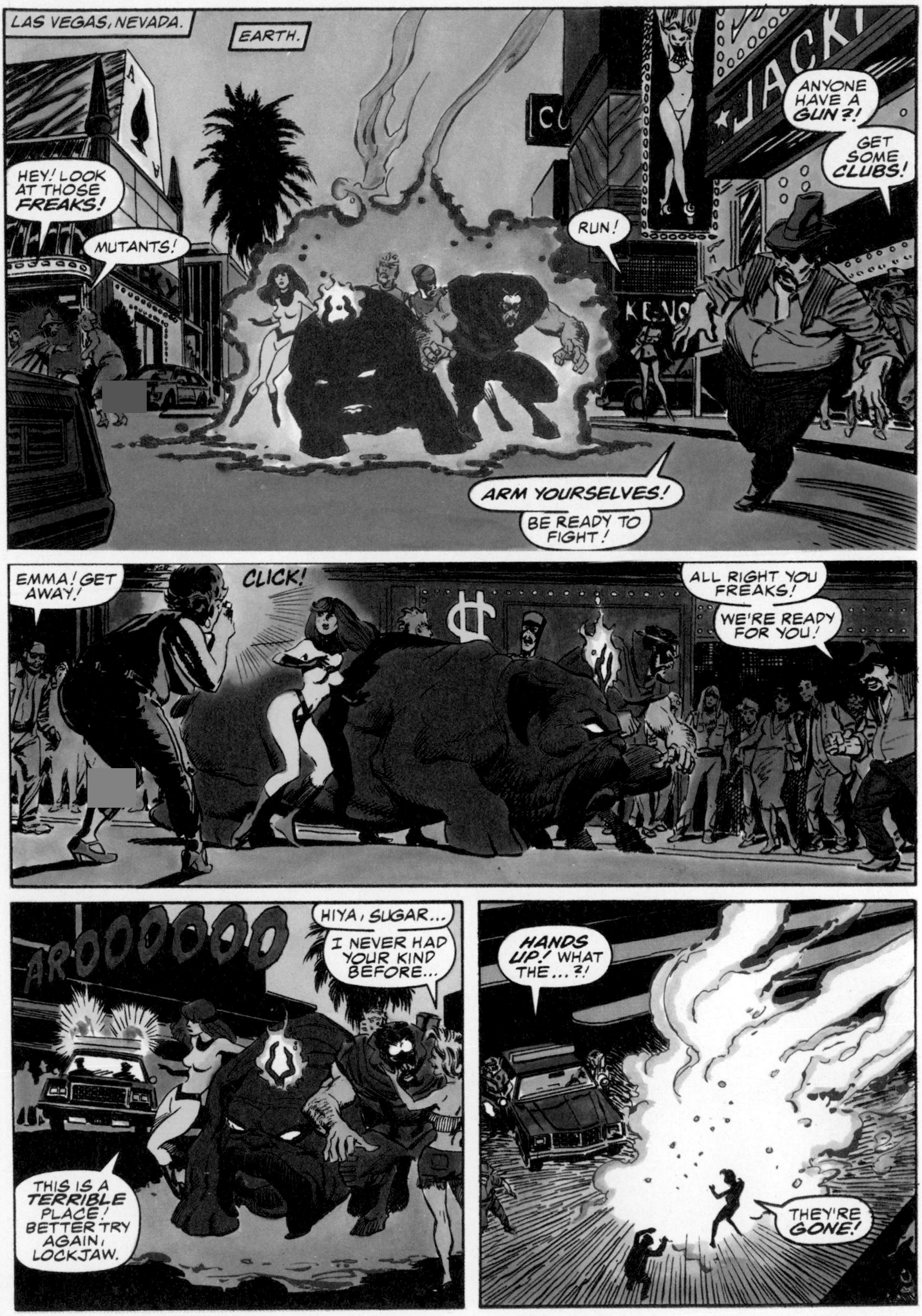
LAS VEGAS, NEVADA.
EARTH.
HEY! LOOK AT THOSE FREAKS!
MUTANTS!
RUN!
ANYONE HAVE A GUN?!
GET SOME CLUBS!
ARM YOURSELVES!
BE READY TO FIGHT!
EMMA! GET AWAY!
CLICK!
ALL RIGHT YOU FREAKS!
WE'RE READY FOR YOU!
AROOOOOO
HIYA, SUGAR...
I NEVER HAD YOUR KIND BEFORE...
THIS IS A TERRIBLE PLACE! BETTER TRY AGAIN, LOCKJAW.
HANDS UP! WHAT THE...?!
THEY'RE GONE!

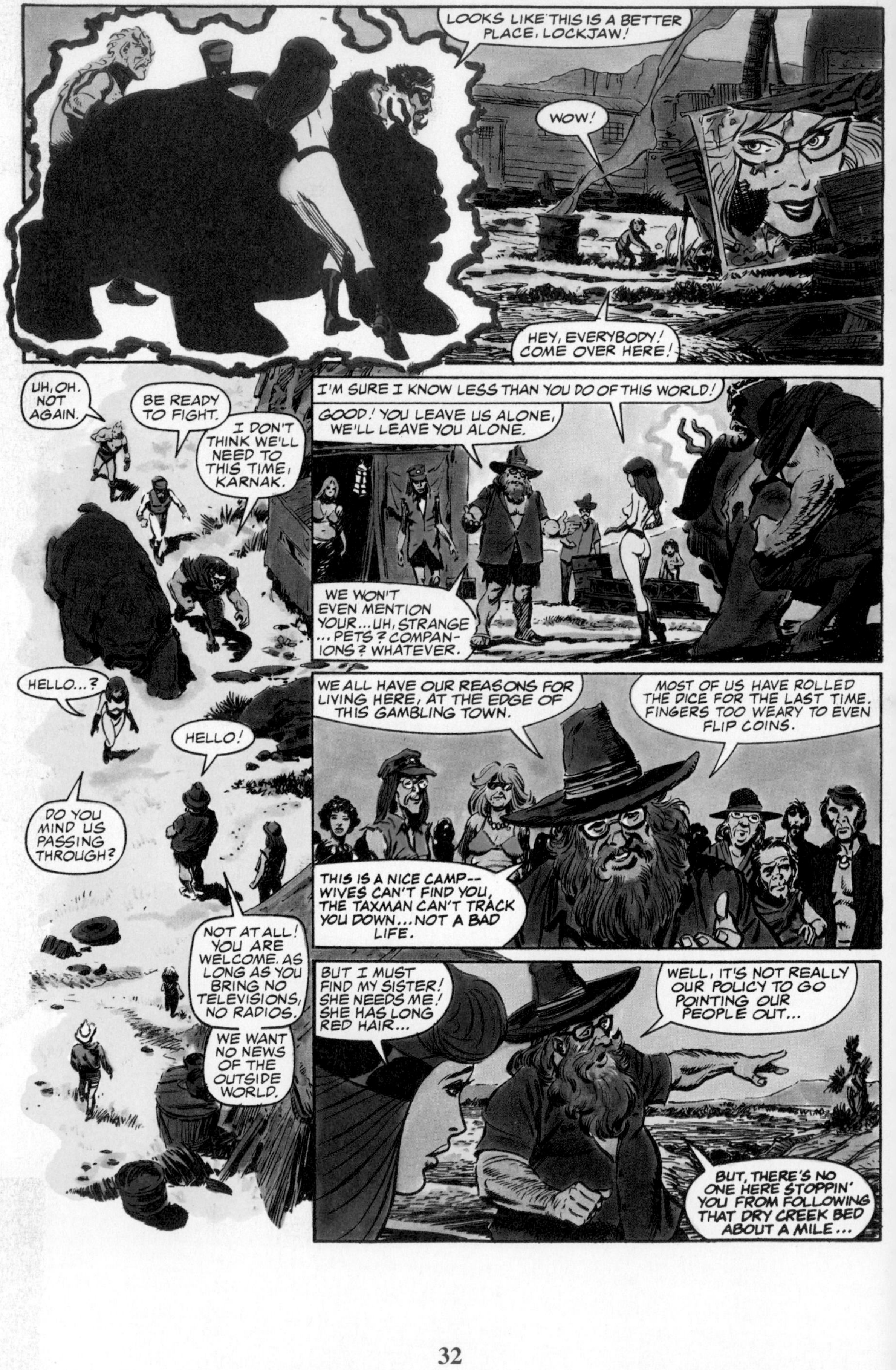
LOOKS LIKE THIS IS A BETTER PLACE, LOCKJAW!
WOW!
HEY, EVERYBODY! COME OVER HERE!
UH, OH. NOT AGAIN.
BE READY TO FIGHT.
I DON'T THINK WE'LL NEED TO THIS TIME, KARNAK.
I'M SURE I KNOW LESS THAN YOU DO OF THIS WORLD!
GOOD! YOU LEAVE US ALONE, WE'LL LEAVE YOU ALONE.
WE WON'T EVEN MENTION YOUR... UH, STRANGE ... PETS? COMPANIONS? WHATEVER.
HELLO...?
HELLO!
DO YOU MIND US PASSING THROUGH?
NOT AT ALL! YOU ARE WELCOME. AS LONG AS YOU BRING NO TELEVISIONS, NO RADIOS.
WE WANT NO NEWS OF THE OUTSIDE WORLD.
WE ALL HAVE OUR REASONS FOR LIVING HERE, AT THE EDGE OF THIS GAMBLING TOWN.
MOST OF US HAVE ROLLED THE DICE FOR THE LAST TIME. FINGERS TOO WEARY TO EVEN FLIP COINS.
THIS IS A NICE CAMP-- WIVES CAN'T FIND YOU, THE TAXMAN CAN'T TRACK YOU DOWN... NOT A BAD LIFE.
BUT I MUST FIND MY SISTER! SHE NEEDS ME! SHE HAS LONG RED HAIR...
WELL, IT'S NOT REALLY OUR POLICY TO GO POINTING OUR PEOPLE OUT...
BUT, THERE'S NO ONE HERE STOPPIN' YOU FROM FOLLOWING THAT DRY CREEK BED ABOUT A MILE...

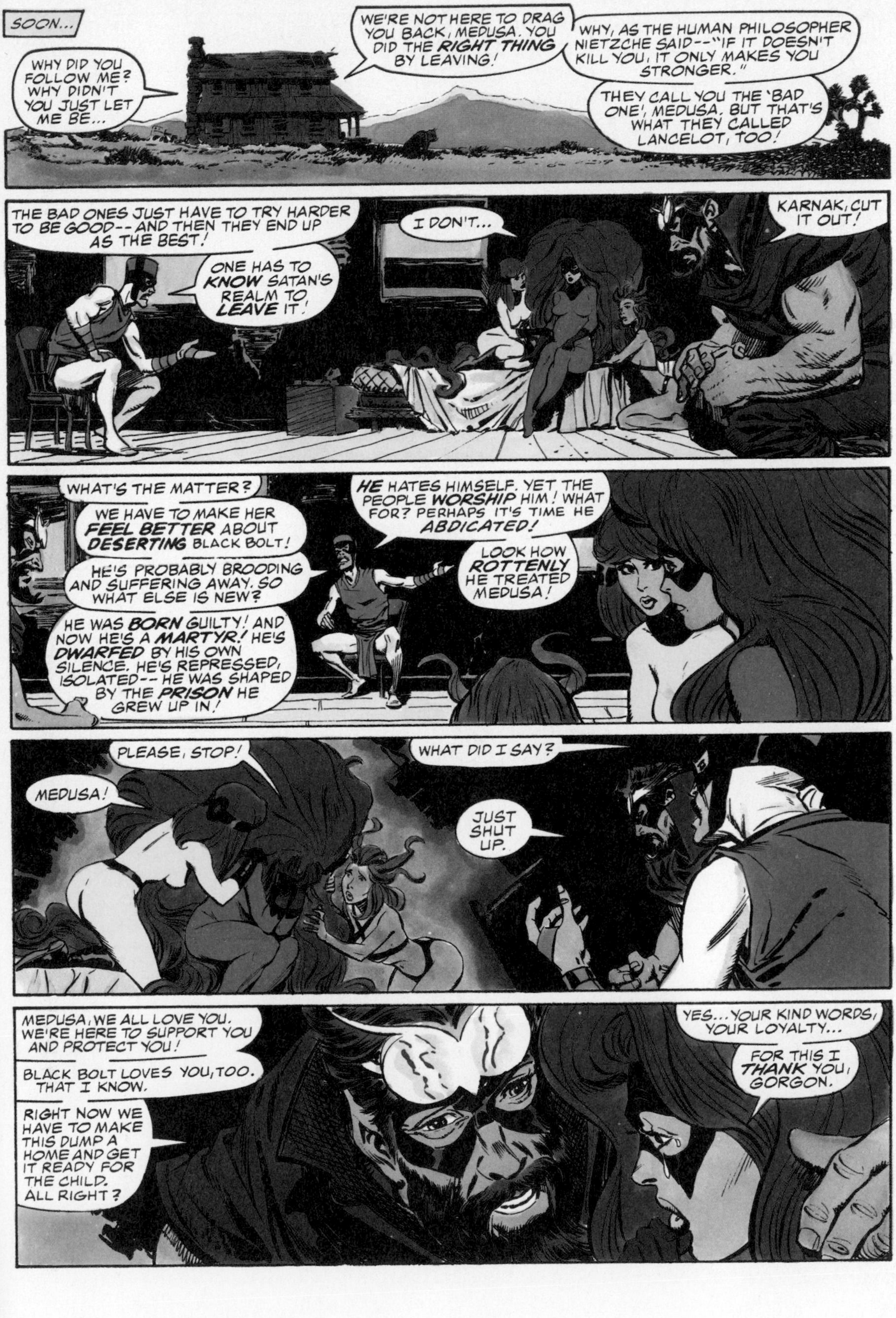
SOON...
WHY DID YOU FOLLOW ME? WHY DIDN'T YOU JUST LET ME BE...
WE'RE NOT HERE TO DRAG YOU BACK, MEDUSA. YOU DID THE RIGHT THING BY LEAVING!
WHY, AS THE HUMAN PHILOSOPHER NIETZCHE SAID--"IF IT DOESN'T KILL YOU, IT ONLY MAKES YOU STRONGER."
THEY CALL YOU THE 'BAD ONE', MEDUSA, BUT THAT'S WHAT THEY CALLED LANCELOT, TOO!
THE BAD ONES JUST HAVE TO TRY HARDER TO BE GOOD-- AND THEN THEY END UP AS THE BEST!
ONE HAS TO KNOW SATAN'S REALM TO LEAVE IT!
I DON'T...
KARNAK, CUT IT OUT!
WHAT'S THE MATTER?
WE HAVE TO MAKE HER FEEL BETTER ABOUT DESERTING BLACK BOLT!
HE'S PROBABLY BROODING AND SUFFERING AWAY. SO WHAT ELSE IS NEW?
HE WAS BORN GUILTY! AND NOW HE'S A MARTYR! HE'S DWARFED BY HIS OWN SILENCE. HE'S REPRESSED, ISOLATED-- HE WAS SHAPED BY THE PRISON HE GREW UP IN!
HE HATES HIMSELF. YET THE PEOPLE WORSHIP HIM! WHAT FOR? PERHAPS IT'S TIME HE ABDICATED!
LOOK HOW ROTTENLY HE TREATED MEDUSA!
PLEASE, STOP!
WHAT DID I SAY?
MEDUSA!
JUST SHUT UP.
MEDUSA, WE ALL LOVE YOU. WE'RE HERE TO SUPPORT YOU AND PROTECT YOU!
BLACK BOLT LOVES YOU, TOO. THAT I KNOW.
RIGHT NOW WE HAVE TO MAKE THIS DUMP A HOME AND GET IT READY FOR THE CHILD. ALL RIGHT?
YES... YOUR KIND WORDS, YOUR LOYALTY...
FOR THIS I THANK YOU, GORGON.

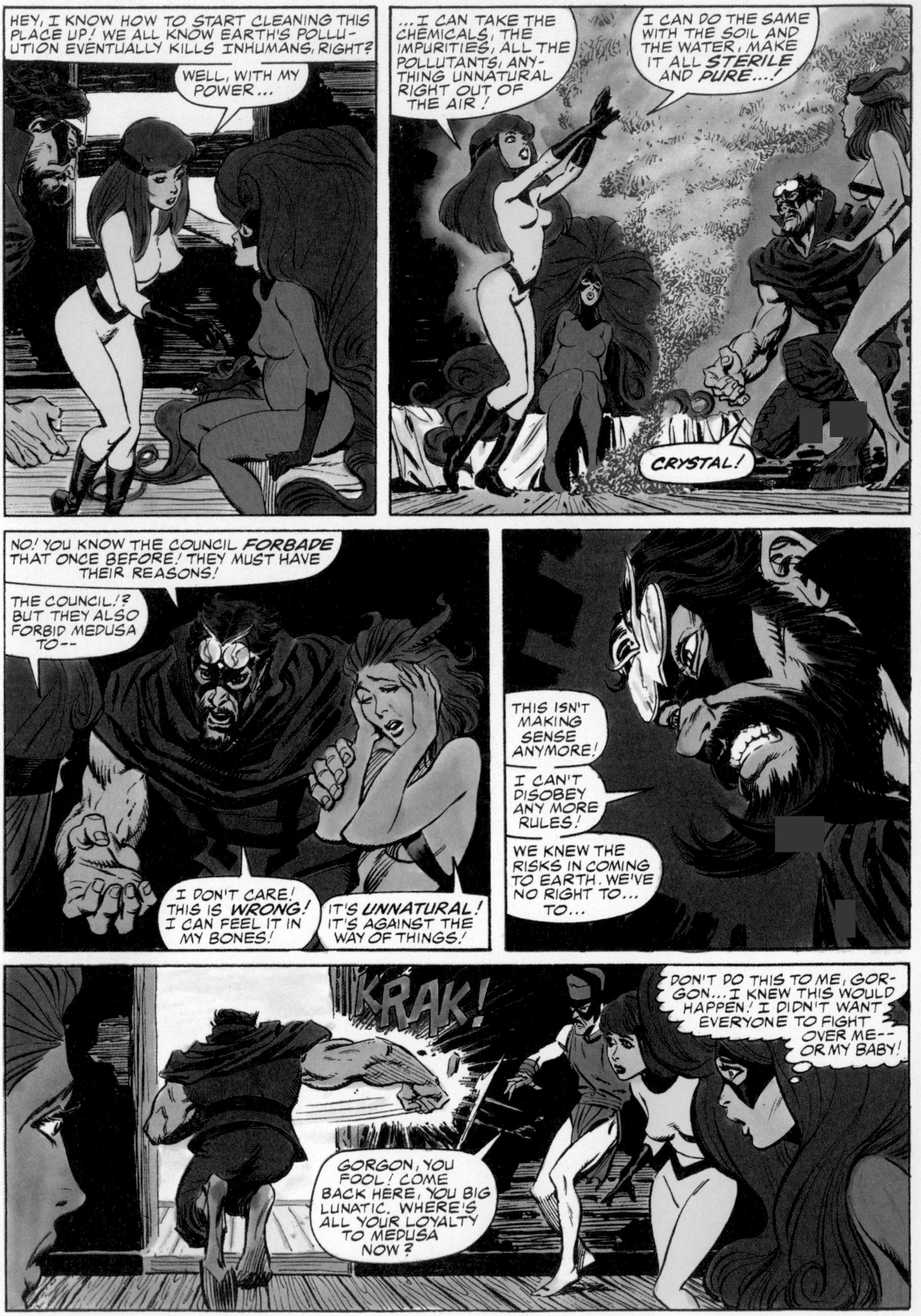
HEY, I KNOW HOW TO START CLEANING THIS PLACE UP! WE ALL KNOW EARTH'S POLLUTION EVENTUALLY KILLS INHUMANS, RIGHT?
WELL, WITH MY POWER...
...I CAN TAKE THE CHEMICALS, THE IMPURITIES, ALL THE POLLUTANTS, ANYTHING UNNATURAL RIGHT OUT OF THE AIR!
I CAN DO THE SAME WITH THE SOIL AND THE WATER, MAKE IT ALL STERILE AND PURE...!
CRYSTAL!
NO! YOU KNOW THE COUNCIL FORBADE THAT ONCE BEFORE! THEY MUST HAVE THEIR REASONS!
THE COUNCIL!? BUT THEY ALSO FORBID MEDUSA TO--
I DON'T CARE! THIS IS WRONG! I CAN FEEL IT IN MY BONES!
IT'S UNNATURAL! IT'S AGAINST THE WAY OF THINGS!
THIS ISN'T MAKING SENSE ANYMORE!
I CAN'T DISOBEY ANY MORE RULES!
WE KNEW THE RISKS IN COMING TO EARTH. WE'VE NO RIGHT TO... TO...
KRAK!
GORGON, YOU FOOL! COME BACK HERE, YOU BIG LUNATIC. WHERE'S ALL YOUR LOYALTY TO MEDUSA NOW?
DON'T DO THIS TO ME, GORGON... I KNEW THIS WOULD HAPPEN! I DIDN'T WANT EVERYONE TO FIGHT OVER ME-- OR MY BABY!

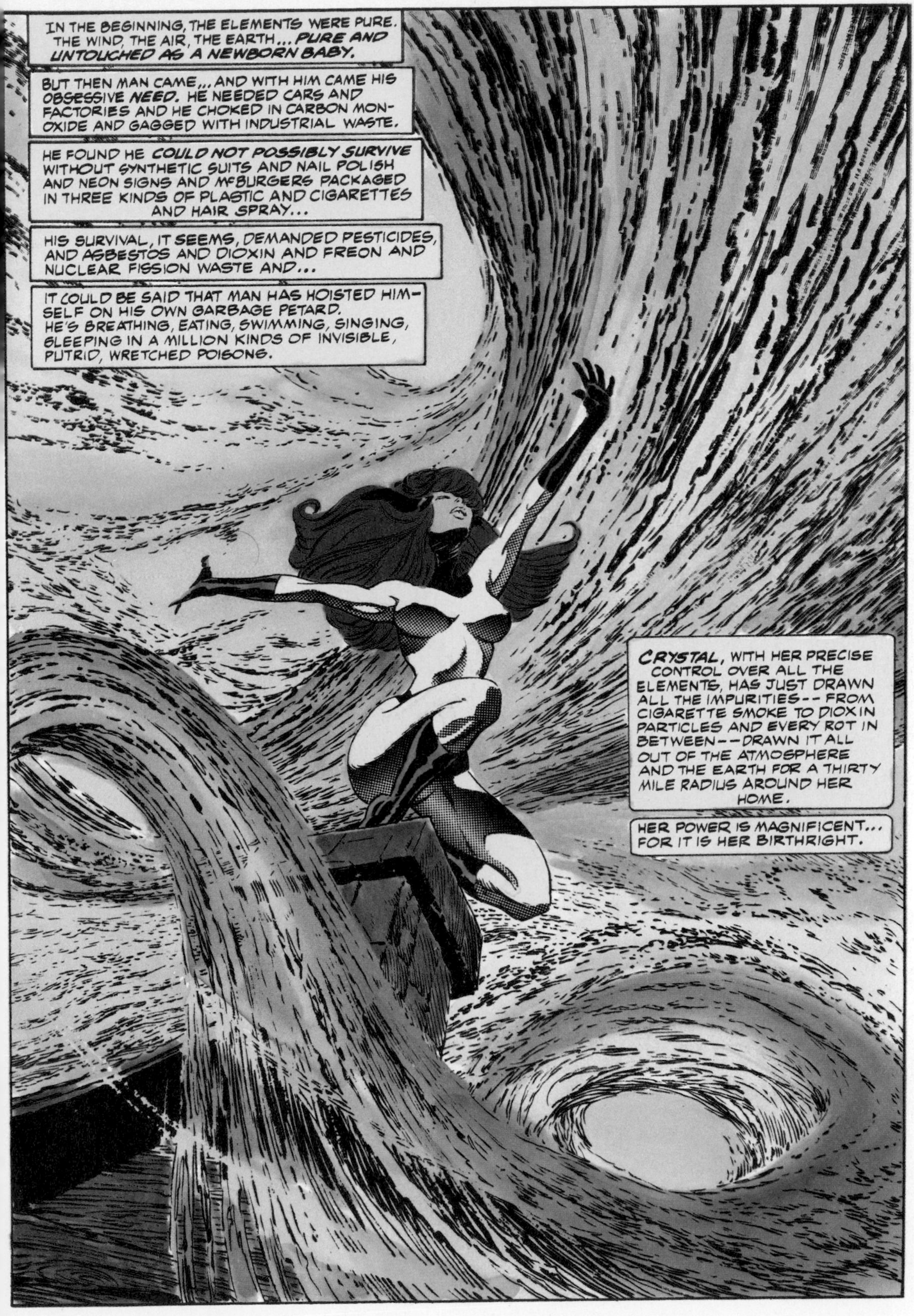
IN THE BEGINNING, THE ELEMENTS WERE PURE. THE WIND, THE AIR, THE EARTH... PURE AND UNTOUCHED AS A NEWBORN BABY.
BUT THEN MAN CAME... AND WITH HIM CAME HIS OBSESSIVE NEED. HE NEEDED CARS AND FACTORIES AND HE CHOKED IN CARBON MONOXIDE AND GAGGED WITH INDUSTRIAL WASTE.
HE FOUND HE COULD NOT POSSIBLY SURVIVE WITHOUT SYNTHETIC SUITS AND NAIL POLISH AND NEON SIGNS AND McBURGERS PACKAGED IN THREE KINDS OF PLASTIC AND CIGARETTES AND HAIR SPRAY...
HIS SURVIVAL, IT SEEMS, DEMANDED PESTICIDES, AND ASBESTOS AND DIOXIN AND FREON AND NUCLEAR FISSION WASTE AND...
IT COULD BE SAID THAT MAN HAS HOISTED HIMSELF ON HIS OWN GARBAGE PETARD. HE'S BREATHING, EATING, SWIMMING, SINGING, SLEEPING IN A MILLION KINDS OF INVISIBLE, PUTRID, WRETCHED POISONS.
CRYSTAL, WITH HER PRECISE CONTROL OVER ALL THE ELEMENTS, HAS JUST DRAWN ALL THE IMPURITIES-- FROM CIGARETTE SMOKE TO DIOXIN PARTICLES AND EVERY ROT IN BETWEEN--DRAWN IT ALL OUT OF THE ATMOSPHERE AND THE EARTH FOR A THIRTY MILE RADIUS AROUND HER HOME.
HER POWER IS MAGNIFICENT... FOR IT IS HER BIRTHRIGHT.

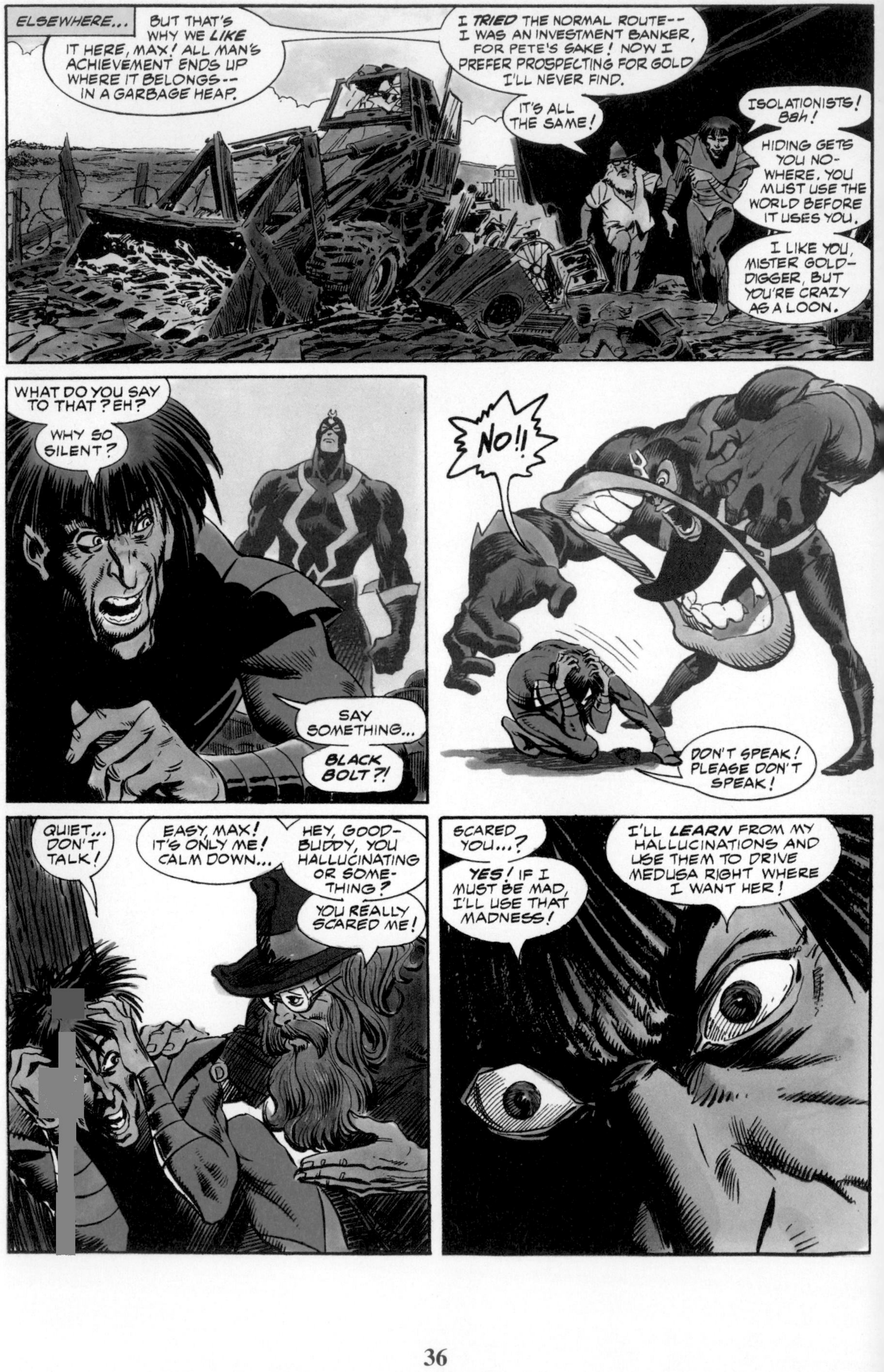

ELSEWHERE...
BUT THAT'S WHY WE *LIKE* IT HERE, MAX! ALL MAN'S ACHIEVEMENT ENDS UP WHERE IT BELONGS-- IN A GARBAGE HEAP.
I *TRIED* THE NORMAL ROUTE-- I WAS AN INVESTMENT BANKER, FOR PETE'S SAKE! NOW I PREFER PROSPECTING FOR GOLD I'LL NEVER FIND.
IT'S ALL THE SAME!
ISOLATIONISTS! Bah!
HIDING GETS YOU NO-WHERE. YOU MUST USE THE WORLD BEFORE IT USES YOU.
I LIKE YOU, MISTER GOLD-DIGGER, BUT YOU'RE CRAZY AS A LOON.
WHAT DO YOU SAY TO THAT? EH?
WHY SO SILENT?
SAY SOMETHING...
BLACK BOLT?!
NO!!
DON'T SPEAK! PLEASE DON'T SPEAK!
QUIET... DON'T TALK!
EASY, MAX! IT'S ONLY ME! CALM DOWN...
HEY, GOOD-BUDDY, YOU HALLUCINATING OR SOME-THING?
YOU REALLY SCARED ME!
SCARED YOU...?
YES! IF I MUST BE MAD, I'LL USE THAT MADNESS!
I'LL *LEARN* FROM MY HALLUCINATIONS AND USE THEM TO DRIVE MEDUSA RIGHT WHERE I WANT HER!

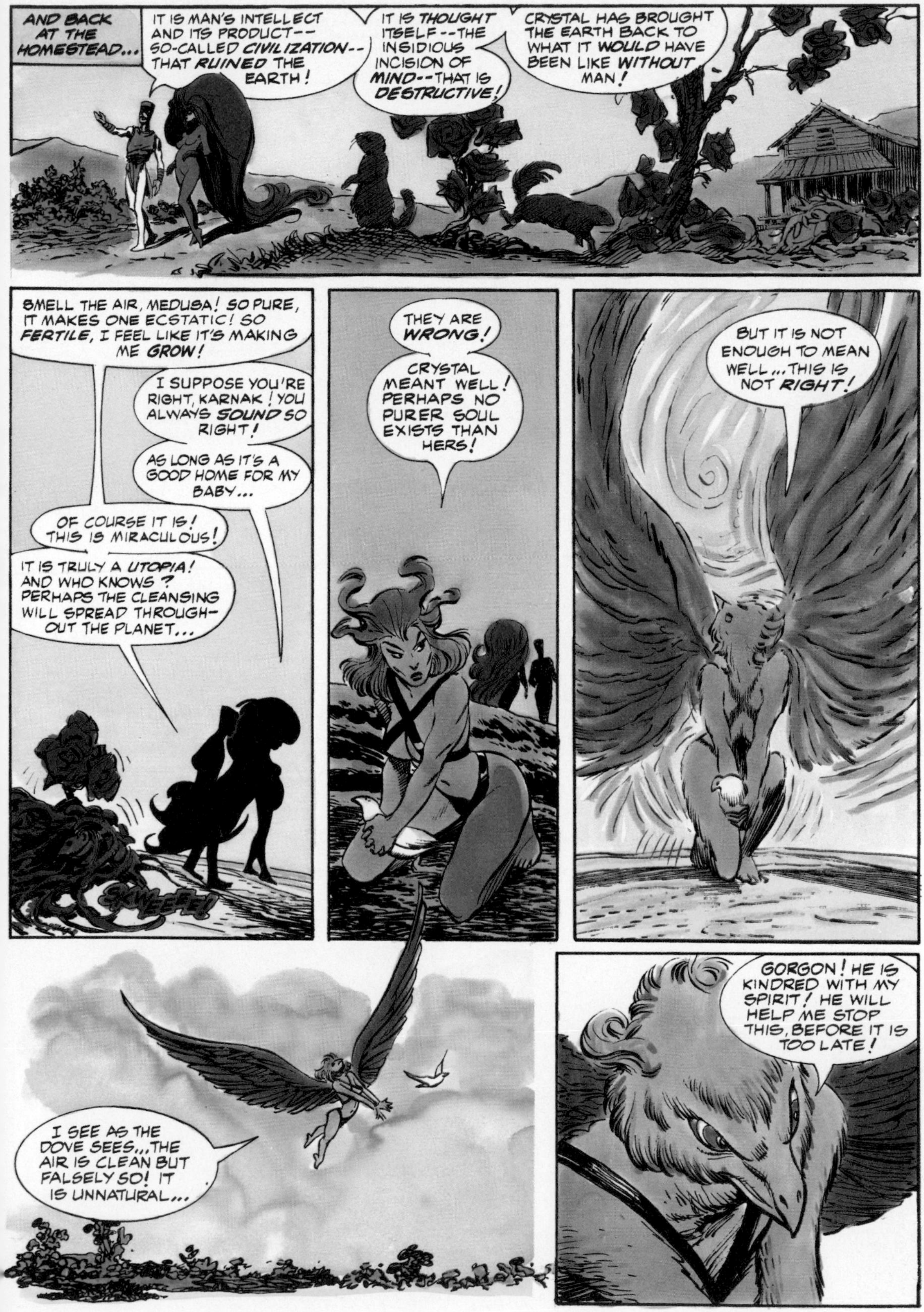
AND BACK AT THE HOMESTEAD...
IT IS MAN'S INTELLECT AND ITS PRODUCT-- SO-CALLED CIVILIZATION-- THAT RUINED THE EARTH!
IT IS THOUGHT ITSELF--THE INSIDIOUS INCISION OF MIND--THAT IS DESTRUCTIVE!
CRYSTAL HAS BROUGHT THE EARTH BACK TO WHAT IT WOULD HAVE BEEN LIKE WITHOUT MAN!
SMELL THE AIR, MEDUSA! SO PURE, IT MAKES ONE ECSTATIC! SO FERTILE, I FEEL LIKE IT'S MAKING ME GROW!
I SUPPOSE YOU'RE RIGHT, KARNAK! YOU ALWAYS SOUND SO RIGHT!
AS LONG AS IT'S A GOOD HOME FOR MY BABY...
OF COURSE IT IS! THIS IS MIRACULOUS!
IT IS TRULY A UTOPIA! AND WHO KNOWS? PERHAPS THE CLEANSING WILL SPREAD THROUGH-OUT THE PLANET...
SKWEEEE!
THEY ARE WRONG!
CRYSTAL MEANT WELL! PERHAPS NO PURER SOUL EXISTS THAN HERS!
BUT IT IS NOT ENOUGH TO MEAN WELL... THIS IS NOT RIGHT!
I SEE AS THE DOVE SEES... THE AIR IS CLEAN BUT FALSELY SO! IT IS UNNATURAL...
GORGON! HE IS KINDRED WITH MY SPIRIT! HE WILL HELP ME STOP THIS, BEFORE IT IS TOO LATE!

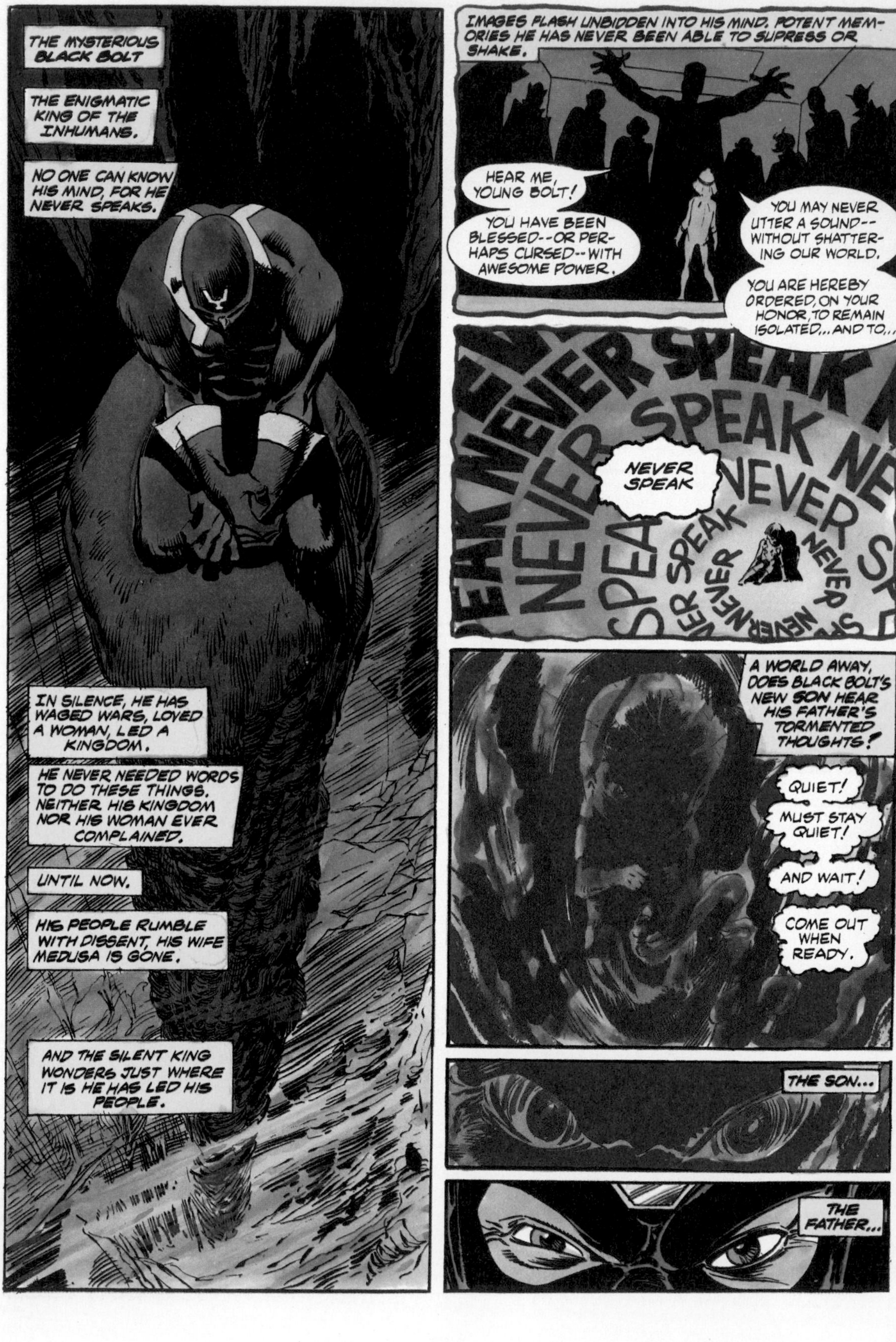
THE MYSTERIOUS BLACK BOLT
THE ENIGMATIC KING OF THE INHUMANS.
NO ONE CAN KNOW HIS MIND, FOR HE NEVER SPEAKS.
IN SILENCE, HE HAS WAGED WARS, LOVED A WOMAN, LED A KINGDOM.
HE NEVER NEEDED WORDS TO DO THESE THINGS. NEITHER HIS KINGDOM NOR HIS WOMAN EVER COMPLAINED.
UNTIL NOW.
HIS PEOPLE RUMBLE WITH DISSENT, HIS WIFE MEDUSA IS GONE.
AND THE SILENT KING WONDERS JUST WHERE IT IS HE HAS LED HIS PEOPLE.
IMAGES FLASH UNBIDDEN INTO HIS MIND, POTENT MEMORIES HE HAS NEVER BEEN ABLE TO SUPRESS OR SHAKE.
HEAR ME, YOUNG BOLT!
YOU HAVE BEEN BLESSED--OR PERHAPS CURSED--WITH AWESOME POWER.
YOU MAY NEVER UTTER A SOUND--WITHOUT SHATTERING OUR WORLD.
YOU ARE HEREBY ORDERED, ON YOUR HONOR, TO REMAIN ISOLATED... AND TO...
NEVER SPEAK
NEVER SPEAK
A WORLD AWAY, DOES BLACK BOLT'S NEW SON HEAR HIS FATHER'S TORMENTED THOUGHTS?
QUIET!
MUST STAY QUIET!
AND WAIT!
COME OUT WHEN READY.
THE SON...
THE FATHER...

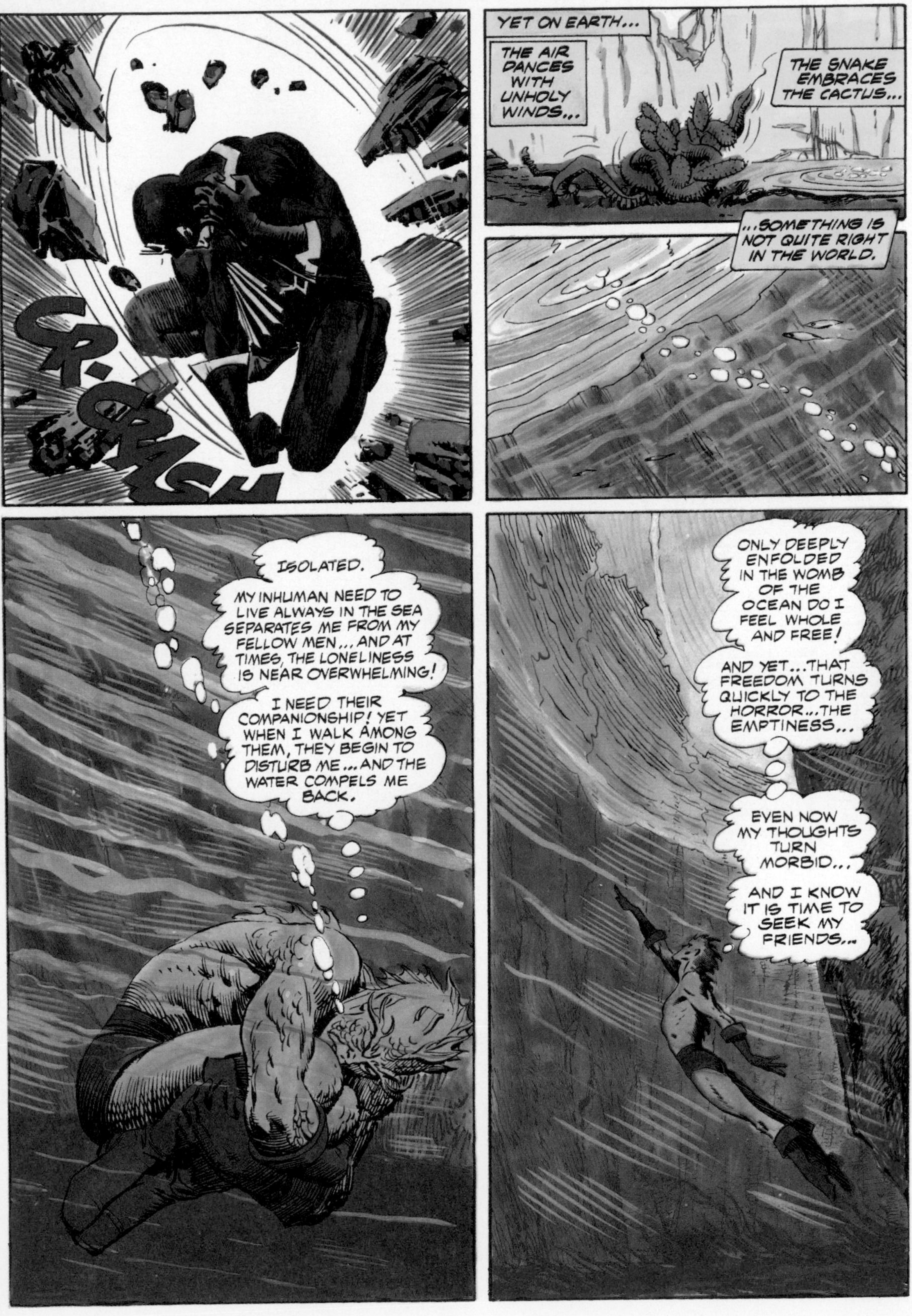
CR-CRASH
YET ON EARTH...
THE AIR DANCES WITH UNHOLY WINDS...
THE SNAKE EMBRACES THE CACTUS...
...SOMETHING IS NOT QUITE RIGHT IN THE WORLD.
ISOLATED.
MY INHUMAN NEED TO LIVE ALWAYS IN THE SEA SEPARATES ME FROM MY FELLOW MEN... AND AT TIMES, THE LONELINESS IS NEAR OVERWHELMING!
I NEED THEIR COMPANIONSHIP! YET WHEN I WALK AMONG THEM, THEY BEGIN TO DISTURB ME... AND THE WATER COMPELS ME BACK.
ONLY DEEPLY ENFOLDED IN THE WOMB OF THE OCEAN DO I FEEL WHOLE AND FREE!
AND YET... THAT FREEDOM TURNS QUICKLY TO THE HORROR... THE EMPTINESS...
EVEN NOW MY THOUGHTS TURN MORBID...
AND I KNOW IT IS TIME TO SEEK MY FRIENDS...

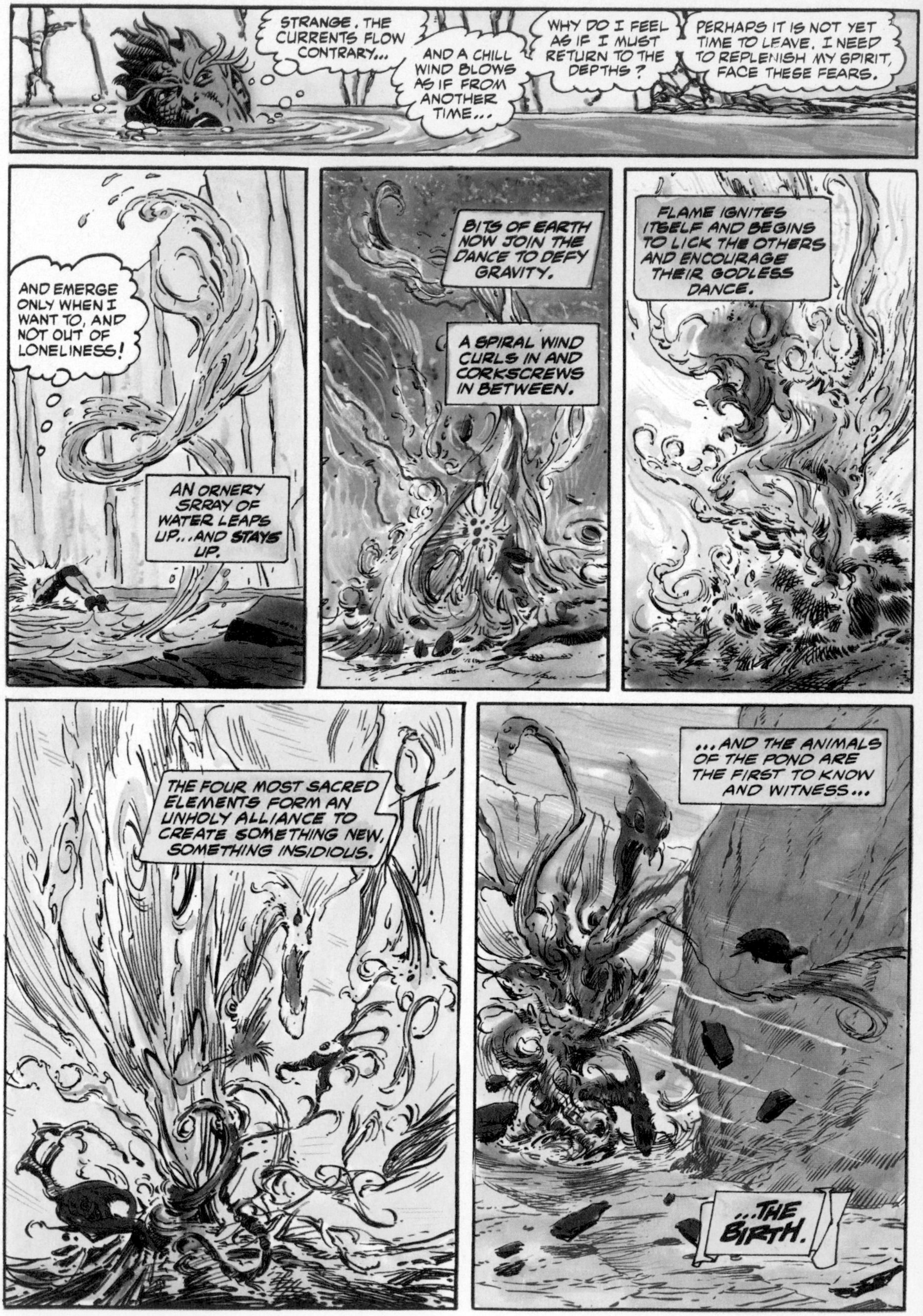
STRANGE. THE CURRENTS FLOW CONTRARY...
AND A CHILL WIND BLOWS AS IF FROM ANOTHER TIME...
WHY DO I FEEL AS IF I MUST RETURN TO THE DEPTHS?
PERHAPS IT IS NOT YET TIME TO LEAVE. I NEED TO REPLENISH MY SPIRIT, FACE THESE FEARS.
AND EMERGE ONLY WHEN I WANT TO, AND NOT OUT OF LONELINESS!
AN ORNERY SRRAY OF WATER LEAPS UP...AND STAYS UP.
BITS OF EARTH NOW JOIN THE DANCE TO DEFY GRAVITY.
A SPIRAL WIND CURLS IN AND CORKSCREWS IN BETWEEN.
FLAME IGNITES ITSELF AND BEGINS TO LICK THE OTHERS AND ENCOURAGE THEIR GODLESS DANCE.
THE FOUR MOST SACRED ELEMENTS FORM AN UNHOLY ALLIANCE TO CREATE SOMETHING NEW, SOMETHING INSIDIOUS.
...AND THE ANIMALS OF THE POND ARE THE FIRST TO KNOW AND WITNESS...
...THE BIRTH.

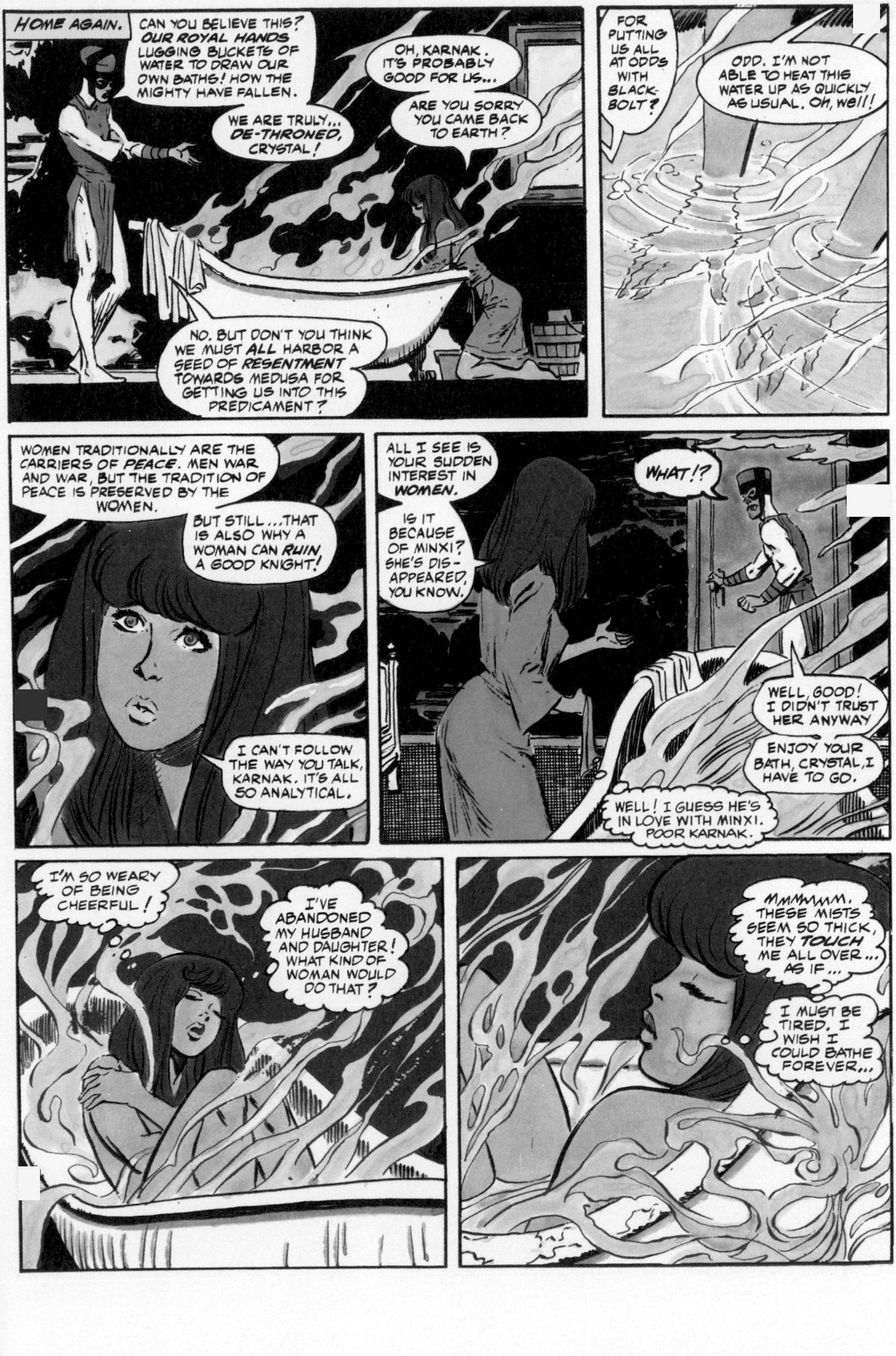
HOME AGAIN.
CAN YOU BELIEVE THIS? OUR ROYAL HANDS LUGGING BUCKETS OF WATER TO DRAW OUR OWN BATHS! HOW THE MIGHTY HAVE FALLEN.
WE ARE TRULY... DE-THRONED, CRYSTAL!
OH, KARNAK. IT'S PROBABLY GOOD FOR US...
ARE YOU SORRY YOU CAME BACK TO EARTH?
NO. BUT DON'T YOU THINK WE MUST ALL HARBOR A SEED OF RESENTMENT TOWARDS MEDUSA FOR GETTING US INTO THIS PREDICAMENT?
FOR PUTTING US ALL AT ODDS WITH BLACK-BOLT?
ODD. I'M NOT ABLE TO HEAT THIS WATER UP AS QUICKLY AS USUAL. OH, WELL!
WOMEN TRADITIONALLY ARE THE CARRIERS OF PEACE. MEN WAR AND WAR, BUT THE TRADITION OF PEACE IS PRESERVED BY THE WOMEN.
BUT STILL... THAT IS ALSO WHY A WOMAN CAN RUIN A GOOD KNIGHT!
I CAN'T FOLLOW THE WAY YOU TALK, KARNAK. IT'S ALL SO ANALYTICAL.
ALL I SEE IS YOUR SUDDEN INTEREST IN WOMEN.
IS IT BECAUSE OF MINXI? SHE'S DIS-APPEARED, YOU KNOW.
WHAT!?
WELL, GOOD! I DIDN'T TRUST HER ANYWAY
ENJOY YOUR BATH, CRYSTAL, I HAVE TO GO.
WELL! I GUESS HE'S IN LOVE WITH MINXI. POOR KARNAK.
I'M SO WEARY OF BEING CHEERFUL!
I'VE ABANDONED MY HUSBAND AND DAUGHTER! WHAT KIND OF WOMAN WOULD DO THAT?
MMMMMM. THESE MISTS SEEM SO THICK, THEY TOUCH ME ALL OVER... AS IF...
I MUST BE TIRED. I WISH I COULD BATHE FOREVER...

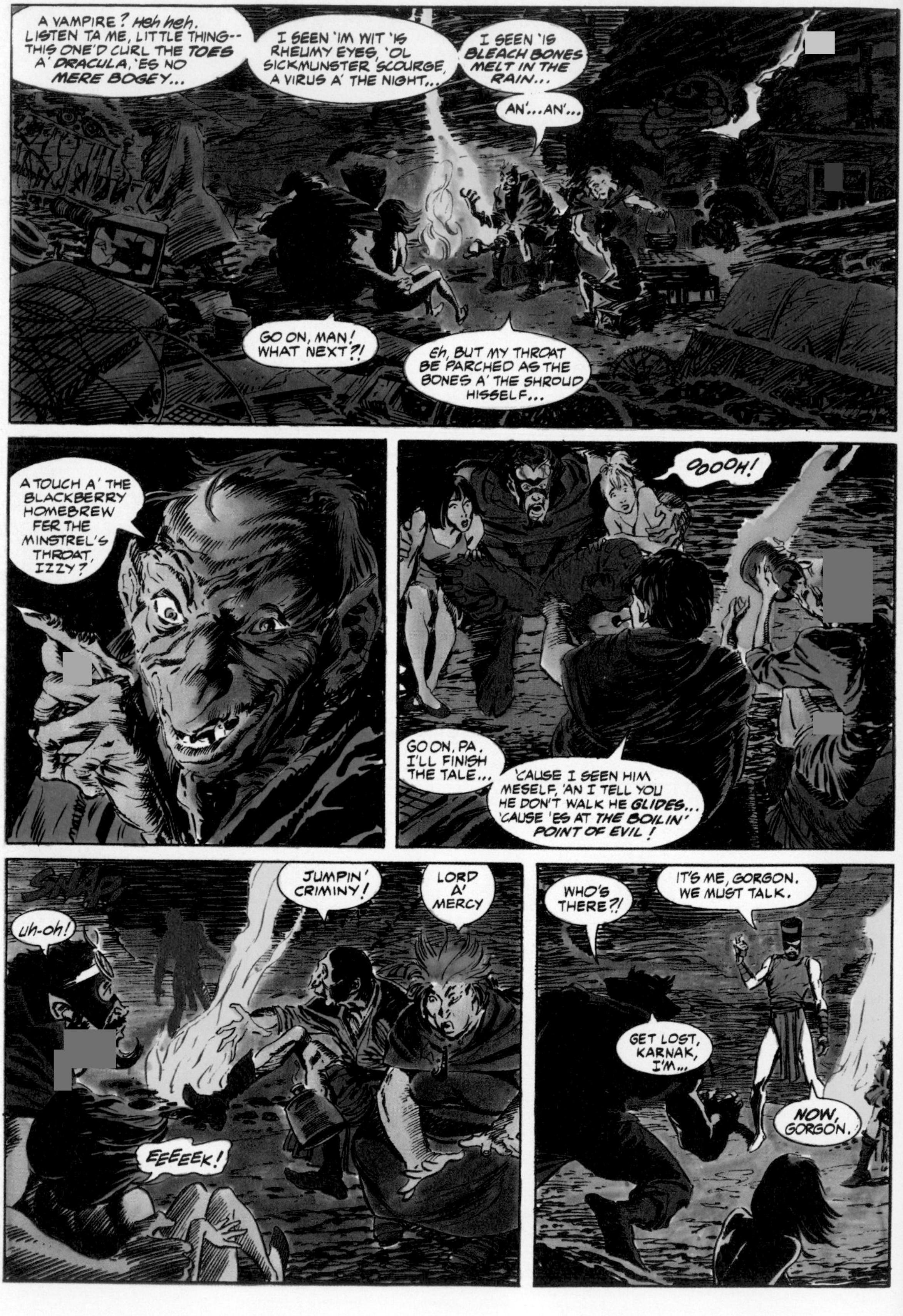
A VAMPIRE? heh heh. LISTEN TA ME, LITTLE THING-- THIS ONE'D CURL THE TOES A' DRACULA, 'ES NO MERE BOGEY...
I SEEN 'IM WIT 'IS RHEUMY EYES, 'OL SICKMUNSTER 'SCOURGE, A VIRUS A' THE NIGHT...
I SEEN 'IS BLEACH BONES MELT IN THE RAIN...
AN'... AN'...
GO ON, MAN! WHAT NEXT?!
eh, BUT MY THROAT BE PARCHED AS THE BONES A' THE SHROUD HISSELF...
A TOUCH A' THE BLACKBERRY HOMEBREW FER THE MINSTREL'S THROAT, IZZY?
OOOOH!
GO ON, PA. I'LL FINISH THE TALE...
'CAUSE I SEEN HIM MESELF, 'AN I TELL YOU HE DON'T WALK HE GLIDES... 'CAUSE 'ES AT THE BOILIN' POINT OF EVIL!
SNAP!
uh-oh!
JUMPIN' CRIMINY!
LORD A' MERCY
EEEEEK!
WHO'S THERE?!
IT'S ME, GORGON. WE MUST TALK.
GET LOST, KARNAK, I'M...
NOW, GORGON.

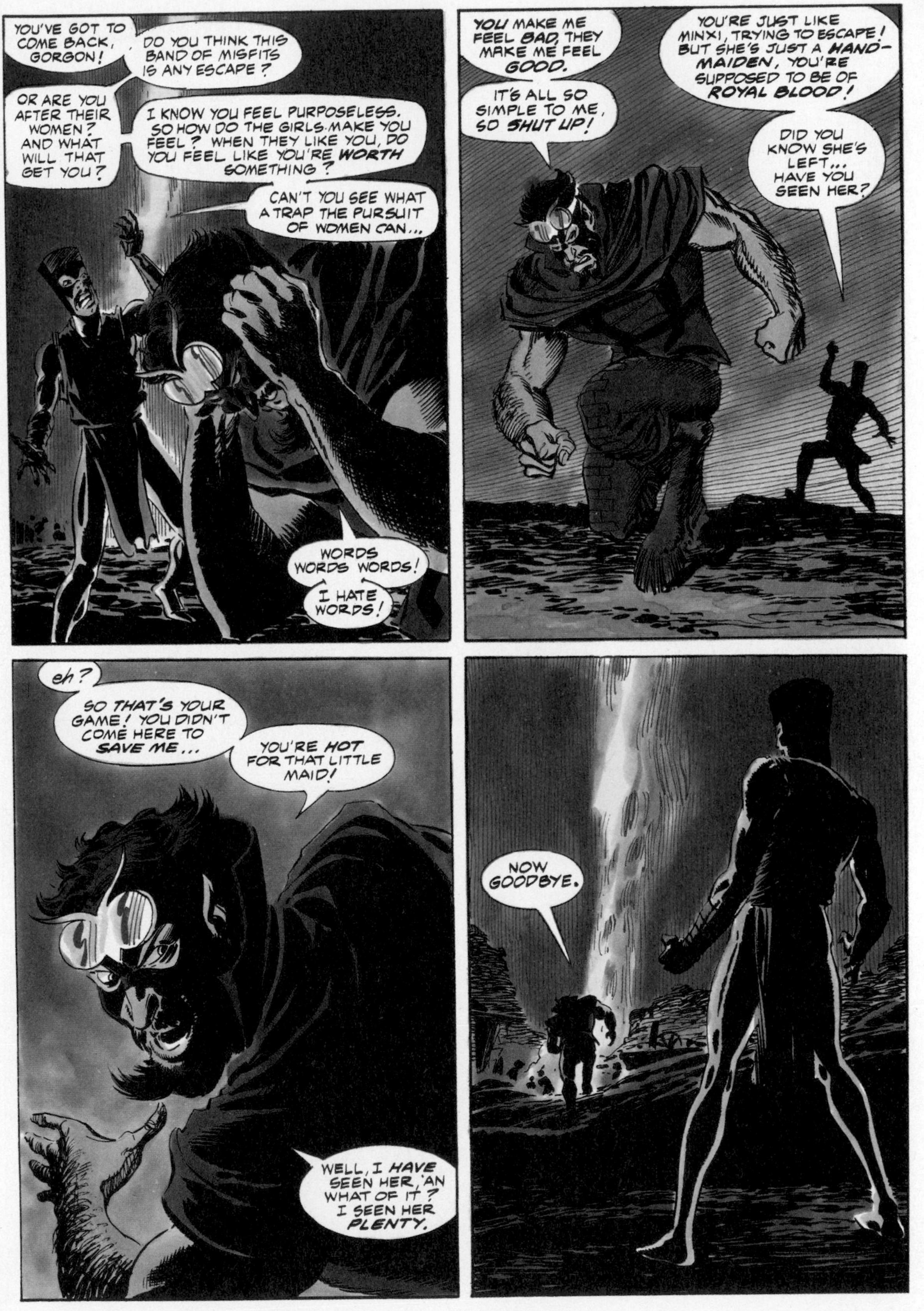
YOU'VE GOT TO COME BACK, GORGON!
DO YOU THINK THIS BAND OF MISFITS IS ANY ESCAPE?
OR ARE YOU AFTER THEIR WOMEN? AND WHAT WILL THAT GET YOU?
I KNOW YOU FEEL PURPOSELESS. SO HOW DO THE GIRLS MAKE YOU FEEL? WHEN THEY LIKE YOU, DO YOU FEEL LIKE YOU'RE WORTH SOMETHING?
CAN'T YOU SEE WHAT A TRAP THE PURSUIT OF WOMEN CAN...
WORDS WORDS WORDS!
I HATE WORDS!
YOU MAKE ME FEEL BAD, THEY MAKE ME FEEL GOOD.
IT'S ALL SO SIMPLE TO ME, SO SHUT UP!
YOU'RE JUST LIKE MINXI, TRYING TO ESCAPE! BUT SHE'S JUST A HAND-MAIDEN, YOU'RE SUPPOSED TO BE OF ROYAL BLOOD!
DID YOU KNOW SHE'S LEFT... HAVE YOU SEEN HER?
eh?
SO THAT'S YOUR GAME! YOU DIDN'T COME HERE TO SAVE ME...
YOU'RE HOT FOR THAT LITTLE MAID!
WELL, I HAVE SEEN HER, 'AN WHAT OF IT? I SEEN HER PLENTY.
NOW GOODBYE.

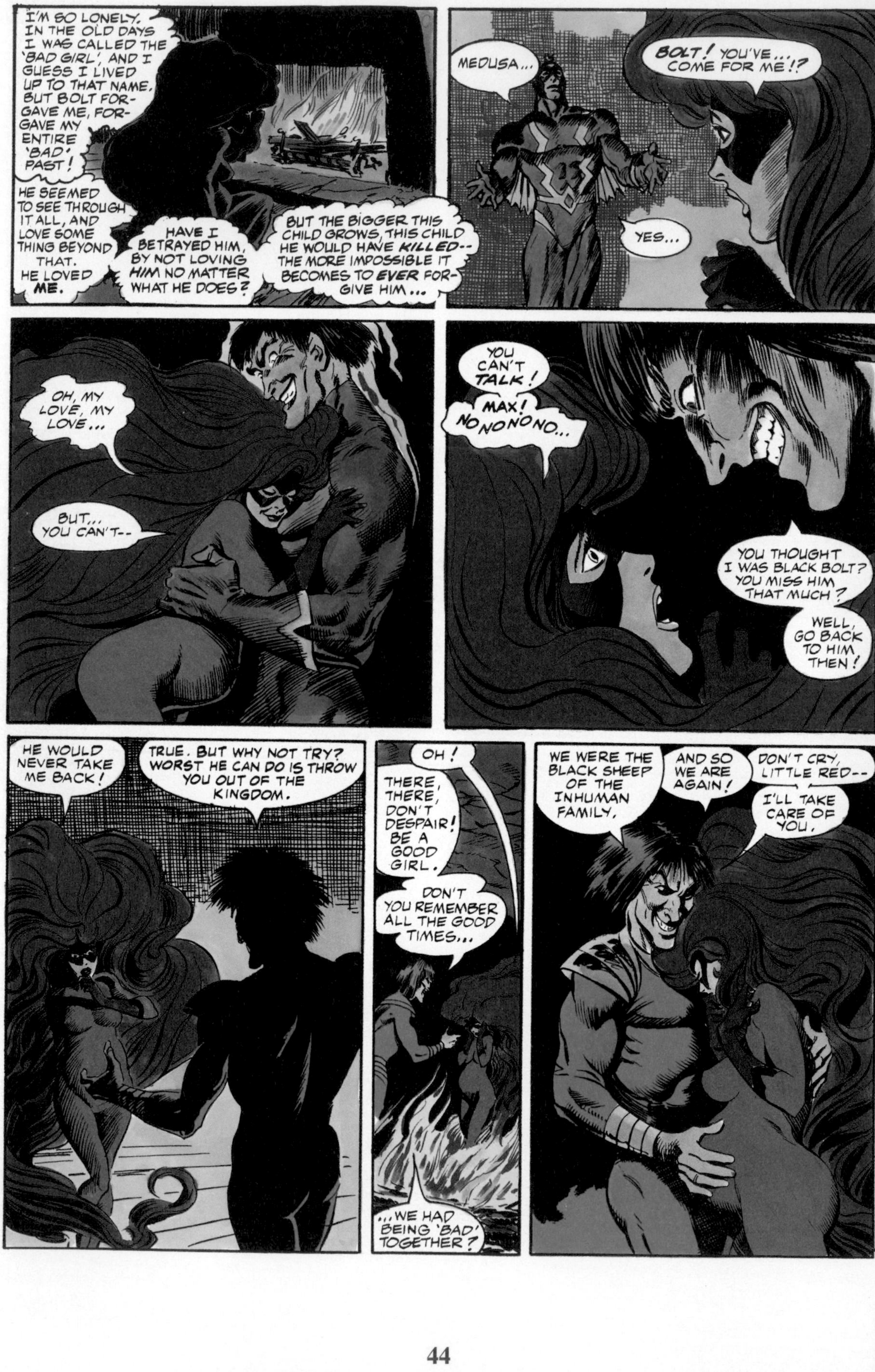
I'M SO LONELY. IN THE OLD DAYS I WAS CALLED THE 'BAD GIRL', AND I GUESS I LIVED UP TO THAT NAME. BUT BOLT FORGAVE ME, FORGAVE MY ENTIRE 'BAD' PAST!
HE SEEMED TO SEE THROUGH IT ALL, AND LOVE SOME THING BEYOND THAT. HE LOVED ME.
HAVE I BETRAYED HIM, BY NOT LOVING HIM NO MATTER WHAT HE DOES?
BUT THE BIGGER THIS CHILD GROWS, THIS CHILD HE WOULD HAVE KILLED-- THE MORE IMPOSSIBLE IT BECOMES TO EVER FORGIVE HIM...
MEDUSA...
BOLT! YOU'VE... COME FOR ME!?
YES...
OH, MY LOVE, MY LOVE...
BUT,.. YOU CAN'T--
YOU CAN'T TALK!
MAX! NONONONO...
YOU THOUGHT I WAS BLACK BOLT? YOU MISS HIM THAT MUCH?
WELL, GO BACK TO HIM THEN!
HE WOULD NEVER TAKE ME BACK!
TRUE. BUT WHY NOT TRY? WORST HE CAN DO IS THROW YOU OUT OF THE KINGDOM.
OH!
THERE, THERE, DON'T DESPAIR! BE A GOOD GIRL.
DON'T YOU REMEMBER ALL THE GOOD TIMES...
...WE HAD BEING 'BAD' TOGETHER?
WE WERE THE BLACK SHEEP OF THE INHUMAN FAMILY,
AND SO WE ARE AGAIN!
DON'T CRY, LITTLE RED--
I'LL TAKE CARE OF YOU.

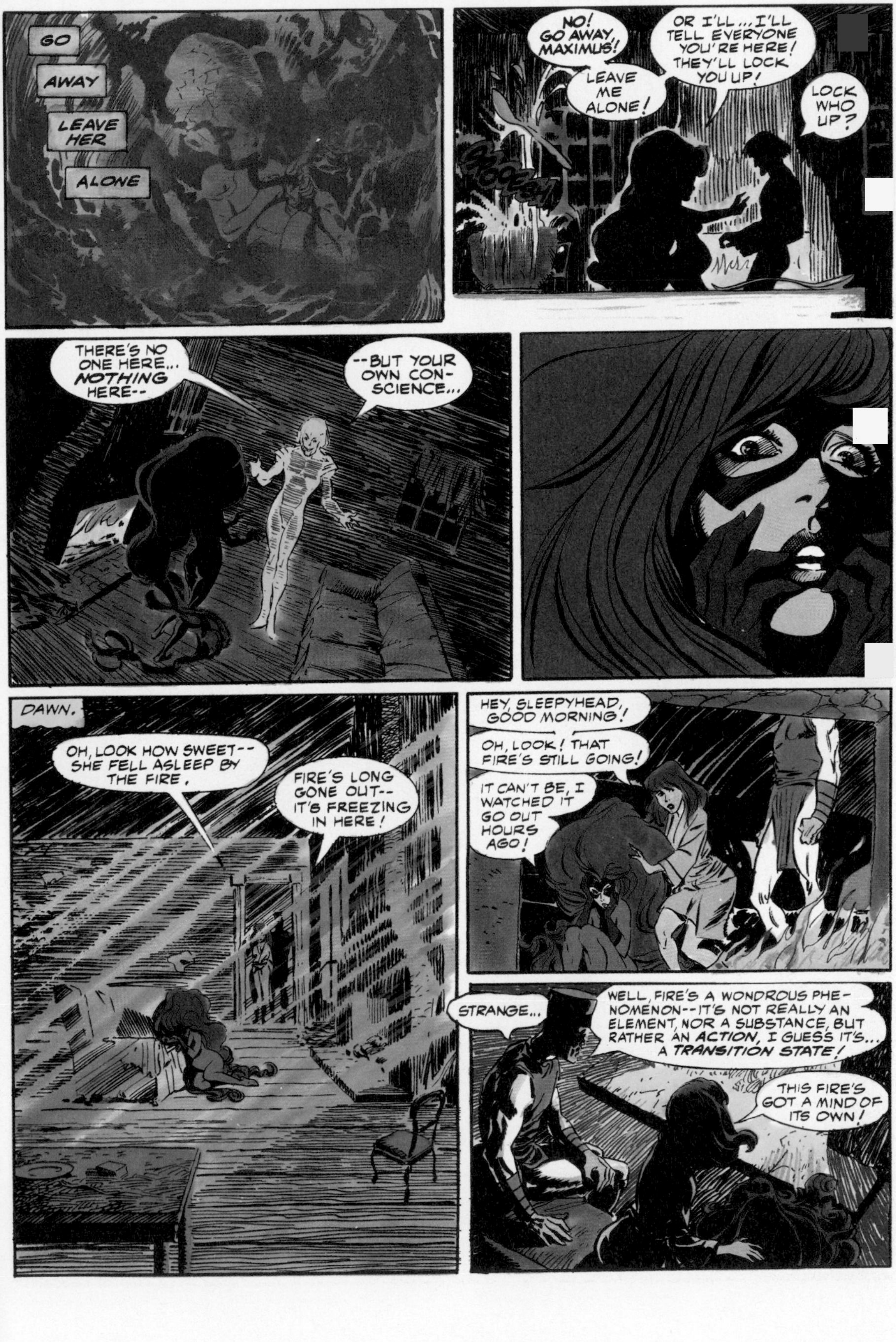

GO
AWAY
LEAVE HER
ALONE
NO! GO AWAY, MAXIMUS!
LEAVE ME ALONE!
OR I'LL... I'LL TELL EVERYONE YOU'RE HERE! THEY'LL LOCK YOU UP!
LOCK WHO UP?
THERE'S NO ONE HERE... NOTHING HERE--
--BUT YOUR OWN CON-SCIENCE...
DAWN.
OH, LOOK HOW SWEET-- SHE FELL ASLEEP BY THE FIRE.
FIRE'S LONG GONE OUT-- IT'S FREEZING IN HERE!
HEY, SLEEPYHEAD, GOOD MORNING!
OH, LOOK! THAT FIRE'S STILL GOING!
IT CAN'T BE, I WATCHED IT GO OUT HOURS AGO!
STRANGE...
WELL, FIRE'S A WONDROUS PHE-NOMENON--IT'S NOT REALLY AN ELEMENT, NOR A SUBSTANCE, BUT RATHER AN ACTION, I GUESS IT'S... A TRANSITION STATE!
THIS FIRE'S GOT A MIND OF ITS OWN!

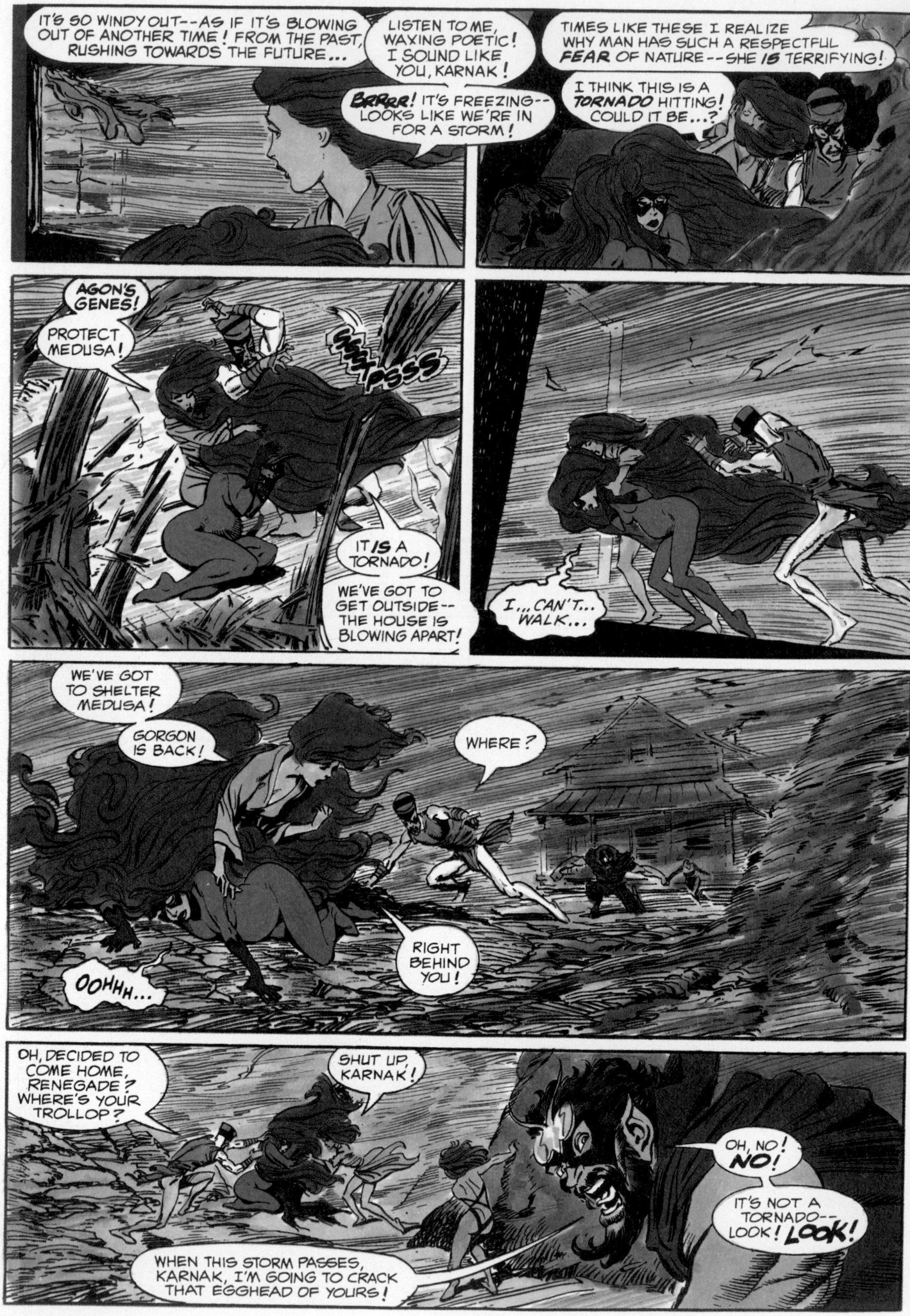
IT'S SO WINDY OUT--AS IF IT'S BLOWING OUT OF ANOTHER TIME! FROM THE PAST, RUSHING TOWARDS THE FUTURE...
LISTEN TO ME, WAXING POETIC! I SOUND LIKE YOU, KARNAK!
BRRRR! IT'S FREEZING-- LOOKS LIKE WE'RE IN FOR A STORM!
TIMES LIKE THESE I REALIZE WHY MAN HAS SUCH A RESPECTFUL FEAR OF NATURE--SHE IS TERRIFYING!
I THINK THIS IS A TORNADO HITTING! COULD IT BE...?
AGON'S GENES!
PROTECT MEDUSA!
SSSST PSSS
IT IS A TORNADO!
WE'VE GOT TO GET OUTSIDE-- THE HOUSE IS BLOWING APART!
I...CAN'T... WALK...
WE'VE GOT TO SHELTER MEDUSA!
GORGON IS BACK!
WHERE?
RIGHT BEHIND YOU!
OOHHH...
OH, DECIDED TO COME HOME, RENEGADE? WHERE'S YOUR TROLLOP?
SHUT UP, KARNAK!
OH, NO! NO!
IT'S NOT A TORNADO-- LOOK! LOOK!
WHEN THIS STORM PASSES, KARNAK, I'M GOING TO CRACK THAT EGGHEAD OF YOURS!

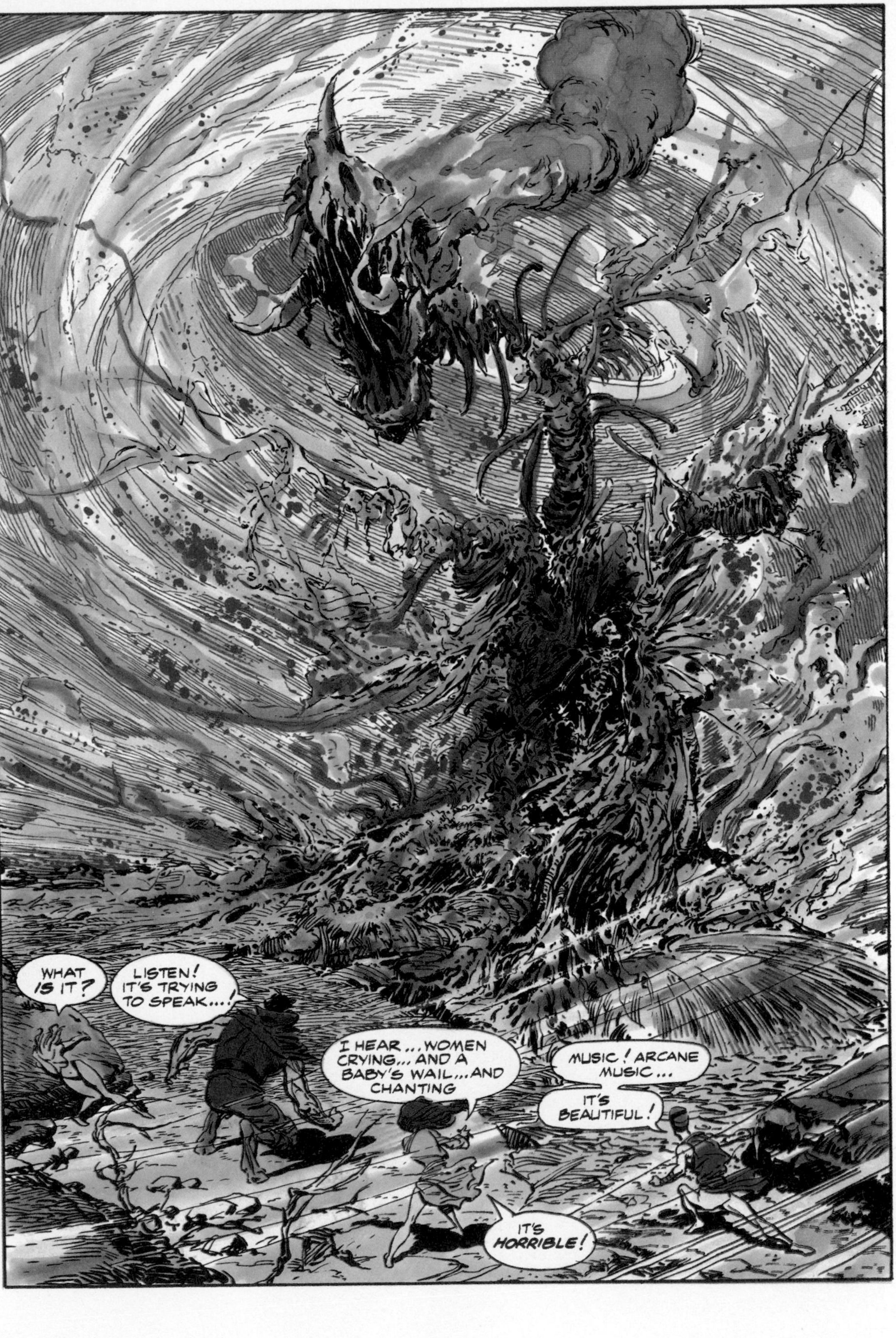
WHAT IS IT?
LISTEN! IT'S TRYING TO SPEAK...!
I HEAR... WOMEN CRYING... AND A BABY'S WAIL... AND CHANTING
MUSIC! ARCANE MUSIC...
IT'S BEAUTIFUL!
IT'S HORRIBLE!

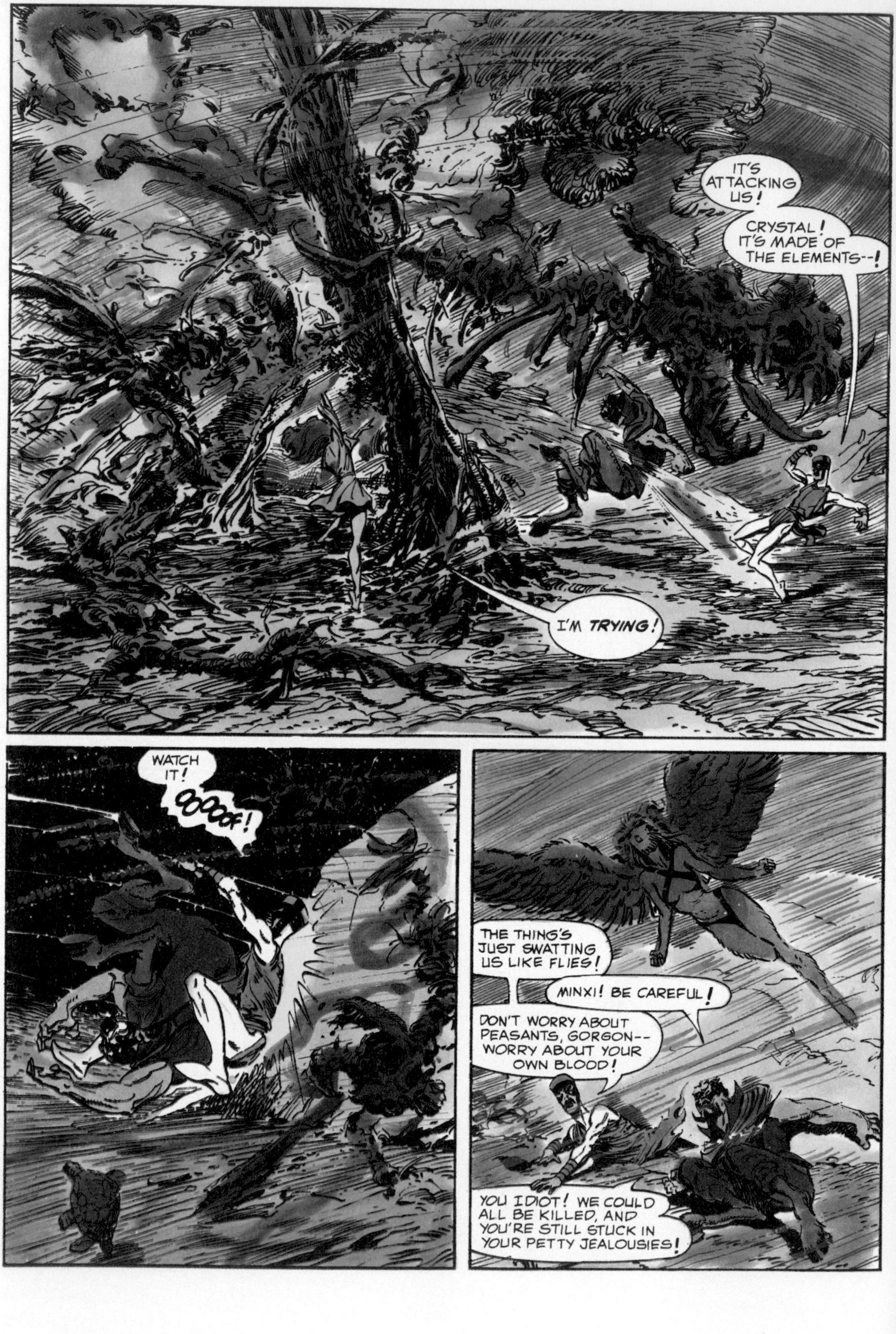

IT'S ATTACKING US!
CRYSTAL! IT'S MADE OF THE ELEMENTS--!
I'M TRYING!
WATCH IT!
OOOOOF!
THE THING'S JUST SWATTING US LIKE FLIES!
MINXI! BE CAREFUL!
DON'T WORRY ABOUT PEASANTS, GORGON-- WORRY ABOUT YOUR OWN BLOOD!
YOU IDIOT! WE COULD ALL BE KILLED, AND YOU'RE STILL STUCK IN YOUR PETTY JEALOUSIES!

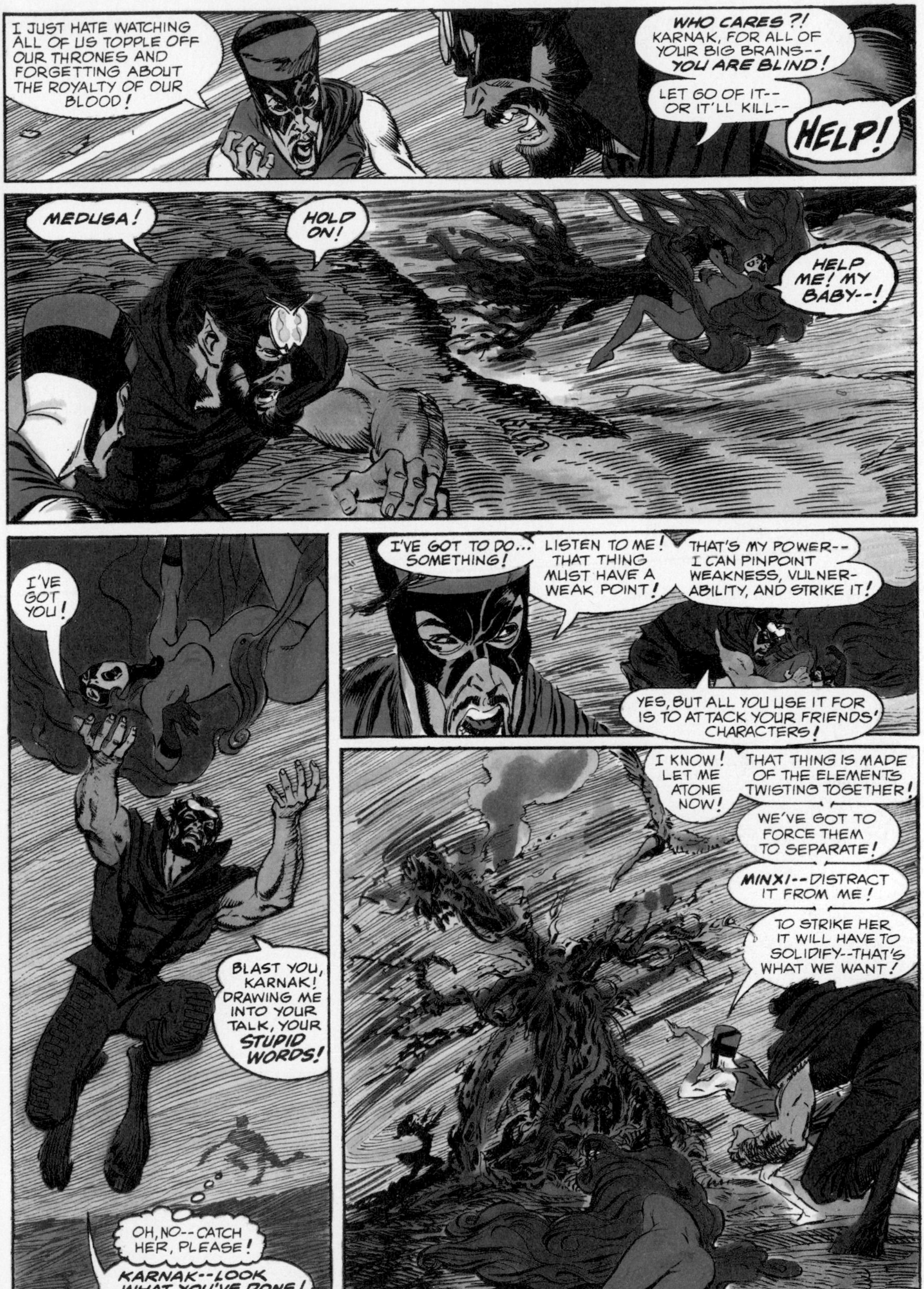
I JUST HATE WATCHING ALL OF US TOPPLE OFF OUR THRONES AND FORGETTING ABOUT THE ROYALTY OF OUR BLOOD!
WHO CARES?! KARNAK, FOR ALL OF YOUR BIG BRAINS-- YOU ARE BLIND!
LET GO OF IT-- OR IT'LL KILL--
HELP!
MEDUSA!
HOLD ON!
HELP ME! MY BABY--!
I'VE GOT YOU!
BLAST YOU, KARNAK! DRAWING ME INTO YOUR TALK, YOUR STUPID WORDS!
OH, NO--CATCH HER, PLEASE!
KARNAK--LOOK WHAT YOU'VE DONE!
I'VE GOT TO DO... SOMETHING!
LISTEN TO ME! THAT THING MUST HAVE A WEAK POINT!
THAT'S MY POWER-- I CAN PINPOINT WEAKNESS, VULNER-ABILITY, AND STRIKE IT!
YES, BUT ALL YOU USE IT FOR IS TO ATTACK YOUR FRIENDS' CHARACTERS!
I KNOW! LET ME ATONE NOW!
THAT THING IS MADE OF THE ELEMENTS TWISTING TOGETHER!
WE'VE GOT TO FORCE THEM TO SEPARATE!
MINXI--DISTRACT IT FROM ME!
TO STRIKE HER IT WILL HAVE TO SOLIDIFY--THAT'S WHAT WE WANT!

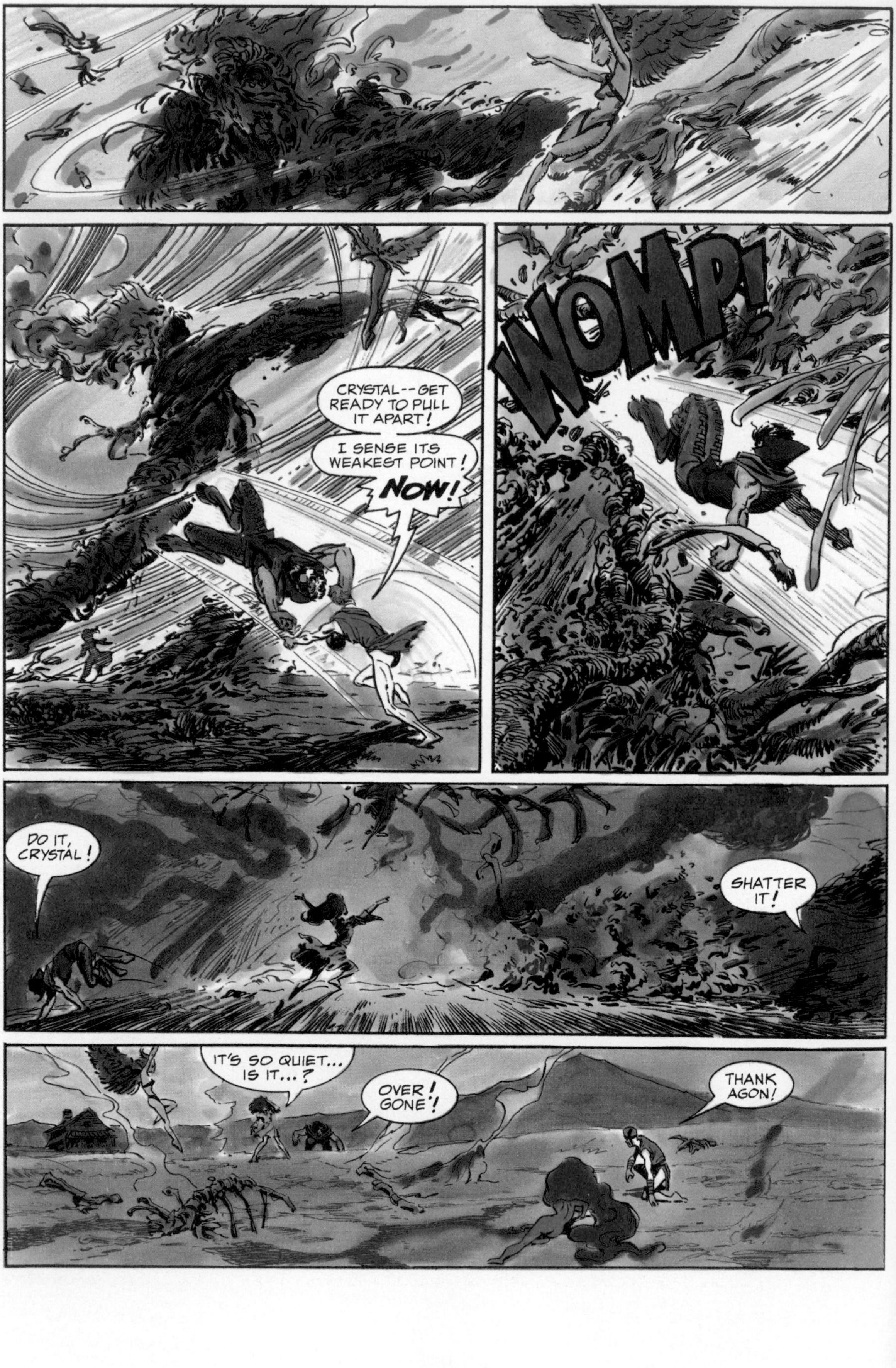
CRYSTAL--GET READY TO PULL IT APART!
I SENSE ITS WEAKEST POINT!
NOW!
WOMP!
DO IT, CRYSTAL!
SHATTER IT!
IT'S SO QUIET... IS IT...?
OVER! GONE!
THANK AGON!

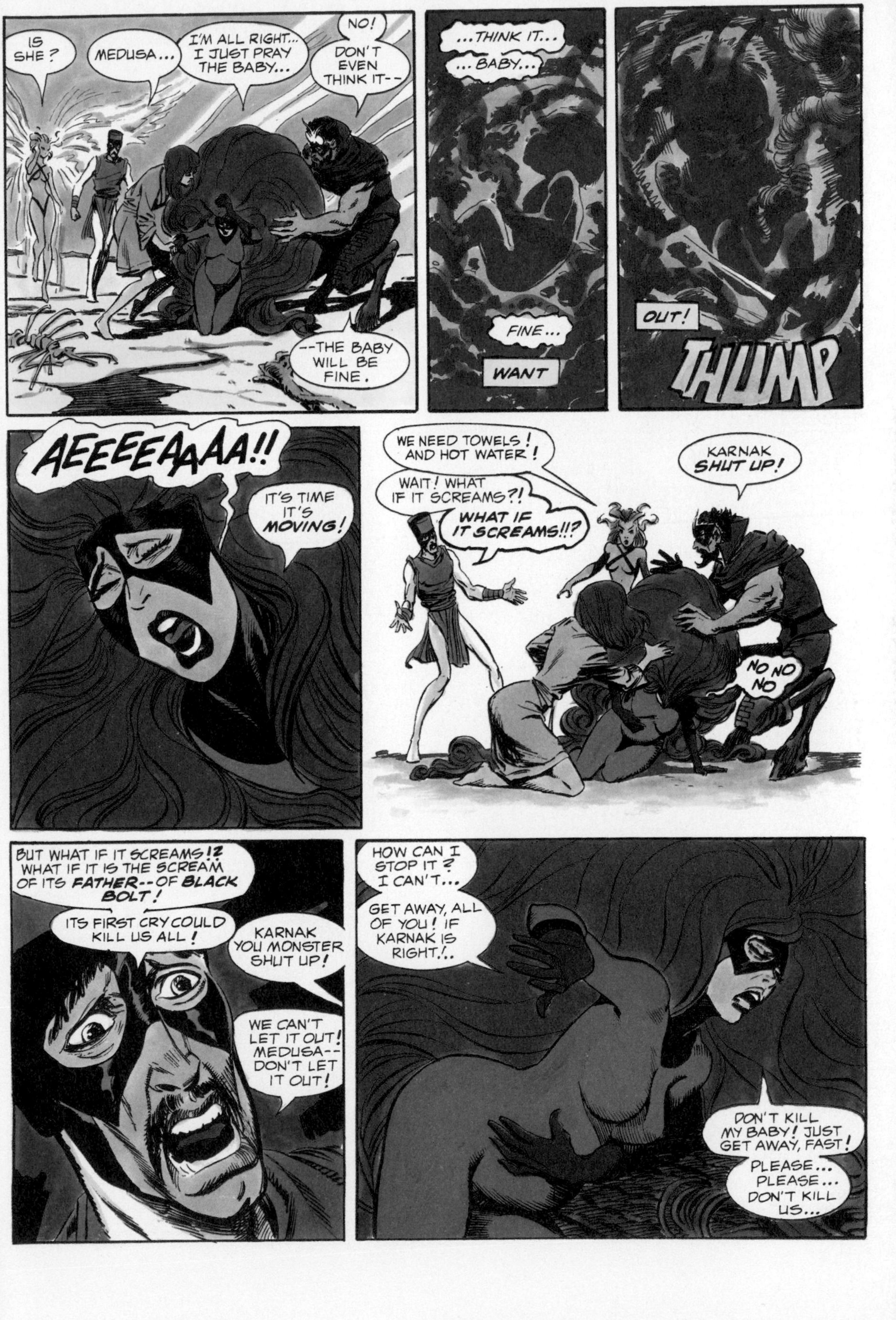
IS SHE ?
MEDUSA...
I'M ALL RIGHT... I JUST PRAY THE BABY...
NO! DON'T EVEN THINK IT--
--THE BABY WILL BE FINE.
...THINK IT...
...BABY...
FINE...
WANT
OUT!
THUMP
AEEEEAAAA!!
IT'S TIME IT'S MOVING!
WE NEED TOWELS! AND HOT WATER!
WAIT! WHAT IF IT SCREAMS?! WHAT IF IT SCREAMS!!?
KARNAK SHUT UP!
NO NO NO
BUT WHAT IF IT SCREAMS!? WHAT IF IT IS THE SCREAM OF ITS FATHER--OF BLACK BOLT!
ITS FIRST CRY COULD KILL US ALL!
KARNAK YOU MONSTER SHUT UP!
WE CAN'T LET IT OUT! MEDUSA-- DON'T LET IT OUT!
HOW CAN I STOP IT? I CAN'T...
GET AWAY, ALL OF YOU! IF KARNAK IS RIGHT!..
DON'T KILL MY BABY! JUST GET AWAY, FAST!
PLEASE... PLEASE... DON'T KILL US...

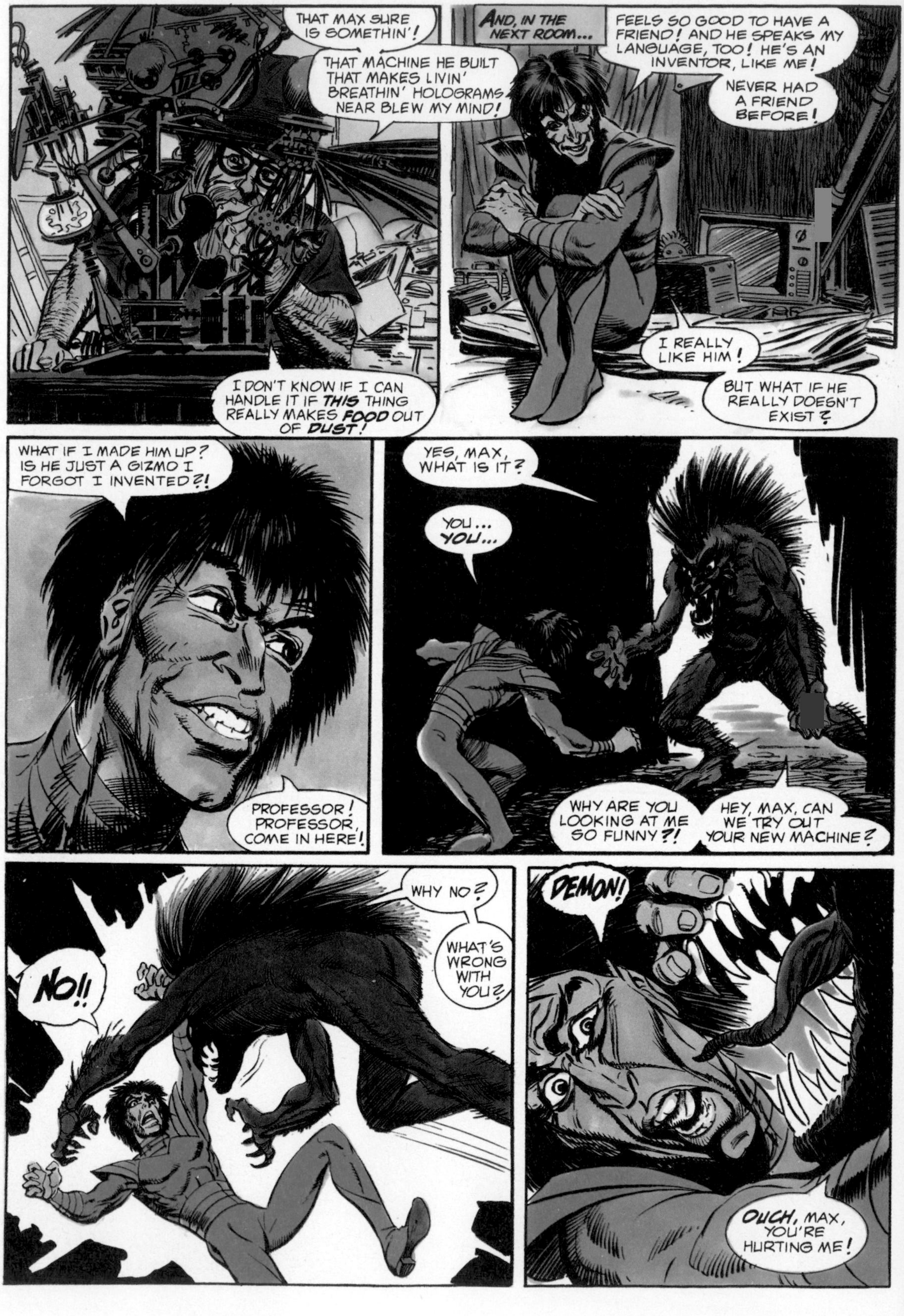
THAT MAX SURE IS SOMETHIN'!
THAT MACHINE HE BUILT THAT MAKES LIVIN' BREATHIN' HOLOGRAMS NEAR BLEW MY MIND!
I DON'T KNOW IF I CAN HANDLE IT IF THIS THING REALLY MAKES FOOD OUT OF DUST!
AND, IN THE NEXT ROOM...
FEELS SO GOOD TO HAVE A FRIEND! AND HE SPEAKS MY LANGUAGE, TOO! HE'S AN INVENTOR, LIKE ME!
NEVER HAD A FRIEND BEFORE!
I REALLY LIKE HIM!
BUT WHAT IF HE REALLY DOESN'T EXIST?
WHAT IF I MADE HIM UP? IS HE JUST A GIZMO I FORGOT I INVENTED?!
PROFESSOR! PROFESSOR, COME IN HERE!
YES, MAX, WHAT IS IT?
YOU... YOU...
WHY ARE YOU LOOKING AT ME SO FUNNY?!
HEY, MAX, CAN WE TRY OUT YOUR NEW MACHINE?
NO!!
WHY NO?
WHAT'S WRONG WITH YOU?
DEMON!
OUCH, MAX, YOU'RE HURTING ME!

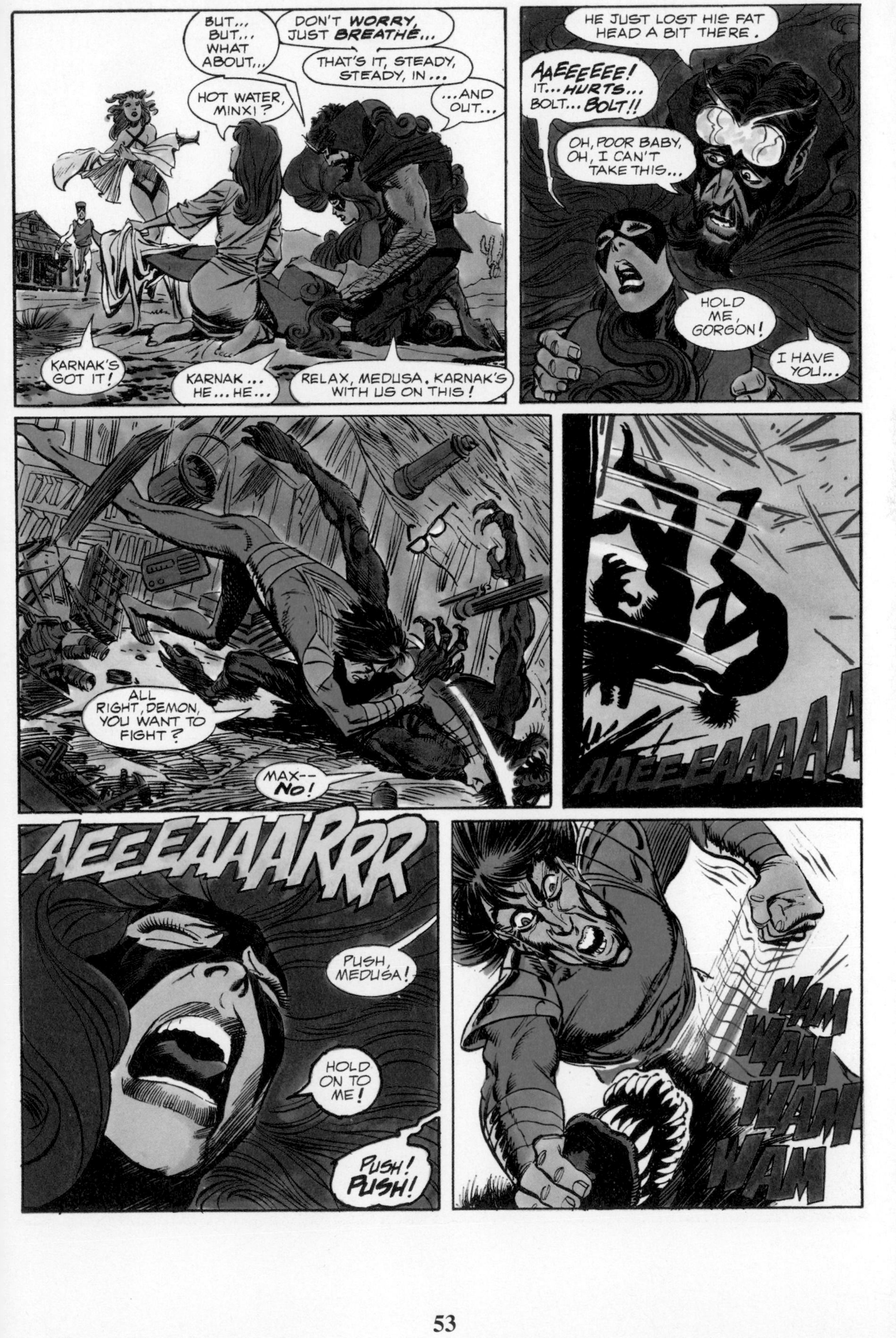
BUT... BUT... WHAT ABOUT...
DON'T WORRY, JUST BREATHE...
THAT'S IT, STEADY, STEADY, IN...
HOT WATER, MINX!?
...AND OUT...
KARNAK'S GOT IT!
KARNAK... HE... HE...
RELAX, MEDUSA. KARNAK'S WITH US ON THIS!
HE JUST LOST HIS FAT HEAD A BIT THERE.
AAEEEEEE! IT... HURTS... BOLT... BOLT!!
OH, POOR BABY, OH, I CAN'T TAKE THIS...
HOLD ME, GORGON!
I HAVE YOU...
ALL RIGHT, DEMON, YOU WANT TO FIGHT?
MAX-- NO!
AAEEEAAAAA
AEEEAAAARRR
PUSH, MEDUSA!
HOLD ON TO ME!
PUSH! PUSH!
WAM WAM WAM WAM WAM

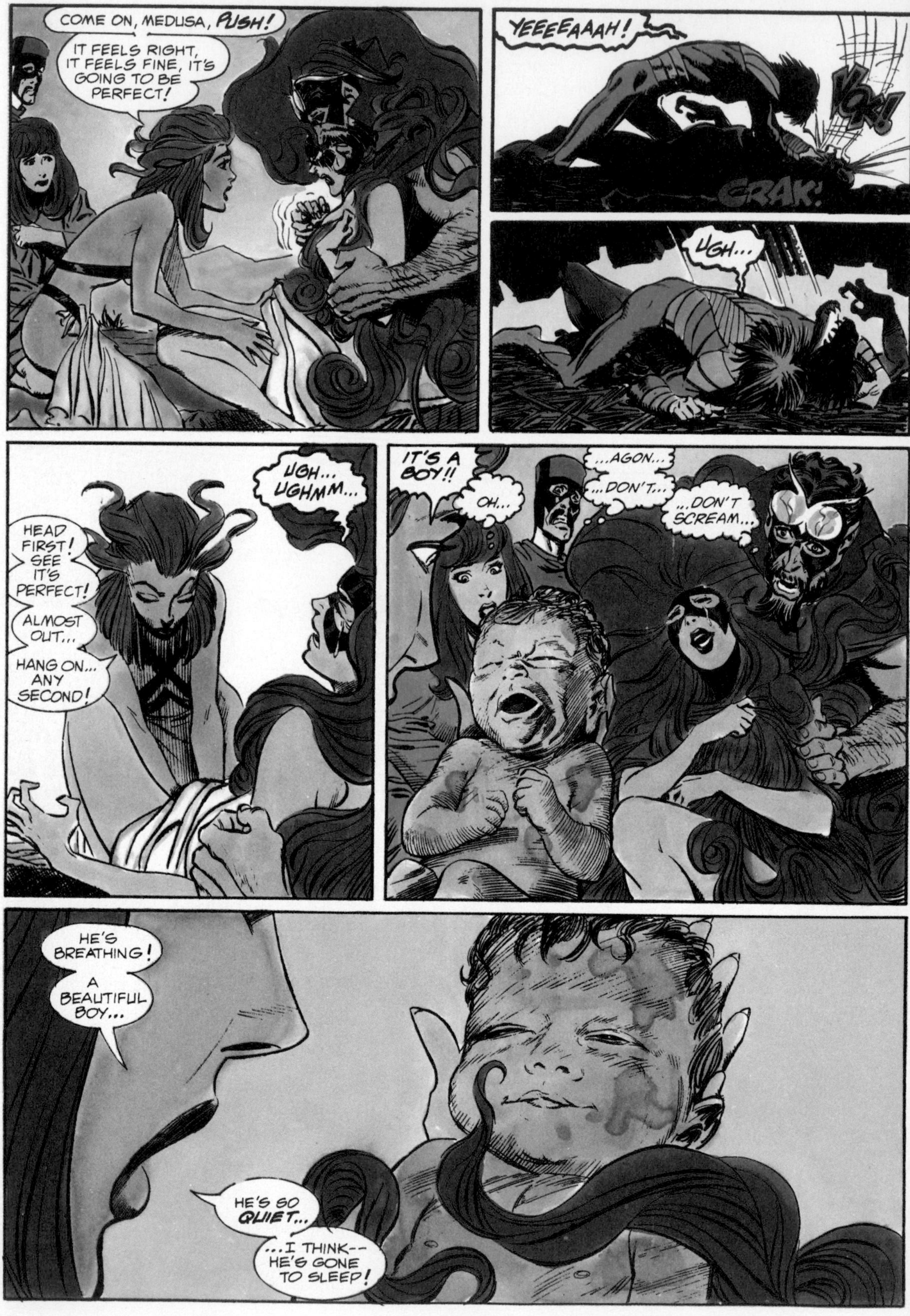
COME ON, MEDUSA, PUSH!
IT FEELS RIGHT, IT FEELS FINE, IT'S GOING TO BE PERFECT!
YEEEEAAAH!
YOW!
CRAK!
UGH...
UGH... UGHMM...
HEAD FIRST! SEE IT'S PERFECT!
ALMOST OUT...
HANG ON... ANY SECOND!
IT'S A BOY!!
OH...
...AGON...
...DON'T...
...DON'T SCREAM...
HE'S BREATHING!
A BEAUTIFUL BOY...
HE'S SO QUIET...
...I THINK-- HE'S GONE TO SLEEP!

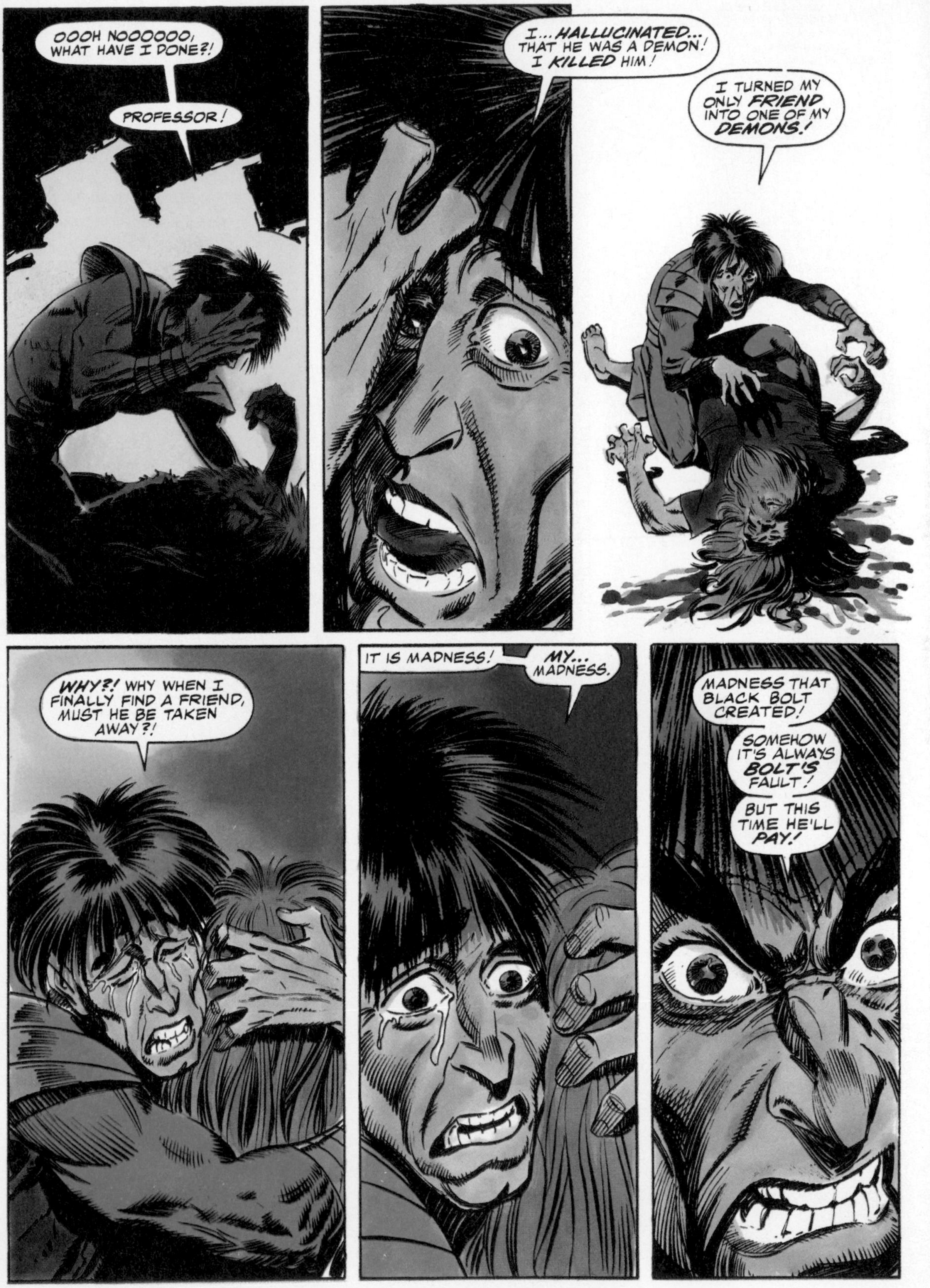
OOOH NOOOOOO, WHAT HAVE I DONE?!
PROFESSOR!
I... HALLUCINATED... THAT HE WAS A DEMON! I KILLED HIM!
I TURNED MY ONLY FRIEND INTO ONE OF MY DEMONS!
WHY?! WHY WHEN I FINALLY FIND A FRIEND, MUST HE BE TAKEN AWAY?!
IT IS MADNESS!
MY... MADNESS.
MADNESS THAT BLACK BOLT CREATED!
SOMEHOW IT'S ALWAYS BOLT'S FAULT!
BUT THIS TIME HE'LL PAY!

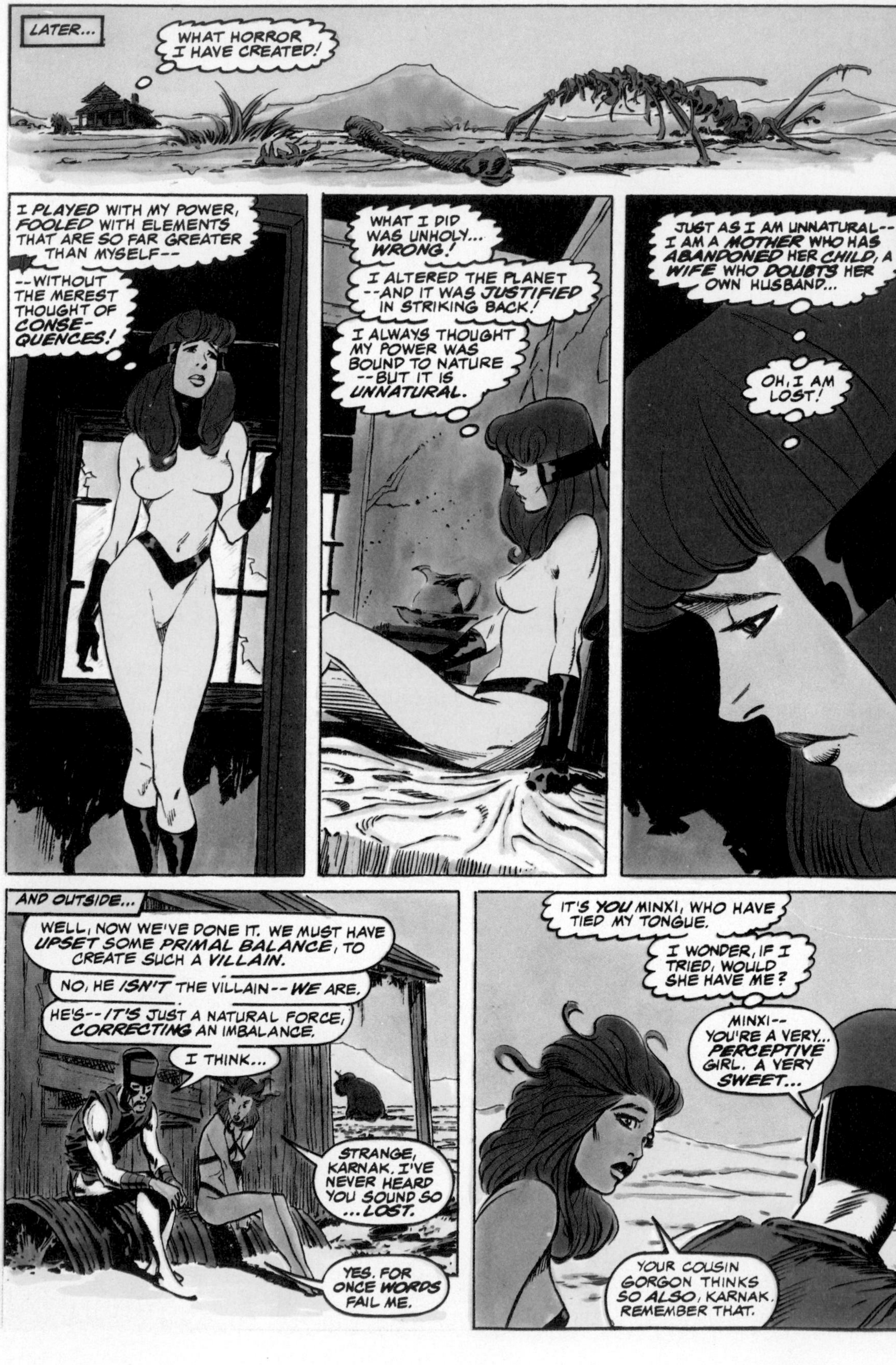
LATER...
WHAT HORROR I HAVE CREATED!
I PLAYED WITH MY POWER, FOOLED WITH ELEMENTS THAT ARE SO FAR GREATER THAN MYSELF--
--WITHOUT THE MEREST THOUGHT OF CONSE-QUENCES!
WHAT I DID WAS UNHOLY... WRONG!
I ALTERED THE PLANET --AND IT WAS JUSTIFIED IN STRIKING BACK!
I ALWAYS THOUGHT MY POWER WAS BOUND TO NATURE --BUT IT IS UNNATURAL.
JUST AS I AM UNNATURAL-- I AM A MOTHER WHO HAS ABANDONED HER CHILD, A WIFE WHO DOUBTS HER OWN HUSBAND...
OH, I AM LOST!
AND OUTSIDE...
WELL, NOW WE'VE DONE IT. WE MUST HAVE UPSET SOME PRIMAL BALANCE, TO CREATE SUCH A VILLAIN.
NO, HE ISN'T THE VILLAIN--WE ARE.
HE'S--IT'S JUST A NATURAL FORCE, CORRECTING AN IMBALANCE.
I THINK...
STRANGE, KARNAK. I'VE NEVER HEARD YOU SOUND SO ...LOST.
YES. FOR ONCE WORDS FAIL ME.
IT'S YOU MINXI, WHO HAVE TIED MY TONGUE.
I WONDER, IF I TRIED, WOULD SHE HAVE ME?
MINXI-- YOU'RE A VERY... PERCEPTIVE GIRL. A VERY SWEET...
YOUR COUSIN GORGON THINKS SO ALSO, KARNAK. REMEMBER THAT.

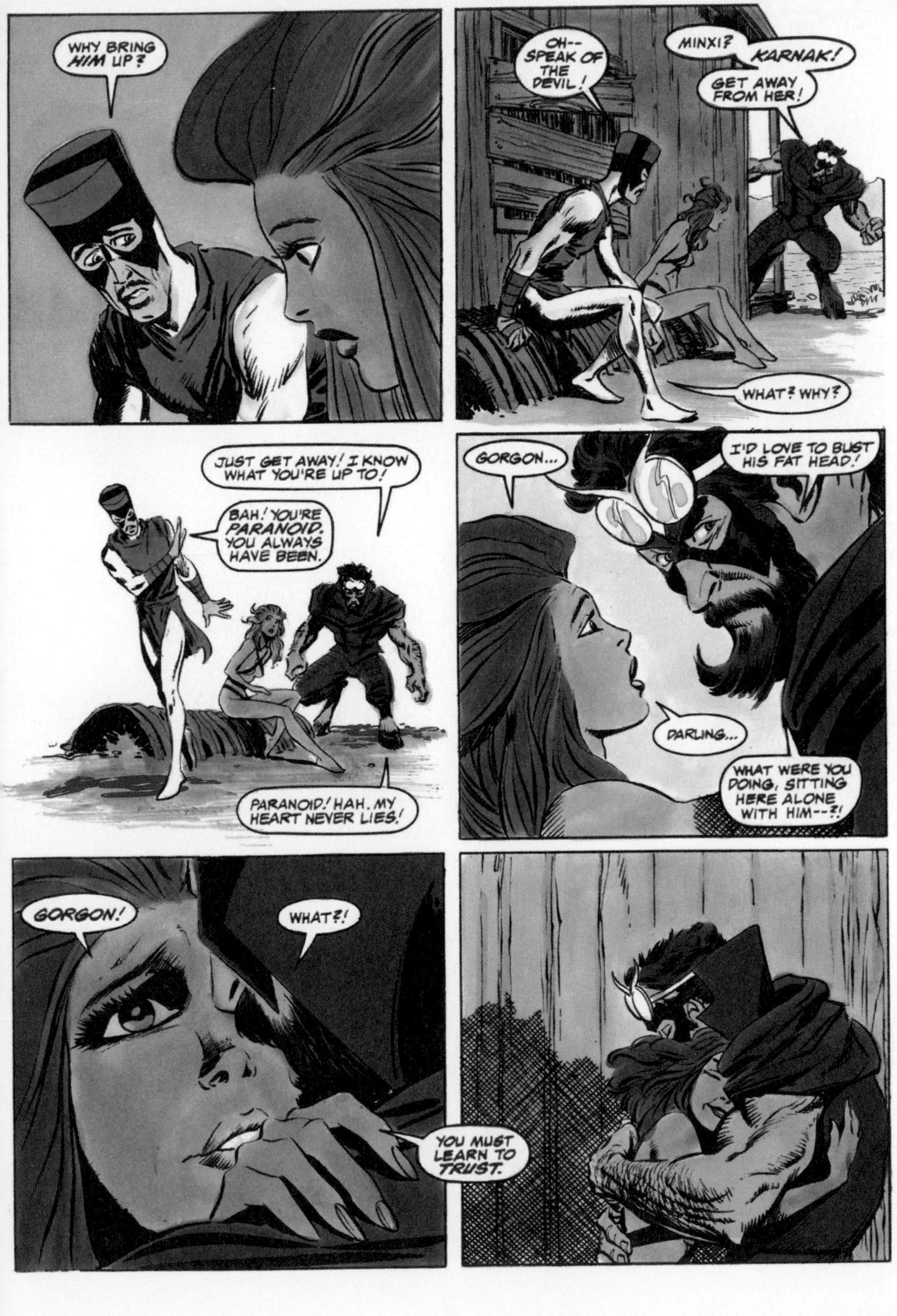
WHY BRING HIM UP?
OH-- SPEAK OF THE DEVIL!
MINXI?
KARNAK!
GET AWAY FROM HER!
WHAT? WHY?
JUST GET AWAY! I KNOW WHAT YOU'RE UP TO!
BAH! YOU'RE PARANOID. YOU ALWAYS HAVE BEEN.
PARANOID! HAH. MY HEART NEVER LIES!
GORGON...
I'D LOVE TO BUST HIS FAT HEAD!
DARLING...
WHAT WERE YOU DOING, SITTING HERE ALONE WITH HIM--?!
GORGON!
WHAT?!
YOU MUST LEARN TO TRUST.

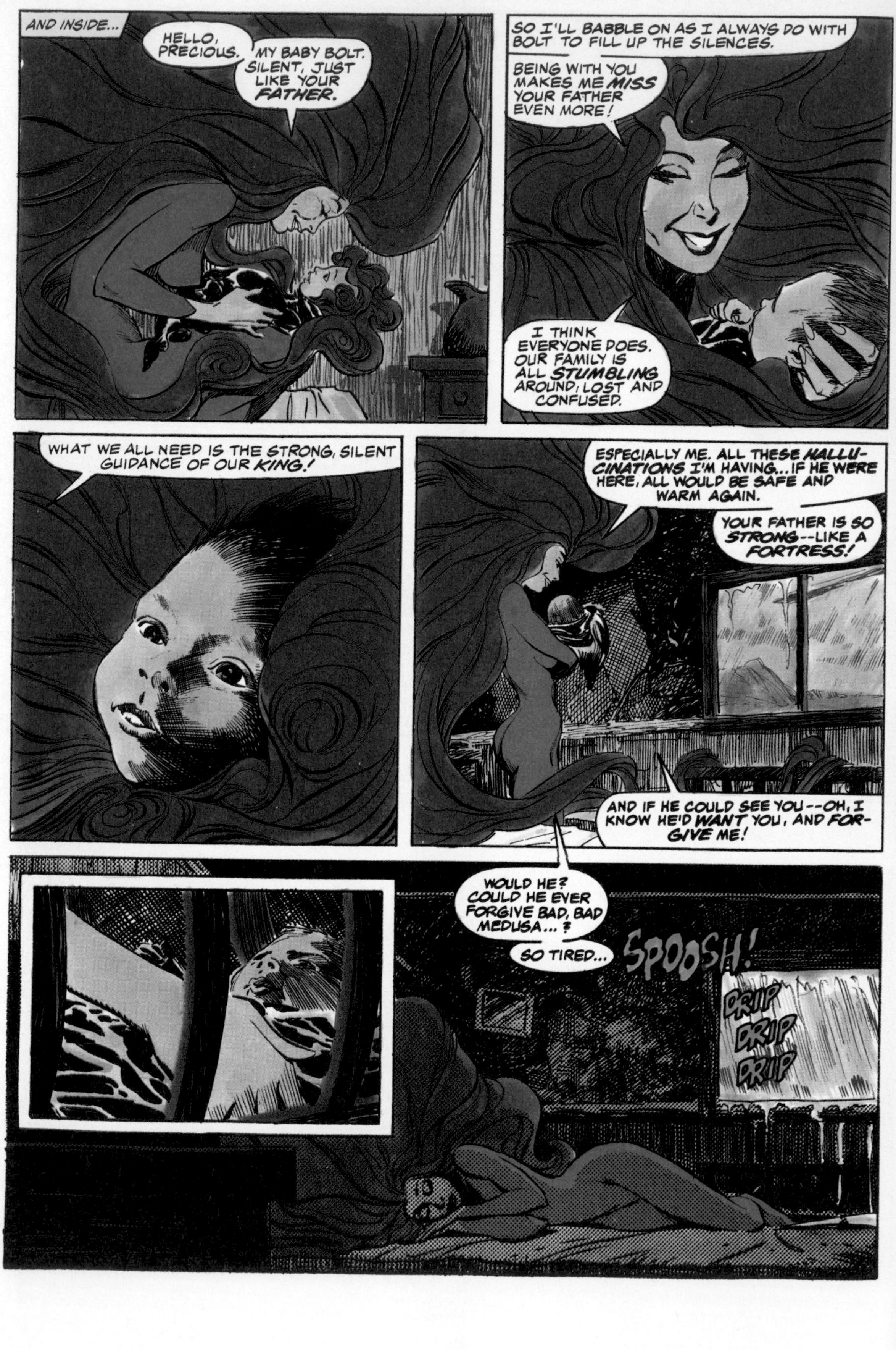
AND INSIDE...
HELLO, PRECIOUS.
MY BABY BOLT. SILENT, JUST LIKE YOUR FATHER.
SO I'LL BABBLE ON AS I ALWAYS DO WITH BOLT TO FILL UP THE SILENCES.
BEING WITH YOU MAKES ME MISS YOUR FATHER EVEN MORE!
I THINK EVERYONE DOES. OUR FAMILY IS ALL STUMBLING AROUND; LOST AND CONFUSED.
WHAT WE ALL NEED IS THE STRONG, SILENT GUIDANCE OF OUR KING!
ESPECIALLY ME. ALL THESE HALLUCINATIONS I'M HAVING... IF HE WERE HERE, ALL WOULD BE SAFE AND WARM AGAIN.
YOUR FATHER IS SO STRONG--LIKE A FORTRESS!
AND IF HE COULD SEE YOU--OH, I KNOW HE'D WANT YOU, AND FORGIVE ME!
WOULD HE? COULD HE EVER FORGIVE BAD, BAD MEDUSA... ?
SO TIRED...
SPOOSH!
DRIP DRIP DRIP

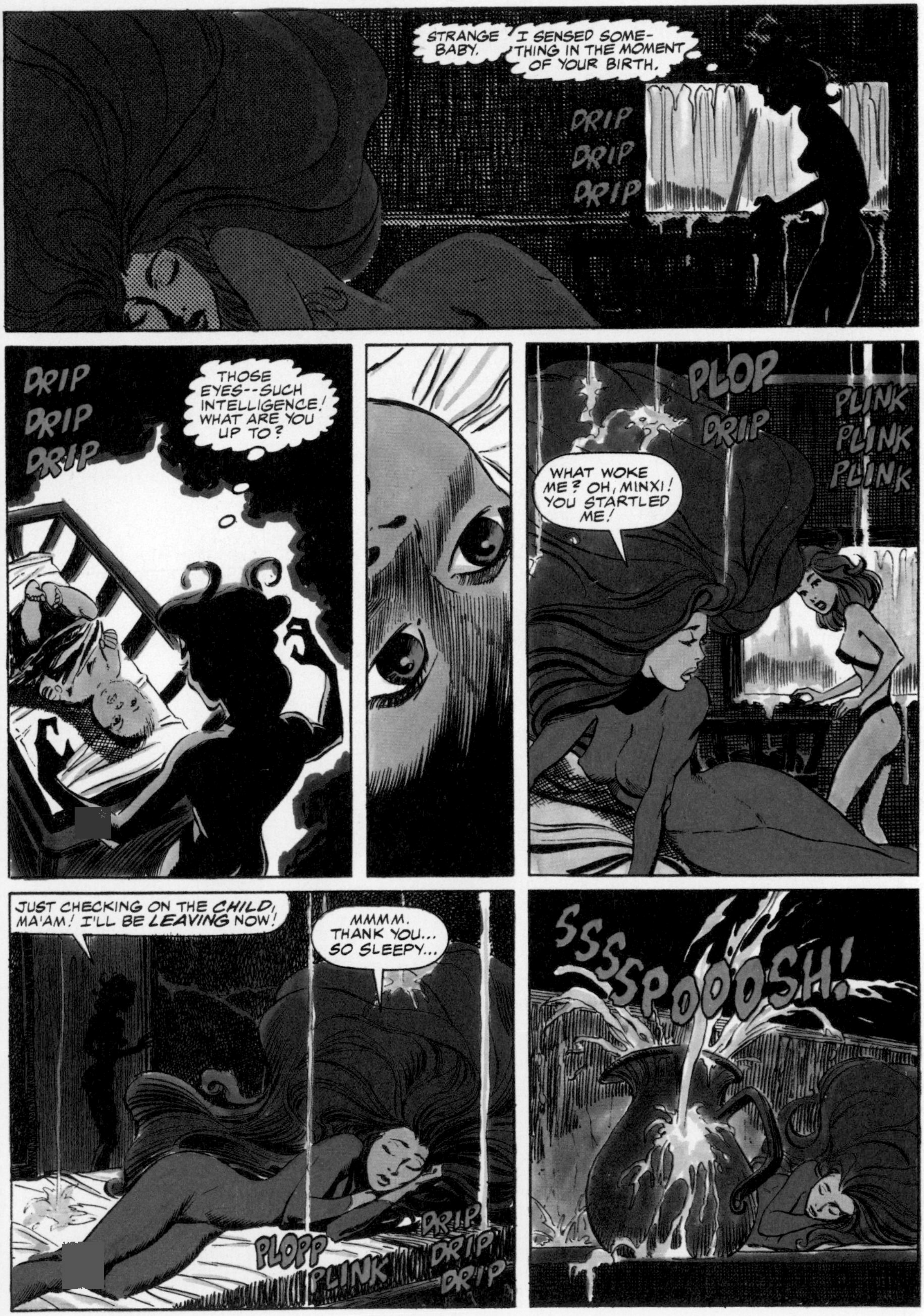

STRANGE BABY.
I SENSED SOMETHING IN THE MOMENT OF YOUR BIRTH.
DRIP
DRIP
DRIP
DRIP
DRIP
DRIP
THOSE EYES--SUCH INTELLIGENCE! WHAT ARE YOU UP TO?
PLOP
DRIP
PLINK
PLINK
PLINK
WHAT WOKE ME? OH, MINXI! YOU STARTLED ME!
JUST CHECKING ON THE CHILD, MA'AM! I'LL BE LEAVING NOW!
MMMM. THANK YOU... SO SLEEPY...
PLOPP
PLINK
DRIP
DRIP
DRIP
SSSSPOOOSH!

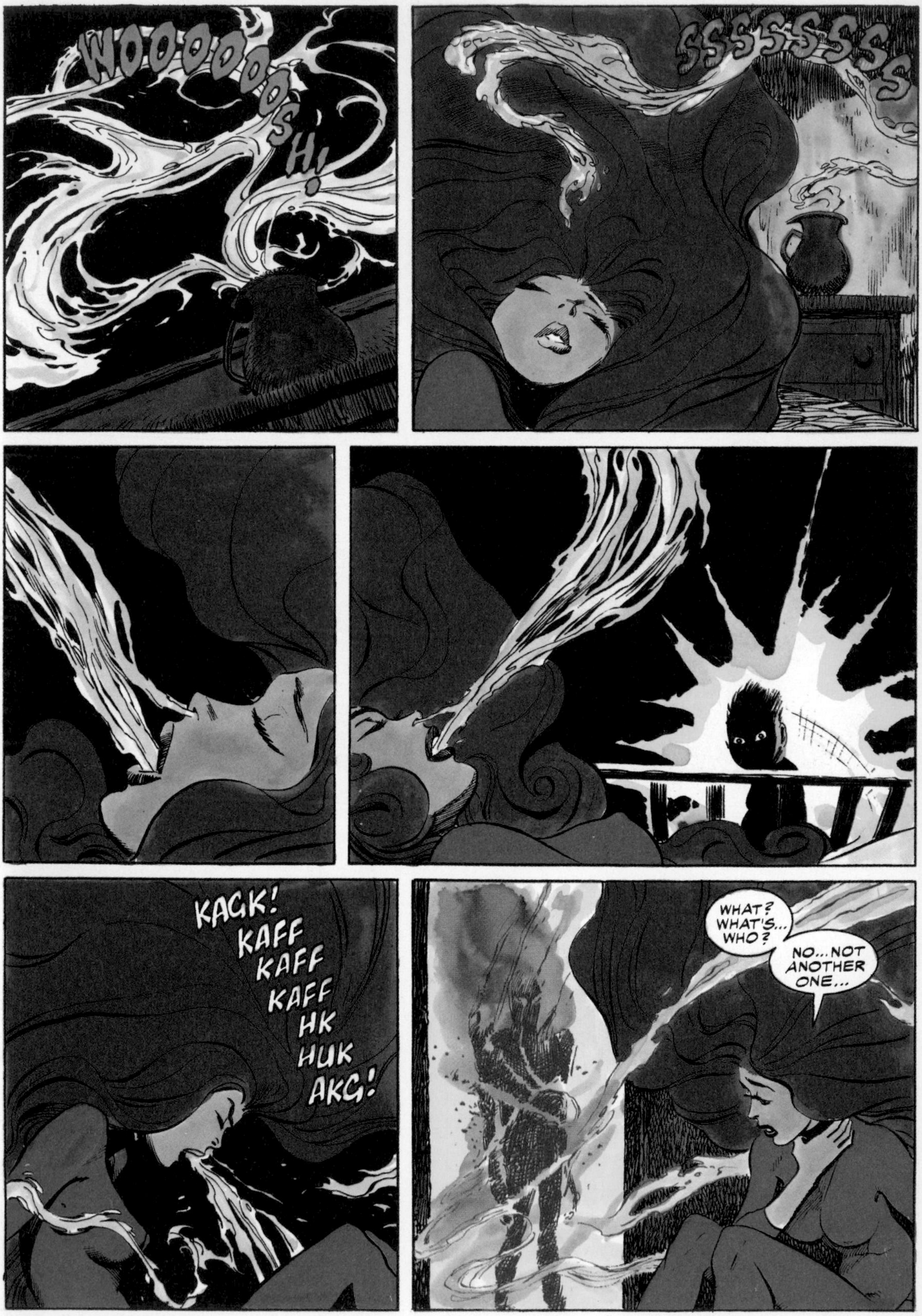
WOOOOOOOSH!
SSSSSSSSS
KAGK! KAFF KAFF KAFF HK HUK AKG!
WHAT? WHAT'S... WHO?
NO...NOT ANOTHER ONE...

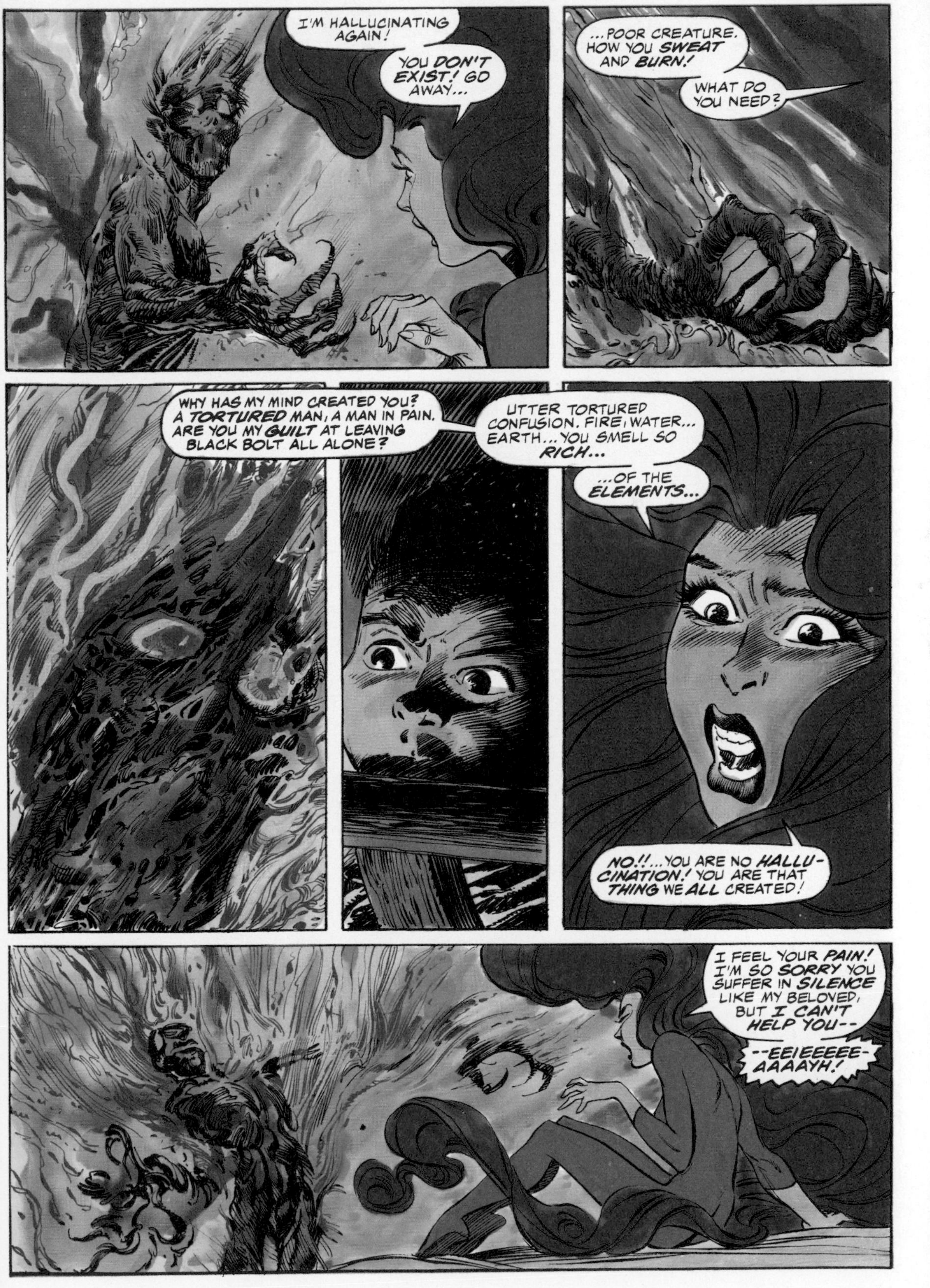
I'M HALLUCINATING AGAIN!
YOU DON'T EXIST! GO AWAY...
...POOR CREATURE. HOW YOU SWEAT AND BURN!
WHAT DO YOU NEED?
WHY HAS MY MIND CREATED YOU? A TORTURED MAN, A MAN IN PAIN. ARE YOU MY GUILT AT LEAVING BLACK BOLT ALL ALONE?
UTTER TORTURED CONFUSION. FIRE, WATER... EARTH... YOU SMELL SO RICH...
...OF THE ELEMENTS...
NO!!...YOU ARE NO HALLUCINATION! YOU ARE THAT THING WE ALL CREATED!
I FEEL YOUR PAIN! I'M SO SORRY YOU SUFFER IN SILENCE LIKE MY BELOVED, BUT I CAN'T HELP YOU--
--EEIEEEEE-AAAAYH!

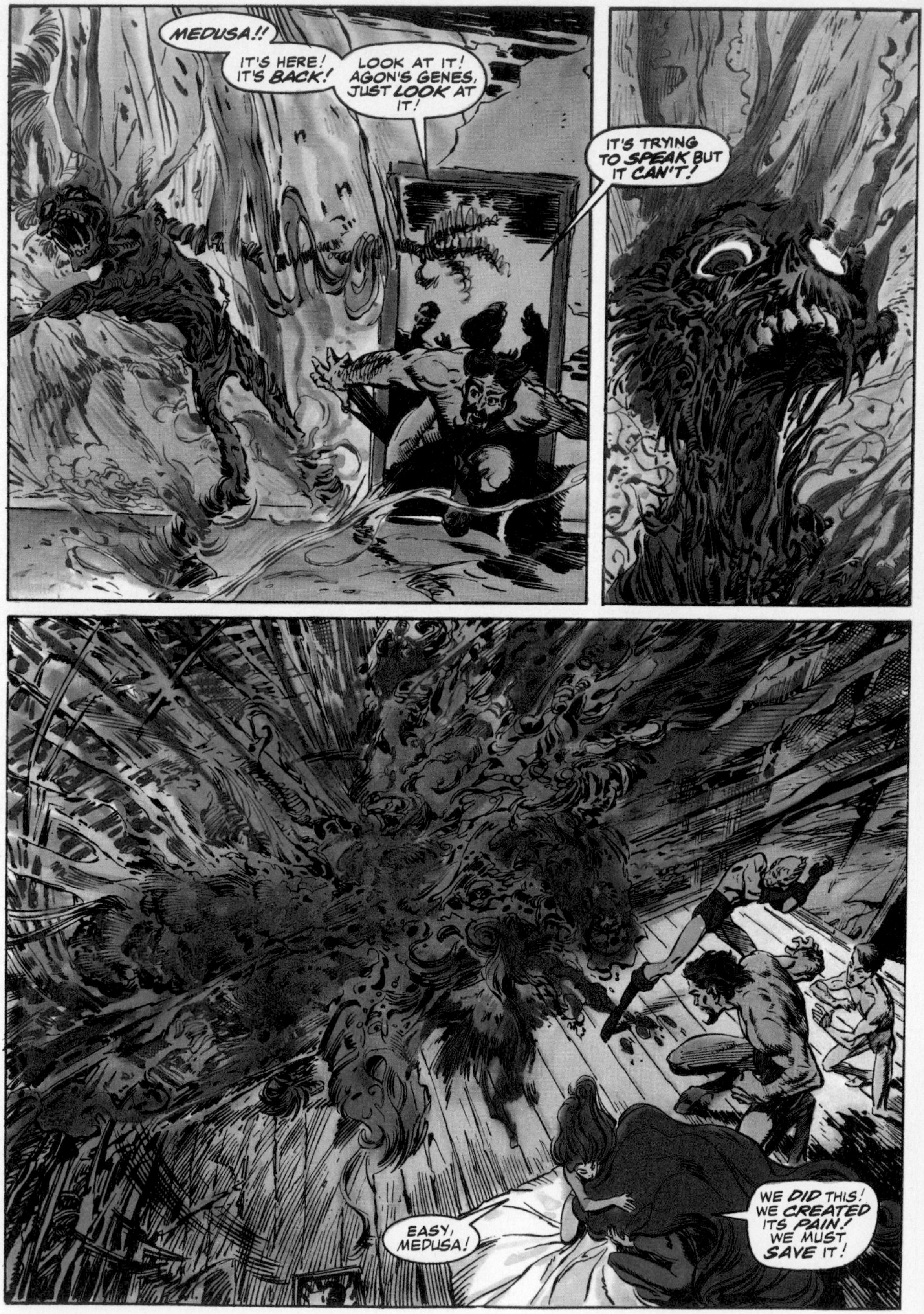
MEDUSA!!
IT'S HERE! IT'S BACK!
LOOK AT IT! AGON'S GENES, JUST LOOK AT IT!
IT'S TRYING TO SPEAK BUT IT CAN'T!
EASY, MEDUSA!
WE DID THIS! WE CREATED ITS PAIN! WE MUST SAVE IT!

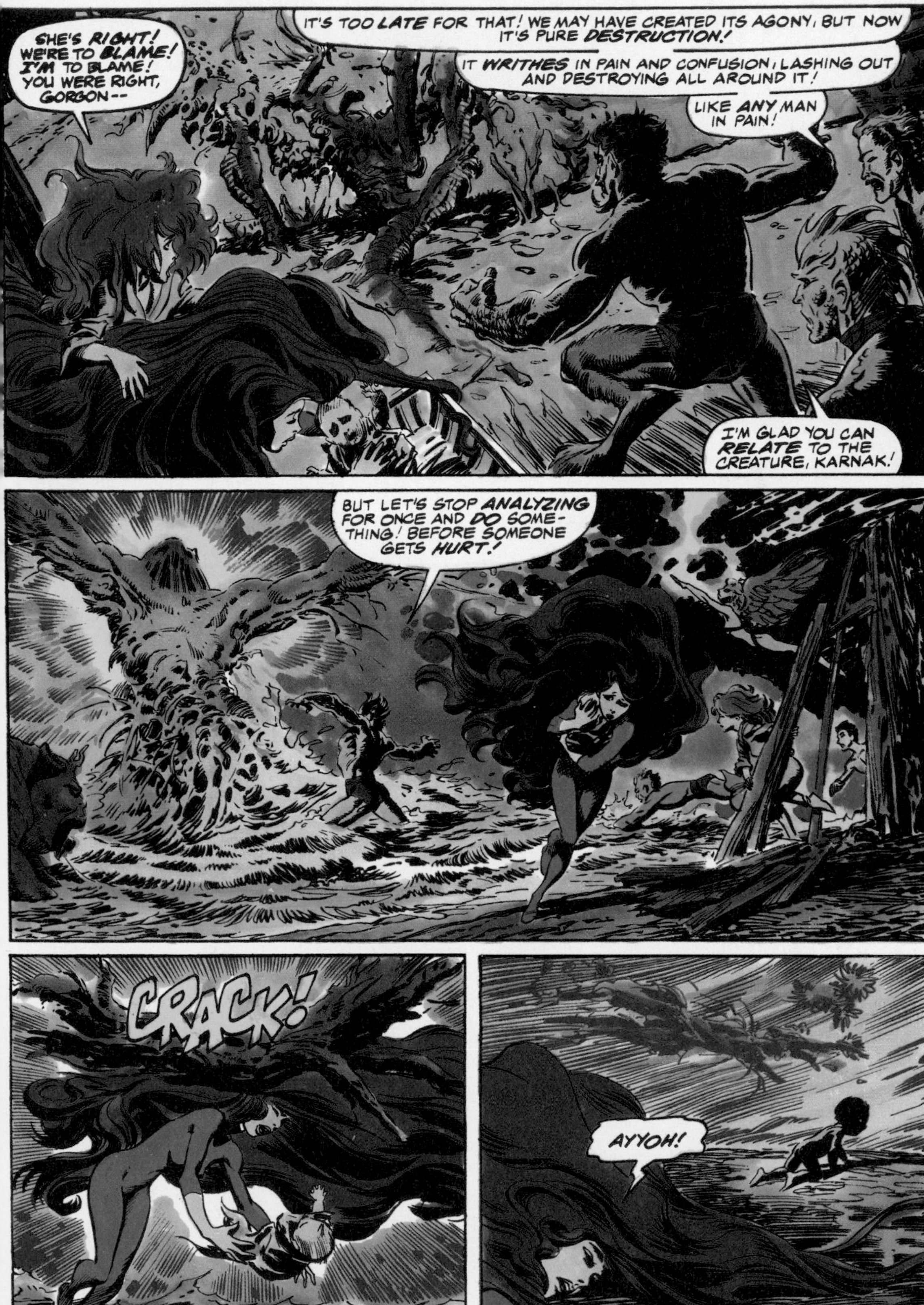
SHE'S RIGHT! WE'RE TO BLAME! I'M TO BLAME! YOU WERE RIGHT, GORGON--
IT'S TOO LATE FOR THAT! WE MAY HAVE CREATED ITS AGONY, BUT NOW IT'S PURE DESTRUCTION!
IT WRITHES IN PAIN AND CONFUSION, LASHING OUT AND DESTROYING ALL AROUND IT!
LIKE ANY MAN IN PAIN!
I'M GLAD YOU CAN RELATE TO THE CREATURE, KARNAK!
BUT LET'S STOP ANALYZING FOR ONCE AND DO SOMETHING! BEFORE SOMEONE GETS HURT!
CRACK!
AYYOH!

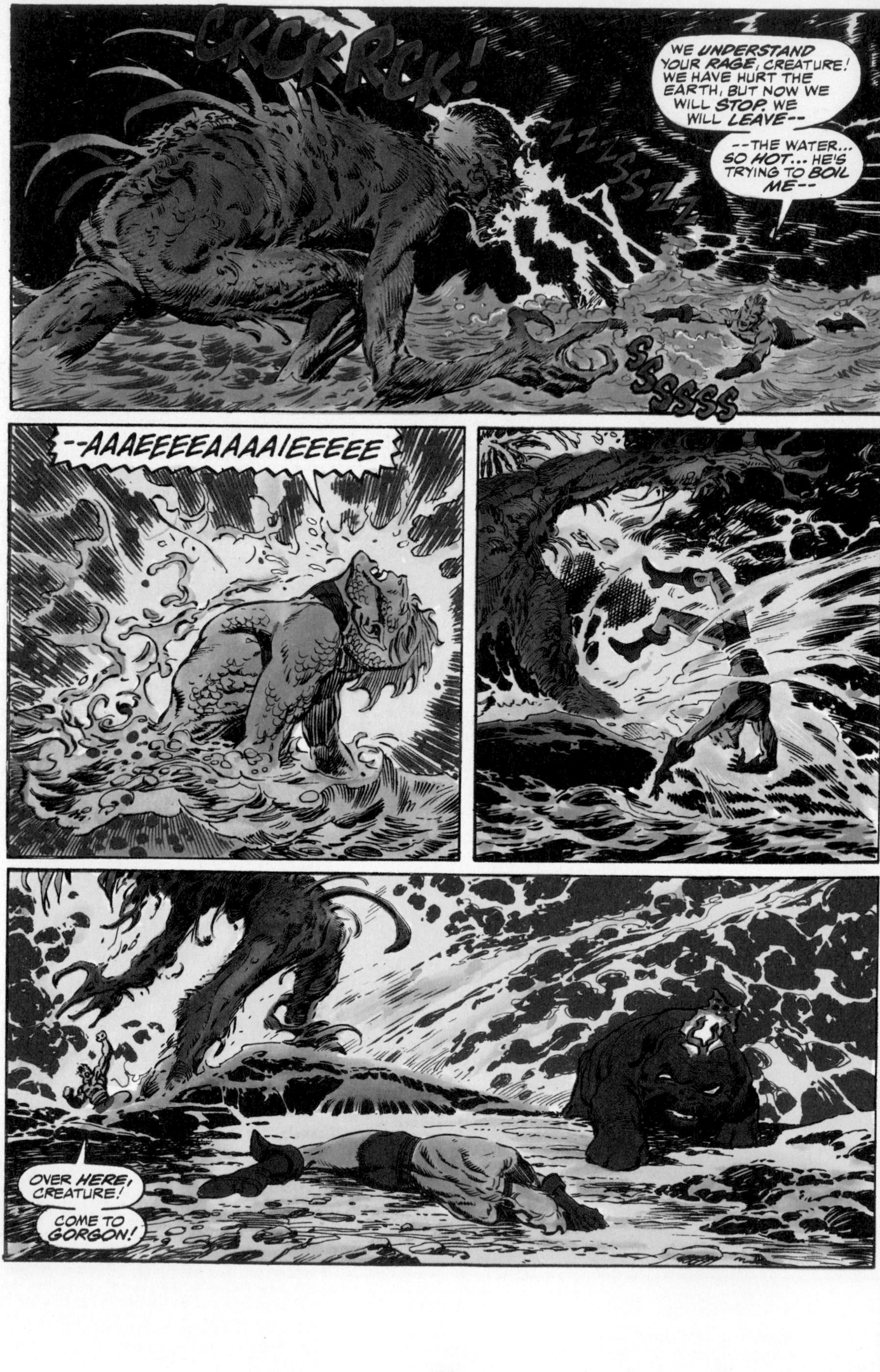
CKCKRCK!
WE UNDERSTAND YOUR RAGE, CREATURE! WE HAVE HURT THE EARTH, BUT NOW WE WILL STOP. WE WILL LEAVE--
--THE WATER... SO HOT... HE'S TRYING TO BOIL ME--
ZZZSSZZ
SSSSSS
--AAAEEEEAAAAIEEEEE
OVER HERE, CREATURE!
COME TO GORGON!

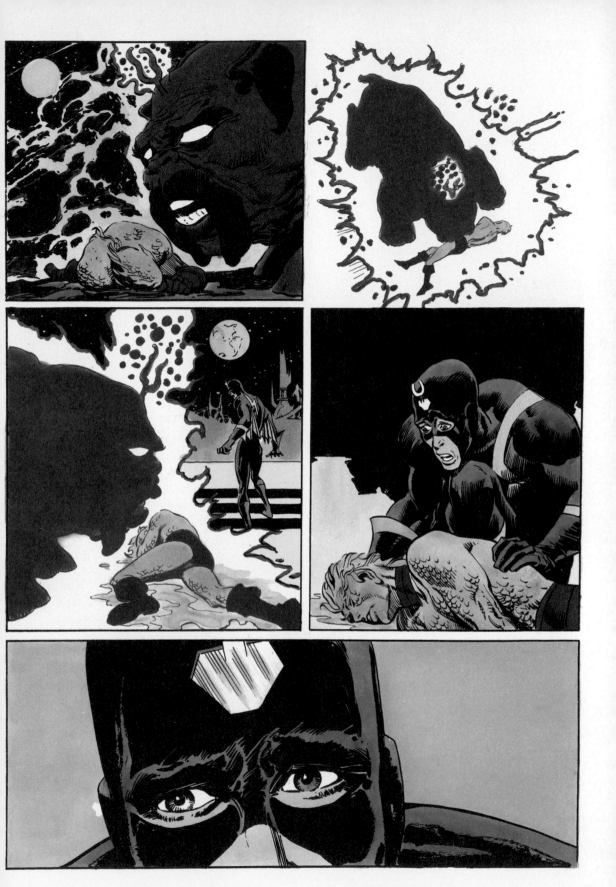

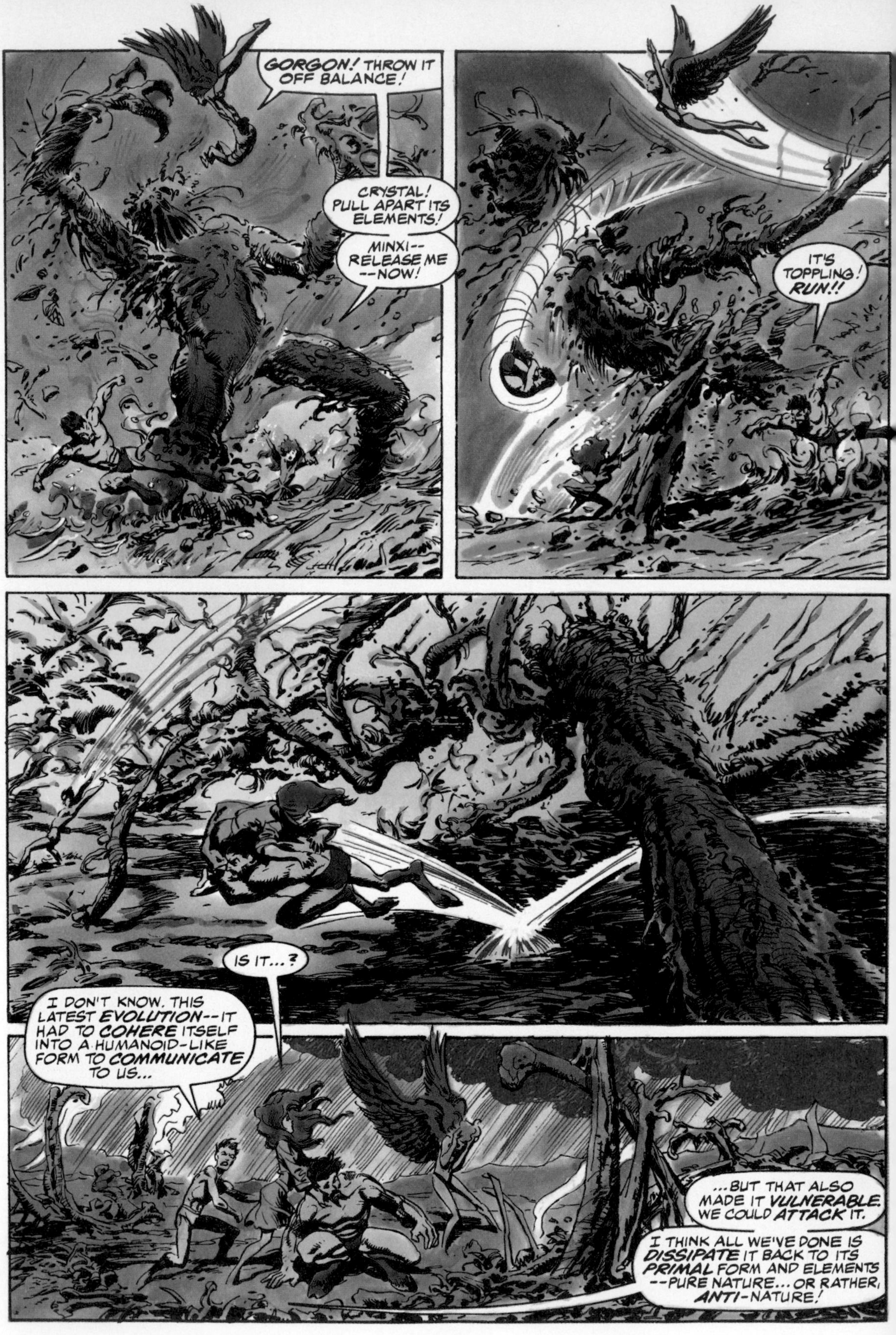
GORGON! THROW IT OFF BALANCE!
CRYSTAL! PULL APART ITS ELEMENTS!
MINXI-- RELEASE ME --NOW!
IT'S TOPPLING! RUN!!
IS IT...?
I DON'T KNOW. THIS LATEST EVOLUTION--IT HAD TO COHERE ITSELF INTO A HUMANOID-LIKE FORM TO COMMUNICATE TO US...
...BUT THAT ALSO MADE IT VULNERABLE. WE COULD ATTACK IT.
I THINK ALL WE'VE DONE IS DISSIPATE IT BACK TO ITS PRIMAL FORM AND ELEMENTS --PURE NATURE... OR RATHER, ANTI-NATURE!

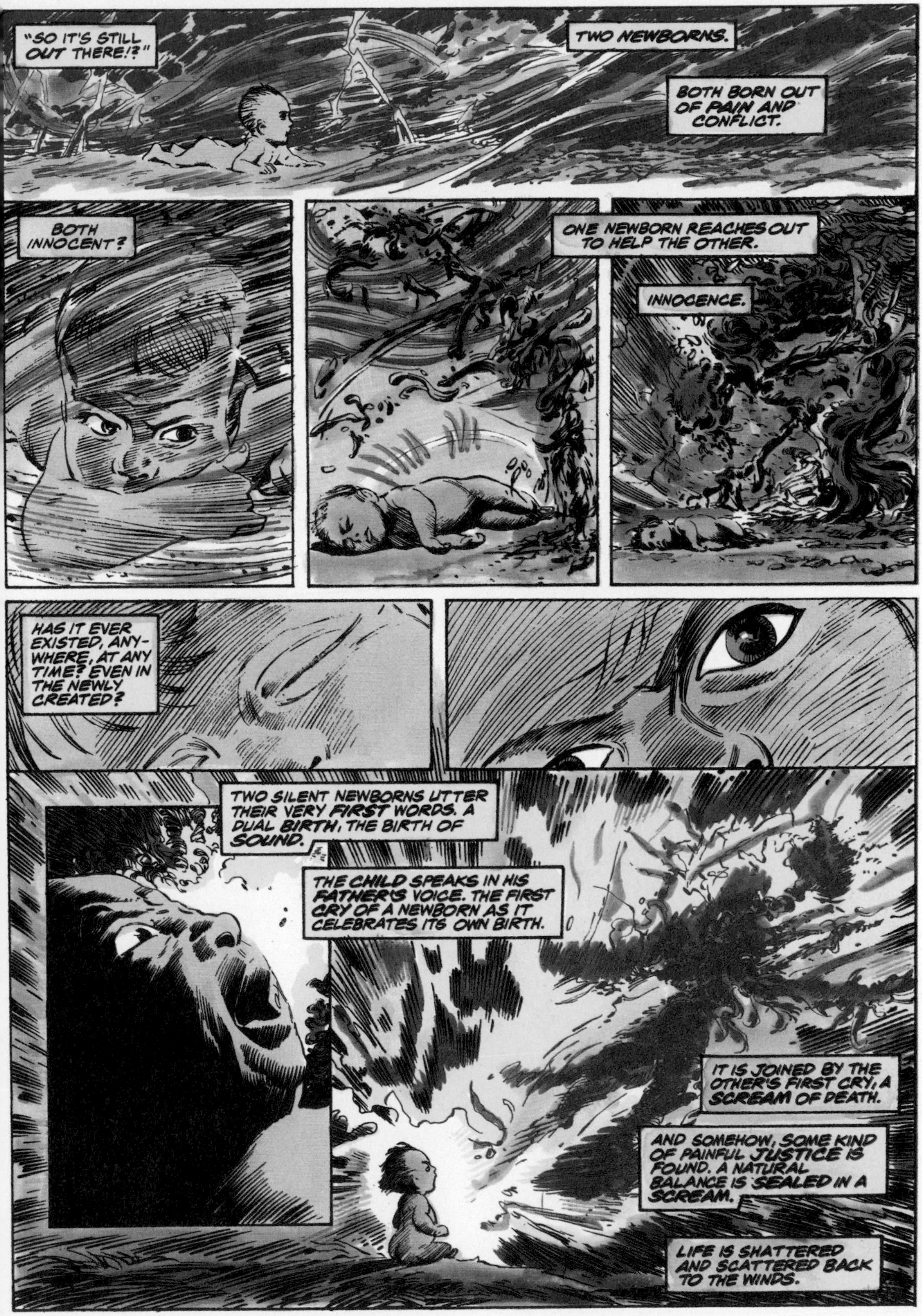
"SO IT'S STILL OUT THERE!?"
TWO NEWBORNS.
BOTH BORN OUT OF PAIN AND CONFLICT.
BOTH INNOCENT?
ONE NEWBORN REACHES OUT TO HELP THE OTHER.
INNOCENCE.
HAS IT EVER EXISTED, ANYWHERE, AT ANY TIME? EVEN IN THE NEWLY CREATED?
TWO SILENT NEWBORNS UTTER THEIR VERY FIRST WORDS. A DUAL BIRTH, THE BIRTH OF SOUND.
THE CHILD SPEAKS IN HIS FATHER'S VOICE. THE FIRST CRY OF A NEWBORN AS IT CELEBRATES ITS OWN BIRTH.
IT IS JOINED BY THE OTHER'S FIRST CRY, A SCREAM OF DEATH.
AND SOMEHOW, SOME KIND OF PAINFUL JUSTICE IS FOUND. A NATURAL BALANCE IS SEALED IN A SCREAM.
LIFE IS SHATTERED AND SCATTERED BACK TO THE WINDS.

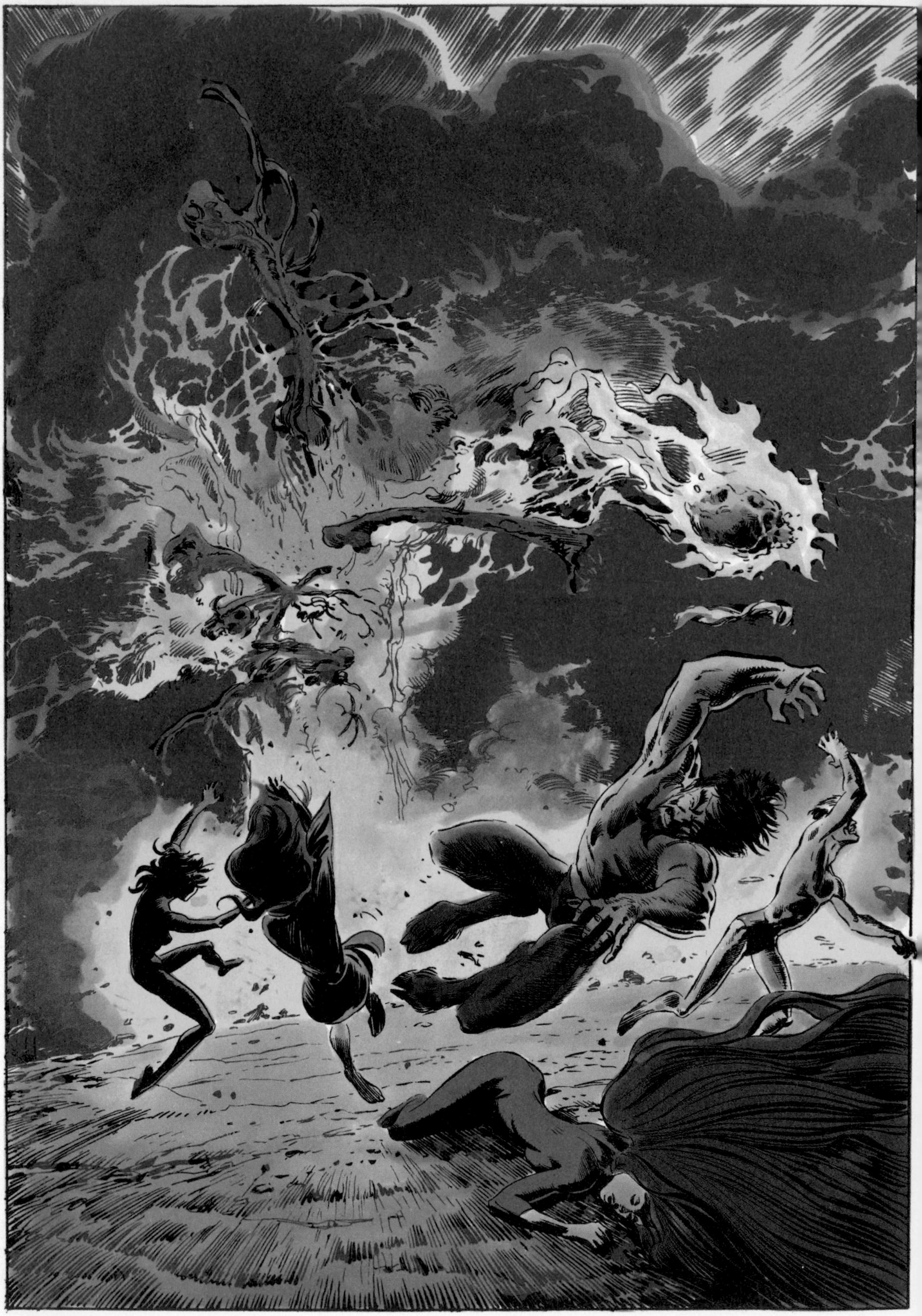

OOOOH...

OOOO ...UH? WHERE?

MY BABY!

RIGHT HERE, MEDUSA! YOU'VE BEEN OUT FOR HOURS!

IS IT... ALL OVER?

YES, WE CHASED THE "ELEMENTAL MAN" OFF INTO THE DESERT, AND HE SIMPLY EXPLODED!

WHERE WAS MY BABY?

CURLED UP BY YOUR SIDE. ASLEEP THROUGH THE WHOLE THING, I GUESS.

HELLO, MY DARLING--

OH!

YOU LOOK... DIFFERENT!

HIS EYES...SOMETHING ...REMINDS ME OF BLACK BOLT'S EYES, THE DEPTH THAT COMES WITH WISDOM, EXPERI-ENCE... AND PAIN!

WHAT HAVE YOU DONE?!

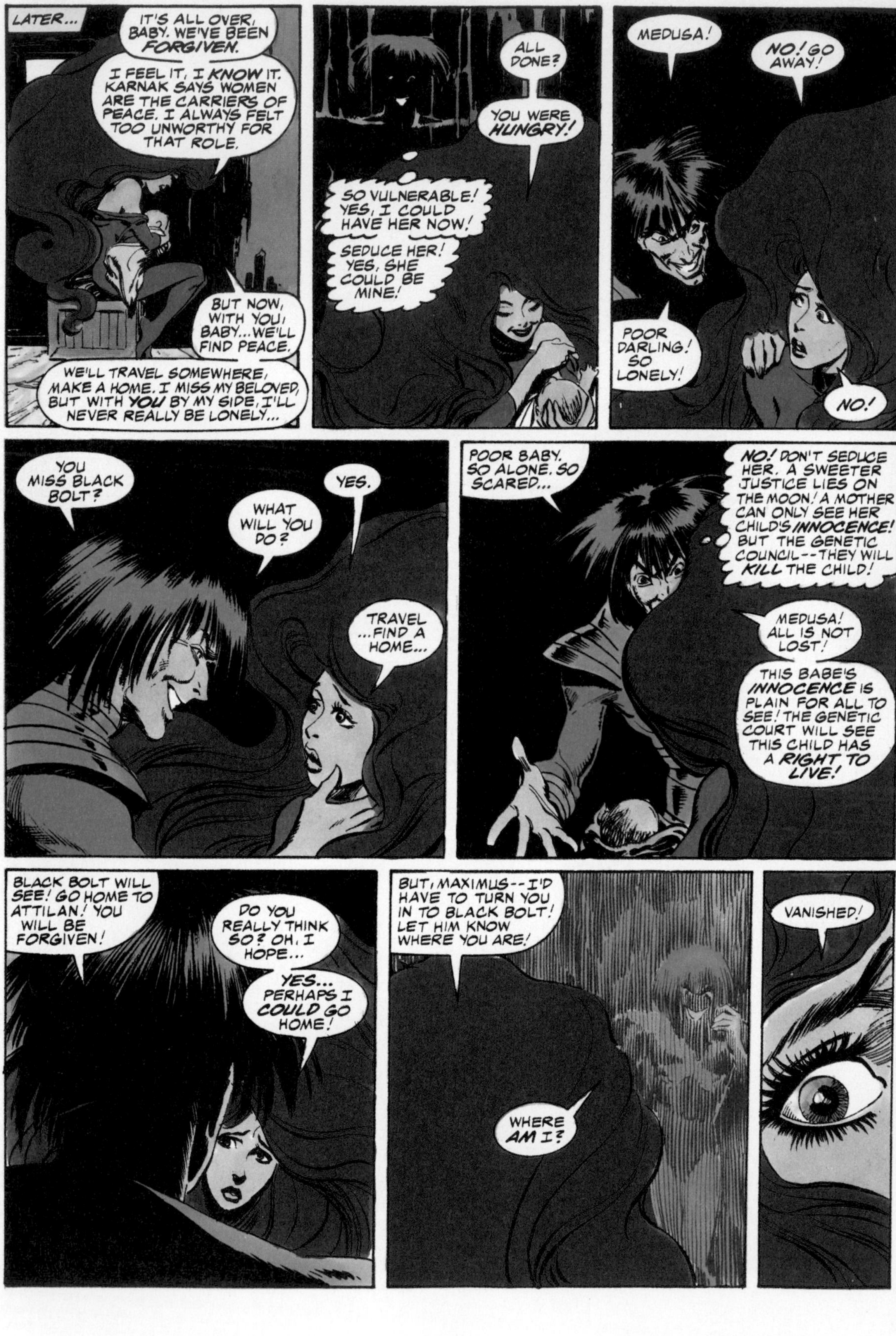

LATER...
IT'S ALL OVER, BABY. WE'VE BEEN FORGIVEN.
I FEEL IT, I KNOW IT. KARNAK SAYS WOMEN ARE THE CARRIERS OF PEACE. I ALWAYS FELT TOO UNWORTHY FOR THAT ROLE.
BUT NOW, WITH YOU, BABY... WE'LL FIND PEACE.
WE'LL TRAVEL SOMEWHERE, MAKE A HOME. I MISS MY BELOVED, BUT WITH YOU BY MY SIDE, I'LL NEVER REALLY BE LONELY...
ALL DONE?
YOU WERE HUNGRY!
SO VULNERABLE! YES, I COULD HAVE HER NOW!
SEDUCE HER! YES, SHE COULD BE MINE!
MEDUSA!
NO! GO AWAY!
POOR DARLING! SO LONELY!
NO!
YOU MISS BLACK BOLT?
YES.
WHAT WILL YOU DO?
TRAVEL ...FIND A HOME...
POOR BABY. SO ALONE. SO SCARED...
NO! DON'T SEDUCE HER. A SWEETER JUSTICE LIES ON THE MOON! A MOTHER CAN ONLY SEE HER CHILD'S INNOCENCE! BUT THE GENETIC COUNCIL--THEY WILL KILL THE CHILD!
MEDUSA! ALL IS NOT LOST!
THIS BABE'S INNOCENCE IS PLAIN FOR ALL TO SEE! THE GENETIC COURT WILL SEE THIS CHILD HAS A RIGHT TO LIVE!
BLACK BOLT WILL SEE! GO HOME TO ATTILAN! YOU WILL BE FORGIVEN!
DO YOU REALLY THINK SO? OH, I HOPE...
YES... PERHAPS I COULD GO HOME!
BUT, MAXIMUS--I'D HAVE TO TURN YOU IN TO BLACK BOLT! LET HIM KNOW WHERE YOU ARE!
WHERE AM I?
VANISHED!

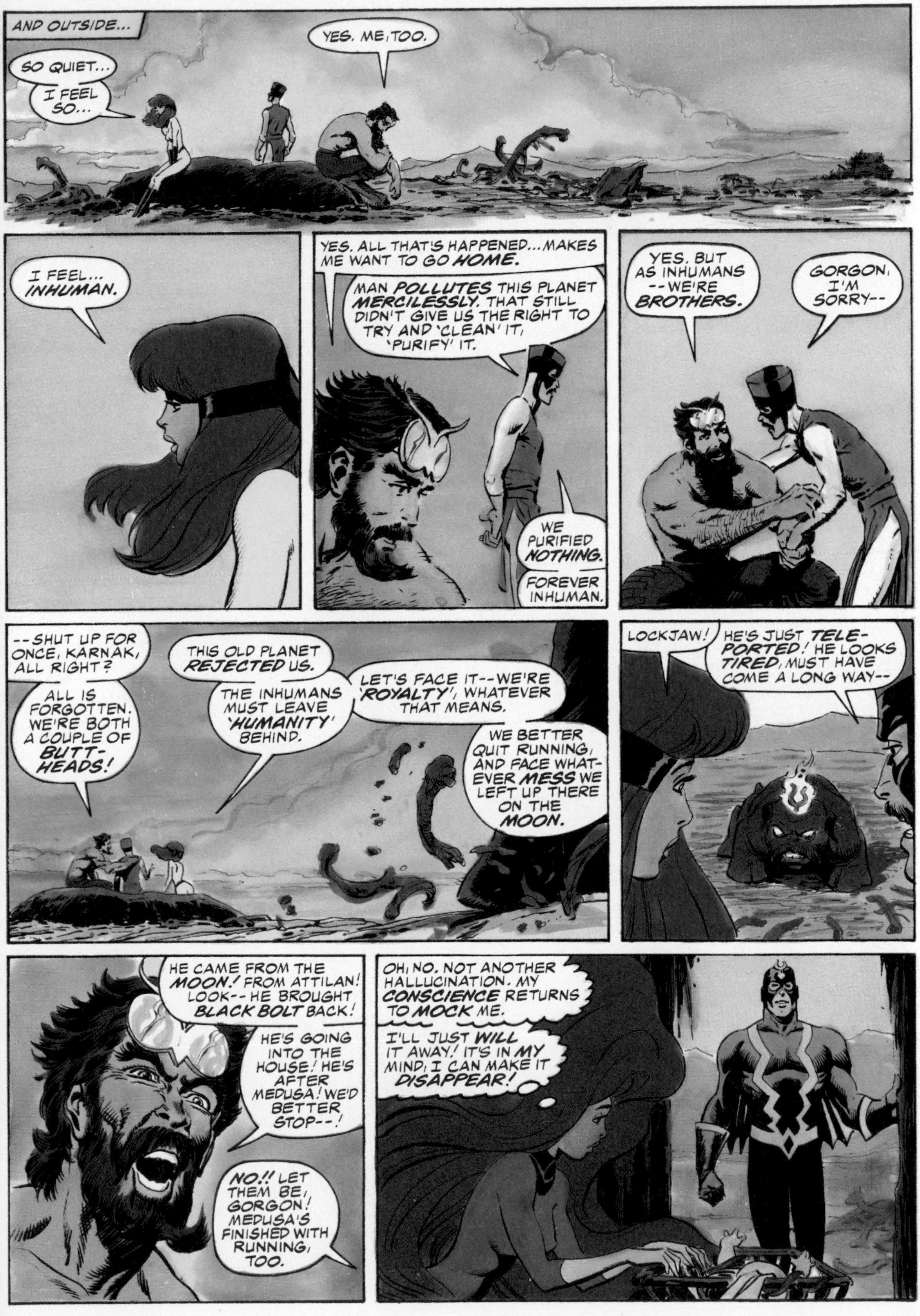

AND OUTSIDE...
SO QUIET...
I FEEL SO...
YES. ME, TOO.
I FEEL... INHUMAN.
YES. ALL THAT'S HAPPENED... MAKES ME WANT TO GO HOME.
MAN POLLUTES THIS PLANET MERCILESSLY. THAT STILL DIDN'T GIVE US THE RIGHT TO TRY AND 'CLEAN' IT, 'PURIFY' IT.
WE PURIFIED NOTHING.
FOREVER INHUMAN.
YES. BUT AS INHUMANS --WE'RE BROTHERS.
GORGON, I'M SORRY--
--SHUT UP FOR ONCE, KARNAK, ALL RIGHT?
ALL IS FORGOTTEN. WE'RE BOTH A COUPLE OF BUTT-HEADS!
THIS OLD PLANET REJECTED US.
THE INHUMANS MUST LEAVE 'HUMANITY' BEHIND.
LET'S FACE IT--WE'RE 'ROYALTY', WHATEVER THAT MEANS.
WE BETTER QUIT RUNNING, AND FACE WHATEVER MESS WE LEFT UP THERE ON THE MOON.
LOCKJAW!
HE'S JUST TELEPORTED! HE LOOKS TIRED, MUST HAVE COME A LONG WAY--
HE CAME FROM THE MOON! FROM ATTILAN! LOOK--HE BROUGHT BLACK BOLT BACK!
HE'S GOING INTO THE HOUSE! HE'S AFTER MEDUSA! WE'D BETTER STOP--!
NO!! LET THEM BE, GORGON! MEDUSA'S FINISHED WITH RUNNING, TOO.
OH, NO. NOT ANOTHER HALLUCINATION. MY CONSCIENCE RETURNS TO MOCK ME.
I'LL JUST WILL IT AWAY! IT'S IN MY MIND, I CAN MAKE IT DISAPPEAR!

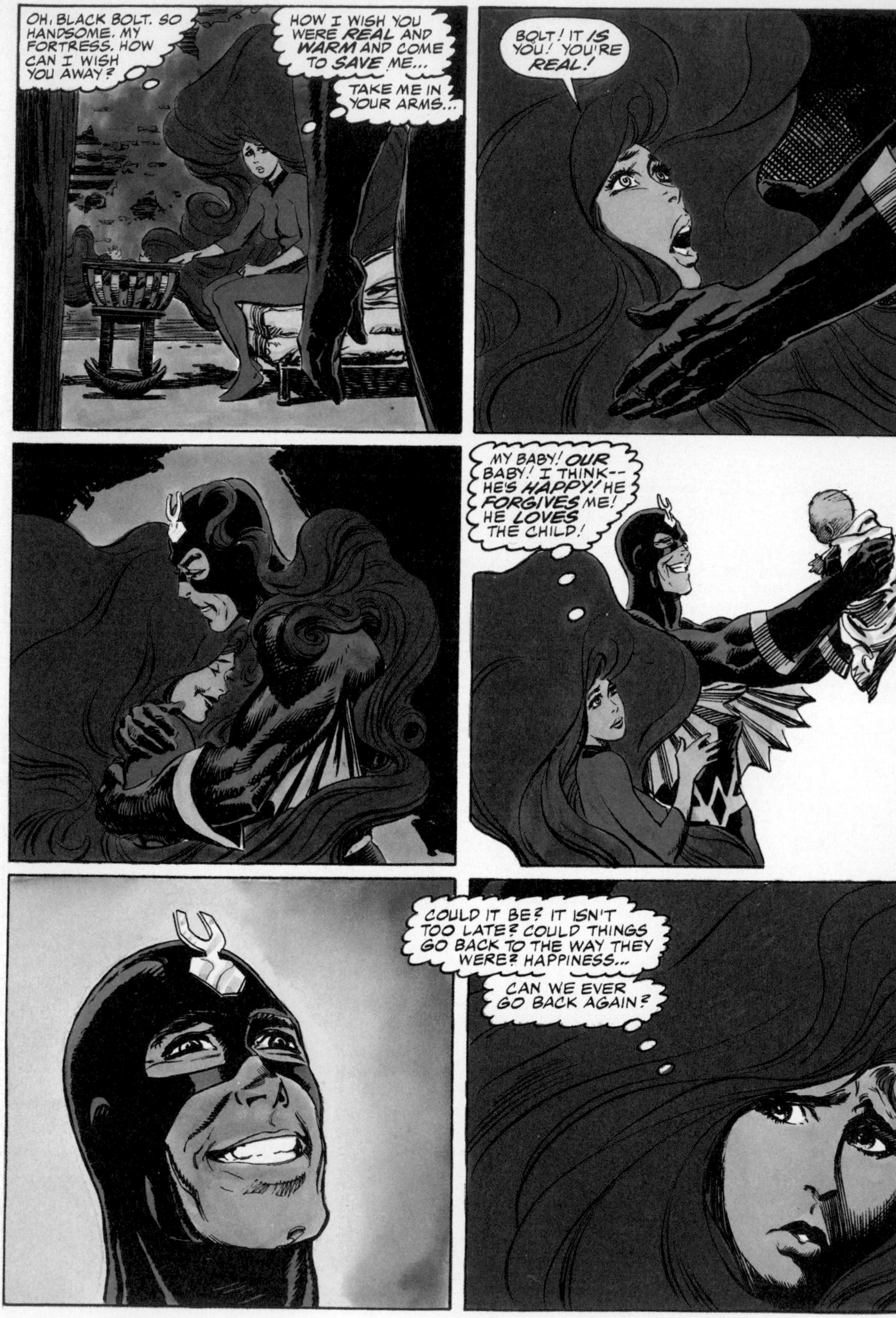
OH, BLACK BOLT. SO HANDSOME. MY FORTRESS. HOW CAN I WISH YOU AWAY?
HOW I WISH YOU WERE REAL AND WARM AND COME TO SAVE ME...
TAKE ME IN YOUR ARMS...
BOLT! IT IS YOU! YOU'RE REAL!
MY BABY! OUR BABY! I THINK-- HE'S HAPPY! HE FORGIVES ME! HE LOVES THE CHILD!
COULD IT BE? IT ISN'T TOO LATE? COULD THINGS GO BACK TO THE WAY THEY WERE? HAPPINESS...
CAN WE EVER GO BACK AGAIN?

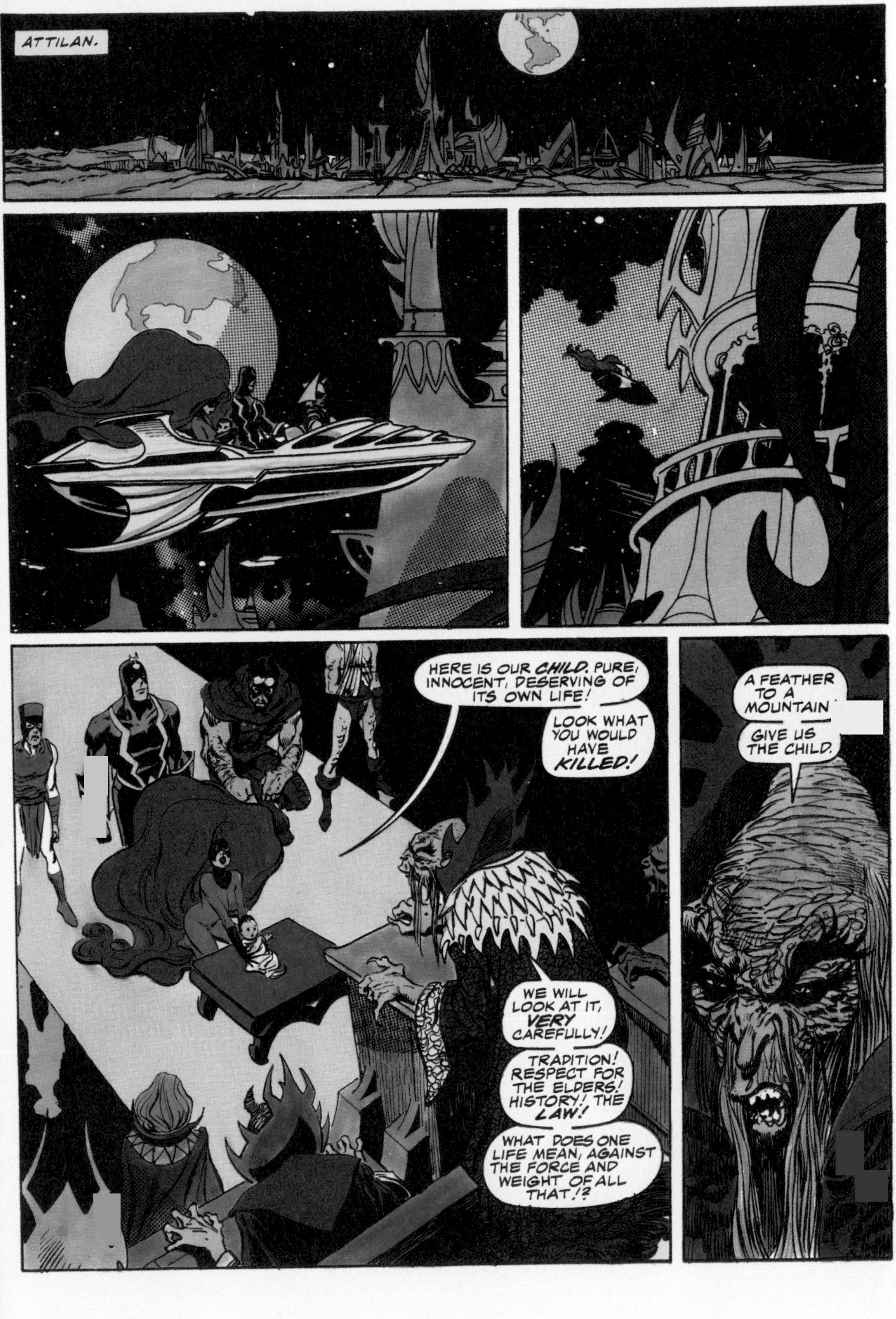
ATTILAN.
HERE IS OUR CHILD. PURE, INNOCENT, DESERVING OF ITS OWN LIFE!
LOOK WHAT YOU WOULD HAVE KILLED!
WE WILL LOOK AT IT, VERY CAREFULLY!
TRADITION! RESPECT FOR THE ELDERS! HISTORY! THE LAW!
WHAT DOES ONE LIFE MEAN, AGAINST THE FORCE AND WEIGHT OF ALL THAT!?
A FEATHER TO A MOUNTAIN
GIVE US THE CHILD.

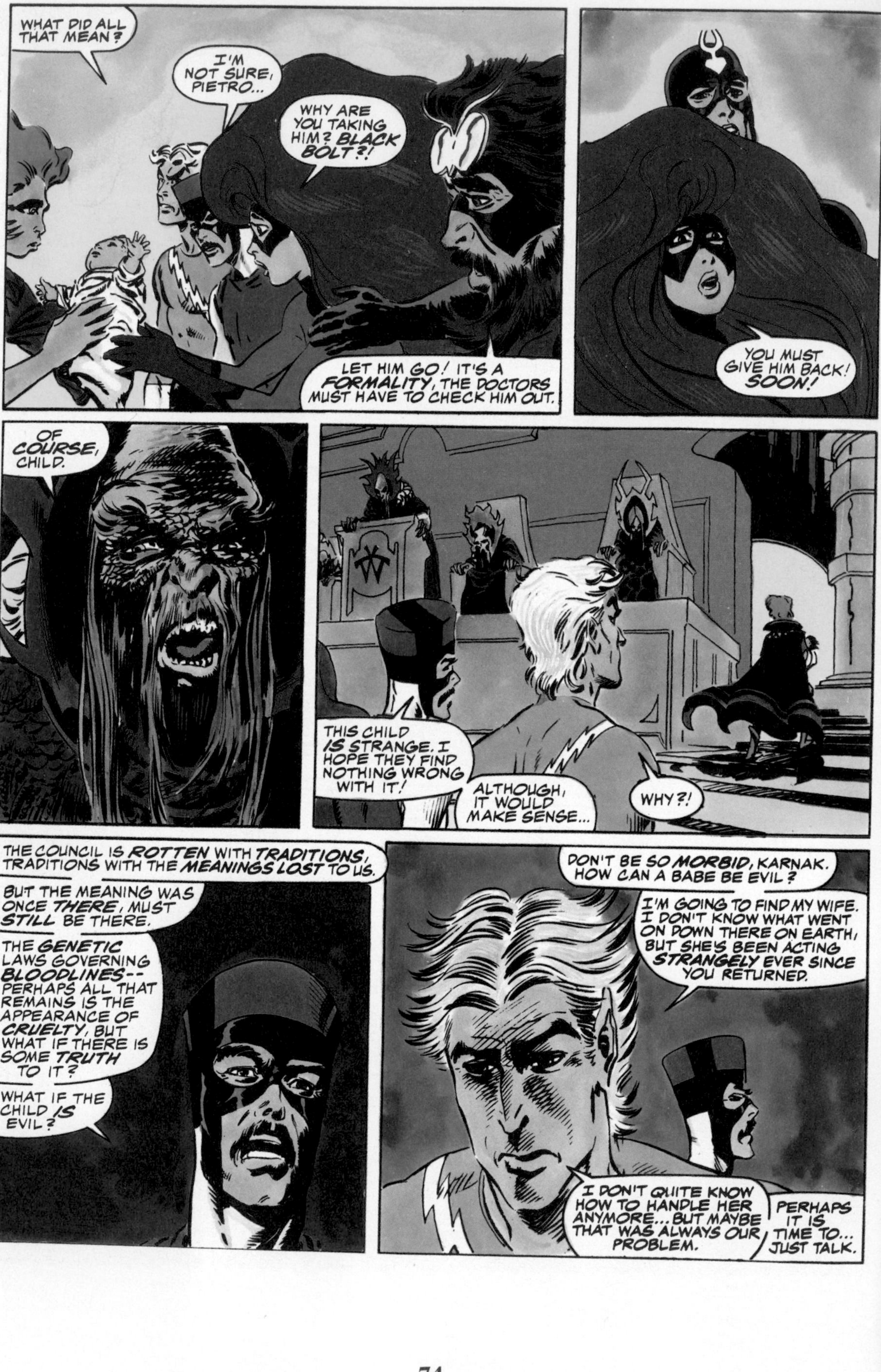
WHAT DID ALL THAT MEAN?
I'M NOT SURE, PIETRO...
WHY ARE YOU TAKING HIM? BLACK BOLT?!
LET HIM GO! IT'S A FORMALITY, THE DOCTORS MUST HAVE TO CHECK HIM OUT.
YOU MUST GIVE HIM BACK! SOON!
OF COURSE, CHILD.
THIS CHILD IS STRANGE. I HOPE THEY FIND NOTHING WRONG WITH IT!
ALTHOUGH, IT WOULD MAKE SENSE...
WHY?!
THE COUNCIL IS ROTTEN WITH TRADITIONS, TRADITIONS WITH THE MEANINGS LOST TO US.
BUT THE MEANING WAS ONCE THERE, MUST STILL BE THERE.
THE GENETIC LAWS GOVERNING BLOODLINES-- PERHAPS ALL THAT REMAINS IS THE APPEARANCE OF CRUELTY, BUT WHAT IF THERE IS SOME TRUTH TO IT?
WHAT IF THE CHILD IS EVIL?
DON'T BE SO MORBID, KARNAK. HOW CAN A BABE BE EVIL?
I'M GOING TO FIND MY WIFE. I DON'T KNOW WHAT WENT ON DOWN THERE ON EARTH, BUT SHE'S BEEN ACTING STRANGELY EVER SINCE YOU RETURNED.
I DON'T QUITE KNOW HOW TO HANDLE HER ANYMORE... BUT MAYBE THAT WAS ALWAYS OUR PROBLEM.
PERHAPS IT IS TIME TO... JUST TALK.

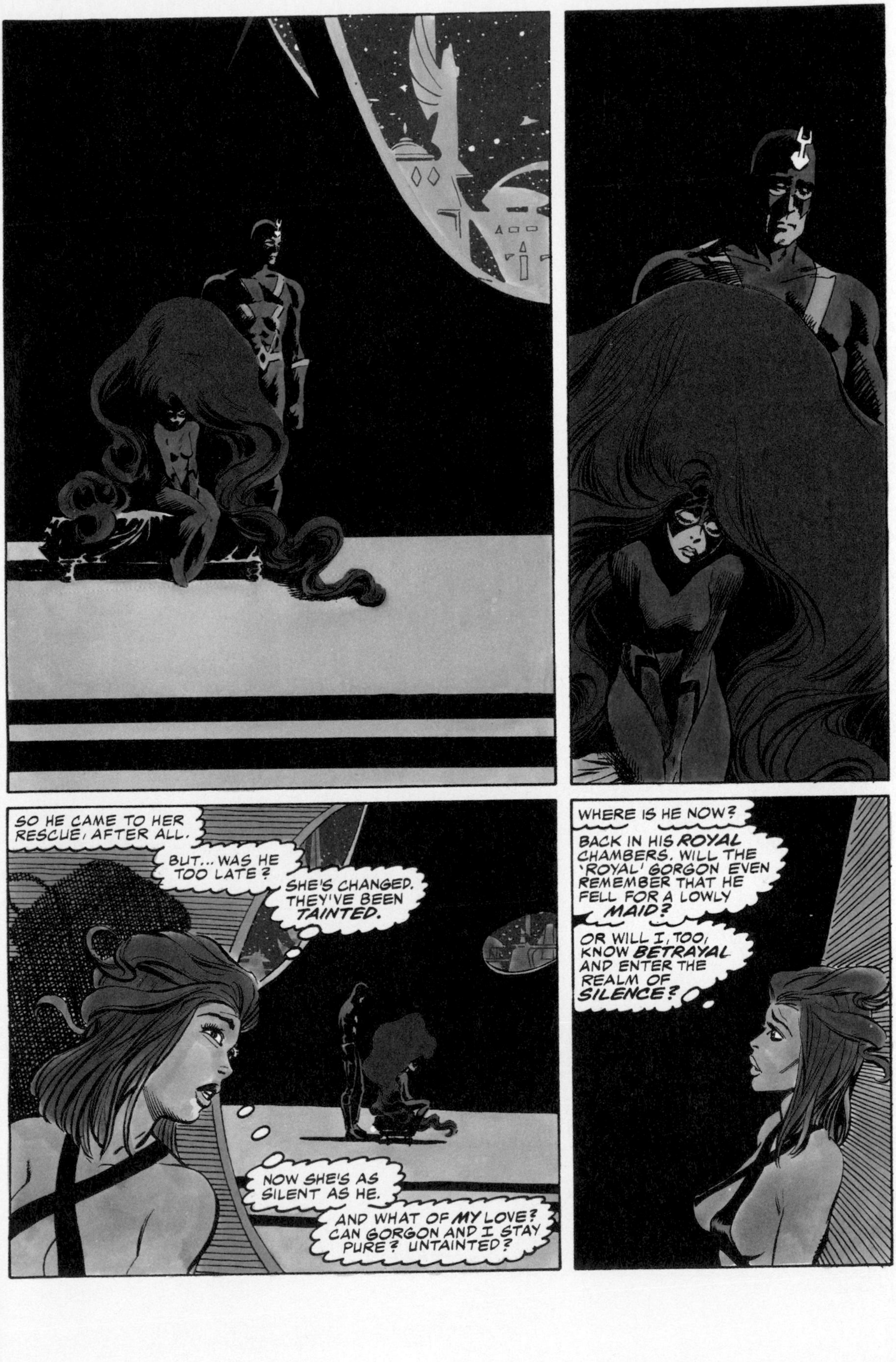
SO HE CAME TO HER RESCUE, AFTER ALL.
BUT... WAS HE TOO LATE?
SHE'S CHANGED. THEY'VE BEEN TAINTED.
NOW SHE'S AS SILENT AS HE.
AND WHAT OF MY LOVE? CAN GORGON AND I STAY PURE? UNTAINTED?
WHERE IS HE NOW?
BACK IN HIS ROYAL CHAMBERS. WILL THE 'ROYAL' GORGON EVEN REMEMBER THAT HE FELL FOR A LOWLY MAID?
OR WILL I, TOO, KNOW BETRAYAL AND ENTER THE REALM OF SILENCE?

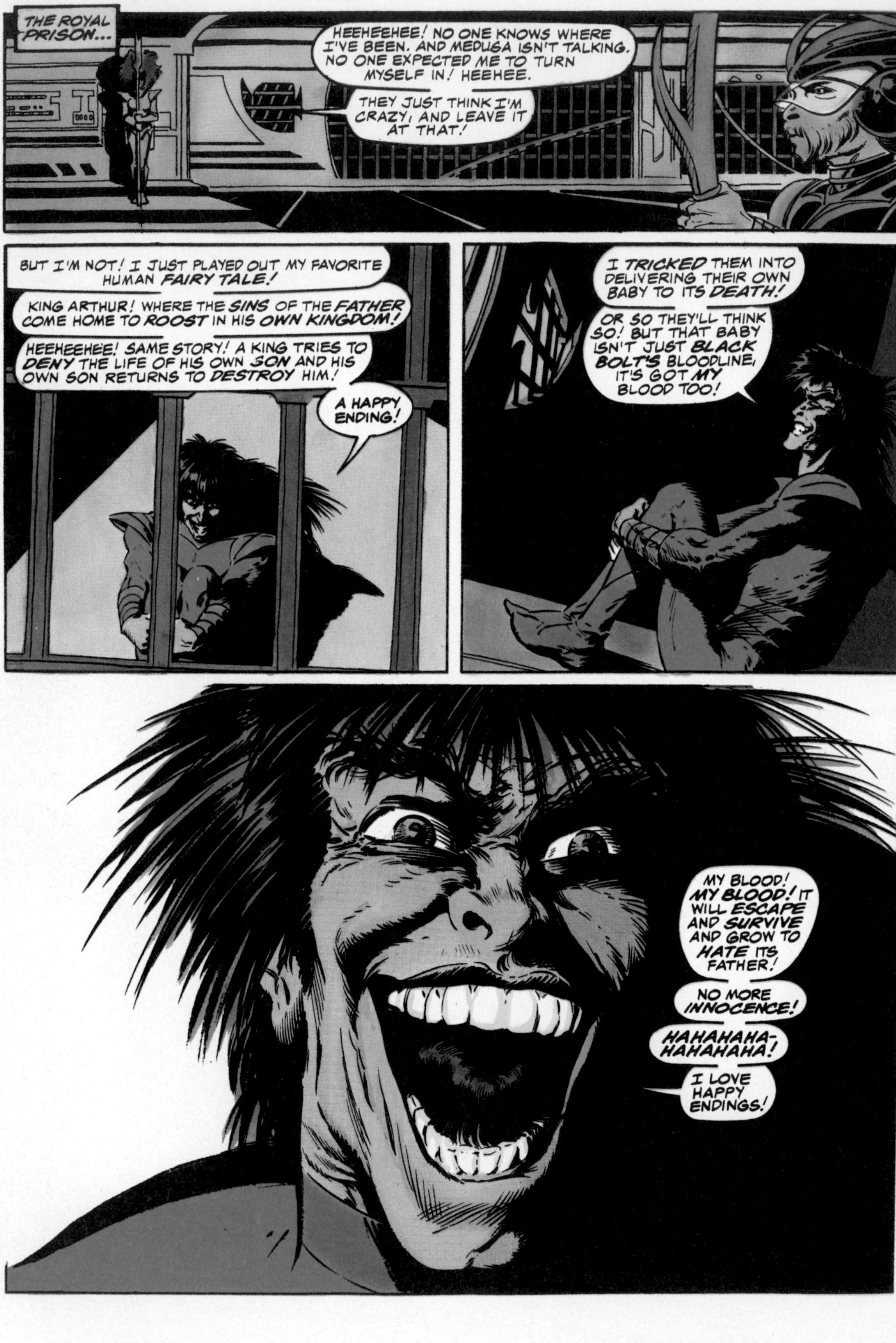
THE ROYAL PRISON...
HEEHEEHEE! NO ONE KNOWS WHERE I'VE BEEN. AND MEDUSA ISN'T TALKING. NO ONE EXPECTED ME TO TURN MYSELF IN! HEEHEE.
THEY JUST THINK I'M CRAZY, AND LEAVE IT AT THAT!
BUT I'M NOT! I JUST PLAYED OUT MY FAVORITE HUMAN FAIRY TALE!
KING ARTHUR! WHERE THE SINS OF THE FATHER COME HOME TO ROOST IN HIS OWN KINGDOM!
HEEHEEHEE! SAME STORY! A KING TRIES TO DENY THE LIFE OF HIS OWN SON AND HIS OWN SON RETURNS TO DESTROY HIM!
A HAPPY ENDING!
I TRICKED THEM INTO DELIVERING THEIR OWN BABY TO ITS DEATH!
OR SO THEY'LL THINK SO! BUT THAT BABY ISN'T JUST BLACK BOLT'S BLOODLINE, IT'S GOT MY BLOOD TOO!
MY BLOOD! MY BLOOD! IT WILL ESCAPE AND SURVIVE AND GROW TO HATE ITS FATHER!
NO MORE INNOCENCE!
HAHAHAHA-HAHAHAHA!
I LOVE HAPPY ENDINGS!

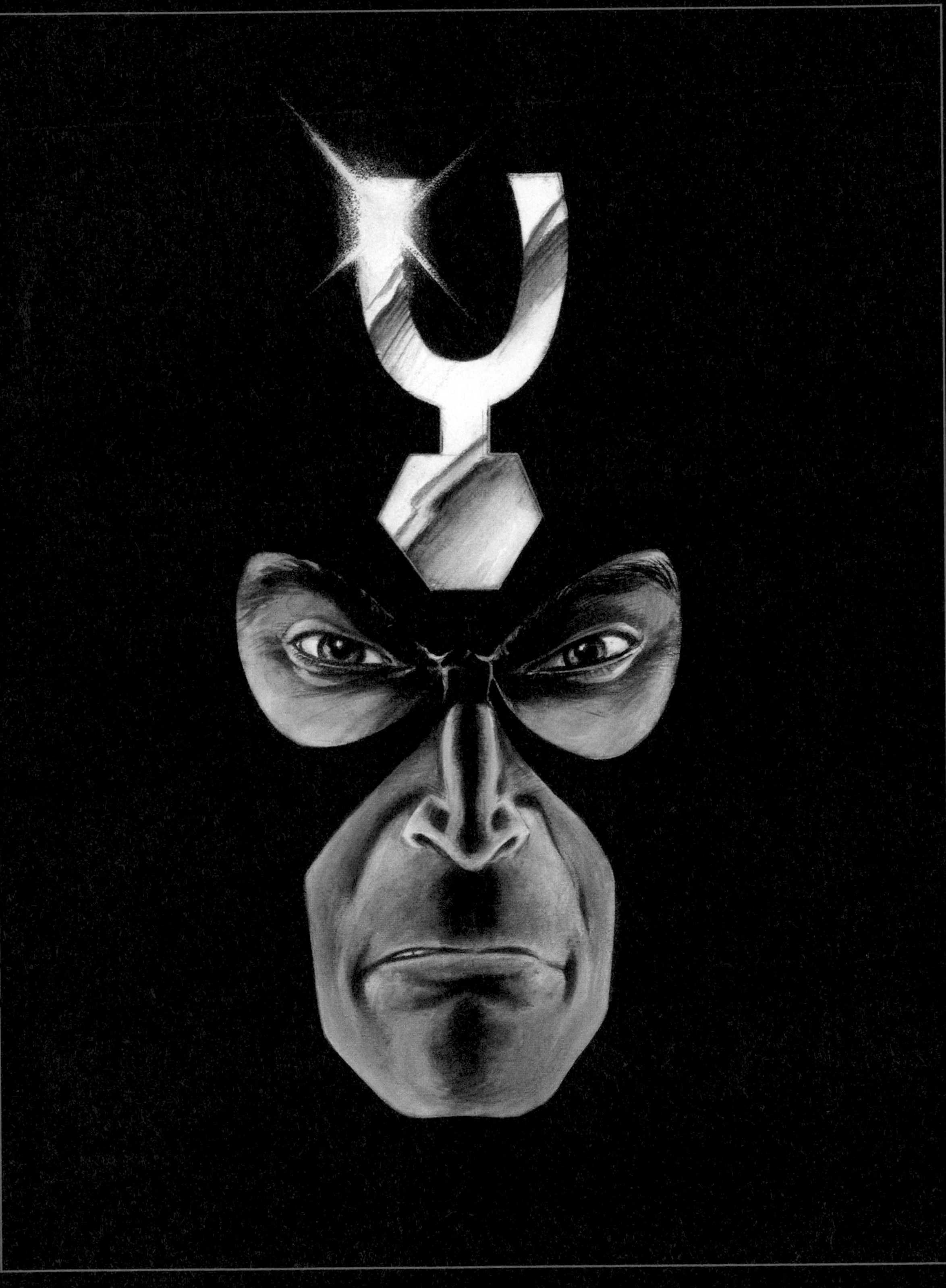

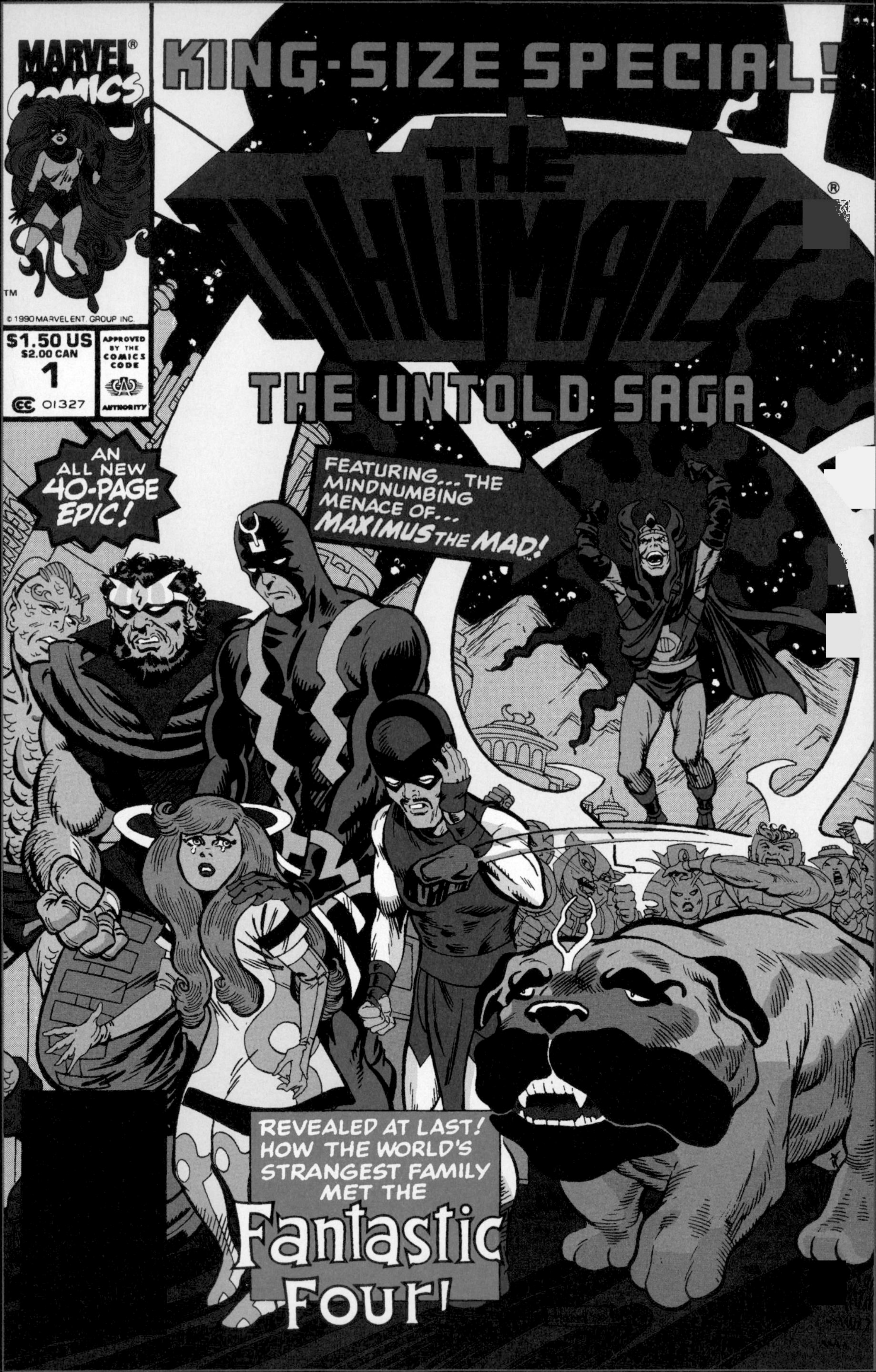
MARVEL® COMICS
KING-SIZE SPECIAL!
THE INHUMANS®
THE UNTOLD SAGA
TM
© 1990 MARVEL ENT. GROUP INC.
$1.50 US
$2.00 CAN
1
APPROVED BY THE COMICS CODE AUTHORITY
01327
AN ALL NEW 40-PAGE EPIC!
FEATURING... THE MINDNUMBING MENACE OF... MAXIMUS THE MAD!
REVEALED AT LAST! HOW THE WORLD'S STRANGEST FAMILY MET THE
Fantastic Four!

Stan Lee PRESENTS: THE UNCANNY INHUMANS™

REMEMBRANCES OF REVOLUTIONS PAST

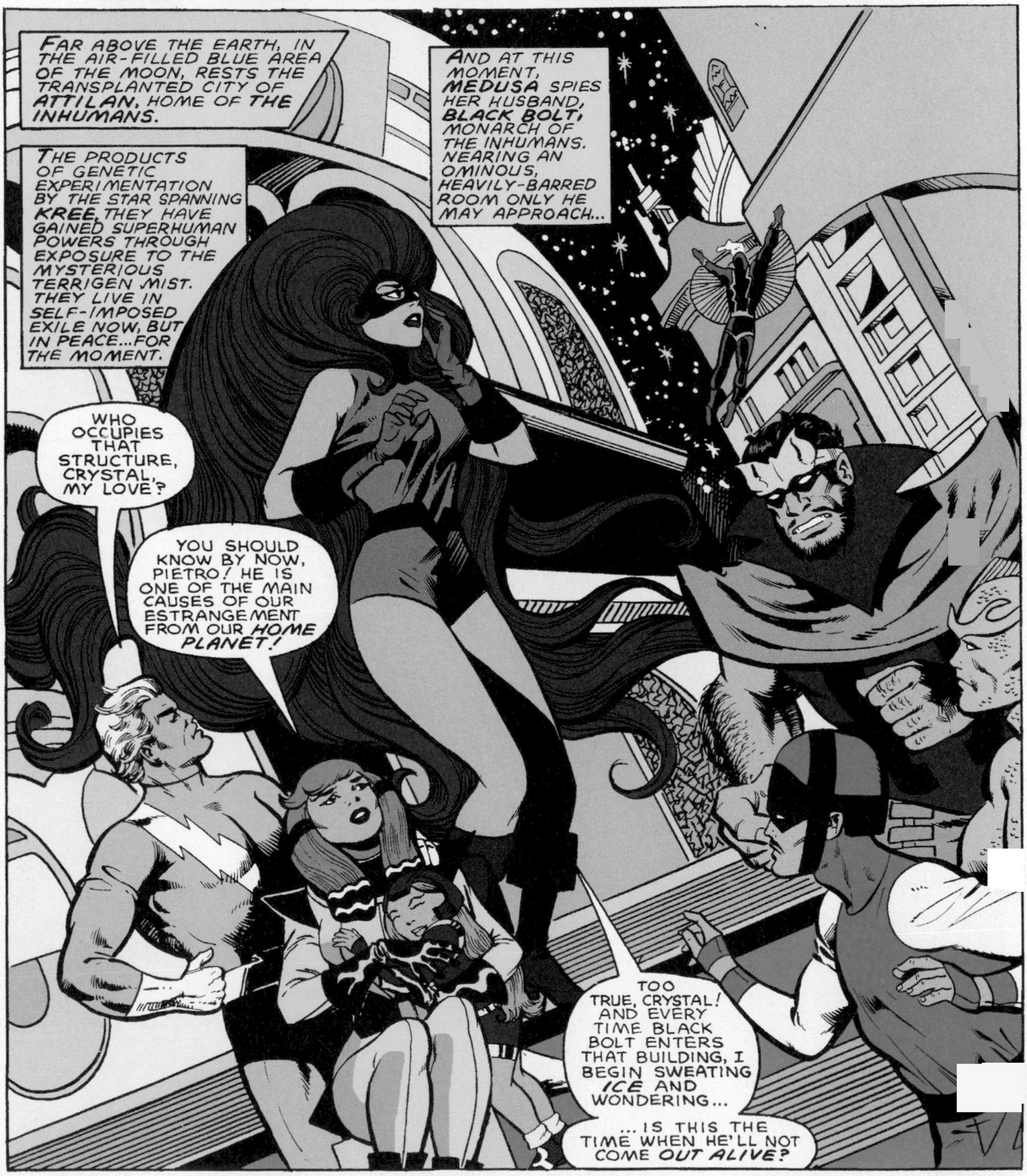
FAR ABOVE THE EARTH, IN THE AIR-FILLED BLUE AREA OF THE MOON, RESTS THE TRANSPLANTED CITY OF ATTILAN, HOME OF THE INHUMANS.
THE PRODUCTS OF GENETIC EXPERIMENTATION BY THE STAR SPANNING KREE, THEY HAVE GAINED SUPERHUMAN POWERS THROUGH EXPOSURE TO THE MYSTERIOUS TERRIGEN MIST. THEY LIVE IN SELF-IMPOSED EXILE NOW, BUT IN PEACE...FOR THE MOMENT.
AND AT THIS MOMENT, MEDUSA SPIES HER HUSBAND, BLACK BOLT, MONARCH OF THE INHUMANS. NEARING AN OMINOUS, HEAVILY-BARRED ROOM ONLY HE MAY APPROACH...
WHO OCCUPIES THAT STRUCTURE, CRYSTAL, MY LOVE?
YOU SHOULD KNOW BY NOW, PIETRO! HE IS ONE OF THE MAIN CAUSES OF OUR ESTRANGEMENT FROM OUR HOME PLANET!
TOO TRUE, CRYSTAL! AND EVERY TIME BLACK BOLT ENTERS THAT BUILDING, I BEGIN SWEATING ICE AND WONDERING...
...IS THIS THE TIME WHEN HE'LL NOT COME OUT ALIVE?

LOU MOUGIN	RICHARD HOWELL	VINCE COLLETTA	DIANA ALBERS	MARK GRUENWALD	TOM DeFALCO
WRITER	PENCILER/COLORIST	INKER	LETTERER	EDITOR	EDITOR IN CHIEF

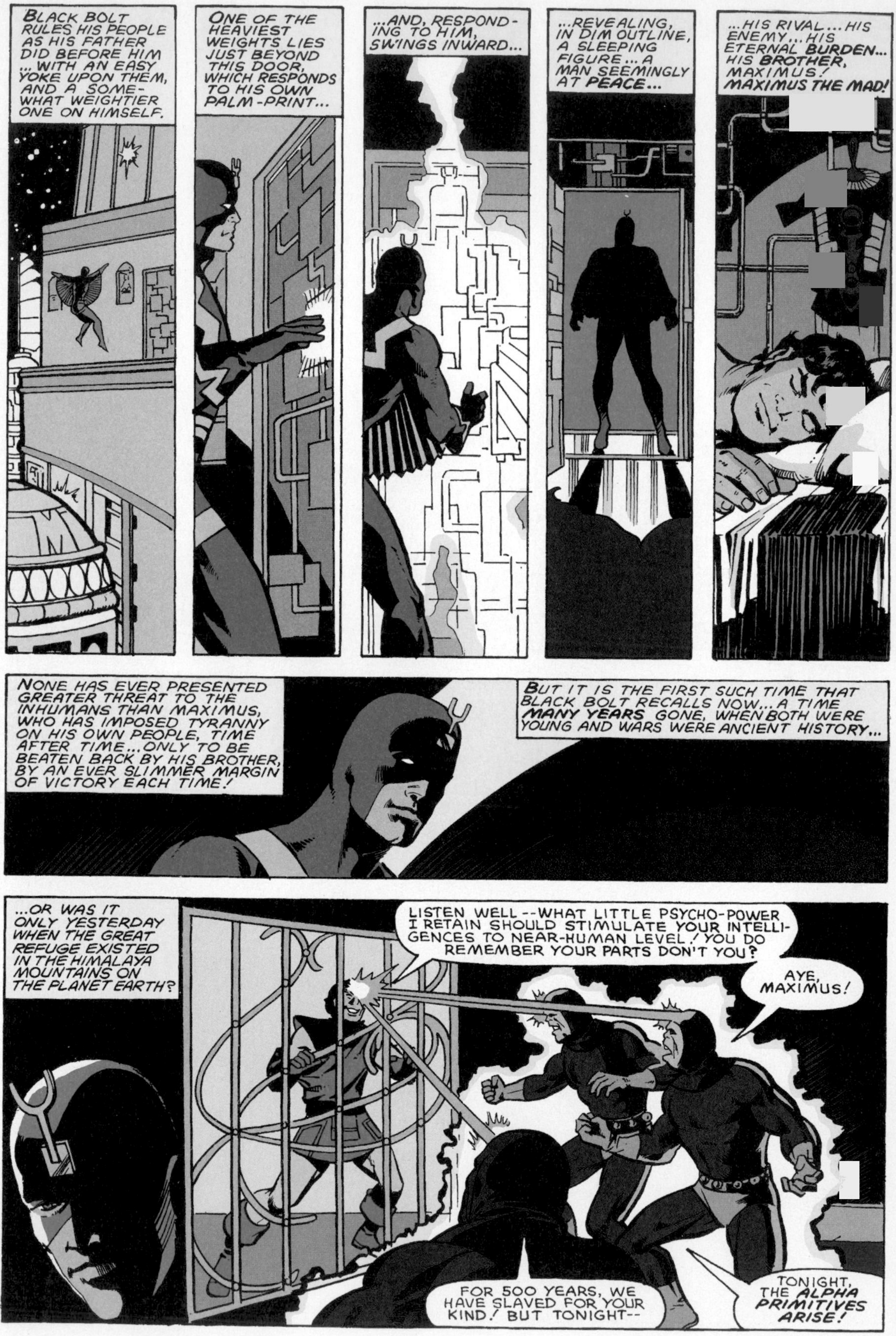
BLACK BOLT RULES HIS PEOPLE AS HIS FATHER DID BEFORE HIM ...WITH AN EASY YOKE UPON THEM, AND A SOME-WHAT WEIGHTIER ONE ON HIMSELF.
ONE OF THE HEAVIEST WEIGHTS LIES JUST BEYOND THIS DOOR, WHICH RESPONDS TO HIS OWN PALM-PRINT...
...AND, RESPOND-ING TO HIM, SWINGS INWARD...
...REVEALING, IN DIM OUTLINE, A SLEEPING FIGURE... A MAN SEEMINGLY AT PEACE...
...HIS RIVAL... HIS ENEMY... HIS ETERNAL BURDEN... HIS BROTHER, MAXIMUS! MAXIMUS THE MAD!
NONE HAS EVER PRESENTED GREATER THREAT TO THE INHUMANS THAN MAXIMUS, WHO HAS IMPOSED TYRANNY ON HIS OWN PEOPLE, TIME AFTER TIME... ONLY TO BE BEATEN BACK BY HIS BROTHER, BY AN EVER SLIMMER MARGIN OF VICTORY EACH TIME!
BUT IT IS THE FIRST SUCH TIME THAT BLACK BOLT RECALLS NOW... A TIME MANY YEARS GONE, WHEN BOTH WERE YOUNG AND WARS WERE ANCIENT HISTORY...
...OR WAS IT ONLY YESTERDAY WHEN THE GREAT REFUGE EXISTED IN THE HIMALAYA MOUNTAINS ON THE PLANET EARTH?
LISTEN WELL--WHAT LITTLE PSYCHO-POWER I RETAIN SHOULD STIMULATE YOUR INTELLI-GENCES TO NEAR-HUMAN LEVEL! YOU DO REMEMBER YOUR PARTS DON'T YOU?
AYE, MAXIMUS!
FOR 500 YEARS, WE HAVE SLAVED FOR YOUR KIND! BUT TONIGHT--
TONIGHT, THE ALPHA PRIMITIVES ARISE!

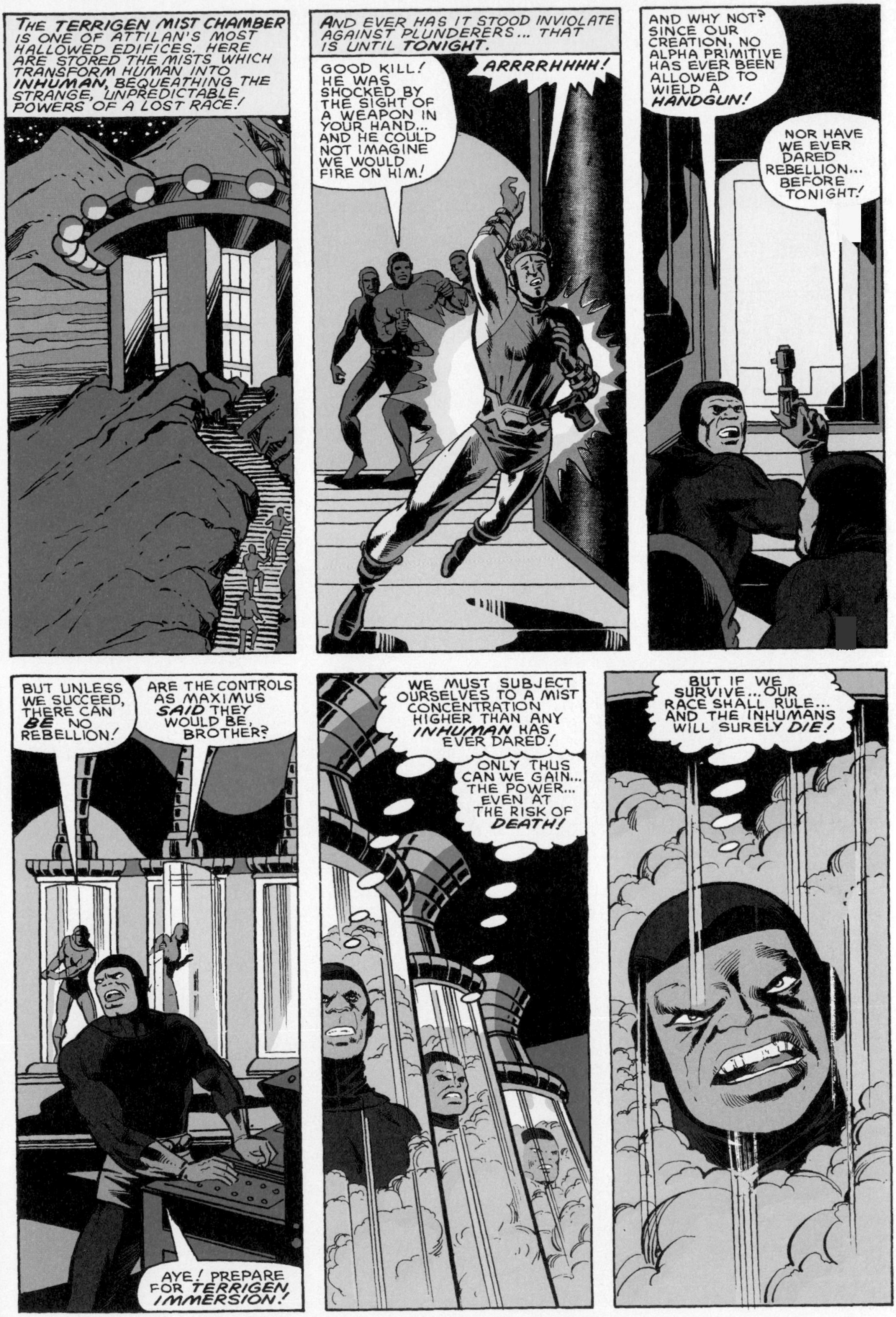
THE TERRIGEN MIST CHAMBER IS ONE OF ATTILAN'S MOST HALLOWED EDIFICES. HERE ARE STORED THE MISTS WHICH TRANSFORM HUMAN INTO INHUMAN, BEQUEATHING THE STRANGE, UNPREDICTABLE POWERS OF A LOST RACE!
AND EVER HAS IT STOOD INVIOLATE AGAINST PLUNDERERS... THAT IS UNTIL TONIGHT.
GOOD KILL! HE WAS SHOCKED BY THE SIGHT OF A WEAPON IN YOUR HAND... AND HE COULD NOT IMAGINE WE WOULD FIRE ON HIM!
ARRRRHHHH!
AND WHY NOT? SINCE OUR CREATION, NO ALPHA PRIMITIVE HAS EVER BEEN ALLOWED TO WIELD A HANDGUN!
NOR HAVE WE EVER DARED REBELLION... BEFORE TONIGHT!
BUT UNLESS WE SUCCEED, THERE CAN BE NO REBELLION!
ARE THE CONTROLS AS MAXIMUS SAID THEY WOULD BE, BROTHER?
AYE! PREPARE FOR TERRIGEN IMMERSION!
WE MUST SUBJECT OURSELVES TO A MIST CONCENTRATION HIGHER THAN ANY INHUMAN HAS EVER DARED!
ONLY THUS CAN WE GAIN... THE POWER... EVEN AT THE RISK OF DEATH!
BUT IF WE SURVIVE... OUR RACE SHALL RULE... AND THE INHUMANS WILL SURELY DIE!

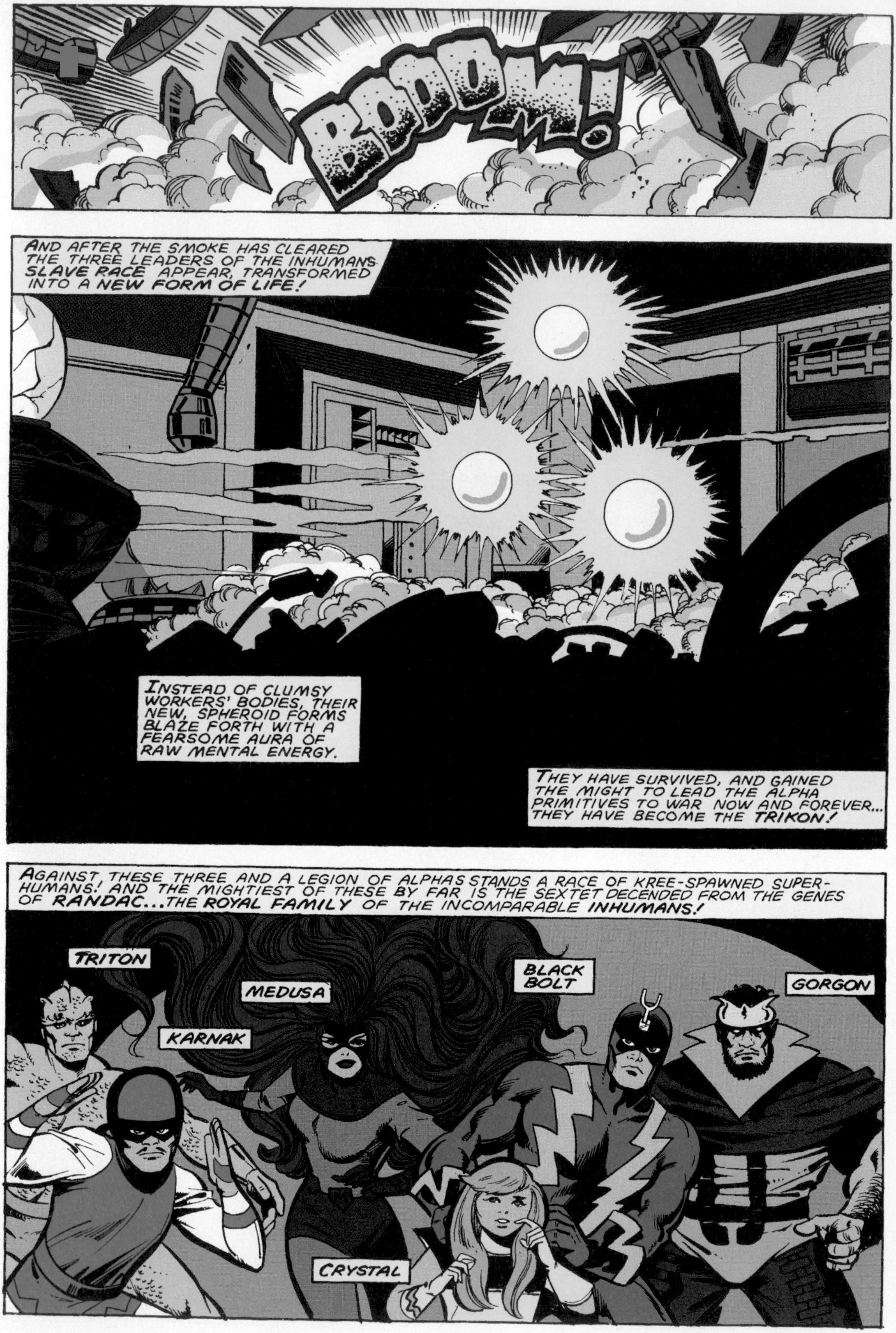
BOOOM!
AND AFTER THE SMOKE HAS CLEARED THE THREE LEADERS OF THE INHUMANS' SLAVE RACE APPEAR, TRANSFORMED INTO A NEW FORM OF LIFE!
INSTEAD OF CLUMSY WORKERS' BODIES, THEIR NEW, SPHEROID FORMS BLAZE FORTH WITH A FEARSOME AURA OF RAW MENTAL ENERGY.
THEY HAVE SURVIVED, AND GAINED THE MIGHT TO LEAD THE ALPHA PRIMITIVES TO WAR NOW AND FOREVER... THEY HAVE BECOME THE TRIKON!
AGAINST THESE THREE AND A LEGION OF ALPHAS STANDS A RACE OF KREE-SPAWNED SUPER-HUMANS! AND THE MIGHTIEST OF THESE BY FAR IS THE SEXTET DECENDED FROM THE GENES OF RANDAC...THE ROYAL FAMILY OF THE INCOMPARABLE INHUMANS!
TRITON
MEDUSA
KARNAK
BLACK BOLT
GORGON
CRYSTAL

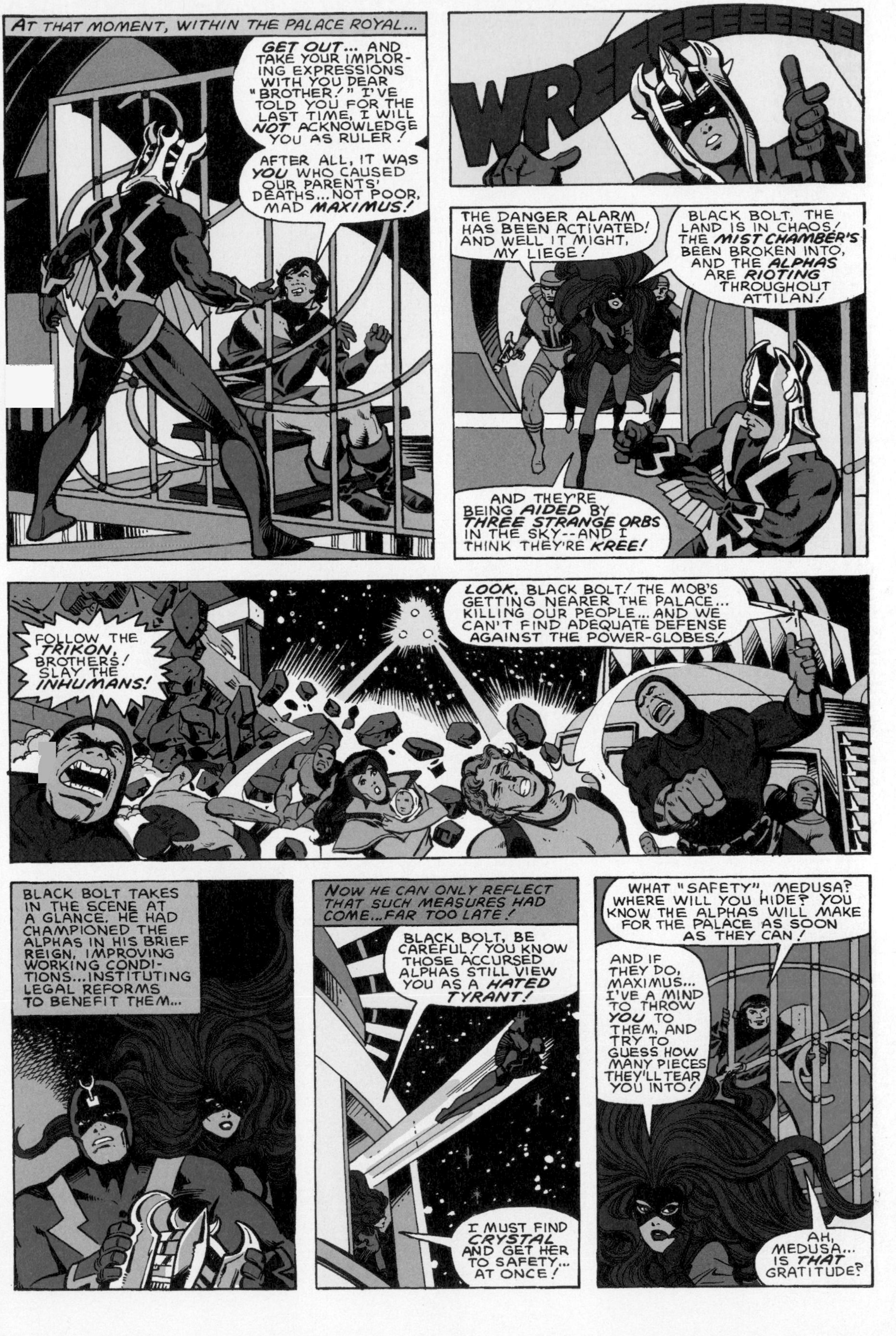
AT THAT MOMENT, WITHIN THE PALACE ROYAL...
GET OUT... AND TAKE YOUR IMPLORING EXPRESSIONS WITH YOU DEAR "BROTHER!" I'VE TOLD YOU FOR THE LAST TIME, I WILL NOT ACKNOWLEDGE YOU AS RULER!
AFTER ALL, IT WAS YOU WHO CAUSED OUR PARENTS' DEATHS... NOT POOR, MAD MAXIMUS!
WREEEEEEEEEEE
THE DANGER ALARM HAS BEEN ACTIVATED! AND WELL IT MIGHT, MY LIEGE!
BLACK BOLT, THE LAND IS IN CHAOS! THE MIST CHAMBER'S BEEN BROKEN INTO, AND THE ALPHAS ARE RIOTING THROUGHOUT ATTILAN!
AND THEY'RE BEING AIDED BY THREE STRANGE ORBS IN THE SKY--AND I THINK THEY'RE KREE!
FOLLOW THE TRIKON, BROTHERS! SLAY THE INHUMANS!
LOOK, BLACK BOLT! THE MOB'S GETTING NEARER THE PALACE... KILLING OUR PEOPLE... AND WE CAN'T FIND ADEQUATE DEFENSE AGAINST THE POWER-GLOBES!
BLACK BOLT TAKES IN THE SCENE AT A GLANCE. HE HAD CHAMPIONED THE ALPHAS IN HIS BRIEF REIGN, IMPROVING WORKING CONDITIONS... INSTITUTING LEGAL REFORMS TO BENEFIT THEM...
NOW HE CAN ONLY REFLECT THAT SUCH MEASURES HAD COME... FAR TOO LATE!
BLACK BOLT, BE CAREFUL! YOU KNOW THOSE ACCURSED ALPHAS STILL VIEW YOU AS A HATED TYRANT!
I MUST FIND CRYSTAL AND GET HER TO SAFETY... AT ONCE!
WHAT "SAFETY", MEDUSA? WHERE WILL YOU HIDE? YOU KNOW THE ALPHAS WILL MAKE FOR THE PALACE AS SOON AS THEY CAN!
AND IF THEY DO, MAXIMUS... I'VE A MIND TO THROW YOU TO THEM, AND TRY TO GUESS HOW MANY PIECES THEY'LL TEAR YOU INTO!
AH, MEDUSA... IS THAT GRATITUDE?

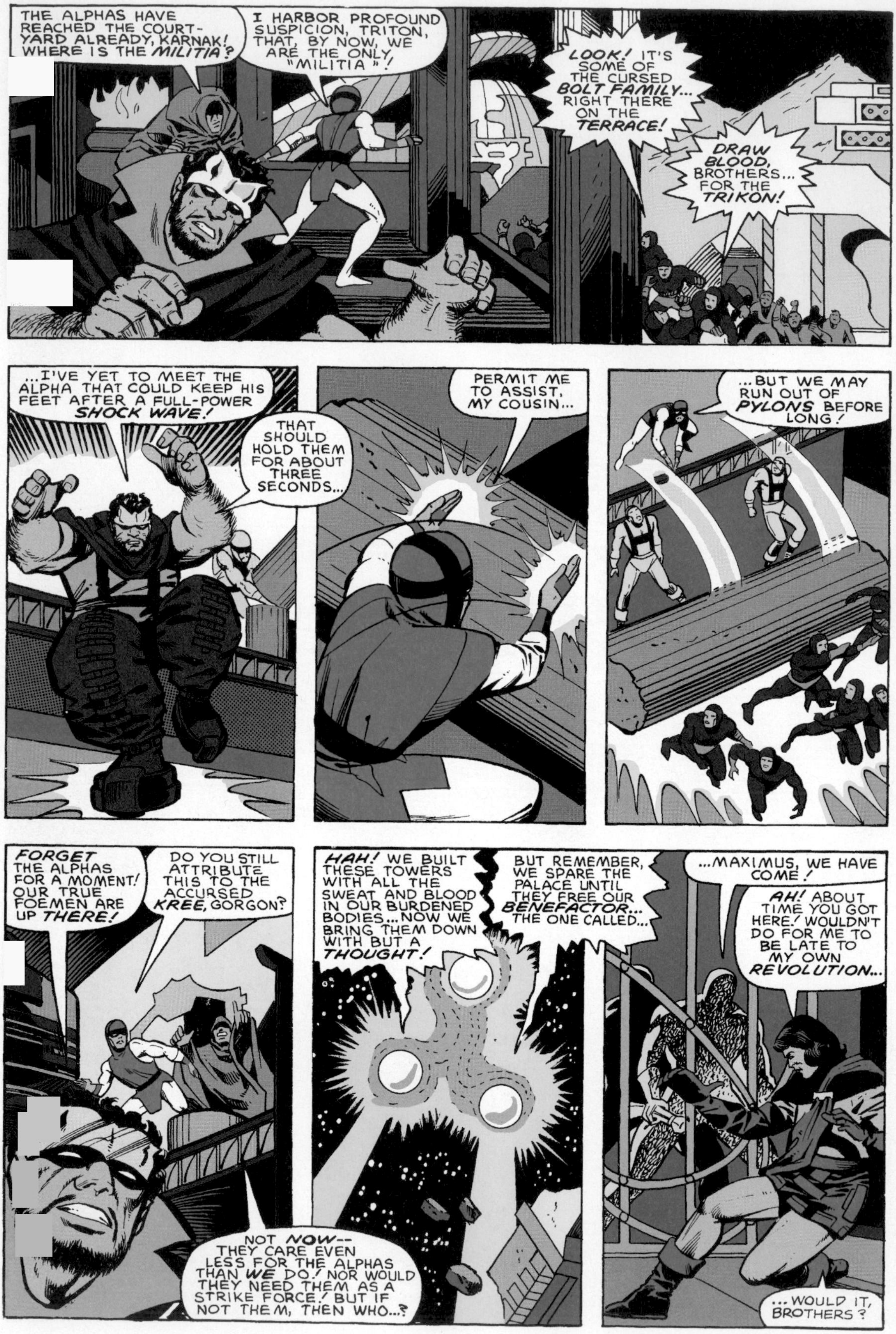
THE ALPHAS HAVE REACHED THE COURT-YARD ALREADY, KARNAK! WHERE IS THE MILITIA?
I HARBOR PROFOUND SUSPICION, TRITON, THAT, BY NOW, WE ARE THE ONLY "MILITIA"!
LOOK! IT'S SOME OF THE CURSED BOLT FAMILY... RIGHT THERE ON THE TERRACE!
DRAW BLOOD, BROTHERS... FOR THE TRIKON!
...I'VE YET TO MEET THE ALPHA THAT COULD KEEP HIS FEET AFTER A FULL-POWER SHOCK WAVE!
THAT SHOULD HOLD THEM FOR ABOUT THREE SECONDS...
PERMIT ME TO ASSIST, MY COUSIN...
...BUT WE MAY RUN OUT OF PYLONS BEFORE LONG!
FORGET THE ALPHAS FOR A MOMENT! OUR TRUE FOEMEN ARE UP THERE!
DO YOU STILL ATTRIBUTE THIS TO THE ACCURSED KREE, GORGON?
NOT NOW-- THEY CARE EVEN LESS FOR THE ALPHAS THAN WE DO! NOR WOULD THEY NEED THEM AS A STRIKE FORCE! BUT IF NOT THEM, THEN WHO...?
HAH! WE BUILT THESE TOWERS WITH ALL THE SWEAT AND BLOOD IN OUR BURDENED BODIES... NOW WE BRING THEM DOWN WITH BUT A THOUGHT!
BUT REMEMBER, WE SPARE THE PALACE UNTIL THEY FREE OUR BENEFACTOR... THE ONE CALLED...
...MAXIMUS, WE HAVE COME!
AH! ABOUT TIME YOU GOT HERE! WOULDN'T DO FOR ME TO BE LATE TO MY OWN REVOLUTION...
...WOULD IT, BROTHERS?

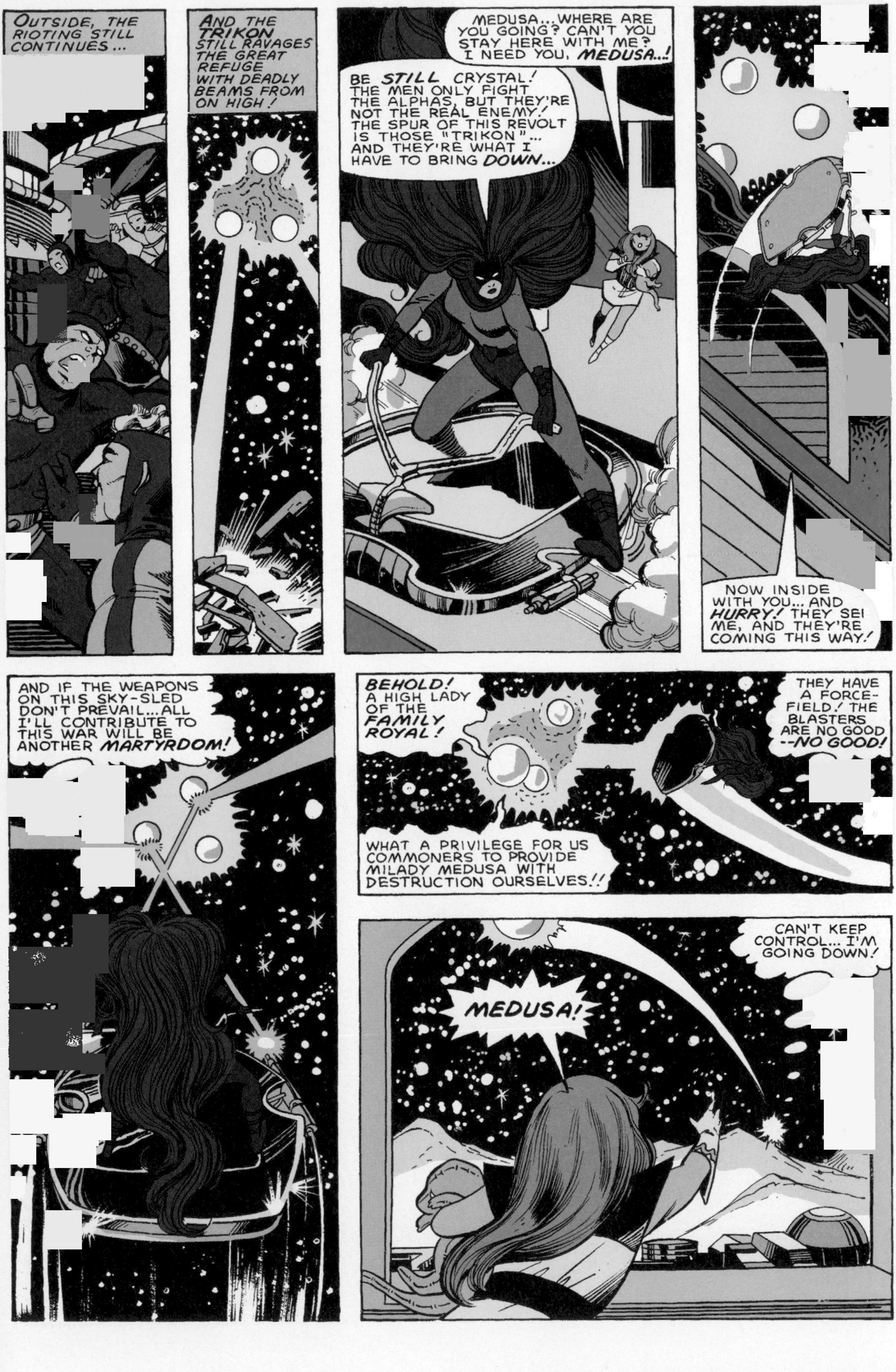

OUTSIDE, THE RIOTING STILL CONTINUES...
AND THE TRIKON STILL RAVAGES THE GREAT REFUGE WITH DEADLY BEAMS FROM ON HIGH!
MEDUSA... WHERE ARE YOU GOING? CAN'T YOU STAY HERE WITH ME? I NEED YOU, MEDUSA...!
BE STILL CRYSTAL! THE MEN ONLY FIGHT THE ALPHAS, BUT THEY'RE NOT THE REAL ENEMY! THE SPUR OF THIS REVOLT IS THOSE "TRIKON"... AND THEY'RE WHAT I HAVE TO BRING DOWN...
NOW INSIDE WITH YOU... AND HURRY! THEY SEI ME, AND THEY'RE COMING THIS WAY!
AND IF THE WEAPONS ON THIS SKY-SLED DON'T PREVAIL... ALL I'LL CONTRIBUTE TO THIS WAR WILL BE ANOTHER MARTYRDOM!
BEHOLD! A HIGH LADY OF THE FAMILY ROYAL!
WHAT A PRIVILEGE FOR US COMMONERS TO PROVIDE MILADY MEDUSA WITH DESTRUCTION OURSELVES!!
THEY HAVE A FORCE-FIELD! THE BLASTERS ARE NO GOOD --NO GOOD!
CAN'T KEEP CONTROL... I'M GOING DOWN!
MEDUSA!

BLACK BOLT! DID YOU SEE HER? OH, PLEASE, YOU'VE GOT TO HELP MEDUSA... WHAT?

YOU WANT... LOCKJAW? Y-YES, I'LL CALL HIM!

LOCKJAW! HERE HE IS! LOCKJAW... UNCLE BOLT NEEDS YOUR AID!

THEN, CRYSTAL CAN ONLY WONDER HOW THE SILENT MAN IN BLACK CAN MAKE HIS WISHES PERFECTLY UNDERSTOOD BY LOCKJAW...

BUT THEN, SHE REALIZES THAT SHE HERSELF NEVER FAILS TO COMPREHEND BLACK BOLT'S COMMANDS, THOUGH HE SPEAKS NOT A WORD... AND CRYSTAL BEGINS TO UNDERSTAND.

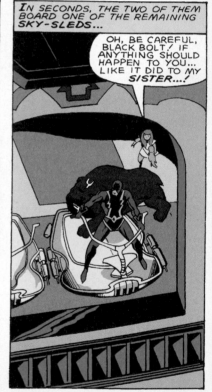

IN SECONDS, THE TWO OF THEM BOARD ONE OF THE REMAINING SKY-SLEDS...

OH, BE CAREFUL, BLACK BOLT! IF ANYTHING SHOULD HAPPEN TO YOU... LIKE IT DID TO MY SISTER...!

SILENTLY, THE MUTE MONARCH AND HIS LOYAL COMPANION LAUNCH THEIR ATTACK AGAINST THE THREE GLOWING BALLS OF DEATH!

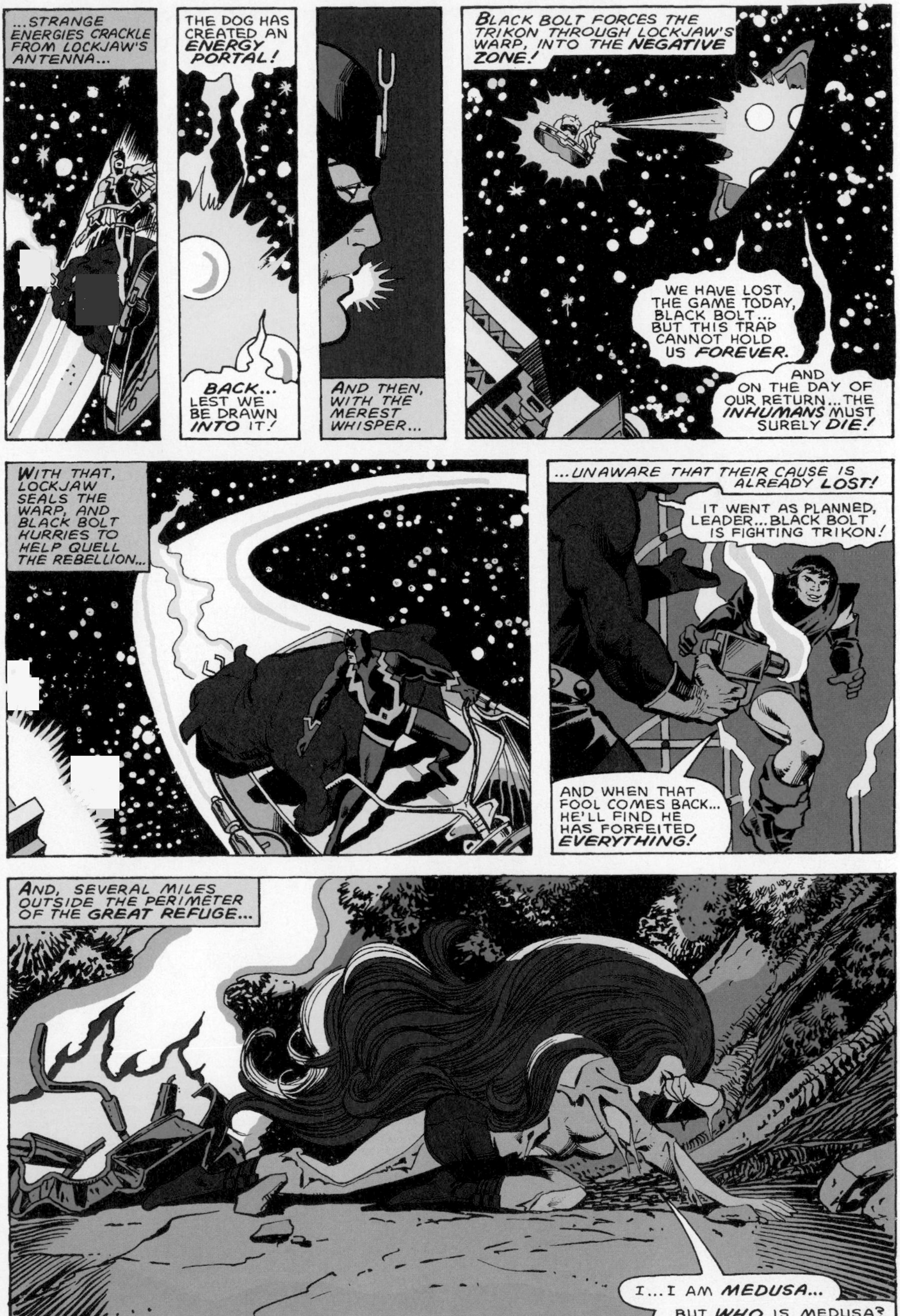
...STRANGE ENERGIES CRACKLE FROM LOCKJAW'S ANTENNA...
THE DOG HAS CREATED AN ENERGY PORTAL!
BACK... LEST WE BE DRAWN INTO IT!
AND THEN, WITH THE MEREST WHISPER...
BLACK BOLT FORCES THE TRIKON THROUGH LOCKJAW'S WARP, INTO THE NEGATIVE ZONE!
WE HAVE LOST THE GAME TODAY, BLACK BOLT... BUT THIS TRAP CANNOT HOLD US FOREVER.
AND ON THE DAY OF OUR RETURN... THE INHUMANS MUST SURELY DIE!
WITH THAT, LOCKJAW SEALS THE WARP, AND BLACK BOLT HURRIES TO HELP QUELL THE REBELLION...
...UNAWARE THAT THEIR CAUSE IS ALREADY LOST!
IT WENT AS PLANNED, LEADER... BLACK BOLT IS FIGHTING TRIKON!
AND WHEN THAT FOOL COMES BACK... HE'LL FIND HE HAS FORFEITED EVERYTHING!
AND, SEVERAL MILES OUTSIDE THE PERIMETER OF THE GREAT REFUGE...
I... I AM MEDUSA...
BUT WHO IS MEDUSA?

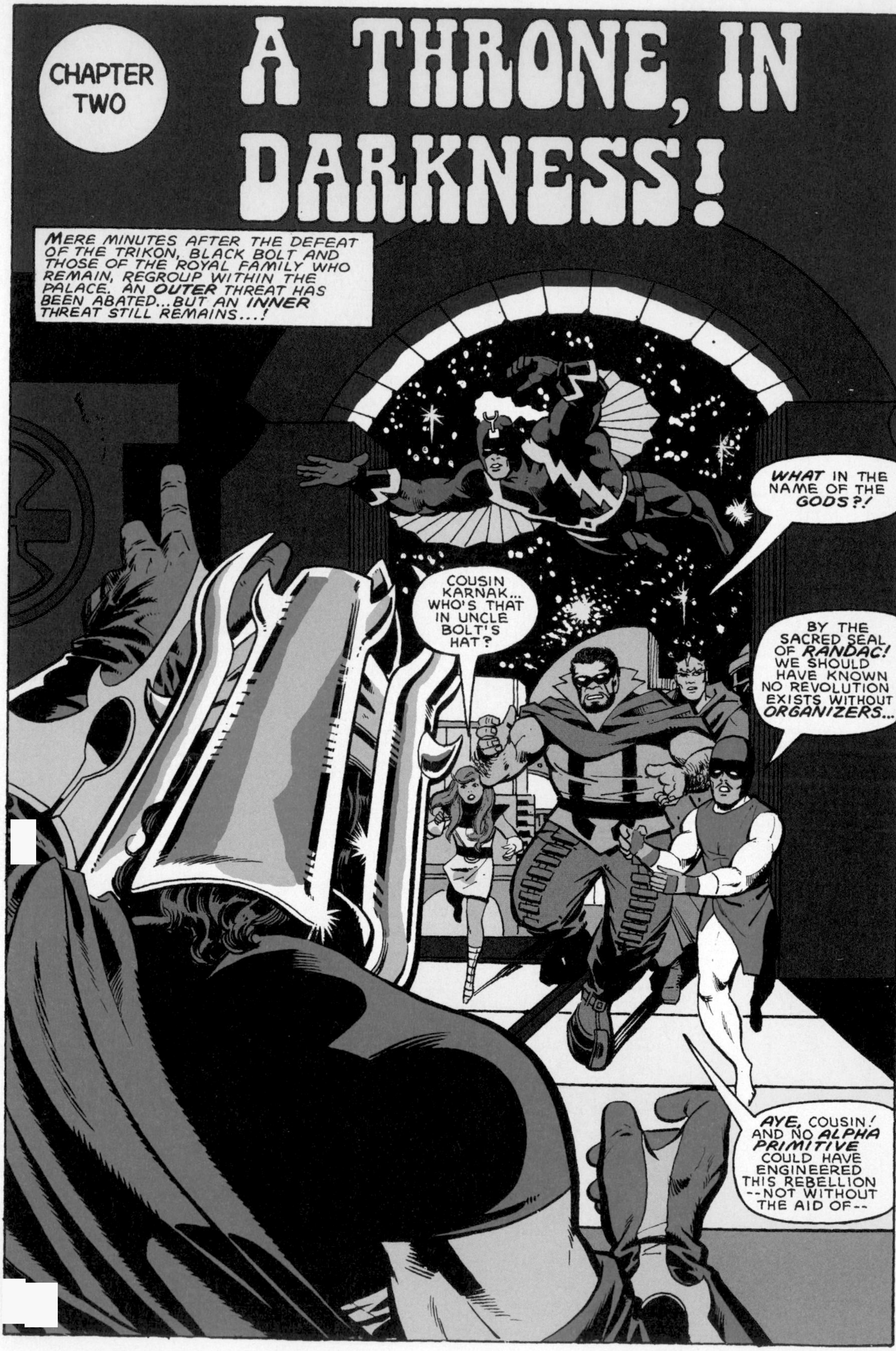
CHAPTER TWO
A THRONE, IN DARKNESS!
MERE MINUTES AFTER THE DEFEAT OF THE TRIKON, BLACK BOLT AND THOSE OF THE ROYAL FAMILY WHO REMAIN, REGROUP WITHIN THE PALACE. AN OUTER THREAT HAS BEEN ABATED...BUT AN INNER THREAT STILL REMAINS...!
WHAT IN THE NAME OF THE GODS?!
COUSIN KARNAK... WHO'S THAT IN UNCLE BOLT'S HAT?
BY THE SACRED SEAL OF RANDAC! WE SHOULD HAVE KNOWN NO REVOLUTION EXISTS WITHOUT ORGANIZERS...
AYE, COUSIN! AND NO ALPHA PRIMITIVE COULD HAVE ENGINEERED THIS REBELLION --NOT WITHOUT THE AID OF--

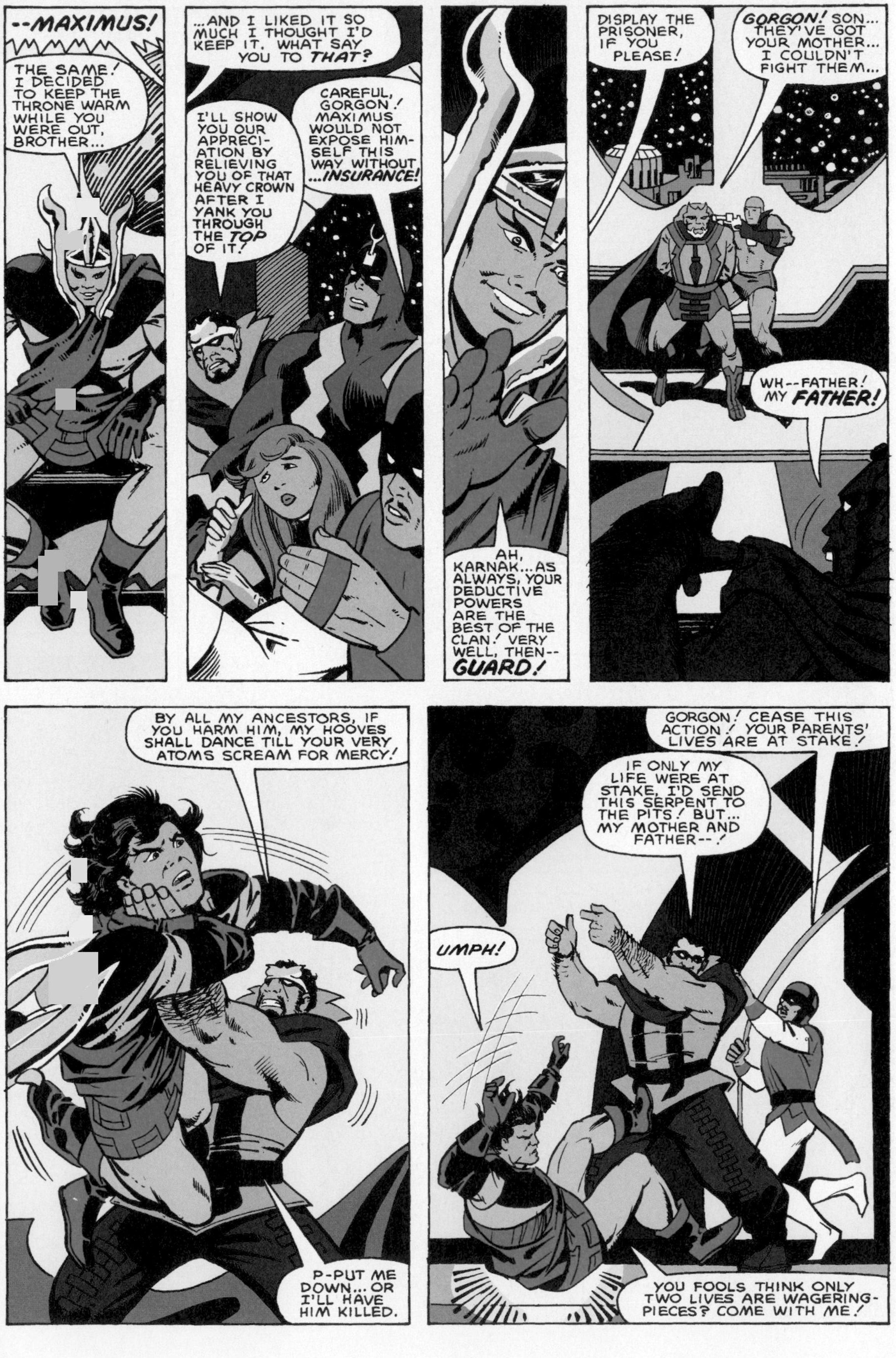
--MAXIMUS!
THE SAME! I DECIDED TO KEEP THE THRONE WARM WHILE YOU WERE OUT, BROTHER...
...AND I LIKED IT SO MUCH I THOUGHT I'D KEEP IT. WHAT SAY YOU TO THAT?
I'LL SHOW YOU OUR APPRECIATION BY RELIEVING YOU OF THAT HEAVY CROWN AFTER I YANK YOU THROUGH THE TOP OF IT!
CAREFUL, GORGON! MAXIMUS WOULD NOT EXPOSE HIMSELF THIS WAY WITHOUT ...INSURANCE!
AH, KARNAK...AS ALWAYS, YOUR DEDUCTIVE POWERS ARE THE BEST OF THE CLAN! VERY WELL, THEN-- GUARD!
DISPLAY THE PRISONER, IF YOU PLEASE!
GORGON! SON... THEY'VE GOT YOUR MOTHER... I COULDN'T FIGHT THEM...
WH--FATHER! MY FATHER!
BY ALL MY ANCESTORS, IF YOU HARM HIM, MY HOOVES SHALL DANCE TILL YOUR VERY ATOMS SCREAM FOR MERCY!
P-PUT ME DOWN... OR I'LL HAVE HIM KILLED.
GORGON! CEASE THIS ACTION! YOUR PARENTS' LIVES ARE AT STAKE!
IF ONLY MY LIFE WERE AT STAKE, I'D SEND THIS SERPENT TO THE PITS! BUT... MY MOTHER AND FATHER--!
UMPH!
YOU FOOLS THINK ONLY TWO LIVES ARE WAGERING-PIECES? COME WITH ME!

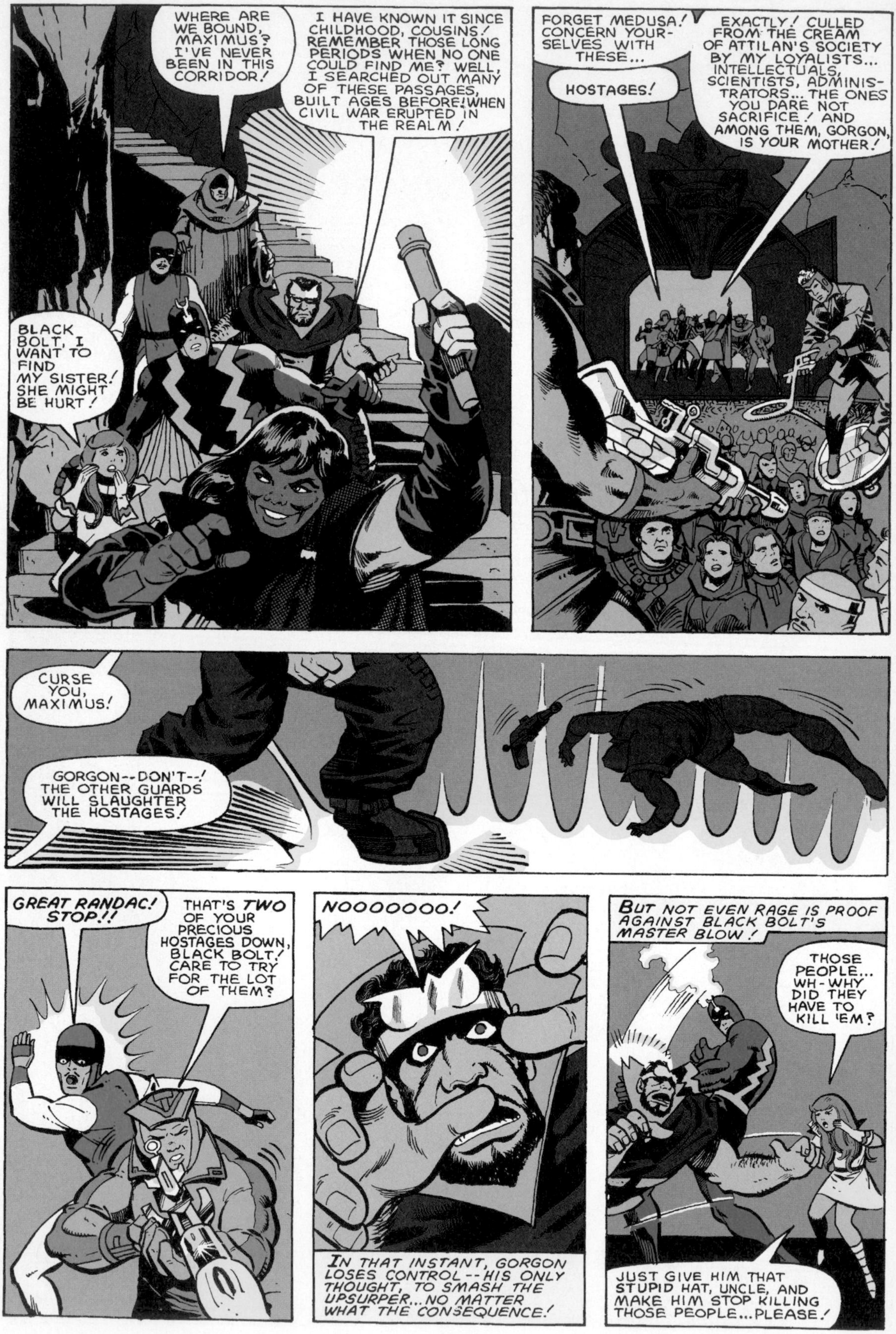
WHERE ARE WE BOUND, MAXIMUS? I'VE NEVER BEEN IN THIS CORRIDOR!
I HAVE KNOWN IT SINCE CHILDHOOD, COUSINS! REMEMBER THOSE LONG PERIODS WHEN NO ONE COULD FIND ME? WELL, I SEARCHED OUT MANY OF THESE PASSAGES, BUILT AGES BEFORE! WHEN CIVIL WAR ERUPTED IN THE REALM!
BLACK BOLT, I WANT TO FIND MY SISTER! SHE MIGHT BE HURT!
FORGET MEDUSA! CONCERN YOURSELVES WITH THESE...
HOSTAGES!
EXACTLY! CULLED FROM THE CREAM OF ATTILAN'S SOCIETY BY MY LOYALISTS... INTELLECTUALS, SCIENTISTS, ADMINISTRATORS... THE ONES YOU DARE NOT SACRIFICE! AND AMONG THEM, GORGON, IS YOUR MOTHER!
CURSE YOU, MAXIMUS!
GORGON--DON'T--! THE OTHER GUARDS WILL SLAUGHTER THE HOSTAGES!
GREAT RANDAC! STOP!!
THAT'S TWO OF YOUR PRECIOUS HOSTAGES DOWN, BLACK BOLT! CARE TO TRY FOR THE LOT OF THEM?
NOOOOOOO!
IN THAT INSTANT, GORGON LOSES CONTROL--HIS ONLY THOUGHT, TO SMASH THE UPSURPER... NO MATTER WHAT THE CONSEQUENCE!
BUT NOT EVEN RAGE IS PROOF AGAINST BLACK BOLT'S MASTER BLOW!
THOSE PEOPLE... WH-WHY DID THEY HAVE TO KILL 'EM?
JUST GIVE HIM THAT STUPID HAT, UNCLE, AND MAKE HIM STOP KILLING THOSE PEOPLE... PLEASE!

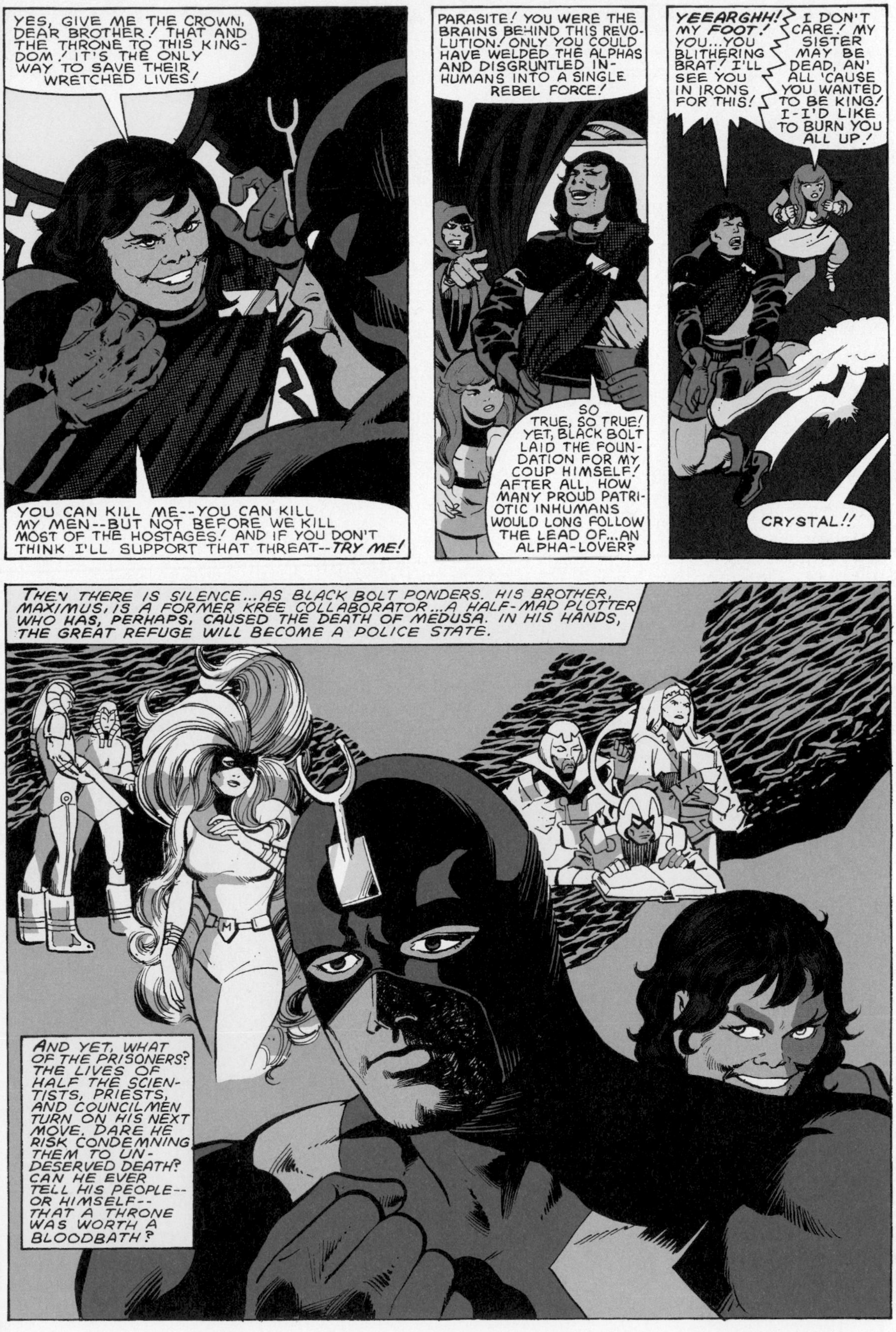

YES, GIVE ME THE CROWN, DEAR BROTHER! THAT AND THE THRONE TO THIS KINGDOM! IT'S THE ONLY WAY TO SAVE THEIR WRETCHED LIVES!
YOU CAN KILL ME--YOU CAN KILL MY MEN--BUT NOT BEFORE WE KILL MOST OF THE HOSTAGES! AND IF YOU DON'T THINK I'LL SUPPORT THAT THREAT--TRY ME!
PARASITE! YOU WERE THE BRAINS BEHIND THIS REVOLUTION! ONLY YOU COULD HAVE WELDED THE ALPHAS AND DISGRUNTLED INHUMANS INTO A SINGLE REBEL FORCE!
SO TRUE, SO TRUE! YET, BLACK BOLT LAID THE FOUNDATION FOR MY COUP HIMSELF! AFTER ALL, HOW MANY PROUD PATRIOTIC INHUMANS WOULD LONG FOLLOW THE LEAD OF...AN ALPHA-LOVER?
YEEARGHH! MY FOOT! YOU...YOU BLITHERING BRAT! I'LL SEE YOU IN IRONS FOR THIS!
I DON'T CARE! MY SISTER MAY BE DEAD, AN' ALL 'CAUSE YOU WANTED TO BE KING! I-I'D LIKE TO BURN YOU ALL UP!
CRYSTAL!!
THEN THERE IS SILENCE... AS BLACK BOLT PONDERS. HIS BROTHER, MAXIMUS, IS A FORMER KREE COLLABORATOR... A HALF-MAD PLOTTER WHO HAS, PERHAPS, CAUSED THE DEATH OF MEDUSA. IN HIS HANDS, THE GREAT REFUGE WILL BECOME A POLICE STATE.
AND YET, WHAT OF THE PRISONERS? THE LIVES OF HALF THE SCIENTISTS, PRIESTS, AND COUNCILMEN TURN ON HIS NEXT MOVE. DARE HE RISK CONDEMNING THEM TO UNDESERVED DEATH? CAN HE EVER TELL HIS PEOPLE--OR HIMSELF--THAT A THRONE WAS WORTH A BLOODBATH?

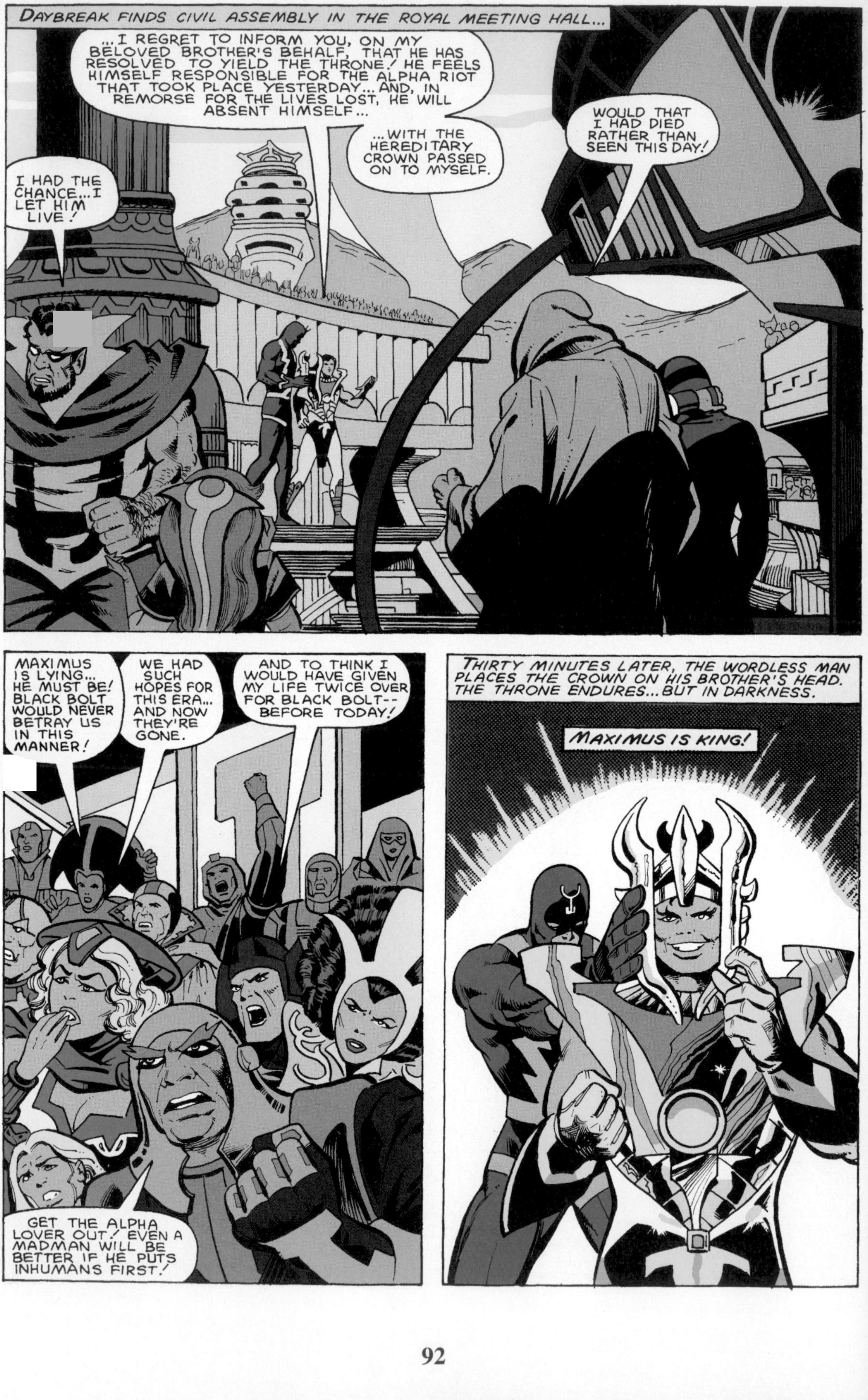

DAYBREAK FINDS CIVIL ASSEMBLY IN THE ROYAL MEETING HALL...
...I REGRET TO INFORM YOU, ON MY BELOVED BROTHER'S BEHALF, THAT HE HAS RESOLVED TO YIELD THE THRONE! HE FEELS HIMSELF RESPONSIBLE FOR THE ALPHA RIOT THAT TOOK PLACE YESTERDAY... AND, IN REMORSE FOR THE LIVES LOST, HE WILL ABSENT HIMSELF...
...WITH THE HEREDITARY CROWN PASSED ON TO MYSELF.
I HAD THE CHANCE... I LET HIM LIVE!
WOULD THAT I HAD DIED RATHER THAN SEEN THIS DAY!
MAXIMUS IS LYING... HE MUST BE! BLACK BOLT WOULD NEVER BETRAY US IN THIS MANNER!
WE HAD SUCH HOPES FOR THIS ERA... AND NOW THEY'RE GONE.
AND TO THINK I WOULD HAVE GIVEN MY LIFE TWICE OVER FOR BLACK BOLT-- BEFORE TODAY!
GET THE ALPHA LOVER OUT! EVEN A MADMAN WILL BE BETTER IF HE PUTS INHUMANS FIRST!
THIRTY MINUTES LATER, THE WORDLESS MAN PLACES THE CROWN ON HIS BROTHER'S HEAD. THE THRONE ENDURES... BUT IN DARKNESS.
MAXIMUS IS KING!

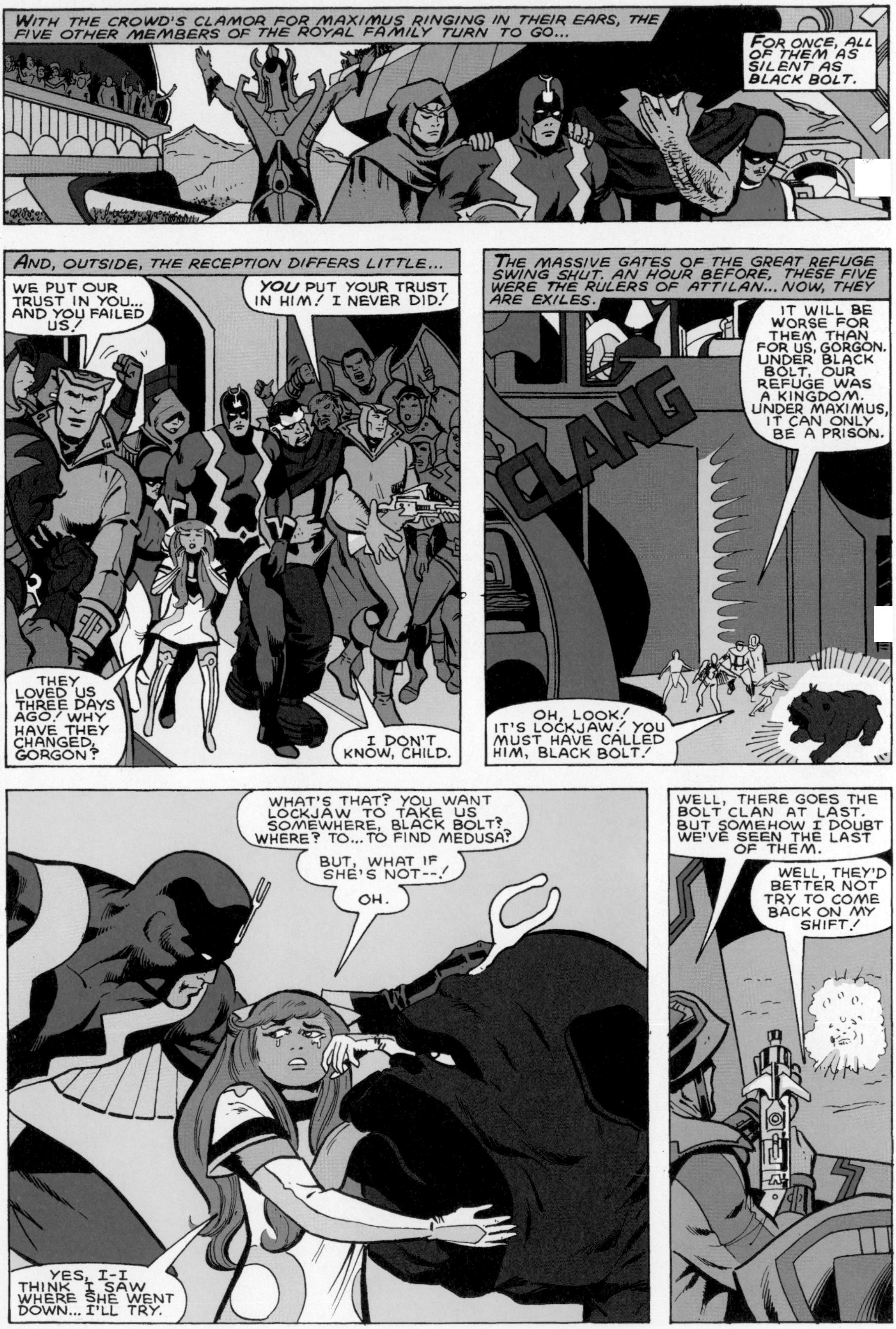

WITH THE CROWD'S CLAMOR FOR MAXIMUS RINGING IN THEIR EARS, THE FIVE OTHER MEMBERS OF THE ROYAL FAMILY TURN TO GO...
FOR ONCE, ALL OF THEM AS SILENT AS BLACK BOLT.
AND, OUTSIDE, THE RECEPTION DIFFERS LITTLE...
WE PUT OUR TRUST IN YOU... AND YOU FAILED US!
YOU PUT YOUR TRUST IN HIM! I NEVER DID!
THEY LOVED US THREE DAYS AGO! WHY HAVE THEY CHANGED, GORGON?
I DON'T KNOW, CHILD.
THE MASSIVE GATES OF THE GREAT REFUGE SWING SHUT. AN HOUR BEFORE, THESE FIVE WERE THE RULERS OF ATTILAN... NOW, THEY ARE EXILES.
IT WILL BE WORSE FOR THEM THAN FOR US, GORGON. UNDER BLACK BOLT, OUR REFUGE WAS A KINGDOM. UNDER MAXIMUS, IT CAN ONLY BE A PRISON.
CLANG
OH, LOOK! IT'S LOCKJAW! YOU MUST HAVE CALLED HIM, BLACK BOLT!
WHAT'S THAT? YOU WANT LOCKJAW TO TAKE US SOMEWHERE, BLACK BOLT? WHERE? TO... TO FIND MEDUSA?
BUT, WHAT IF SHE'S NOT--!
OH.
YES, I-I THINK I SAW WHERE SHE WENT DOWN... I'LL TRY.
WELL, THERE GOES THE BOLT CLAN AT LAST. BUT SOMEHOW I DOUBT WE'VE SEEN THE LAST OF THEM.
WELL, THEY'D BETTER NOT TRY TO COME BACK ON MY SHIFT!

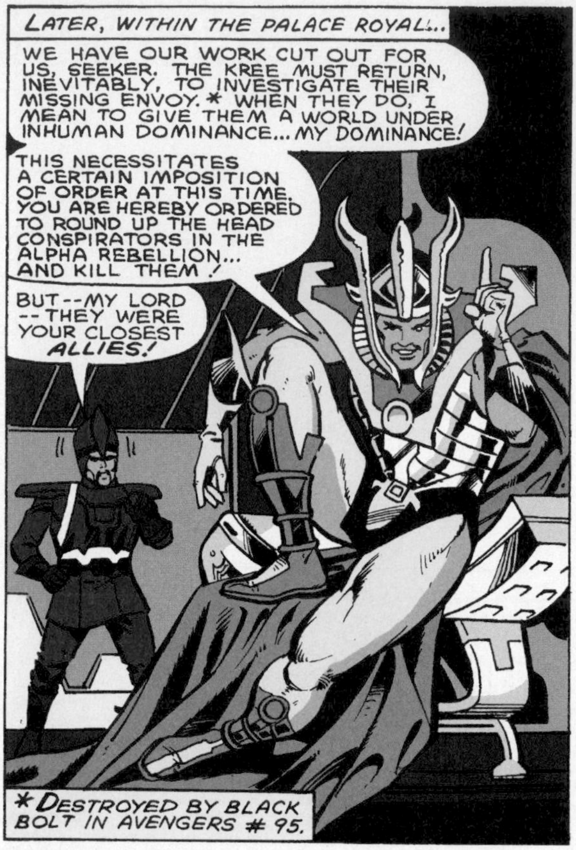
LATER, WITHIN THE PALACE ROYAL...
WE HAVE OUR WORK CUT OUT FOR US, SEEKER. THE KREE MUST RETURN, INEVITABLY, TO INVESTIGATE THEIR MISSING ENVOY.* WHEN THEY DO, I MEAN TO GIVE THEM A WORLD UNDER INHUMAN DOMINANCE... MY DOMINANCE!
THIS NECESSITATES A CERTAIN IMPOSITION OF ORDER AT THIS TIME. YOU ARE HEREBY ORDERED TO ROUND UP THE HEAD CONSPIRATORS IN THE ALPHA REBELLION... AND KILL THEM!
BUT--MY LORD --THEY WERE YOUR CLOSEST ALLIES!
*DESTROYED BY BLACK BOLT IN AVENGERS # 95.

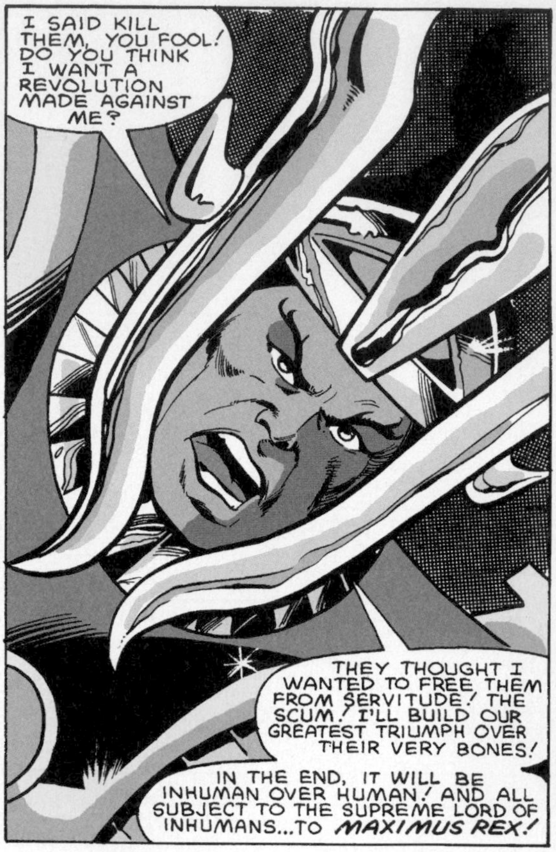
I SAID KILL THEM, YOU FOOL! DO YOU THINK I WANT A REVOLUTION MADE AGAINST ME?
THEY THOUGHT I WANTED TO FREE THEM FROM SERVITUDE! THE SCUM! I'LL BUILD OUR GREATEST TRIUMPH OVER THEIR VERY BONES!
IN THE END, IT WILL BE INHUMAN OVER HUMAN! AND ALL SUBJECT TO THE SUPREME LORD OF INHUMANS...TO MAXIMUS REX!

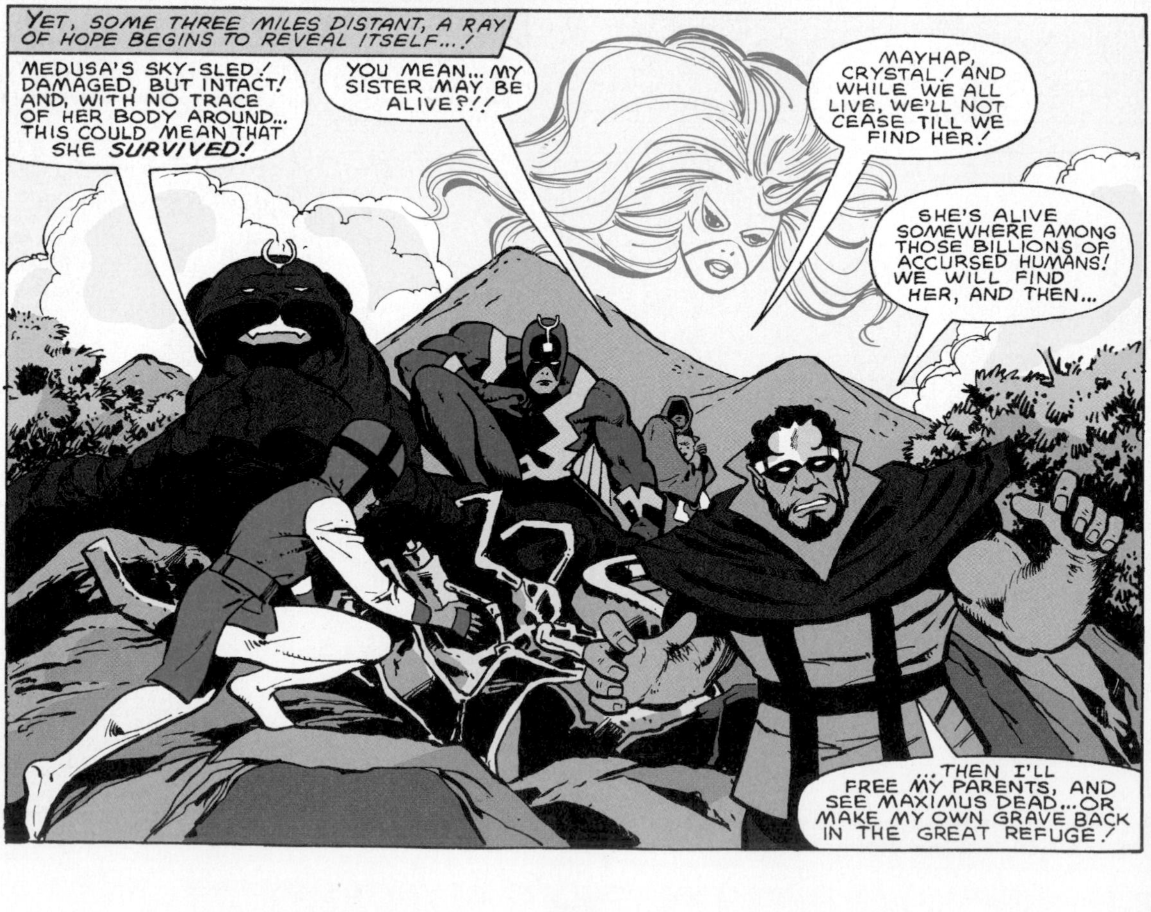
YET, SOME THREE MILES DISTANT, A RAY OF HOPE BEGINS TO REVEAL ITSELF...!
MEDUSA'S SKY-SLED! DAMAGED, BUT INTACT! AND, WITH NO TRACE OF HER BODY AROUND... THIS COULD MEAN THAT SHE SURVIVED!
YOU MEAN... MY SISTER MAY BE ALIVE?!!
MAYHAP, CRYSTAL! AND WHILE WE ALL LIVE, WE'LL NOT CEASE TILL WE FIND HER!
SHE'S ALIVE SOMEWHERE AMONG THOSE BILLIONS OF ACCURSED HUMANS! WE WILL FIND HER, AND THEN...
...THEN I'LL FREE MY PARENTS, AND SEE MAXIMUS DEAD...OR MAKE MY OWN GRAVE BACK IN THE GREAT REFUGE!

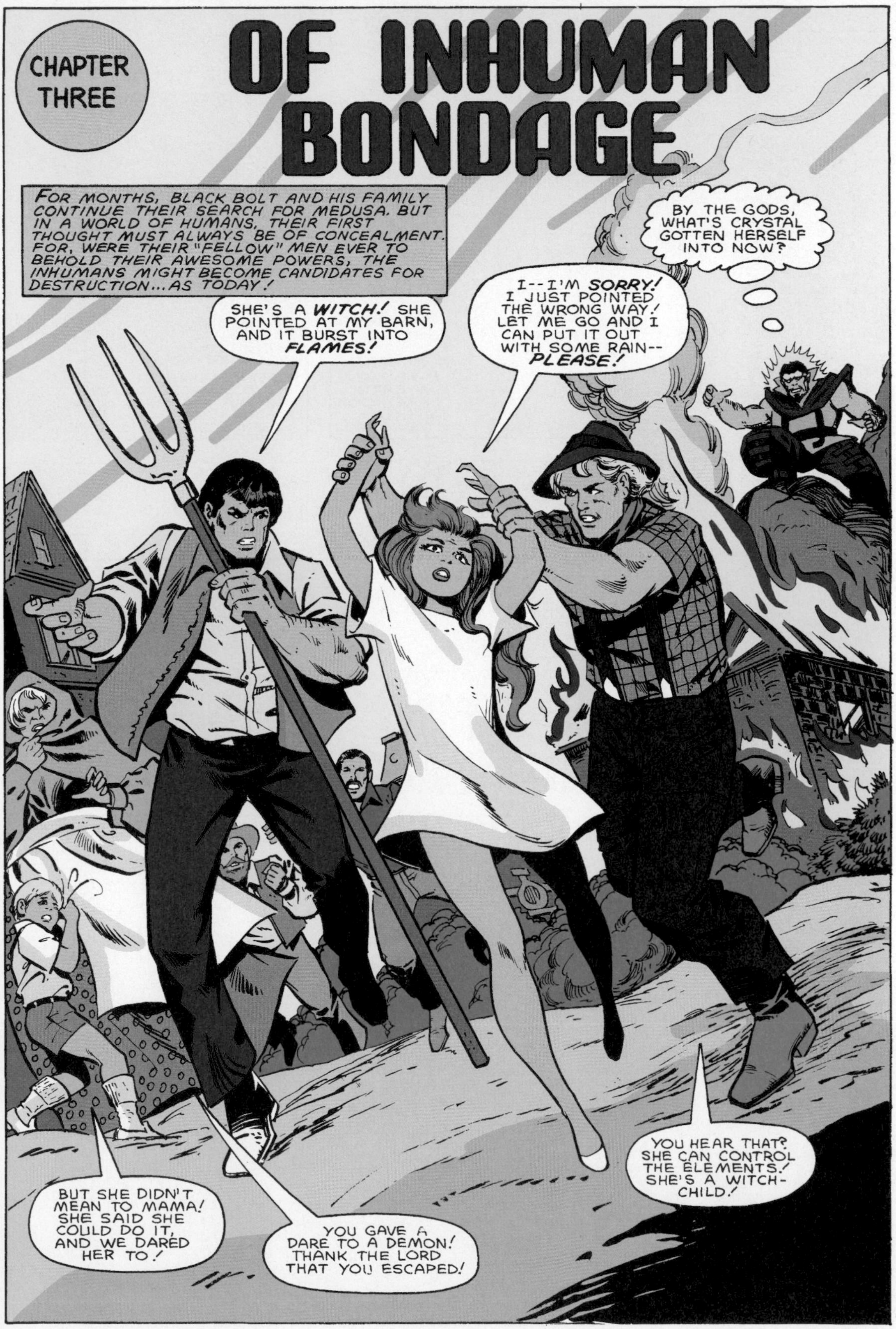
CHAPTER THREE
OF INHUMAN BONDAGE
FOR MONTHS, BLACK BOLT AND HIS FAMILY CONTINUE THEIR SEARCH FOR MEDUSA. BUT IN A WORLD OF HUMANS, THEIR FIRST THOUGHT MUST ALWAYS BE OF CONCEALMENT. FOR, WERE THEIR "FELLOW" MEN EVER TO BEHOLD THEIR AWESOME POWERS, THE INHUMANS MIGHT BECOME CANDIDATES FOR DESTRUCTION...AS TODAY!
BY THE GODS, WHAT'S CRYSTAL GOTTEN HERSELF INTO NOW?
SHE'S A WITCH! SHE POINTED AT MY BARN, AND IT BURST INTO FLAMES!
I--I'M SORRY! I JUST POINTED THE WRONG WAY! LET ME GO AND I CAN PUT IT OUT WITH SOME RAIN-- PLEASE!
BUT SHE DIDN'T MEAN TO MAMA! SHE SAID SHE COULD DO IT, AND WE DARED HER TO!
YOU GAVE A DARE TO A DEMON! THANK THE LORD THAT YOU ESCAPED!
YOU HEAR THAT? SHE CAN CONTROL THE ELEMENTS! SHE'S A WITCH-CHILD!

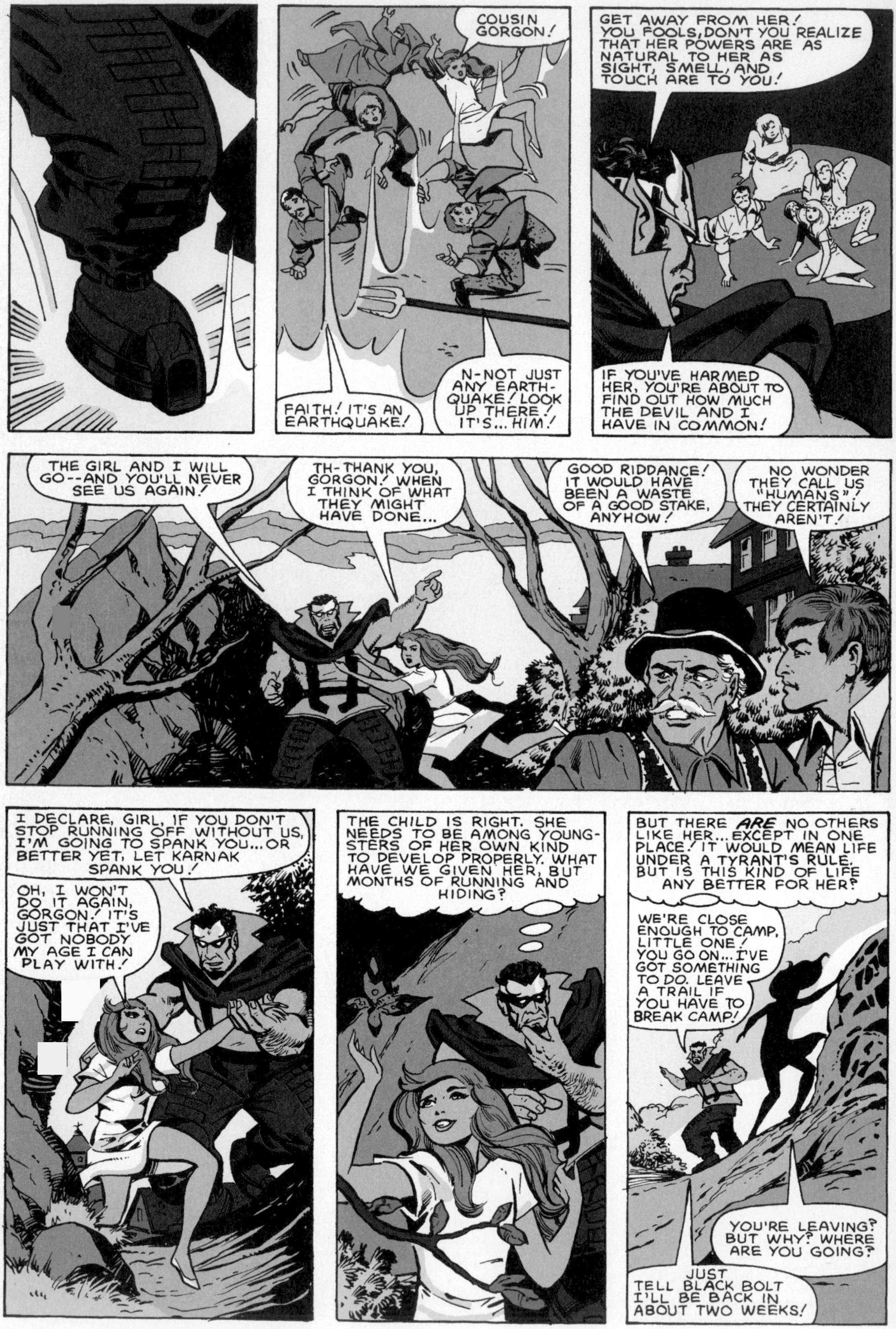
COUSIN GORGON!
FAITH! IT'S AN EARTHQUAKE!
N-NOT JUST ANY EARTH-QUAKE! LOOK UP THERE! IT'S... HIM!
GET AWAY FROM HER! YOU FOOLS, DON'T YOU REALIZE THAT HER POWERS ARE AS NATURAL TO HER AS SIGHT, SMELL, AND TOUCH ARE TO YOU!
IF YOU'VE HARMED HER, YOU'RE ABOUT TO FIND OUT HOW MUCH THE DEVIL AND I HAVE IN COMMON!
THE GIRL AND I WILL GO--AND YOU'LL NEVER SEE US AGAIN!
TH-THANK YOU, GORGON! WHEN I THINK OF WHAT THEY MIGHT HAVE DONE...
GOOD RIDDANCE! IT WOULD HAVE BEEN A WASTE OF A GOOD STAKE, ANYHOW!
NO WONDER THEY CALL US "HUMANS"! THEY CERTAINLY AREN'T!
I DECLARE, GIRL, IF YOU DON'T STOP RUNNING OFF WITHOUT US, I'M GOING TO SPANK YOU... OR BETTER YET, LET KARNAK SPANK YOU!
OH, I WON'T DO IT AGAIN, GORGON! IT'S JUST THAT I'VE GOT NOBODY MY AGE I CAN PLAY WITH!
THE CHILD IS RIGHT. SHE NEEDS TO BE AMONG YOUNG-STERS OF HER OWN KIND TO DEVELOP PROPERLY. WHAT HAVE WE GIVEN HER, BUT MONTHS OF RUNNING AND HIDING?
BUT THERE ARE NO OTHERS LIKE HER... EXCEPT IN ONE PLACE! IT WOULD MEAN LIFE UNDER A TYRANT'S RULE. BUT IS THIS KIND OF LIFE ANY BETTER FOR HER?
WE'RE CLOSE ENOUGH TO CAMP, LITTLE ONE! YOU GO ON... I'VE GOT SOMETHING TO DO. LEAVE A TRAIL IF YOU HAVE TO BREAK CAMP!
YOU'RE LEAVING? BUT WHY? WHERE ARE YOU GOING?
JUST TELL BLACK BOLT I'LL BE BACK IN ABOUT TWO WEEKS!

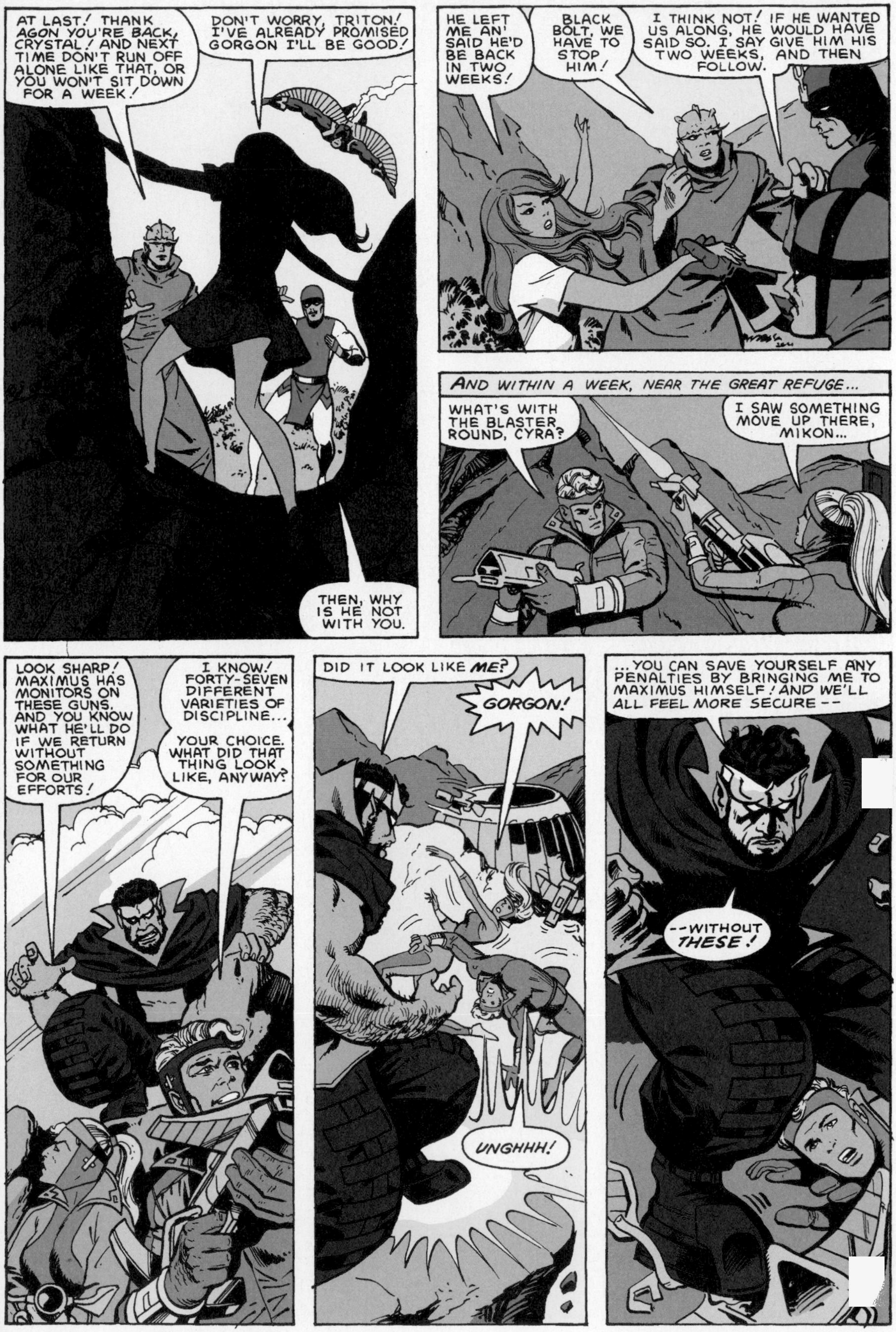
AT LAST! THANK AGON YOU'RE BACK, CRYSTAL! AND NEXT TIME DON'T RUN OFF ALONE LIKE THAT, OR YOU WON'T SIT DOWN FOR A WEEK!
DON'T WORRY, TRITON! I'VE ALREADY PROMISED GORGON I'LL BE GOOD!
THEN, WHY IS HE NOT WITH YOU.
HE LEFT ME AN' SAID HE'D BE BACK IN TWO WEEKS!
BLACK BOLT, WE HAVE TO STOP HIM!
I THINK NOT! IF HE WANTED US ALONG, HE WOULD HAVE SAID SO. I SAY GIVE HIM HIS TWO WEEKS, AND THEN FOLLOW.
AND WITHIN A WEEK, NEAR THE GREAT REFUGE...
WHAT'S WITH THE BLASTER ROUND, CYRA?
I SAW SOMETHING MOVE UP THERE, MIKON...
LOOK SHARP! MAXIMUS HAS MONITORS ON THESE GUNS. AND YOU KNOW WHAT HE'LL DO IF WE RETURN WITHOUT SOMETHING FOR OUR EFFORTS!
I KNOW! FORTY-SEVEN DIFFERENT VARIETIES OF DISCIPLINE...
YOUR CHOICE. WHAT DID THAT THING LOOK LIKE, ANYWAY?
DID IT LOOK LIKE ME?
GORGON!
UNGHHH!
...YOU CAN SAVE YOURSELF ANY PENALTIES BY BRINGING ME TO MAXIMUS HIMSELF! AND WE'LL ALL FEEL MORE SECURE --
--WITHOUT THESE!

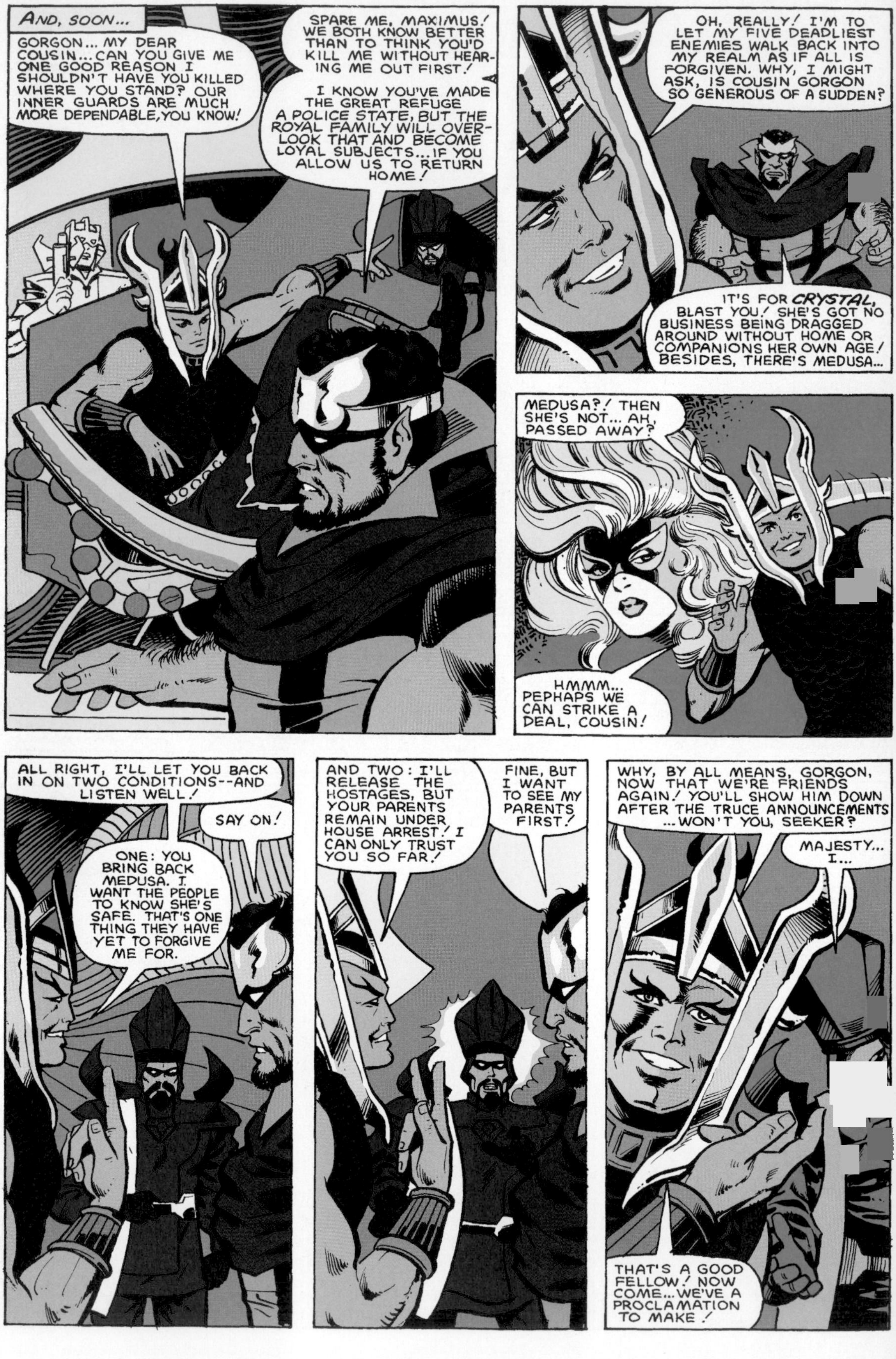
AND, SOON...
GORGON... MY DEAR COUSIN... CAN YOU GIVE ME ONE GOOD REASON I SHOULDN'T HAVE YOU KILLED WHERE YOU STAND? OUR INNER GUARDS ARE MUCH MORE DEPENDABLE, YOU KNOW!
SPARE ME, MAXIMUS! WE BOTH KNOW BETTER THAN TO THINK YOU'D KILL ME WITHOUT HEARING ME OUT FIRST!
I KNOW YOU'VE MADE THE GREAT REFUGE A POLICE STATE, BUT THE ROYAL FAMILY WILL OVERLOOK THAT AND BECOME LOYAL SUBJECTS... IF YOU ALLOW US TO RETURN HOME!
OH, REALLY! I'M TO LET MY FIVE DEADLIEST ENEMIES WALK BACK INTO MY REALM AS IF ALL IS FORGIVEN. WHY, I MIGHT ASK, IS COUSIN GORGON SO GENEROUS OF A SUDDEN?
IT'S FOR CRYSTAL, BLAST YOU! SHE'S GOT NO BUSINESS BEING DRAGGED AROUND WITHOUT HOME OR COMPANIONS HER OWN AGE! BESIDES, THERE'S MEDUSA...
MEDUSA?! THEN SHE'S NOT... AH, PASSED AWAY?
HMMM... PEPHAPS WE CAN STRIKE A DEAL, COUSIN!
ALL RIGHT, I'LL LET YOU BACK IN ON TWO CONDITIONS--AND LISTEN WELL!
SAY ON!
ONE: YOU BRING BACK MEDUSA. I WANT THE PEOPLE TO KNOW SHE'S SAFE. THAT'S ONE THING THEY HAVE YET TO FORGIVE ME FOR.
AND TWO: I'LL RELEASE THE HOSTAGES, BUT YOUR PARENTS REMAIN UNDER HOUSE ARREST! I CAN ONLY TRUST YOU SO FAR!
FINE, BUT I WANT TO SEE MY PARENTS FIRST!
WHY, BY ALL MEANS, GORGON, NOW THAT WE'RE FRIENDS AGAIN! YOU'LL SHOW HIM DOWN AFTER THE TRUCE ANNOUNCEMENTS ...WON'T YOU, SEEKER?
MAJESTY... I...
THAT'S A GOOD FELLOW! NOW COME... WE'VE A PROCLAMATION TO MAKE!

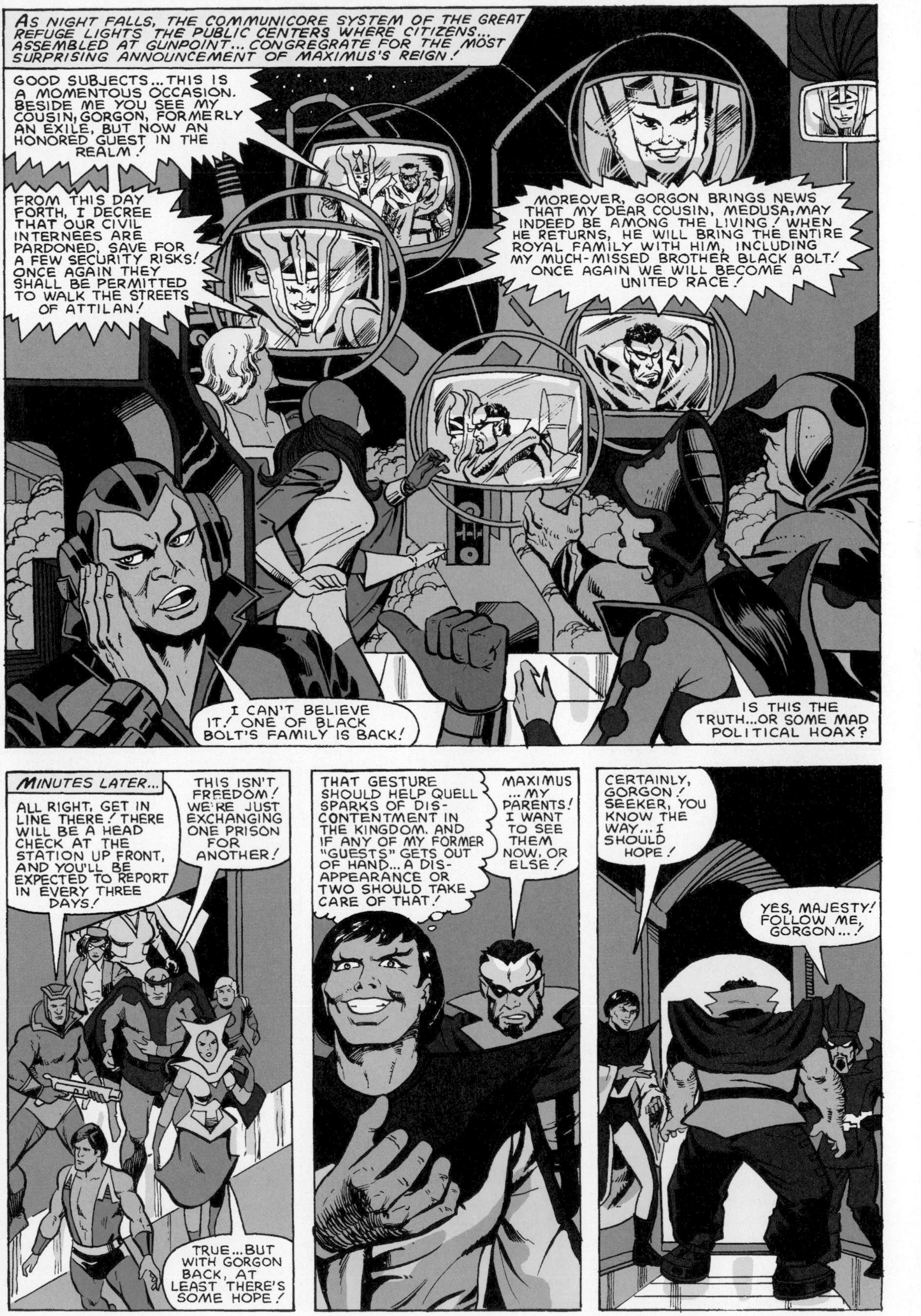
AS NIGHT FALLS, THE COMMUNICORE SYSTEM OF THE GREAT REFUGE LIGHTS THE PUBLIC CENTERS WHERE CITIZENS... ASSEMBLED AT GUNPOINT... CONGREGRATE FOR THE MOST SURPRISING ANNOUNCEMENT OF MAXIMUS'S REIGN!
GOOD SUBJECTS... THIS IS A MOMENTOUS OCCASION. BESIDE ME YOU SEE MY COUSIN, GORGON, FORMERLY AN EXILE, BUT NOW AN HONORED GUEST IN THE REALM!
FROM THIS DAY FORTH, I DECREE THAT OUR CIVIL INTERNEES ARE PARDONED, SAVE FOR A FEW SECURITY RISKS! ONCE AGAIN THEY SHALL BE PERMITTED TO WALK THE STREETS OF ATTILAN!
MOREOVER, GORGON BRINGS NEWS THAT MY DEAR COUSIN, MEDUSA, MAY INDEED BE AMONG THE LIVING! WHEN HE RETURNS, HE WILL BRING THE ENTIRE ROYAL FAMILY WITH HIM, INCLUDING MY MUCH-MISSED BROTHER BLACK BOLT! ONCE AGAIN WE WILL BECOME A UNITED RACE!
I CAN'T BELIEVE IT! ONE OF BLACK BOLT'S FAMILY IS BACK!
IS THIS THE TRUTH...OR SOME MAD POLITICAL HOAX?
MINUTES LATER...
ALL RIGHT, GET IN LINE THERE! THERE WILL BE A HEAD CHECK AT THE STATION UP FRONT, AND YOU'LL BE EXPECTED TO REPORT IN EVERY THREE DAYS!
THIS ISN'T FREEDOM! WE'RE JUST EXCHANGING ONE PRISON FOR ANOTHER!
TRUE... BUT WITH GORGON BACK, AT LEAST THERE'S SOME HOPE!
THAT GESTURE SHOULD HELP QUELL SPARKS OF DIS-CONTENTMENT IN THE KINGDOM. AND IF ANY OF MY FORMER "GUESTS" GETS OUT OF HAND... A DIS-APPEARANCE OR TWO SHOULD TAKE CARE OF THAT!
MAXIMUS ... MY PARENTS! I WANT TO SEE THEM NOW, OR ELSE!
CERTAINLY, GORGON! SEEKER, YOU KNOW THE WAY... I SHOULD HOPE!
YES, MAJESTY! FOLLOW ME, GORGON...!

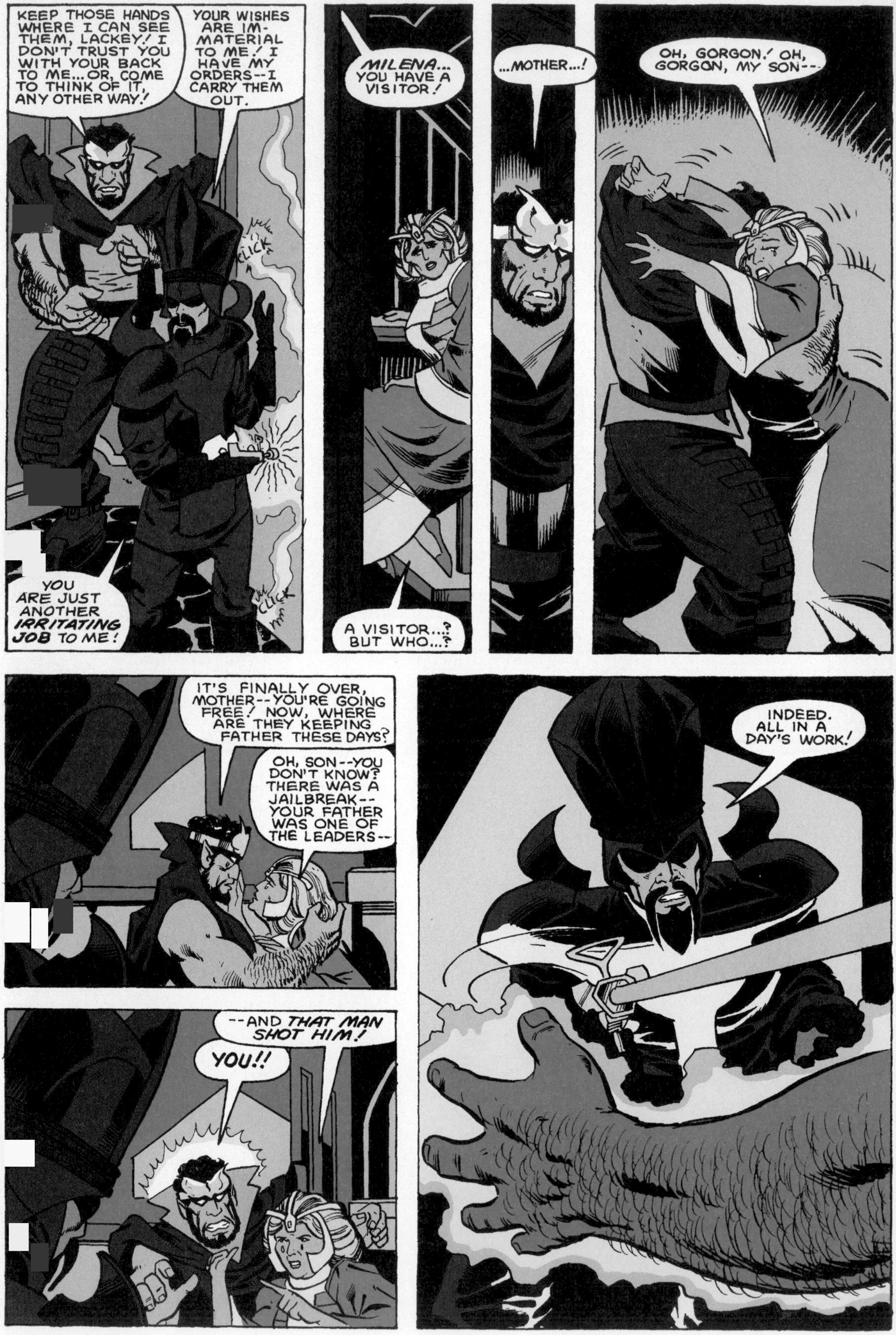

KEEP THOSE HANDS WHERE I CAN SEE THEM, LACKEY! I DON'T TRUST YOU WITH YOUR BACK TO ME...OR, COME TO THINK OF IT, ANY OTHER WAY!
YOUR WISHES ARE IMMATERIAL TO ME! I HAVE MY ORDERS--I CARRY THEM OUT.
CLICK
YOU ARE JUST ANOTHER *IRRITATING JOB* TO ME!
CLICK
MILENA... YOU HAVE A VISITOR!
A VISITOR...? BUT WHO...?
...MOTHER...!
OH, GORGON! OH, GORGON, MY SON--
IT'S FINALLY OVER, MOTHER--YOU'RE GOING FREE! NOW, WHERE ARE THEY KEEPING FATHER THESE DAYS?
OH, SON--YOU DON'T KNOW? THERE WAS A JAILBREAK--YOUR FATHER WAS ONE OF THE LEADERS--
--AND *THAT MAN SHOT HIM!*
YOU!!
INDEED. ALL IN A DAY'S WORK!

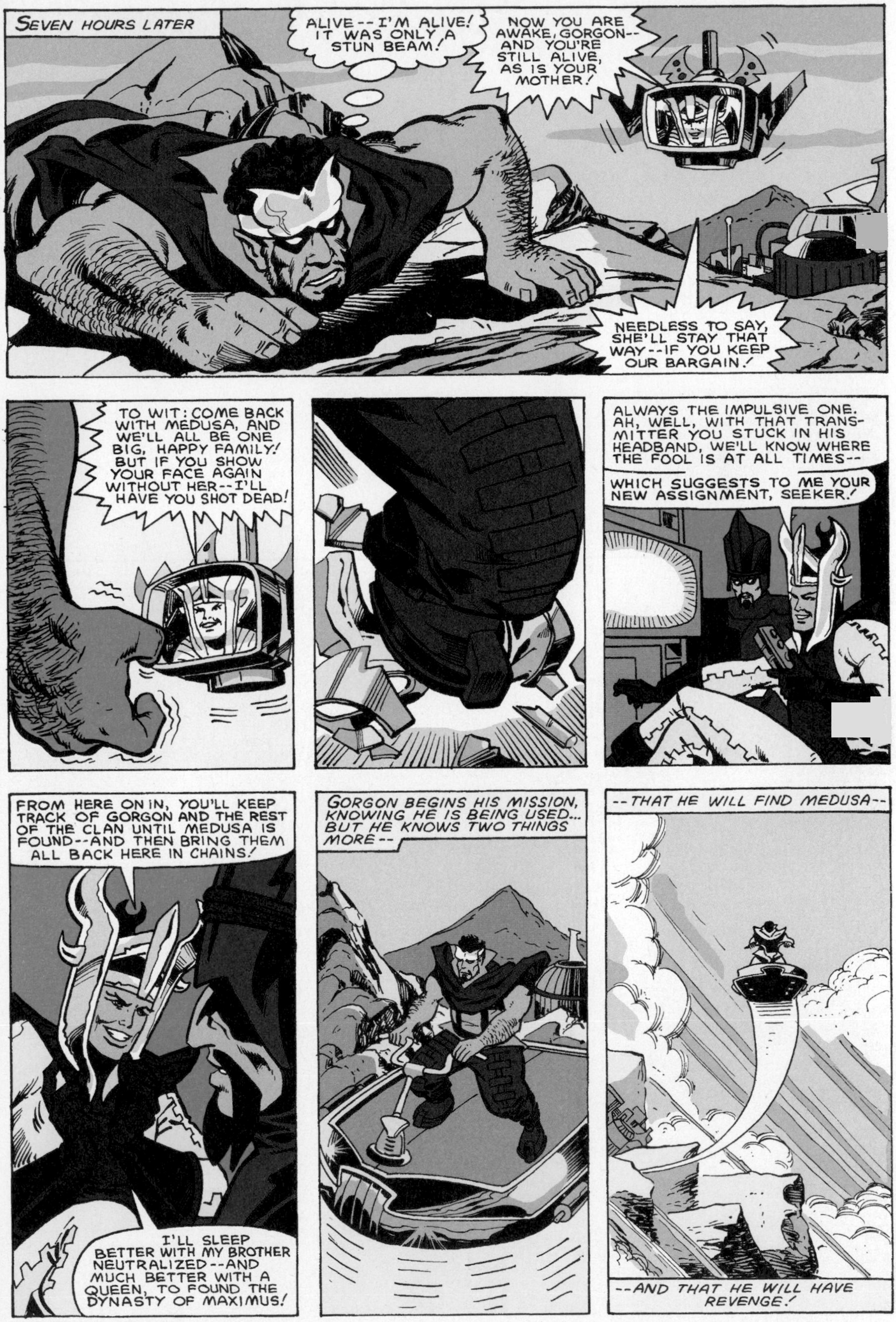
SEVEN HOURS LATER
ALIVE--I'M ALIVE! IT WAS ONLY A STUN BEAM!
NOW YOU ARE AWAKE, GORGON--AND YOU'RE STILL ALIVE, AS IS YOUR MOTHER!
NEEDLESS TO SAY, SHE'LL STAY THAT WAY--IF YOU KEEP OUR BARGAIN!
TO WIT: COME BACK WITH MEDUSA, AND WE'LL ALL BE ONE BIG, HAPPY FAMILY! BUT IF YOU SHOW YOUR FACE AGAIN WITHOUT HER--I'LL HAVE YOU SHOT DEAD!
ALWAYS THE IMPULSIVE ONE. AH, WELL, WITH THAT TRANSMITTER YOU STUCK IN HIS HEADBAND, WE'LL KNOW WHERE THE FOOL IS AT ALL TIMES--
WHICH SUGGESTS TO ME YOUR NEW ASSIGNMENT, SEEKER!
FROM HERE ON IN, YOU'LL KEEP TRACK OF GORGON AND THE REST OF THE CLAN UNTIL MEDUSA IS FOUND--AND THEN BRING THEM ALL BACK HERE IN CHAINS!
I'LL SLEEP BETTER WITH MY BROTHER NEUTRALIZED--AND MUCH BETTER WITH A QUEEN, TO FOUND THE DYNASTY OF MAXIMUS!
GORGON BEGINS HIS MISSION, KNOWING HE IS BEING USED... BUT HE KNOWS TWO THINGS MORE--
--THAT HE WILL FIND MEDUSA--
--AND THAT HE WILL HAVE REVENGE!

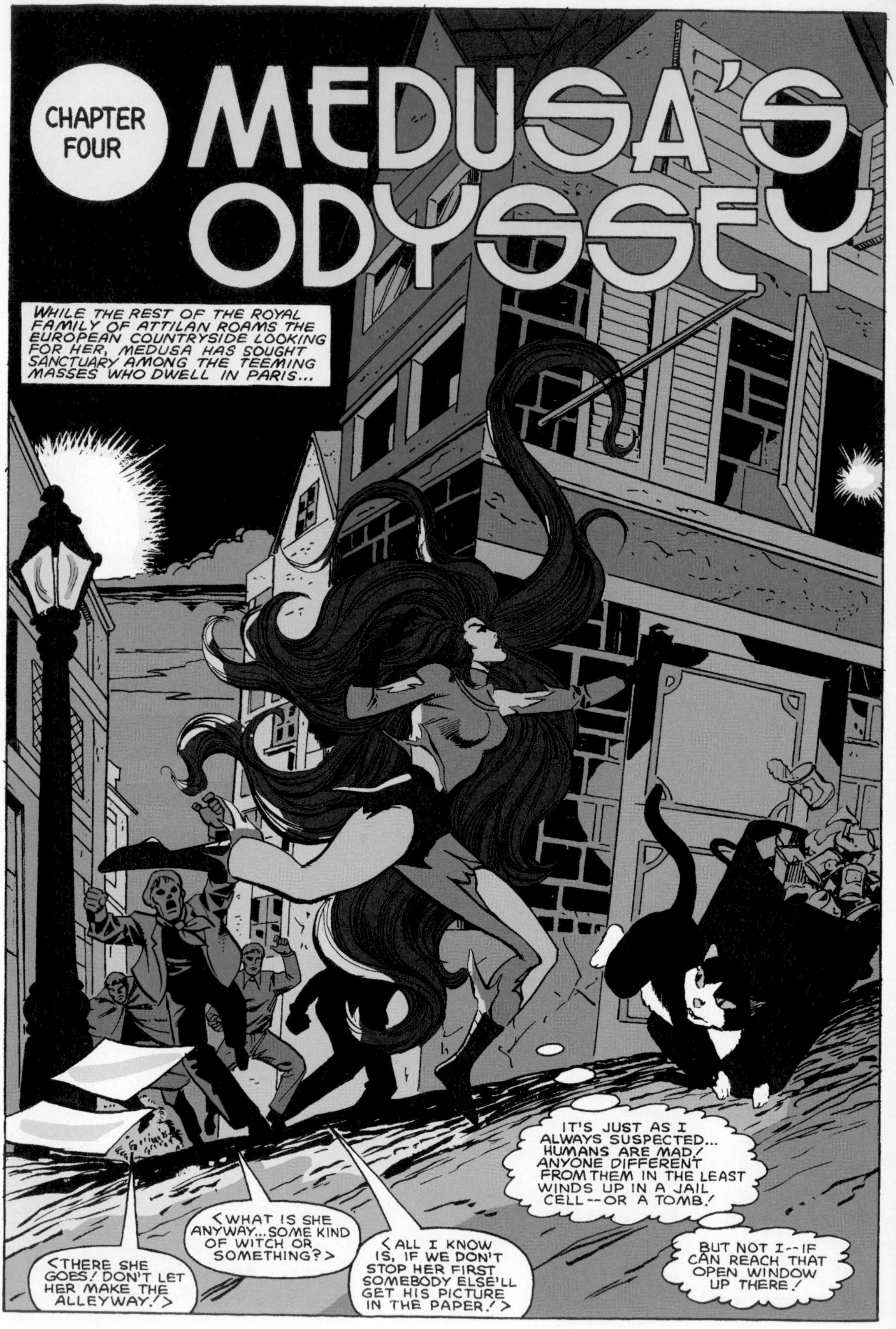
CHAPTER FOUR
MEDUSA'S ODYSSEY
WHILE THE REST OF THE ROYAL FAMILY OF ATTILAN ROAMS THE EUROPEAN COUNTRYSIDE LOOKING FOR HER, MEDUSA HAS SOUGHT SANCTUARY AMONG THE TEEMING MASSES WHO DWELL IN PARIS...
IT'S JUST AS I ALWAYS SUSPECTED... HUMANS ARE MAD! ANYONE DIFFERENT FROM THEM IN THE LEAST WINDS UP IN A JAIL CELL--OR A TOMB!
BUT NOT I--IF CAN REACH THAT OPEN WINDOW UP THERE!
<THERE SHE GOES! DON'T LET HER MAKE THE ALLEYWAY!>
<WHAT IS SHE ANYWAY...SOME KIND OF WITCH OR SOMETHING?>
<ALL I KNOW IS, IF WE DON'T STOP HER FIRST SOMEBODY ELSE'LL GET HIS PICTURE IN THE PAPER!>

IF ONLY THEY DON'T SEE ME UP HERE! I'LL STAND AND FIGHT IF I MUST-- BUT NOT AGAINST A WHOLE CITY!

HOW MUCH EASIER IT WOULD BE IF I COULD *CUT* MY HAIR, AND LOOK LIKE A HUMAN WOMAN! BUT MY TRESSES FEEL PAIN WHEN THEY'RE CUT, AND THEY GROW BACK ALMOST INSTANTLY!

MON DIEU--!!

I-I MEAN YOU NO HARM, BUT I'M BEING PURSUED!

SO IS *PAUL DUMAS,* MADEMOISELLE--BUT BY THE GENDARMES, NOT LADY GODIVA!

I DON'T CARE WHO YOU ARE! JUST PUT DOWN THAT GUN! I'VE HAD ENOUGH OF BEING CHASED AND THREATENED!

YOUR HAIR! YOU CAN USE IT LIKE A LIVING WHIP! WHO ARE YOU, WOMAN?

I AM MEDUSA!

WELL, MY DEAR MADAME MEDUSA-- I THINK WE MAY BE OF USE TO ONE ANOTHER--IF YOU ARE IN NEED OF REFUGE!

REFUGE-- THAT WORD MEANS SOMETHING TO ME, BUT I DON'T KNOW WHAT! I DON'T EVEN KNOW WHERE I AM!

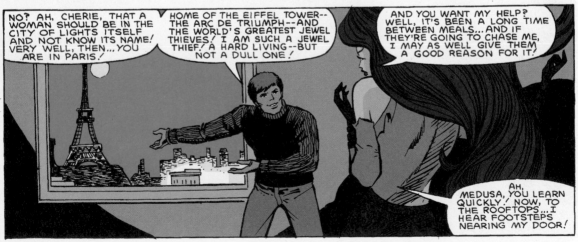

NO? AH, CHERIE, THAT A WOMAN SHOULD BE IN THE CITY OF LIGHTS ITSELF AND NOT KNOW ITS NAME! VERY WELL, THEN...YOU ARE IN PARIS!

HOME OF THE EIFFEL TOWER-- THE ARC DE TRIUMPH--AND THE WORLD'S GREATEST JEWEL THIEVES! I AM SUCH A JEWEL THIEF! A HARD LIVING--BUT NOT A DULL ONE!

AND YOU WANT MY HELP? WELL, IT'S BEEN A LONG TIME BETWEEN MEALS...AND IF THEY'RE GOING TO CHASE ME, I MAY AS WELL GIVE THEM A GOOD REASON FOR IT!

AH, MEDUSA, YOU LEARN QUICKLY! NOW, TO THE ROOFTOPS...I HEAR FOOTSTEPS NEARING MY DOOR!

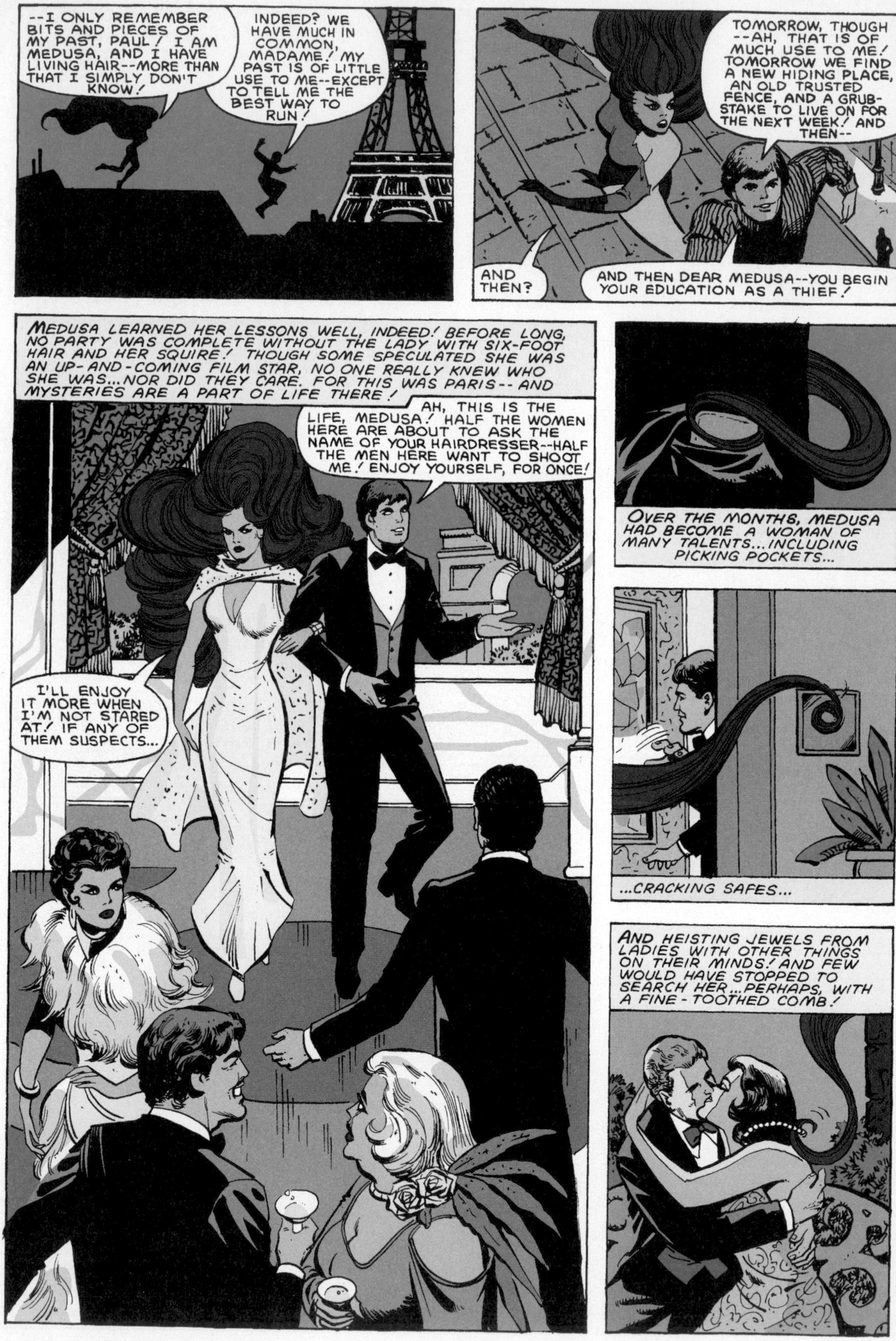
--I ONLY REMEMBER BITS AND PIECES OF MY PAST, PAUL! I AM MEDUSA, AND I HAVE LIVING HAIR--MORE THAN THAT I SIMPLY DON'T KNOW!
INDEED? WE HAVE MUCH IN COMMON, MADAME! MY PAST IS OF LITTLE USE TO ME--EXCEPT TO TELL ME THE BEST WAY TO RUN!
TOMORROW, THOUGH --AH, THAT IS OF MUCH USE TO ME! TOMORROW WE FIND A NEW HIDING PLACE, AN OLD TRUSTED FENCE, AND A GRUB-STAKE TO LIVE ON FOR THE NEXT WEEK! AND THEN--
AND THEN?
AND THEN DEAR MEDUSA--YOU BEGIN YOUR EDUCATION AS A THIEF!
MEDUSA LEARNED HER LESSONS WELL, INDEED! BEFORE LONG, NO PARTY WAS COMPLETE WITHOUT THE LADY WITH SIX-FOOT HAIR AND HER SQUIRE! THOUGH SOME SPECULATED SHE WAS AN UP-AND-COMING FILM STAR, NO ONE REALLY KNEW WHO SHE WAS...NOR DID THEY CARE. FOR THIS WAS PARIS-- AND MYSTERIES ARE A PART OF LIFE THERE!
AH, THIS IS THE LIFE, MEDUSA! HALF THE WOMEN HERE ARE ABOUT TO ASK THE NAME OF YOUR HAIRDRESSER--HALF THE MEN HERE WANT TO SHOOT ME! ENJOY YOURSELF, FOR ONCE!
I'LL ENJOY IT MORE WHEN I'M NOT STARED AT! IF ANY OF THEM SUSPECTS...
OVER THE MONTHS, MEDUSA HAD BECOME A WOMAN OF MANY TALENTS...INCLUDING PICKING POCKETS...
...CRACKING SAFES...
AND HEISTING JEWELS FROM LADIES WITH OTHER THINGS ON THEIR MINDS! AND FEW WOULD HAVE STOPPED TO SEARCH HER...PERHAPS, WITH A FINE-TOOTHED COMB!

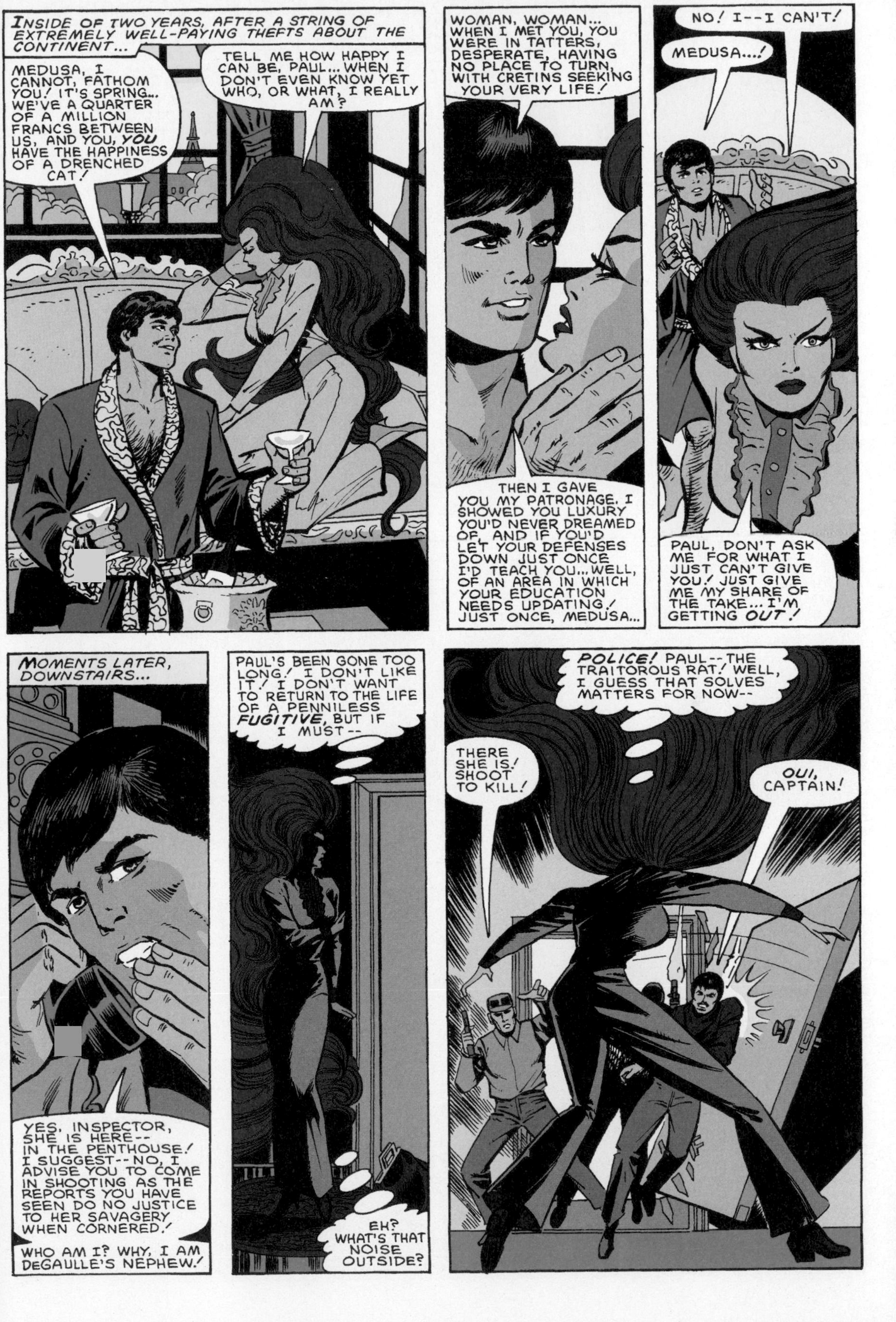

INSIDE OF TWO YEARS, AFTER A STRING OF EXTREMELY WELL-PAYING THEFTS ABOUT THE CONTINENT...
MEDUSA, I CANNOT FATHOM YOU! IT'S SPRING... WE'VE A QUARTER OF A MILLION FRANCS BETWEEN US, AND YOU, YOU HAVE THE HAPPINESS OF A DRENCHED CAT!
TELL ME HOW HAPPY I CAN BE, PAUL... WHEN I DON'T EVEN KNOW YET WHO, OR WHAT, I REALLY AM?
WOMAN, WOMAN... WHEN I MET YOU, YOU WERE IN TATTERS, DESPERATE, HAVING NO PLACE TO TURN, WITH CRETINS SEEKING YOUR VERY LIFE!
THEN I GAVE YOU MY PATRONAGE. I SHOWED YOU LUXURY YOU'D NEVER DREAMED OF, AND IF YOU'D LET YOUR DEFENSES DOWN JUST ONCE I'D TEACH YOU... WELL, OF AN AREA IN WHICH YOUR EDUCATION NEEDS UPDATING! JUST ONCE, MEDUSA...
NO! I--I CAN'T!
MEDUSA...!
PAUL, DON'T ASK ME FOR WHAT I JUST CAN'T GIVE YOU! JUST GIVE ME MY SHARE OF THE TAKE... I'M GETTING OUT!
MOMENTS LATER, DOWNSTAIRS...
YES, INSPECTOR, SHE IS HERE-- IN THE PENTHOUSE! I SUGGEST--NO, I ADVISE YOU TO COME IN SHOOTING AS THE REPORTS YOU HAVE SEEN DO NO JUSTICE TO HER SAVAGERY WHEN CORNERED!
WHO AM I? WHY, I AM DEGAULLE'S NEPHEW!
PAUL'S BEEN GONE TOO LONG! I DON'T LIKE IT! I DON'T WANT TO RETURN TO THE LIFE OF A PENNILESS FUGITIVE, BUT IF I MUST--
EH? WHAT'S THAT NOISE OUTSIDE?
POLICE! PAUL--THE TRAITOROUS RAT! WELL, I GUESS THAT SOLVES MATTERS FOR NOW--
THERE SHE IS! SHOOT TO KILL!
OUI, CAPTAIN!

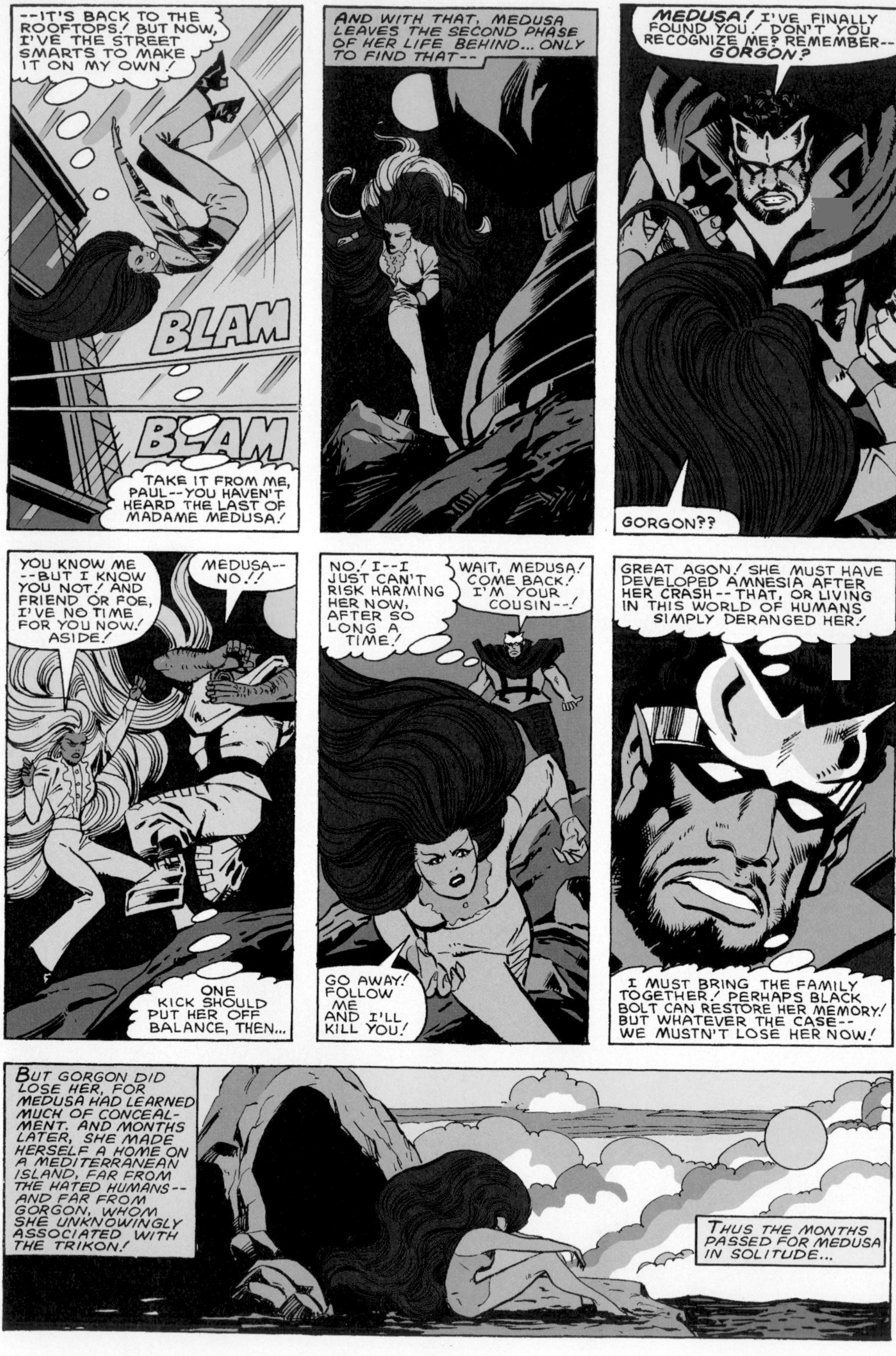

--IT'S BACK TO THE ROOFTOPS! BUT NOW, I'VE THE STREET SMARTS TO MAKE IT ON MY OWN!
BLAM
BLAM
TAKE IT FROM ME, PAUL--YOU HAVEN'T HEARD THE LAST OF MADAME MEDUSA!
AND WITH THAT, MEDUSA LEAVES THE SECOND PHASE OF HER LIFE BEHIND... ONLY TO FIND THAT--
MEDUSA! I'VE FINALLY FOUND YOU! DON'T YOU RECOGNIZE ME? REMEMBER-- GORGON?
GORGON??
YOU KNOW ME --BUT I KNOW YOU NOT! AND FRIEND OR FOE, I'VE NO TIME FOR YOU NOW! ASIDE!
MEDUSA-- NO!!
ONE KICK SHOULD PUT HER OFF BALANCE, THEN...
NO! I--I JUST CAN'T RISK HARMING HER NOW, AFTER SO LONG A TIME!
WAIT, MEDUSA! COME BACK! I'M YOUR COUSIN--!
GO AWAY! FOLLOW ME AND I'LL KILL YOU!
GREAT AGON! SHE MUST HAVE DEVELOPED AMNESIA AFTER HER CRASH--THAT, OR LIVING IN THIS WORLD OF HUMANS SIMPLY DERANGED HER!
I MUST BRING THE FAMILY TOGETHER! PERHAPS BLACK BOLT CAN RESTORE HER MEMORY! BUT WHATEVER THE CASE-- WE MUSTN'T LOSE HER NOW!
BUT GORGON DID LOSE HER, FOR MEDUSA HAD LEARNED MUCH OF CONCEALMENT. AND MONTHS LATER, SHE MADE HERSELF A HOME ON A MEDITERRANEAN ISLAND, FAR FROM THE HATED HUMANS-- AND FAR FROM GORGON, WHOM SHE UNKNOWINGLY ASSOCIATED WITH THE TRIKON!
THUS THE MONTHS PASSED FOR MEDUSA IN SOLITUDE...

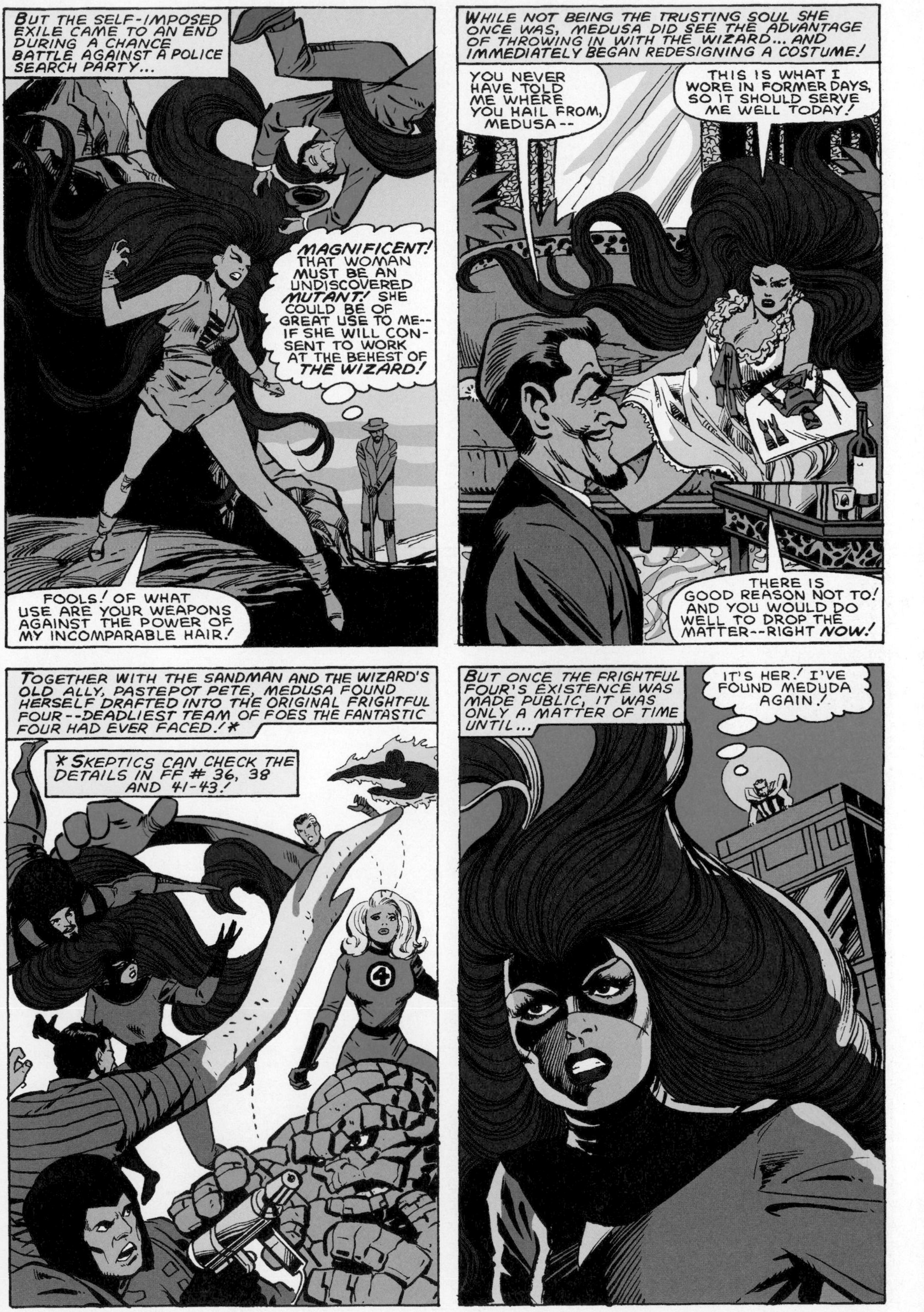

BUT THE SELF-IMPOSED EXILE CAME TO AN END DURING A CHANCE BATTLE AGAINST A POLICE SEARCH PARTY...
MAGNIFICENT! THAT WOMAN MUST BE AN UNDISCOVERED MUTANT! SHE COULD BE OF GREAT USE TO ME--IF SHE WILL CONSENT TO WORK AT THE BEHEST OF THE WIZARD!
FOOLS! OF WHAT USE ARE YOUR WEAPONS AGAINST THE POWER OF MY INCOMPARABLE HAIR!
WHILE NOT BEING THE TRUSTING SOUL SHE ONCE WAS, MEDUSA DID SEE THE ADVANTAGE OF THROWING IN WITH THE WIZARD... AND IMMEDIATELY BEGAN REDESIGNING A COSTUME!
YOU NEVER HAVE TOLD ME WHERE YOU HAIL FROM, MEDUSA--
THIS IS WHAT I WORE IN FORMER DAYS, SO IT SHOULD SERVE ME WELL TODAY!
THERE IS GOOD REASON NOT TO! AND YOU WOULD DO WELL TO DROP THE MATTER--RIGHT NOW!
TOGETHER WITH THE SANDMAN AND THE WIZARD'S OLD ALLY, PASTEPOT PETE, MEDUSA FOUND HERSELF DRAFTED INTO THE ORIGINAL FRIGHTFUL FOUR--DEADLIEST TEAM OF FOES THE FANTASTIC FOUR HAD EVER FACED!*
*SKEPTICS CAN CHECK THE DETAILS IN FF # 36, 38 AND 41-43!
BUT ONCE THE FRIGHTFUL FOUR'S EXISTENCE WAS MADE PUBLIC, IT WAS ONLY A MATTER OF TIME UNTIL...
IT'S HER! I'VE FOUND MEDUDA AGAIN!

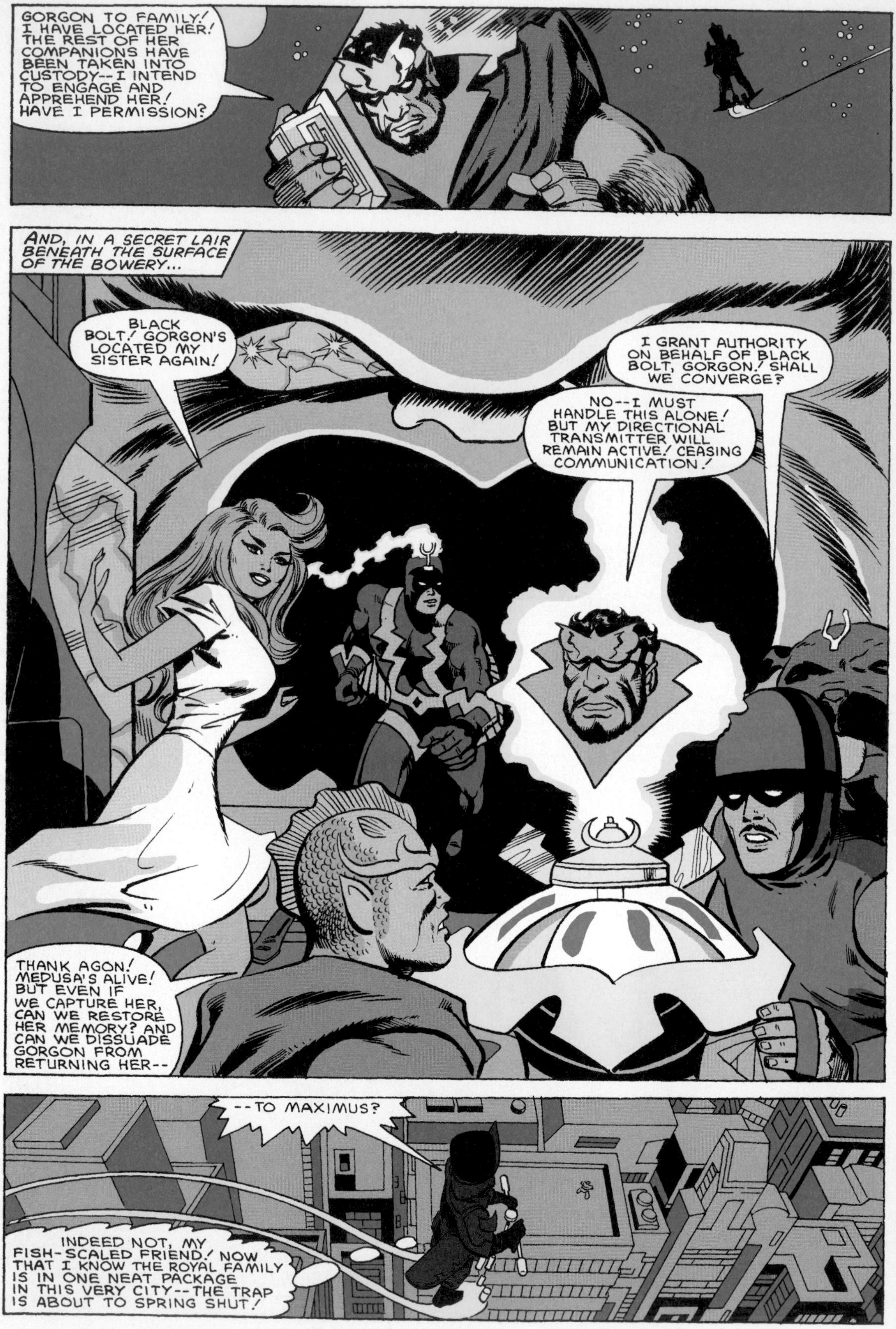
GORGON TO FAMILY! I HAVE LOCATED HER! THE REST OF HER COMPANIONS HAVE BEEN TAKEN INTO CUSTODY--I INTEND TO ENGAGE AND APPREHEND HER! HAVE I PERMISSION?
AND, IN A SECRET LAIR BENEATH THE SURFACE OF THE BOWERY...
BLACK BOLT! GORGON'S LOCATED MY SISTER AGAIN!
I GRANT AUTHORITY ON BEHALF OF BLACK BOLT, GORGON! SHALL WE CONVERGE?
NO--I MUST HANDLE THIS ALONE! BUT MY DIRECTIONAL TRANSMITTER WILL REMAIN ACTIVE! CEASING COMMUNICATION!
THANK AGON! MEDUSA'S ALIVE! BUT EVEN IF WE CAPTURE HER, CAN WE RESTORE HER MEMORY? AND CAN WE DISSUADE GORGON FROM RETURNING HER--
--TO MAXIMUS?
INDEED NOT, MY FISH-SCALED FRIEND! NOW THAT I KNOW THE ROYAL FAMILY IS IN ONE NEAT PACKAGE IN THIS VERY CITY--THE TRAP IS ABOUT TO SPRING SHUT!

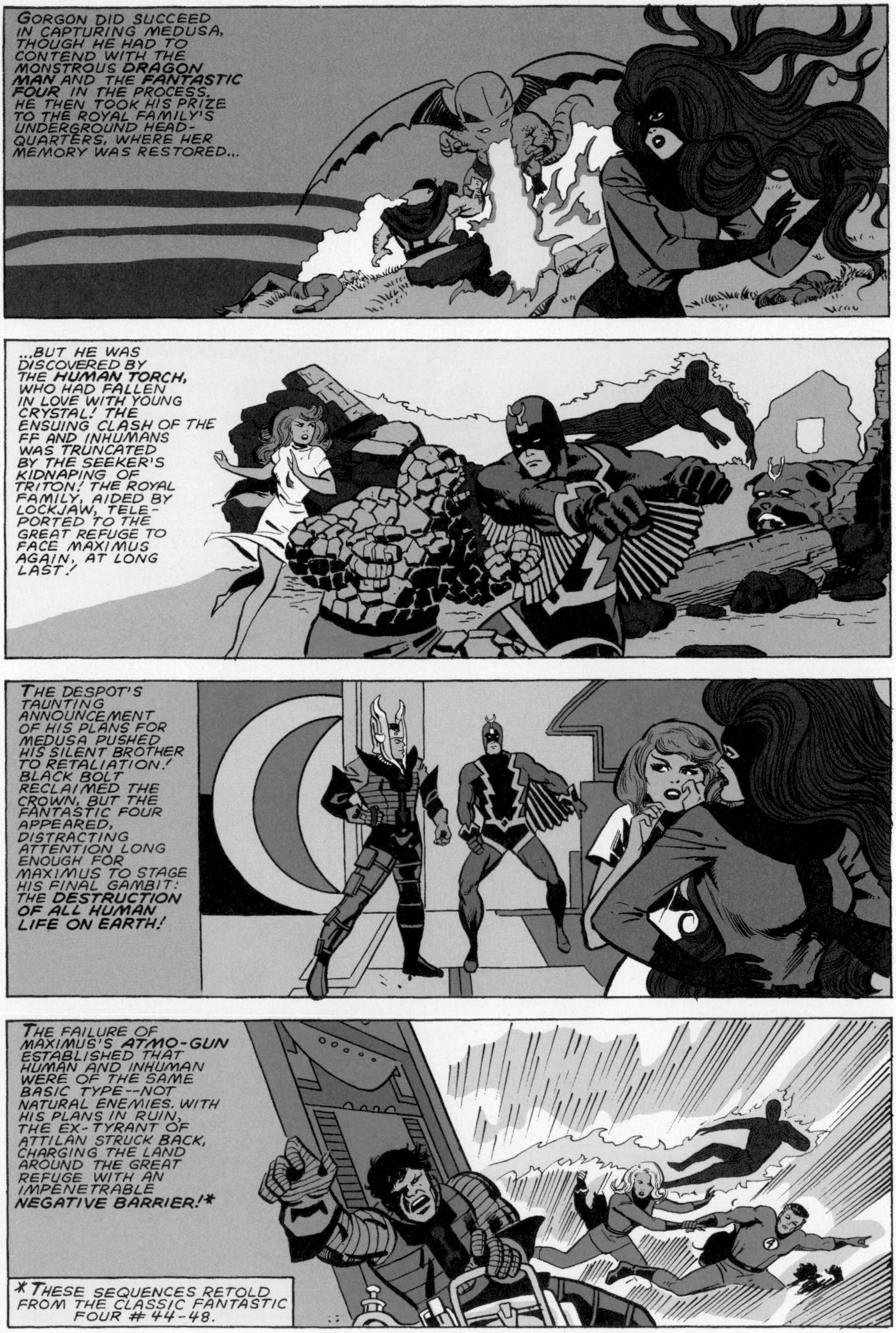
GORGON DID SUCCEED IN CAPTURING MEDUSA, THOUGH HE HAD TO CONTEND WITH THE MONSTROUS DRAGON MAN AND THE FANTASTIC FOUR IN THE PROCESS. HE THEN TOOK HIS PRIZE TO THE ROYAL FAMILY'S UNDERGROUND HEAD-QUARTERS, WHERE HER MEMORY WAS RESTORED...
...BUT HE WAS DISCOVERED BY THE HUMAN TORCH, WHO HAD FALLEN IN LOVE WITH YOUNG CRYSTAL! THE ENSUING CLASH OF THE FF AND INHUMANS WAS TRUNCATED BY THE SEEKER'S KIDNAPING OF TRITON! THE ROYAL FAMILY, AIDED BY LOCKJAW, TELE-PORTED TO THE GREAT REFUGE TO FACE MAXIMUS AGAIN, AT LONG LAST!
THE DESPOT'S TAUNTING ANNOUNCEMENT OF HIS PLANS FOR MEDUSA PUSHED HIS SILENT BROTHER TO RETALIATION! BLACK BOLT RECLAIMED THE CROWN, BUT THE FANTASTIC FOUR APPEARED, DISTRACTING ATTENTION LONG ENOUGH FOR MAXIMUS TO STAGE HIS FINAL GAMBIT: THE DESTRUCTION OF ALL HUMAN LIFE ON EARTH!
THE FAILURE OF MAXIMUS'S ATMO-GUN ESTABLISHED THAT HUMAN AND INHUMAN WERE OF THE SAME BASIC TYPE--NOT NATURAL ENEMIES. WITH HIS PLANS IN RUIN, THE EX-TYRANT OF ATTILAN STRUCK BACK, CHARGING THE LAND AROUND THE GREAT REFUGE WITH AN IMPENETRABLE NEGATIVE BARRIER!*
*THESE SEQUENCES RETOLD FROM THE CLASSIC FANTASTIC FOUR #44-48.

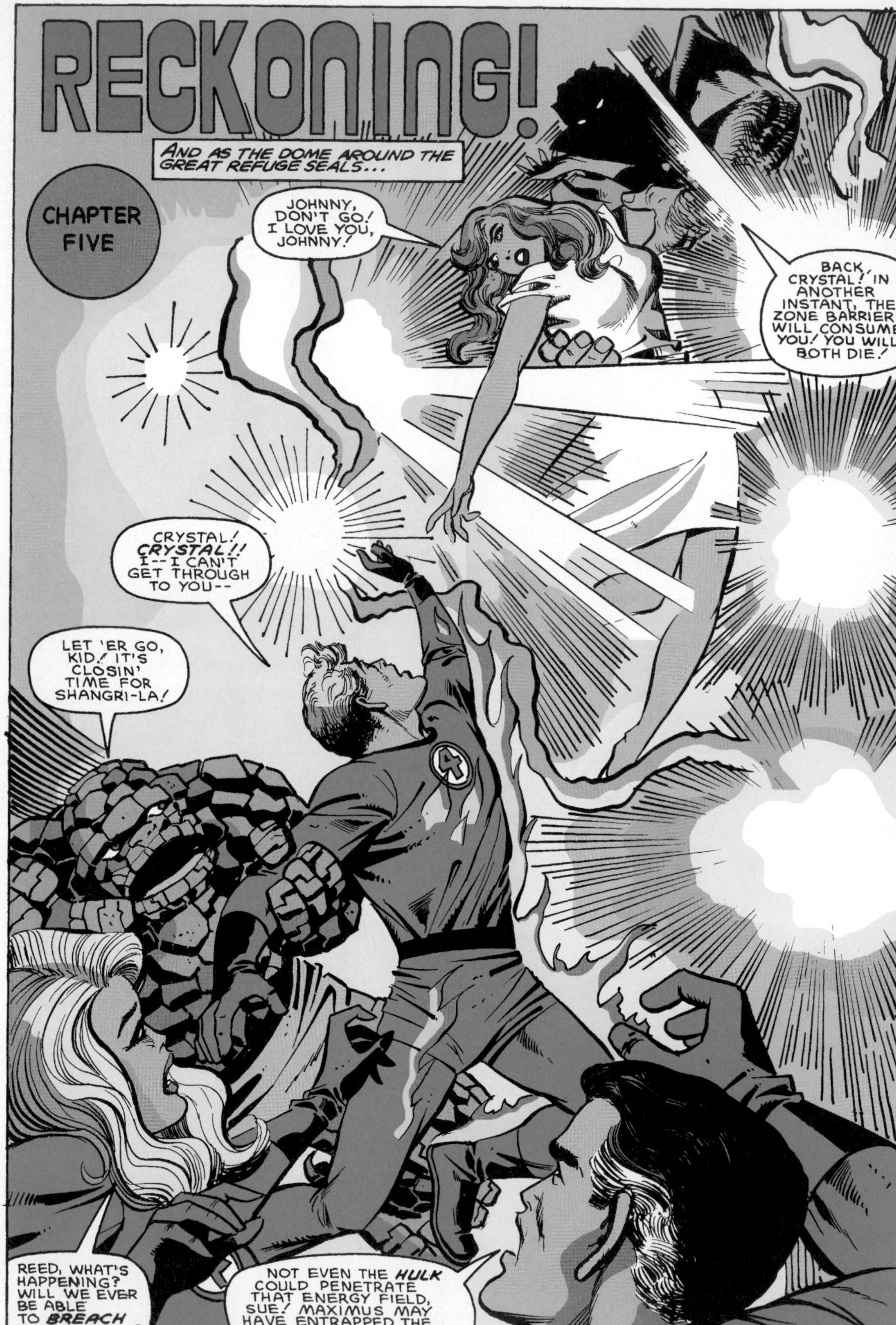
RECKONING!
AND AS THE DOME AROUND THE GREAT REFUGE SEALS...
CHAPTER FIVE
JOHNNY, DON'T GO! I LOVE YOU, JOHNNY!
BACK, CRYSTAL! IN ANOTHER INSTANT, THE ZONE BARRIER WILL CONSUME YOU! YOU WILL BOTH DIE!
CRYSTAL! CRYSTAL!! I--I CAN'T GET THROUGH TO YOU--
LET 'ER GO, KID! IT'S CLOSIN' TIME FOR SHANGRI-LA!
REED, WHAT'S HAPPENING? WILL WE EVER BE ABLE TO BREACH THAT BARRIER?
NOT EVEN THE HULK COULD PENETRATE THAT ENERGY FIELD, SUE! MAXIMUS MAY HAVE ENTRAPPED THE INHUMANS--FOREVER!

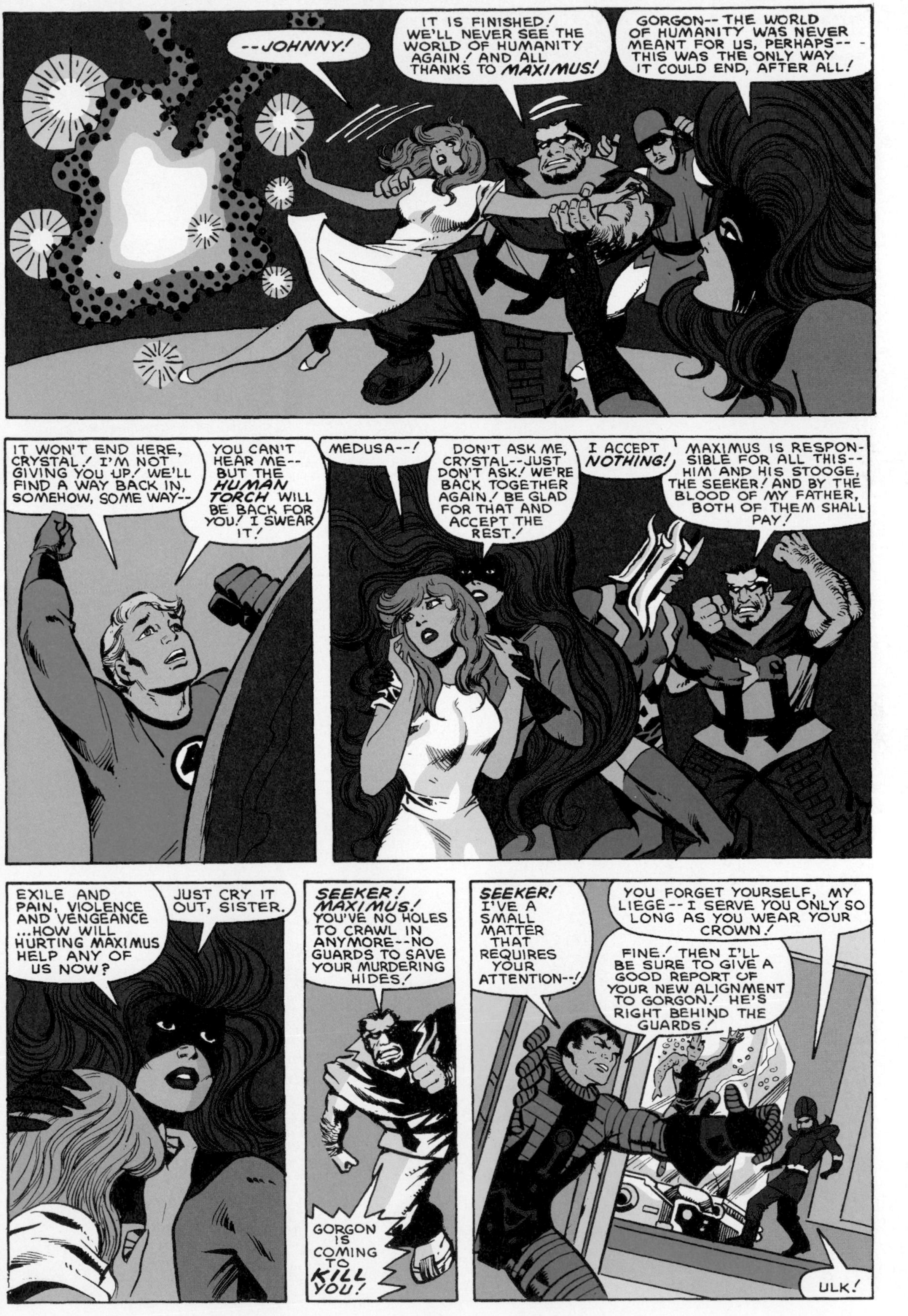
--JOHNNY!
IT IS FINISHED! WE'LL NEVER SEE THE WORLD OF HUMANITY AGAIN! AND ALL THANKS TO MAXIMUS!
GORGON--THE WORLD OF HUMANITY WAS NEVER MEANT FOR US, PERHAPS-- -THIS WAS THE ONLY WAY IT COULD END, AFTER ALL!
IT WON'T END HERE, CRYSTAL! I'M NOT GIVING YOU UP! WE'LL FIND A WAY BACK IN, SOMEHOW, SOME WAY--
YOU CAN'T HEAR ME--BUT THE HUMAN TORCH WILL BE BACK FOR YOU! I SWEAR IT!
MEDUSA--!
DON'T ASK ME, CRYSTAL--JUST DON'T ASK! WE'RE BACK TOGETHER AGAIN! BE GLAD FOR THAT AND ACCEPT THE REST!
I ACCEPT NOTHING!
MAXIMUS IS RESPONSIBLE FOR ALL THIS--HIM AND HIS STOOGE, THE SEEKER! AND BY THE BLOOD OF MY FATHER, BOTH OF THEM SHALL PAY!
EXILE AND PAIN, VIOLENCE AND VENGEANCE ...HOW WILL HURTING MAXIMUS HELP ANY OF US NOW?
JUST CRY IT OUT, SISTER.
SEEKER! MAXIMUS! YOU'VE NO HOLES TO CRAWL IN ANYMORE--NO GUARDS TO SAVE YOUR MURDERING HIDES!
GORGON IS COMING TO KILL YOU!
SEEKER! I'VE A SMALL MATTER THAT REQUIRES YOUR ATTENTION--!
YOU FORGET YOURSELF, MY LIEGE--I SERVE YOU ONLY SO LONG AS YOU WEAR YOUR CROWN!
FINE! THEN I'LL BE SURE TO GIVE A GOOD REPORT OF YOUR NEW ALIGNMENT TO GORGON! HE'S RIGHT BEHIND THE GUARDS!
ULK!

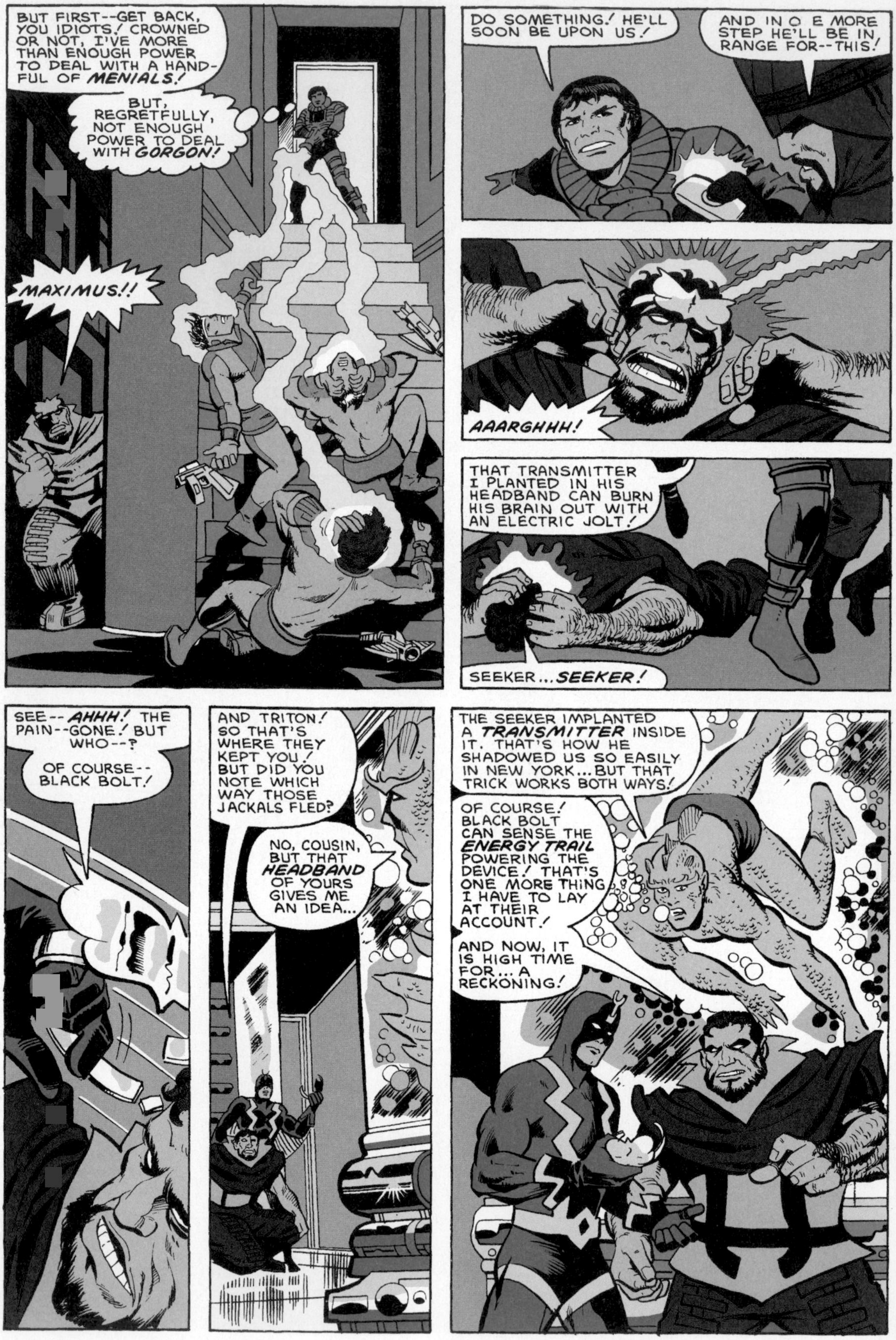
BUT FIRST--GET BACK, YOU IDIOTS! CROWNED OR NOT, I'VE MORE THAN ENOUGH POWER TO DEAL WITH A HANDFUL OF MENIALS!
BUT, REGRETFULLY, NOT ENOUGH POWER TO DEAL WITH GORGON!
MAXIMUS!!
DO SOMETHING! HE'LL SOON BE UPON US!
AND IN O E MORE STEP HE'LL BE IN RANGE FOR--THIS!
AAARGHHH!
THAT TRANSMITTER I PLANTED IN HIS HEADBAND CAN BURN HIS BRAIN OUT WITH AN ELECTRIC JOLT!
SEEKER... SEEKER!
SEE--AHHH! THE PAIN--GONE! BUT WHO--?
OF COURSE--BLACK BOLT!
AND TRITON! SO THAT'S WHERE THEY KEPT YOU! BUT DID YOU NOTE WHICH WAY THOSE JACKALS FLED?
NO, COUSIN, BUT THAT HEADBAND OF YOURS GIVES ME AN IDEA...
THE SEEKER IMPLANTED A TRANSMITTER INSIDE IT. THAT'S HOW HE SHADOWED US SO EASILY IN NEW YORK... BUT THAT TRICK WORKS BOTH WAYS!
OF COURSE! BLACK BOLT CAN SENSE THE ENERGY TRAIL POWERING THE DEVICE! THAT'S ONE MORE THING I HAVE TO LAY AT THEIR ACCOUNT!
AND NOW, IT IS HIGH TIME FOR... A RECKONING!

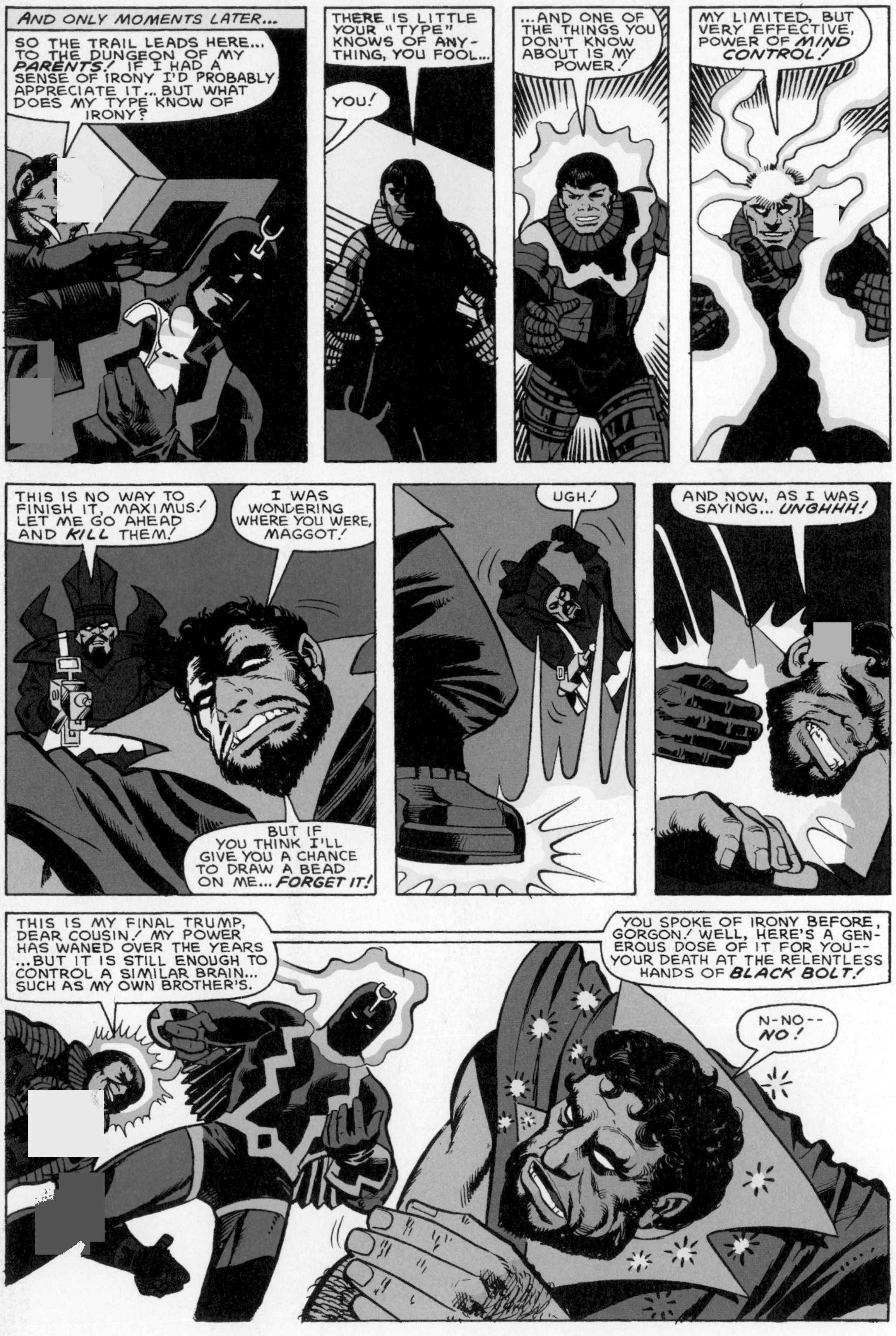
AND ONLY MOMENTS LATER...
SO THE TRAIL LEADS HERE... TO THE DUNGEON OF MY PARENTS! IF I HAD A SENSE OF IRONY I'D PROBABLY APPRECIATE IT... BUT WHAT DOES MY TYPE KNOW OF IRONY?
THERE IS LITTLE YOUR "TYPE" KNOWS OF ANY-THING, YOU FOOL...
YOU!
...AND ONE OF THE THINGS YOU DON'T KNOW ABOUT IS MY POWER!
MY LIMITED, BUT VERY EFFECTIVE, POWER OF MIND CONTROL!
THIS IS NO WAY TO FINISH IT, MAXIMUS! LET ME GO AHEAD AND KILL THEM!
I WAS WONDERING WHERE YOU WERE, MAGGOT!
BUT IF YOU THINK I'LL GIVE YOU A CHANCE TO DRAW A BEAD ON ME... FORGET IT!
UGH!
AND NOW, AS I WAS SAYING... UNGHHH!
THIS IS MY FINAL TRUMP, DEAR COUSIN! MY POWER HAS WANED OVER THE YEARS ...BUT IT IS STILL ENOUGH TO CONTROL A SIMILAR BRAIN... SUCH AS MY OWN BROTHER'S.
YOU SPOKE OF IRONY BEFORE, GORGON! WELL, HERE'S A GEN-EROUS DOSE OF IT FOR YOU-- YOUR DEATH AT THE RELENTLESS HANDS OF BLACK BOLT!
N-NO-- NO!

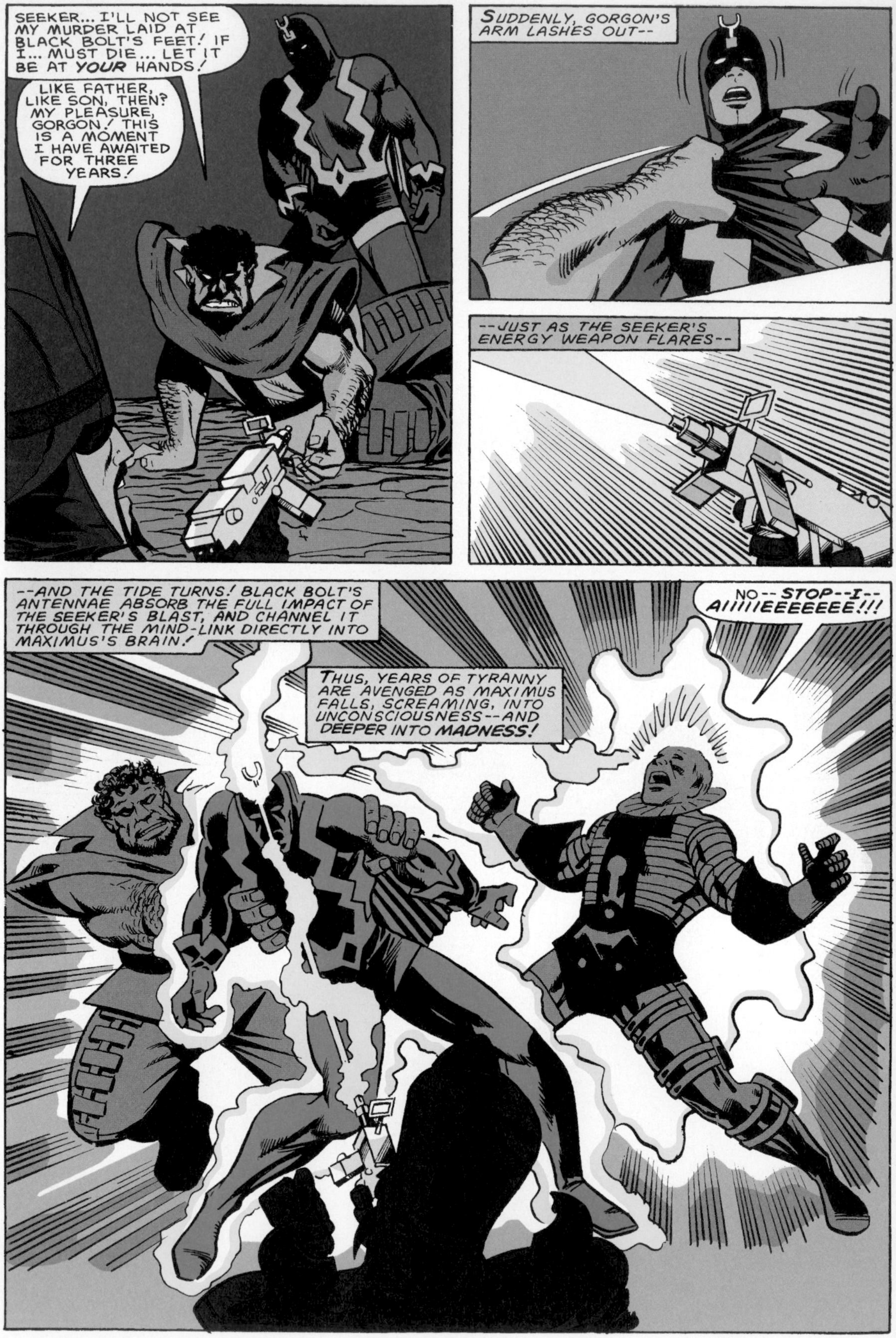
SEEKER... I'LL NOT SEE MY MURDER LAID AT BLACK BOLT'S FEET! IF I... MUST DIE... LET IT BE AT YOUR HANDS!
LIKE FATHER, LIKE SON, THEN? MY PLEASURE, GORGON! THIS IS A MOMENT I HAVE AWAITED FOR THREE YEARS!
SUDDENLY, GORGON'S ARM LASHES OUT--
--JUST AS THE SEEKER'S ENERGY WEAPON FLARES--
--AND THE TIDE TURNS! BLACK BOLT'S ANTENNAE ABSORB THE FULL IMPACT OF THE SEEKER'S BLAST, AND CHANNEL IT THROUGH THE MIND-LINK DIRECTLY INTO MAXIMUS'S BRAIN!
NO--STOP--I-- AIIIIIEEEEEEE!!!
THUS, YEARS OF TYRANNY ARE AVENGED AS MAXIMUS FALLS, SCREAMING, INTO UNCONSCIOUSNESS--AND DEEPER INTO MADNESS!

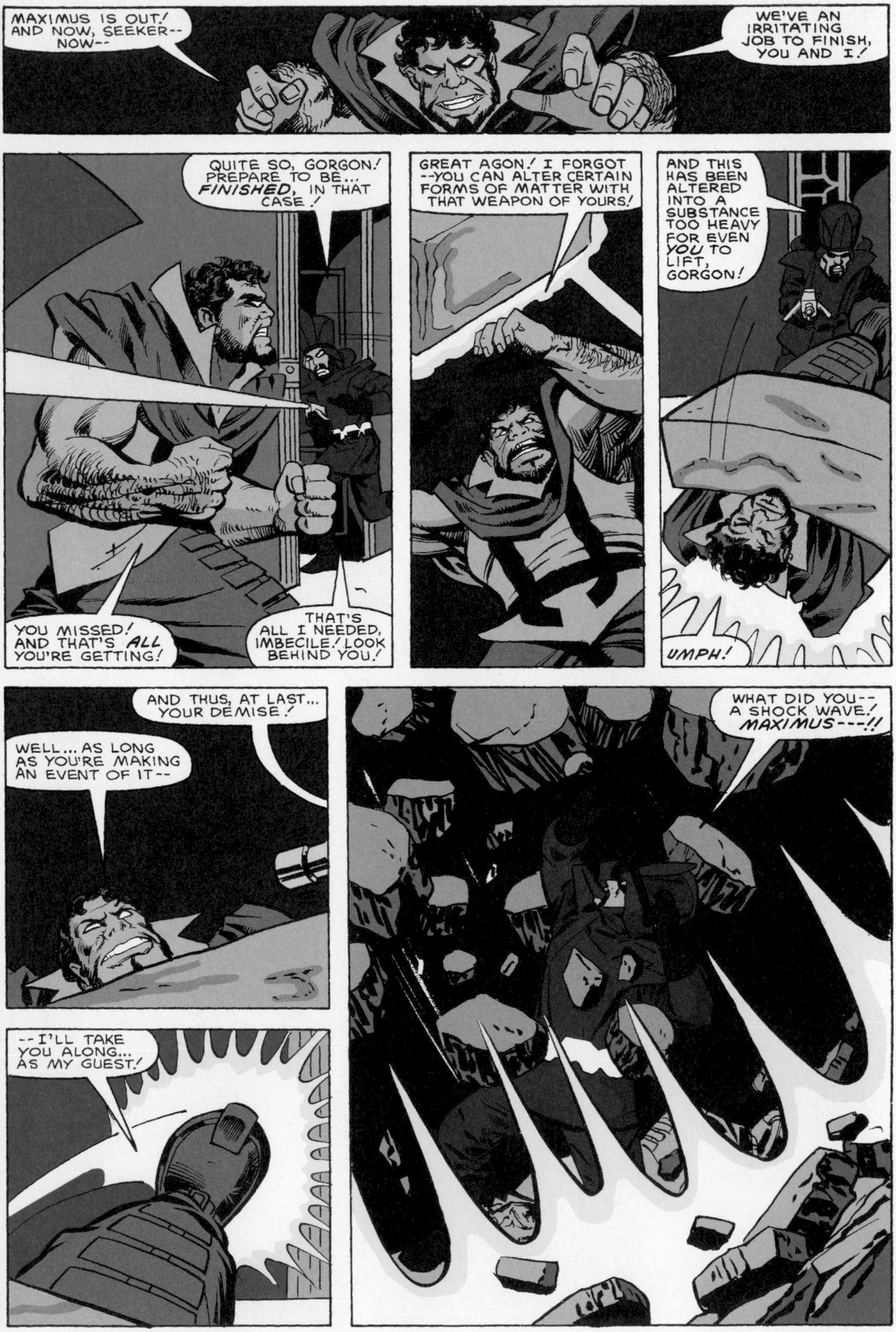

MAXIMUS IS OUT! AND NOW, SEEKER-- NOW--
WE'VE AN IRRITATING JOB TO FINISH, YOU AND I!
QUITE SO, GORGON! PREPARE TO BE... FINISHED, IN THAT CASE!
YOU MISSED! AND THAT'S ALL YOU'RE GETTING!
THAT'S ALL I NEEDED, IMBECILE! LOOK BEHIND YOU!
GREAT AGON! I FORGOT --YOU CAN ALTER CERTAIN FORMS OF MATTER WITH THAT WEAPON OF YOURS!
AND THIS HAS BEEN ALTERED INTO A SUBSTANCE TOO HEAVY FOR EVEN YOU TO LIFT, GORGON!
UMPH!
AND THUS, AT LAST... YOUR DEMISE!
WELL... AS LONG AS YOU'RE MAKING AN EVENT OF IT--
--I'LL TAKE YOU ALONG... AS MY GUEST!
WHAT DID YOU-- A SHOCK WAVE! MAXIMUS---!!

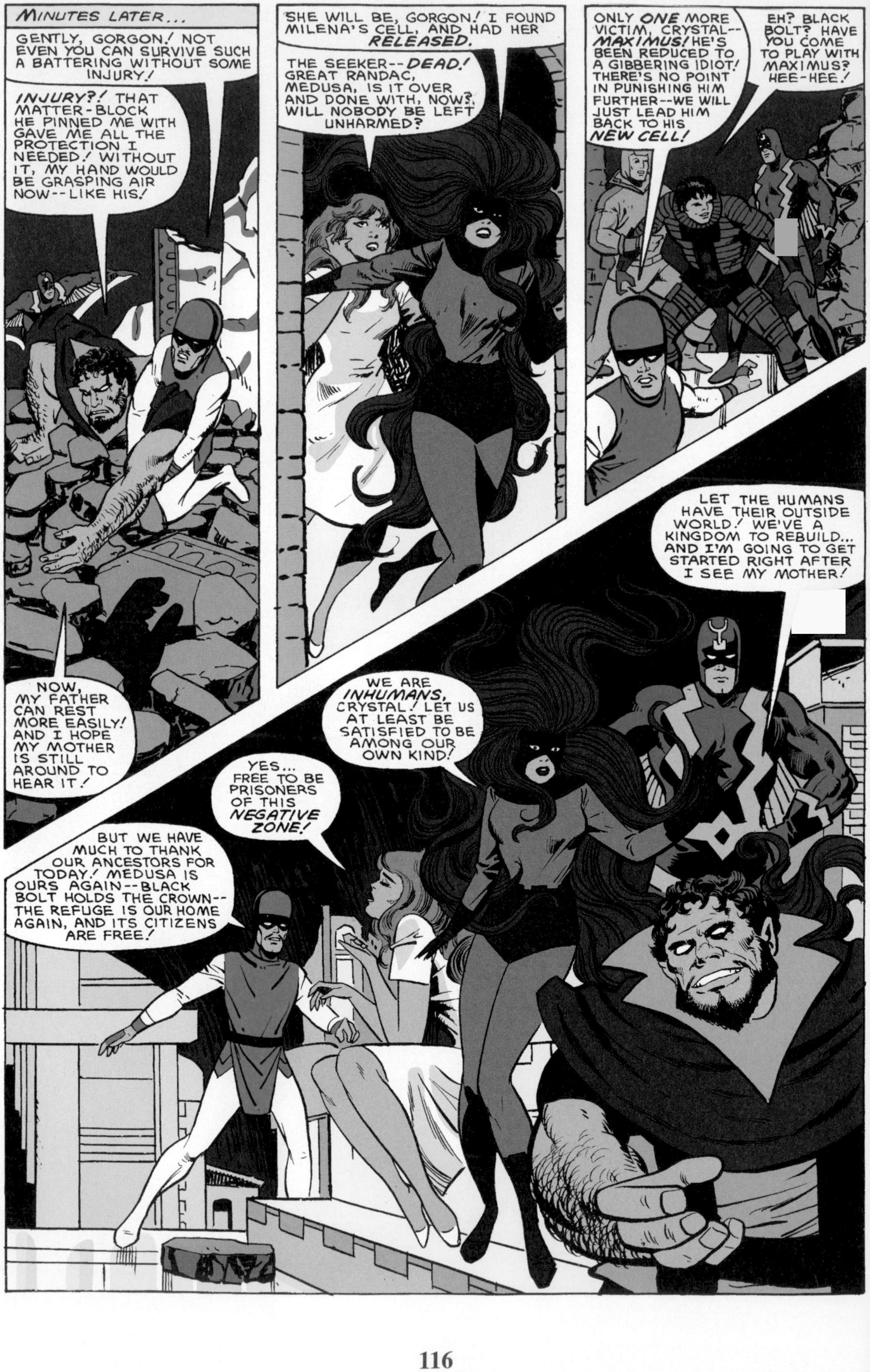
MINUTES LATER...
GENTLY, GORGON! NOT EVEN YOU CAN SURVIVE SUCH A BATTERING WITHOUT SOME INJURY!
INJURY?! THAT MATTER-BLOCK HE PINNED ME WITH GAVE ME ALL THE PROTECTION I NEEDED! WITHOUT IT, MY HAND WOULD BE GRASPING AIR NOW--LIKE HIS!
SHE WILL BE, GORGON! I FOUND MILENA'S CELL, AND HAD HER RELEASED.
THE SEEKER--DEAD! GREAT RANDAC, MEDUSA, IS IT OVER AND DONE WITH, NOW? WILL NOBODY BE LEFT UNHARMED?
ONLY ONE MORE VICTIM, CRYSTAL--MAXIMUS! HE'S BEEN REDUCED TO A GIBBERING IDIOT! THERE'S NO POINT IN PUNISHING HIM FURTHER--WE WILL JUST LEAD HIM BACK TO HIS NEW CELL!
EH? BLACK BOLT? HAVE YOU COME TO PLAY WITH MAXIMUS? HEE-HEE!
NOW, MY FATHER CAN REST MORE EASILY! AND I HOPE MY MOTHER IS STILL AROUND TO HEAR IT!
LET THE HUMANS HAVE THEIR OUTSIDE WORLD! WE'VE A KINGDOM TO REBUILD... AND I'M GOING TO GET STARTED RIGHT AFTER I SEE MY MOTHER!
WE ARE INHUMANS, CRYSTAL! LET US AT LEAST BE SATISFIED TO BE AMONG OUR OWN KIND!
YES... FREE TO BE PRISONERS OF THIS NEGATIVE ZONE!
BUT WE HAVE MUCH TO THANK OUR ANCESTORS FOR TODAY! MEDUSA IS OURS AGAIN--BLACK BOLT HOLDS THE CROWN--THE REFUGE IS OUR HOME AGAIN, AND ITS CITIZENS ARE FREE!

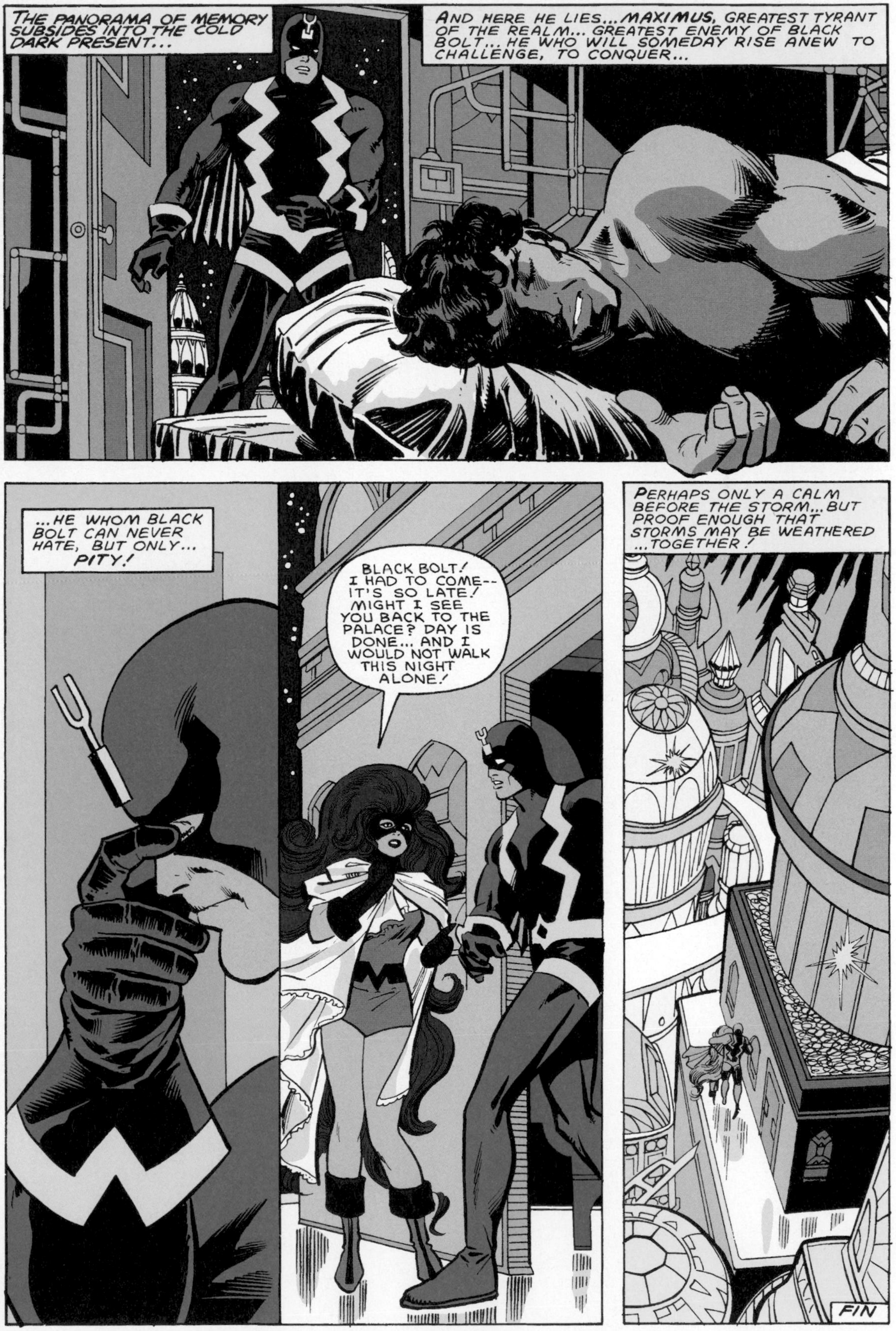
THE PANORAMA OF MEMORY SUBSIDES INTO THE COLD DARK PRESENT...
AND HERE HE LIES... MAXIMUS, GREATEST TYRANT OF THE REALM... GREATEST ENEMY OF BLACK BOLT... HE WHO WILL SOMEDAY RISE ANEW TO CHALLENGE, TO CONQUER...
...HE WHOM BLACK BOLT CAN NEVER HATE, BUT ONLY... PITY!
BLACK BOLT! I HAD TO COME-- IT'S SO LATE! MIGHT I SEE YOU BACK TO THE PALACE? DAY IS DONE... AND I WOULD NOT WALK THIS NIGHT ALONE!
PERHAPS ONLY A CALM BEFORE THE STORM... BUT PROOF ENOUGH THAT STORMS MAY BE WEATHERED ...TOGETHER!
FIN

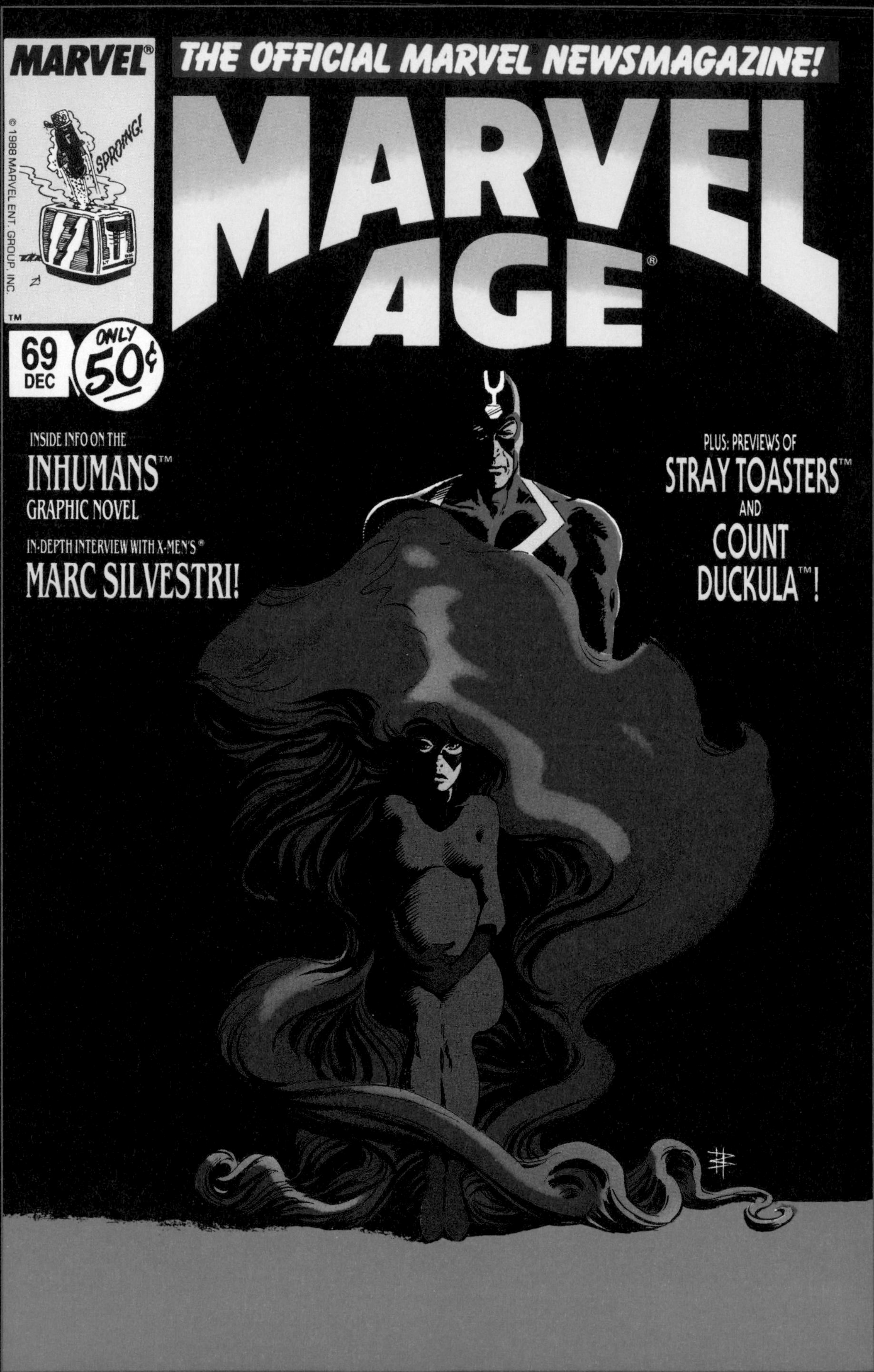
MARVEL®
THE OFFICIAL MARVEL® NEWSMAGAZINE!
MARVEL AGE®
© 1988 MARVEL ENT. GROUP, INC.
SPROING!
TM
69 DEC
ONLY 50¢
INSIDE INFO ON THE
INHUMANS™
GRAPHIC NOVEL
IN-DEPTH INTERVIEW WITH X-MEN'S®
MARC SILVESTRI!
PLUS: PREVIEWS OF
STRAY TOASTERS™
AND
COUNT
DUCKULA™!

THE INHUMANS™

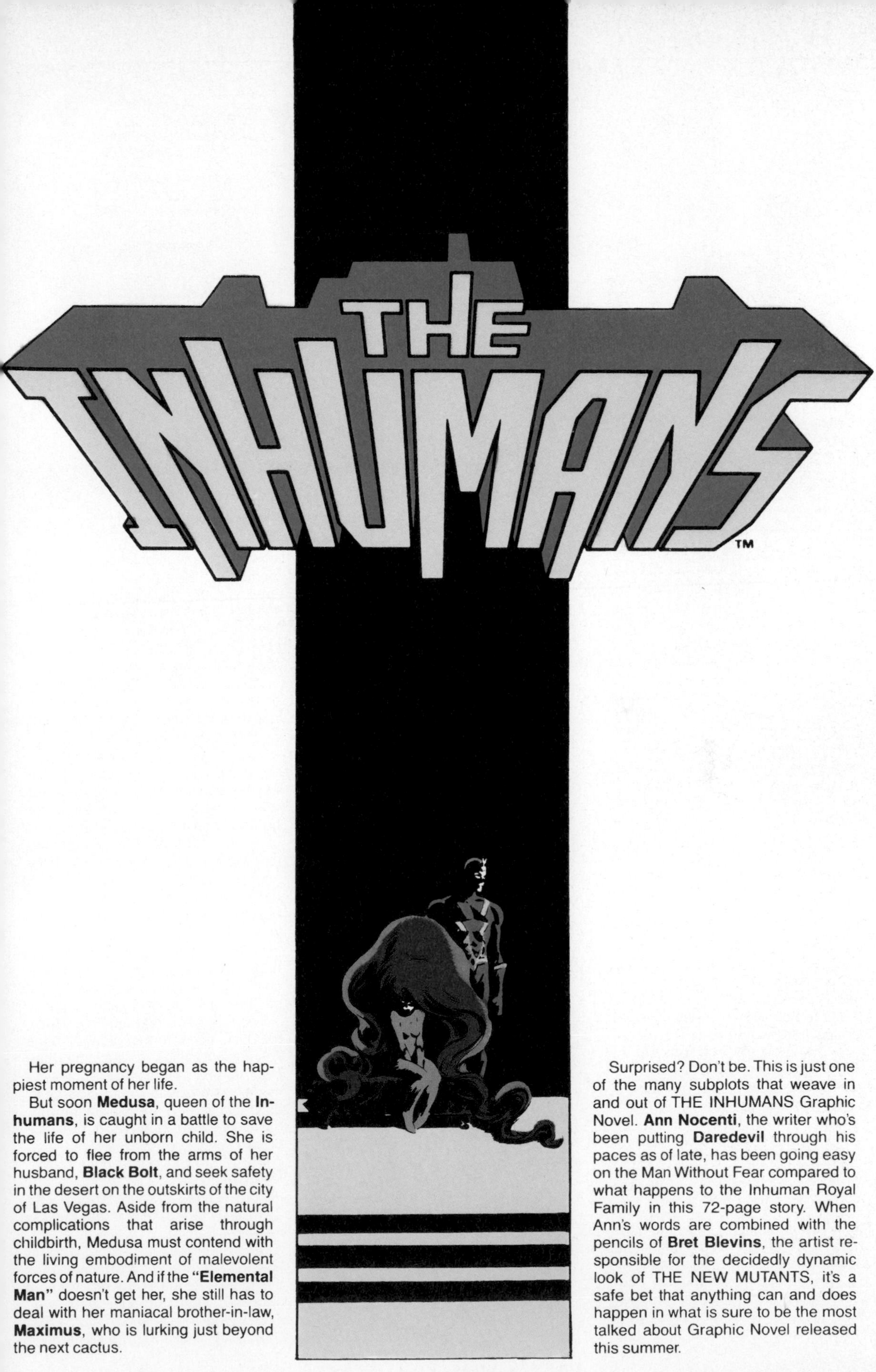

Her pregnancy began as the happiest moment of her life.

But soon **Medusa**, queen of the **Inhumans**, is caught in a battle to save the life of her unborn child. She is forced to flee from the arms of her husband, **Black Bolt**, and seek safety in the desert on the outskirts of the city of Las Vegas. Aside from the natural complications that arise through childbirth, Medusa must contend with the living embodiment of malevolent forces of nature. And if the **"Elemental Man"** doesn't get her, she still has to deal with her maniacal brother-in-law, **Maximus**, who is lurking just beyond the next cactus.

Surprised? Don't be. This is just one of the many subplots that weave in and out of THE INHUMANS Graphic Novel. **Ann Nocenti**, the writer who's been putting **Daredevil** through his paces as of late, has been going easy on the Man Without Fear compared to what happens to the Inhuman Royal Family in this 72-page story. When Ann's words are combined with the pencils of **Bret Blevins**, the artist responsible for the decidedly dynamic look of THE NEW MUTANTS, it's a safe bet that anything can and does happen in what is sure to be the most talked about Graphic Novel released this summer.

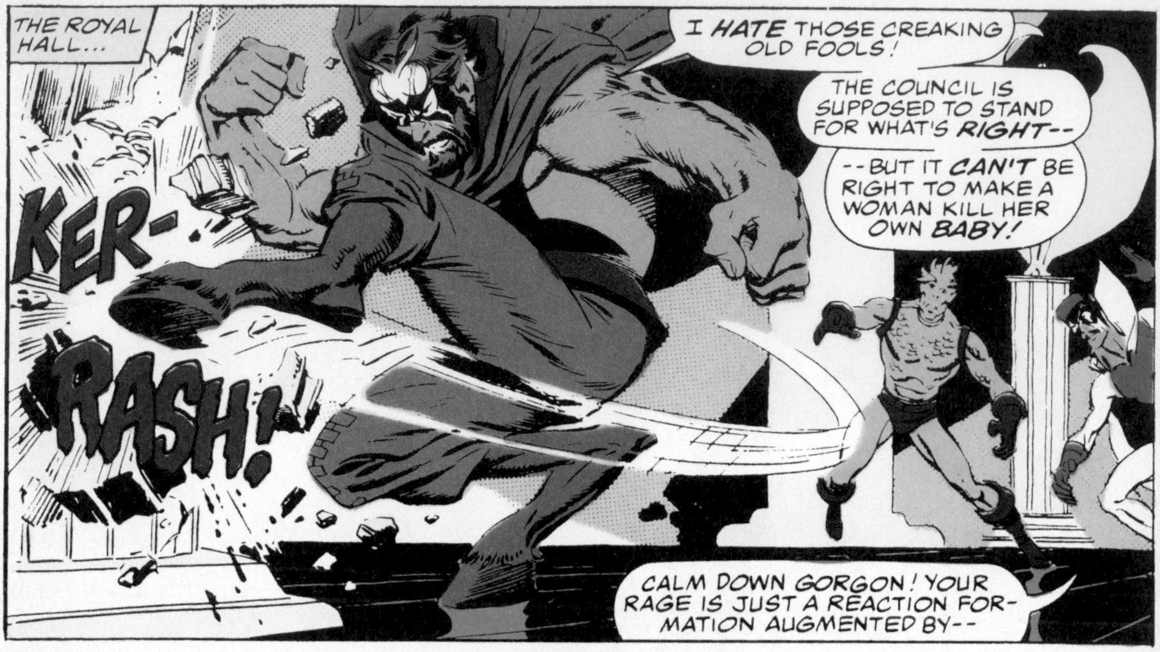
THE ROYAL HALL...
I HATE THOSE CREAKING OLD FOOLS!
THE COUNCIL IS SUPPOSED TO STAND FOR WHAT'S RIGHT--
--BUT IT CAN'T BE RIGHT TO MAKE A WOMAN KILL HER OWN BABY!
KER-RASH!
CALM DOWN GORGON! YOUR RAGE IS JUST A REACTION FORMATION AUGMENTED BY--

Since their first appearance over twenty years ago (in THE FANTASTIC FOUR #45, 1965), the first family of Attilan has always been one of the most intriguing and colorful of all the **Stan Lee** and **Jack Kirby** created characters. In the tradition of their famous anti-heroes, Medusa originally appeared as a member of the **Frightful Four** nine issues before it was revealed she was a member of a race known as the **Inhumans**. Black Bolt, **Gorgon**, **Triton**, **Karnak**, **Crystal**, **Lockjaw**, and the aforementioned Medusa were in exile from the Great Refuge of Attilan, then located in the Himalayas. As the **Fantastic Four** helped Black Bolt wrest control of the kingdom from his insane brother, Maximus, they discovered that the Inhumans had been a race of incredibly powered beings who roamed the Earth while humans were still living in caves. Because these "inhumans" (actually the results of experiments by **Kree** geneticists) were feared, hated, and hunted by humans, they chose to live apart from humanity. In recent years, the polluted environment of Earth forced Black Bolt to move his entire kingdom to the pure atmospheric anomaly that is the Blue Area of the Moon. If that all sounds like enough problems for a single race to encounter, imagine how the Royal Family feels as the story begins . . .

The millennia-old aristocracy of Attilan, a governing body known as the Council of Genetics, is being challenged by the disgruntled youth of the kingdom. Because the race is the result of genetic experimentation over twenty-five thousand years ago, marriages and childbirth are strictly governed by **the Council**. Considering that some of those genetic experiments resulted in such powerful genetic abilities as Black Bolt's voice that is capable of leveling mountains, or that of the scientifically brilliant yet hopelessly insane Maximus, it is understandable that certain restrictions must be followed when couplings or offspring are considered. Unrest abounds as the people demand the right to make their own decisions on these matters. For the second time in his reign as reluctant king of the Inhumans, Black Bolt is confronted by the possibility of a civil war.

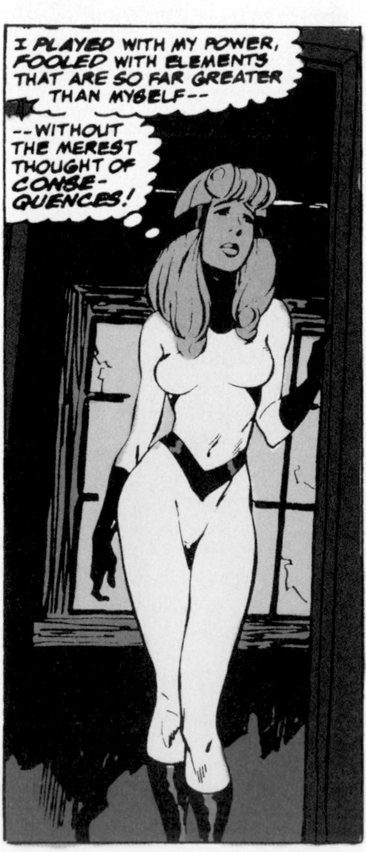
I PLAYED WITH MY POWER, FOOLED WITH ELEMENTS THAT ARE SO FAR GREATER THAN MYSELF--
--WITHOUT THE MEREST THOUGHT OF CONSEQUENCES!

At this point a political hot potato is thrust into his hands when Medusa and Black Bolt announce they're expecting a child, the heir-aparent to the kingdom. Normally this would be time for celebration throughout the land, but instead the Council is outraged and scared! The twelve-member board of Attilan's scientists and geneticists (of which Black Bolt is a member) ask: What will happen if the child possesses the father's power and the uncle's madness? The infant's first innocent cry could destroy the entire city!

Their word being law, they painfully hand down the decree — the unborn child must be destroyed in order to secure the safety of the entire race!

The kingdom threatens to be torn asunder as citizens of all ages question their loyalties to what they consider to be an ancient and oppressive caste system that would cold-heartedly sacrifice an unborn child on the basis of fear. Medusa quickly becomes a symbol for their cause as cries for a revolution echo throughout the Great Refuge. Caught in the middle, between the king and his kingdom, are the rest of the members of the Royal Family.

Medusa's younger sister, **Crystal**, has been ordered back to the Moon so that she might make amends with her husband, **Quicksilver**. Rather than dwell on having to live this mockery of a marriage, her heart belonging with

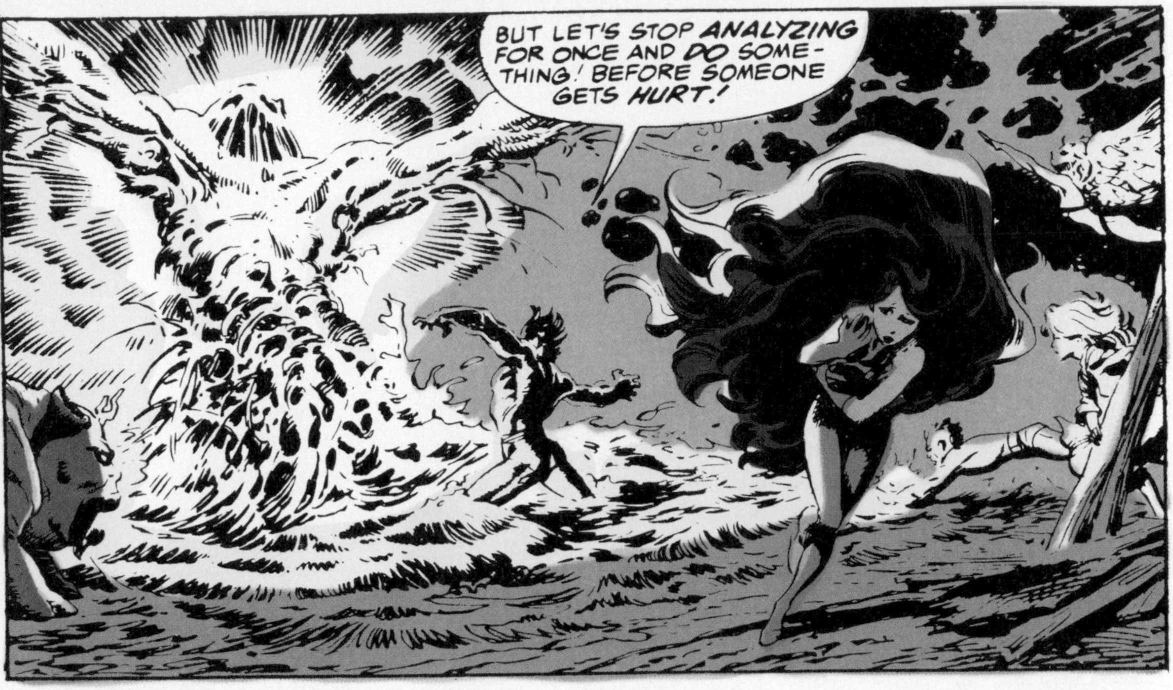
BUT LET'S STOP ANALYZING FOR ONCE AND DO SOME-THING! BEFORE SOMEONE GETS HURT!

her teammates in the Fantastic Four, the young elemental finds relief by looking outside of herself and focusing on the problems that face her sister. When Medusa flees to Earth, willing to risk exposure to deadly pollutants before sacrificing her unborn child to the Council, it is Crystal who convinces **Lockjaw** to teleport the rest of the Royal Family in pursuit.

Nowhere is the conflict between tradition and free-thinking more clearly illustrated than in the relationship between the cousins Gorgon and Karnak. A simple soul with the ability to essentially stomp his feet and get his own way, Gorgon has always looked to the Council for its wisdom and guidance. The very thought that people are questioning the venerable ones is enough to send him into one of his many emotional outbursts. At one point he rants, "We'd all be dead if it weren't for the Council!"

"That was in the past," exclaims the ever analytical Karnak in response. "Now our race is dying *because* of the Council!" Possessed of the ability to destroy any object by finding its weakest point, it seems his ability is also an outward manifestation of his personality. Throughout the story he is constantly but subtly lashing out at everyone as a means of dealing with his anxiety over the changes that threaten to ravage the Royal Family in particular and the aristocracy of the Great Refuge in general.

As the ultimate isolationist by necessity in a kingdom of isolationists by choice, Triton's need to be submerged in water sets him apart from the rest of the Royal Family. From this vantage of distance from his cousins, Triton can clearly see that their decision to flee the Council is only another way for them to avoid their situation rather than deal with the inevitable confrontation between new ideas and old.

When Medusa, Crystal, Triton, Gorgon, and Karnak ultimately decide to stay on Earth (the young elemental uses her ability to purify the air at the cost of manipulating nature) the results are disasterous . . . (Unless one is considering the results from an artistic point of view. The "monster" created by Bret Blevins and inker **Al Williamson**, which appears halfway through the story, is certainly one of the most horrifying creatures to ever appear in the Marvel Universe.)

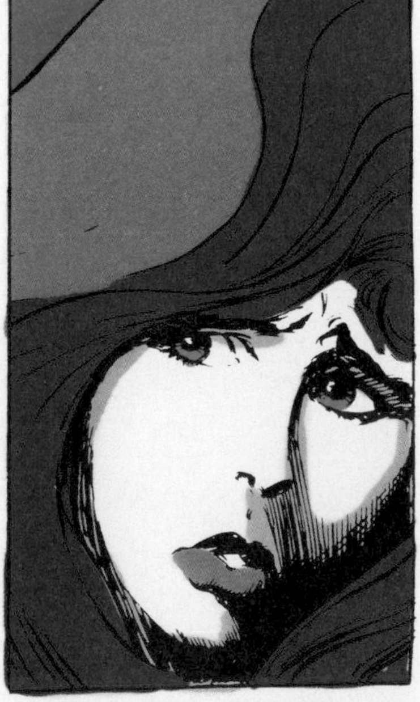

Of course no Inhumans tale would be complete without the inclusion of Maximus. This time, however, the maniacal one manipulates his hated cousins from behind the scenes. In his never-ending attempt to make life miserable for his brother, Black Bolt, Maximus invests in a long-term plan that he's confident will eventually destroy his sibling forever. A plan made all the more sweeter because he's certain the King of the Inhumans will be destroyed by his own child . . .

Though the story's central conflict is resolved by the end of the Graphic Novel, look for more adventures of the Inhumans in the near future. Although they'll be appearing in an upcoming multi-part saga in the pages of MARVEL COMICS PRESENTS (the biweekly book for those readers who might be living on the Blue Area of the Moon), it's likely that Marveldom Assembled will take the Inhumans' cue and hold a revolution of their own. That's it, they can storm the Dreaded Council of Editors and demand an Inhumans' mini-series, or maybe a continuing monthly series! Better yet, a weekly series! No! No! No! A *daily* series! That's right, A DAILY SERIES ABOUT THE INHUMANS! A DAILY SERIES CALLED "THE DEATH OF ALL THE INHUMANS EXCEPT MAXIMUS!"

—*Maximus*

BLACK BOLT

Real Name: Blackagar Boltagon
Occupation: Monarch of the Inhumans
Legal status: Citizen of Attilan
Identity: The existence of the Inhumans is not believed by the general public of Earth.
Place of birth: Island of Attilan, Atlantic Ocean
Marital status: Married
Known relatives: Medusa (wife), Agon (father, deceased), Rynda (mother, deceased), Maximus (brother), Gorgon, Karnak, Triton (cousins)
Group affiliation: Royal Family of the Inhumans
Base of operations: Attilan, Blue Area, Earth's moon
First appearance: FANTASTIC FOUR #45
Origin: THOR #148, 149 and AVENGERS #95
History: Black Bolt was born to two of Attilan's top geneticists, Agon, head of the ruling Council of Genetics, and Rynda, director of the Prenatal Care Center (see *Attilan*). Subjected to the mutagenic Terrigen Mist while still an embryo, Bolt was born with strange powers surpassing even the Inhumans' norm (see *Inhumans*). As an infant, he demonstrated certain energy-manipulative abilities which he could not yet control, particularly that of producing quasi-sonic energy of great destructive potential. To protect the community, he was placed inside a sound-proofed chamber and given an energy-harnessing suit. There he was schooled in the art of controlling his powers until the age of nineteen, when he was permitted to enter society.

A month after being awarded his freedom, Black Bolt discovered his younger brother Maximus in the process of making a treacherous pact with emissaries of the alien Kree (see *Kree*, *Maximus*). Attempting to stop the Kree ship before it escaped, Bolt used the forbidden power of his quasi-sonic voice to knock the ship out of the sky. When the ship crashed to Earth, it landed on the parliament building, killing several key members of the Council of Genetics, including his parents, Agon and Rynda. The reverberations of his brother's shout affected Maximus's sanity and suppressed his nascent mental powers. Despite his guilt and silent protests, Black Bolt was obligated to accept the mantle of leadership of the Inhumans at the age of twenty.

Black Bolt's first crisis in leadership came when his cousin Triton was briefly held captive by humans. Learning of Triton's encounter upon his escape, Black Bolt decided that the Inhumans' island of Attilan was in imminent danger of discovery by humanity. Black Bolt scouted out possible sites to which to move, and settled upon the remote Himalayan mountains. After the great migration, Black Bolt faced his second great crisis when his now mad brother Maximus unleashed the Trikon, three of the Inhumans' worker drones who were transformed into energy-beings. The Trikon enabled Maximus to wrest the rule of the Inhumans from his brother and send Black Bolt and the other members of the Royal Family into exile. For the next few years, Black Bolt and his kinsmen wandered Asia, Europe, and finally America, in search of Medusa, his betrothed mate, who had been separated from the others during the battle with the Trikon (see *Medusa*). Eventually Black Bolt was reunited with Medusa and the Royal Family returned to Attilan and resumed the crown.

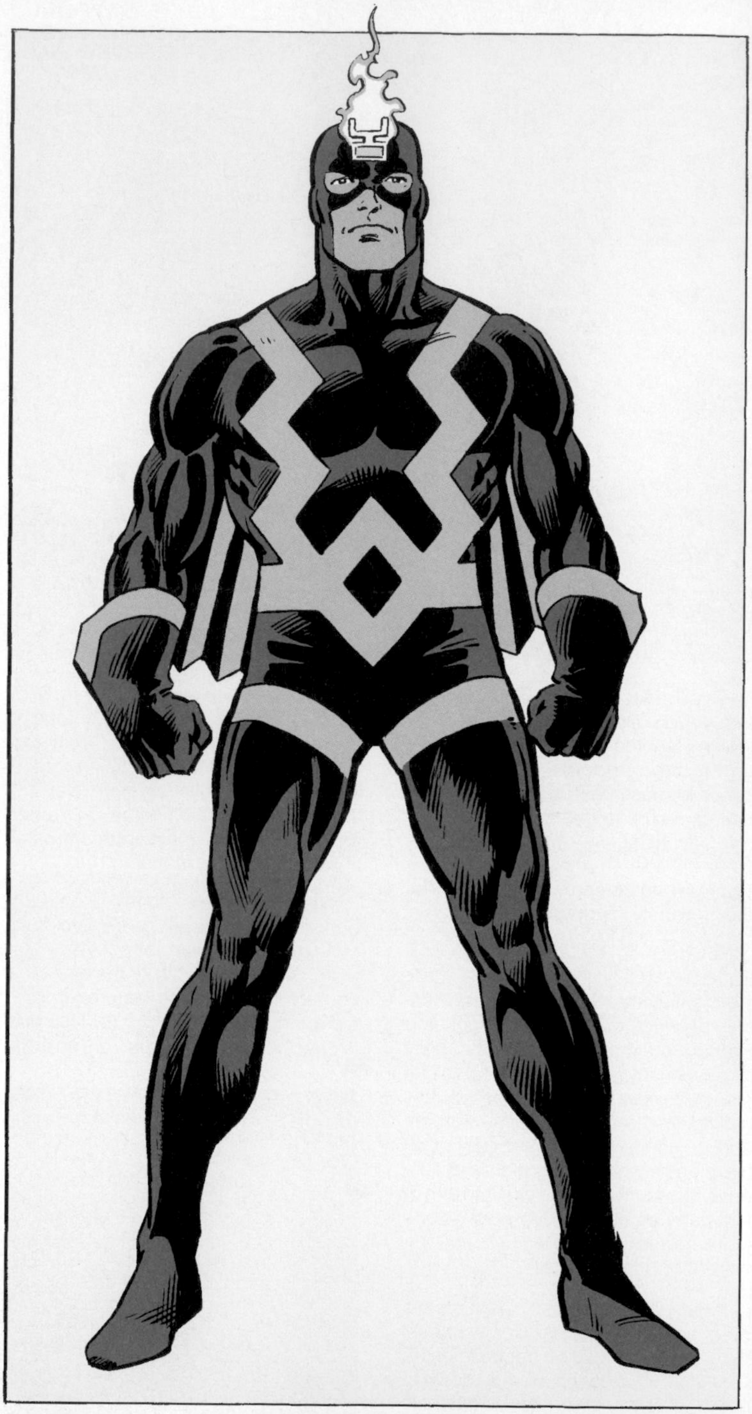

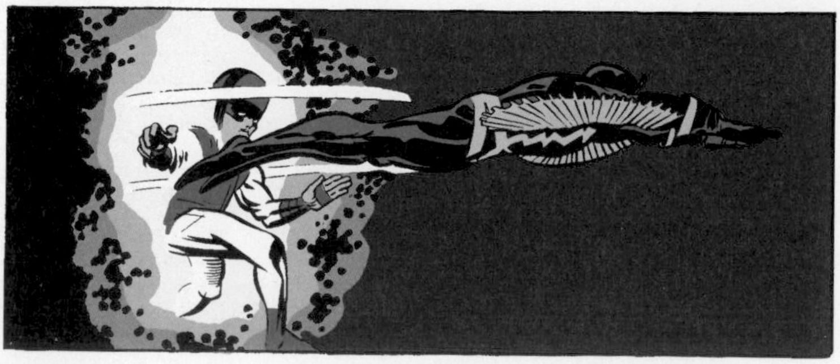

Official Handbook of the Marvel Universe: Deluxe Edition profiles — art by John Byrne & Josef Rubinstein

Black Bolt has led the Inhumans through some of the most turbulent times in their history, including several more attempts by Maximus to usurp the throne, revolts by the worker class, attacks by human renegades, the kidnapping of Medusa, the destruction and rebuilding of Attilan, the revelation of the Inhumans' existence to humanity, and finally the second relocation of Attilan. Recently, following the traditionally lengthy period of betrothal, Black Bolt and Medusa were wed.

Height: 6' 2"
Weight: 210 lbs
Eyes: Blue
Hair: Black

Strength level: Black Bolt possesses superhuman strength, enabling him to lift (press) approximately 1 ton. He is stronger than the average Inhuman due to the particular way in which the mutagenic Terrigen Mist affected his genetic and physical structure. By augmenting his body with his electron power (see below), Black Bolt becomes capable of lifting approximately 60 tons under optimal conditions.

Known superhuman powers: Black Bolt possesses various superhuman powers stemming from his ability to harness free-floating electrons. The speech center of Black Bolt's brain contains an organic mechanism able to generate an as yet unknown type of particle which interacts with ambient electrons to create certain phenomena determined by mental control.

The most devastating of the effects is Black Bolt's quasi-sonic scream. Because his electron-harnessing ability is linked to the speech center of his brain, any attempt to use his vocal cords — from the merest whisper to a full scream — triggers an uncontrollable disturbance of the particle / electron interaction field. This results in a shock wave equivalent, at maximum force, to that caused by the detonation of a nuclear weapon. A whisper has generated sufficient force to rock a battleship, while a scream can reduce a mountain to rubble.

The fork-shaped antenna that Black Bolt has worn upon his brow since childhood enables him to channel his power in more directed, less destructive ways. The antenna monitors his brain's speech center activity and allows him to direct limited quantities of the unknown particle to create a number of controlled phenomena. He can channel this energy inwardly to enhance his own body's speed and strength (see above). Black Bolt is capable of channeling all available energy into one arm for one powerful punch called his Master Blow. This exertion taxes his body's ability to employ the particle / electron energy to its limit and renders him extremely vulnerable following its use.

Black Bolt is also able to direct the unknown particle outwards in ways other than by means of his vocal cords. He can rapidly route particle / electron energy through his arms to create relatively small concussive blasts. He can form a field of highly-active electrons around himself with the wave of a hand, said field being capable of deflecting projectiles up to the mass of an MX missile traveling at its maximum speed. He can create particle / electron interaction fields solid enough to be traversed upon, though this phenomenon is a particularly difficult and exhausting one. He can use these electron fields as extrasensory probes which are highly sensitive to other electromagnetic energy phenomena. He can even manipulate his electron field to jam certain electrical mechanisms.

Black Bolt can also harness the unknown particles his brain generates to interact with electrons to create anti-gravitons that enable him to defy gravity. By emitting a jet of rapidly moving particle / electron interaction by-products while enveloped by anti-gravitons, Black Bolt can fly up to 500 miles per hour for a period of 6 hours before his brain begins to tire appreciably from the effort. The anti-graviton field also serves to protect Black Bolt from the detrimental effects of rapid movement through the atmosphere.

Abilities: Like all Inhumans, Black Bolt is physically superior to normal human beings due to generations of eugenics. Attributes in which Inhumans excel over humans include reaction time, stamina, strength, resistance to injury, and speed. Humans are superior to Inhumans, however, in immunity to disease. ∎

CRYSTAL

Real Name: Crystalia Amaquelin Maximoff
Occupation: Wife and mother
Legal status: Citizen of Attilan
Identity: Publicly known
Former aliases: Briefly mistaken for the Mayan goddess Ixchel
Place of birth: Island of Attilan, Atlantic Ocean
Marital status: Married
Known relatives: Pietro Maximoff (Quicksilver, husband), Luna (daughter), Medusa (sister), Karnak, Triton (cousins), Quelin (father), Ambur (mother)
Group affiliation: Royal Family of the Inhumans, former member of the Fantastic Four
Base of operations: Attilan, Blue Area of the Moon
First appearance: FANTASTIC FOUR #45
History: Crystal was the second child born to the Inhuman nutritionists Quelin and Ambur (see *Inhumans*). Her father Quelin was the brother of Rynda, wife of Agon, king of the Inhumans, and as such she was considered part of the Royal Family of Attilan. Like her older sister Medusa, Crystal was subjected to the Terrigen Mist when she was an infant, and the process endowed her with certain mental powers.

While she was still a child, war erupted, forcing Crystal and her kinsmen to flee Attilan. Crystal passed through adolescence into young adulthood while wandering with her kinsmen through Asia, Europe, and finally America in search of Crystal's amnesiac sister Medusa. When they finally caught up with Medusa in New York, Medusa had sought refuge with the Fantastic Four, mistaking her kinsmen for her enemies. Crystal then met Johnny Storm of the Fantastic Four and the two began a romantic relationship that survived Crystal's return to Attilan and a lengthy separation (see *Fantastic Four, Human Torch*).

Crystal eventually returned to New York, and served as a substitute member of the Fantastic Four during the Invisible Girl's first pregnancy and post-childbirth. Crystal was forced to return to Attilan when her health became impaired by prolonged exposure to pollutants in the atmosphere. However, en route to Attilan, Crystal became a pawn in a plan by the alchemist Diablo, and then happened upon the mutant Quicksilver, who had been wounded in battle with the Sentinels (see *Diablo, Quicksilver*). She brought Quicksilver back to Attilan, nursed him back to health, and became romantically involved with him. The Human Torch soon learned of Crystal's change in affections, and after a futile battle with Quicksilver, terminated his relationship with her. Crystal and Quicksilver were wed shortly thereafter, theirs being the first marriage between an Inhuman and a human (albeit a human mutant) in recorded history. Crystal and Quicksilver conceived a child, a girl bearing no apparent Inhuman or mutant characteristics, whom they named Luna after the world on which she was born. While Quicksilver wanted to exercise the father's right to have his child subjected to the Terrigen Mist, Crystal convinced him to let her grow up "normal." Crystal's relationship with her husband has been strained of late.
Height: 5′ 6″
Weight: 110 lbs
Eyes: Green
Hair: Red

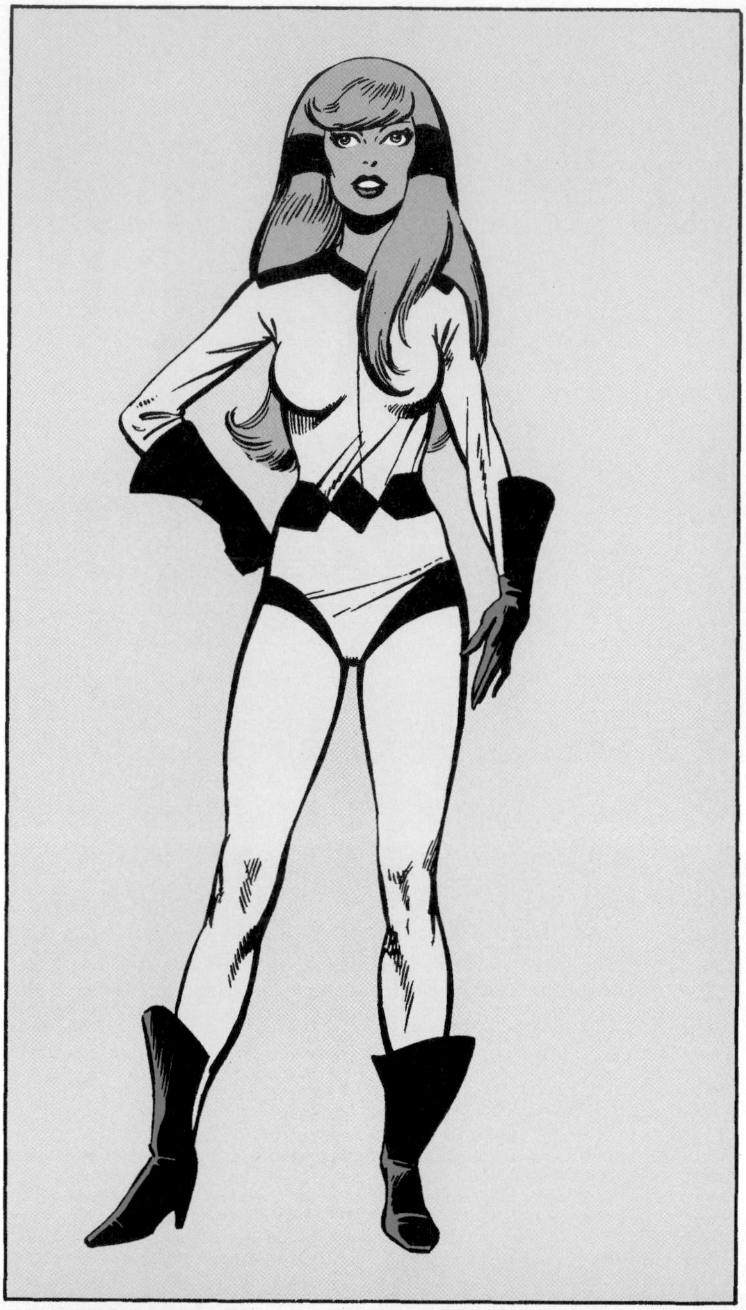

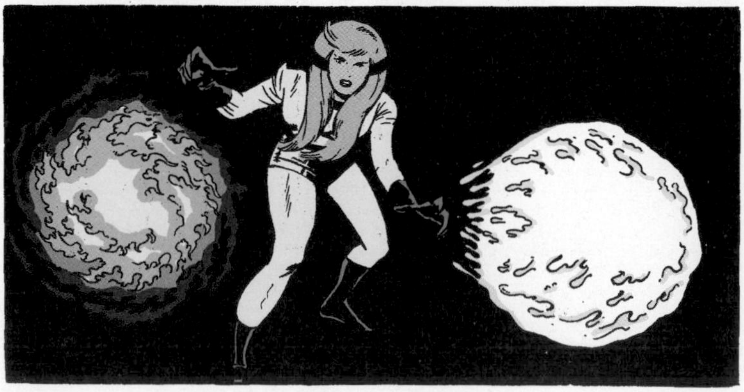

Art by John Byrne & Josef Rubinstein

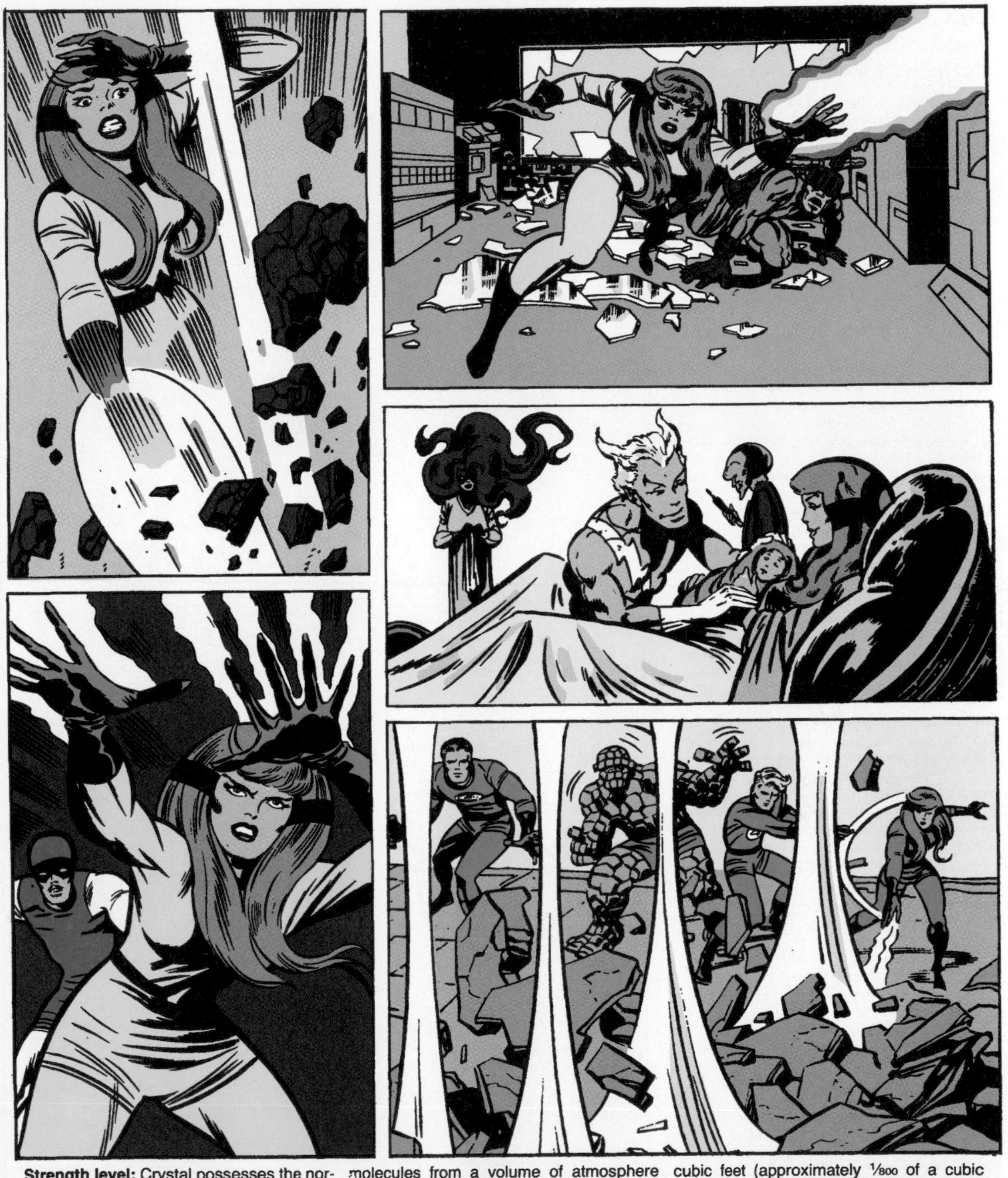

Strength level: Crystal possesses the normal strength of a female Inhuman who engages in moderate regular exercise. Due to generations of eugenics, Inhumans are superior to humans in strength, reaction time, stamina, resistance to injury and speed.

Known superhuman powers: Crystal possesses the ability to mentally manipulate the four basic "elements" of nature: fire, water, earth, and air. She does so by means of a psionic interaction with the substances on a molecular level. By controlling oxygen molecules she can cause fire to spontaneously ignite or she can douse any oxidizing flame by depriving it of oxygen. She can join hydrogen and oxygen molecules to create rain, summoning these molecules from a volume of atmosphere within a radius of approximately two miles.

She can control the movement of water by manipulating surface tension, divining water from the ground and causing it to flow in designated directions. The observed maximum volume of water she can control is approximately 2,000 cubic feet (about 15,000 gallons). Thus, she cannot change the course of rivers or cause the sea to part. She can control the various substances that make up common bedrock (earth: iron, granite, shale, limestone, etc.), creating seismic tremors of up to 6.7 on the Richter scale (greater if tectonic plate fault lines are nearby) by causing a sudden shifting of the earth. The observed maximum volume she can affect at once is 1.8×10^8 cubic feet (approximately $1/800$ of a cubic mile). She can also control oxygen atoms and oxygen-containing molecules to create atmospheric disturbances of various kinds. By intermingling air with earth she can cause a duststorm, air with water a typhoon, and air with fire a firestorm. She is able to create a wind of tornado intensity, approximately 115 miles per hour.

Limitations: Crystal can sustain a certain elemental phenomenon for approximately one hour before her mind begins to tire. She can also create any number of effects in succession for about forty-five minutes before mental fatigue impairs her performance.

GORGON

Real Name: Unrevealed
Occupation: Royal Administrator
Identity: Secret
Legal status: Citizen of Attilan
Other current aliases: None
Place of birth: Island of Attilan, Atlantic Ocean
Marital status: Single
Known relatives: Korath (father, deceased), Milena (mother, deceased), Black Bolt, Maximus (cousins), Agon (paternal uncle)
Group affiliation: Royal Family of the Inhumans
Base of operations: Attilan, Blue Area, Earth's moon
First appearance: FANTASTIC FOUR #44
History: Gorgon was the only son born to the architect Korath and the archivist Milena, leading citizens of the Inhumans' city-state Attilan (see *Inhumans*). Korath was a brother to Agon, king of the Inhumans, and thus his son Gorgon is considered part of the Royal Family of Attilan. Like most of the new generation of the Royal Family, Gorgon was subjected to the Terrigen Mist when he was an infant, and the process endowed him with certain physical adaptations and powers. Gorgon's parents were killed in the war against the Trikon, three of the Inhumans' worker drones who were transformed into energy-beings (see *Appendix: Trikon*).

During this war, Gorgon was forced to flee Attilan along with the deposed ruler Black Bolt and other members of the Royal Family (see *Black Bolt*). For years, Gorgon and his companions wandered Asia, Europe, and finally America in search of their kinsman Medusa, who was separated from them (see *Medusa*). When they finally found her in New York, Medusa mistook Gorgon as her enemy, having suffered from amnesia during her exile. Gorgon was forced to battle the Fantastic Four, among whom she sought protection (see *Fantastic Four*). The misunderstanding was soon resolved, and Gorgon and the Royal Family returned to Attilan where Gorgon's cousin Black Bolt resumed his rightful rule. Gorgon has remained one of Black Bolt's most trusted aides and one of Attilan's staunchest defenders ever since.
Height: 6′ 5″
Weight: 450 lbs
Eyes: Brown
Hair: Black
Unusual features: Gorgon has hooves instead of feet.
Strength level: Gorgon possesses superhuman strength, enabling him to lift (press) approximately 2½ tons. He is stronger than the average Inhuman due to the particular way in which the mutagenic Terrigen Mist affected his genetic and physical structure.
Known superhuman powers: Gorgon's power is centered in his massively-muscled legs and hoof-like feet. Approximately three quarters of Gorgon's total weight is in the lower half of his body, particularly in the thick, dense muscles of his thighs and calves. As a result of having such a low center of gravity, it is extremely difficult to knock Gorgon off balance, and were he to fall from almost any height, he would land on his feet. By natural strength and power alone, he is able to kick through three feet of solid oak with a single blow. However, Gorgon's legs possess far more than great natural strength. As a result of the Terrigen

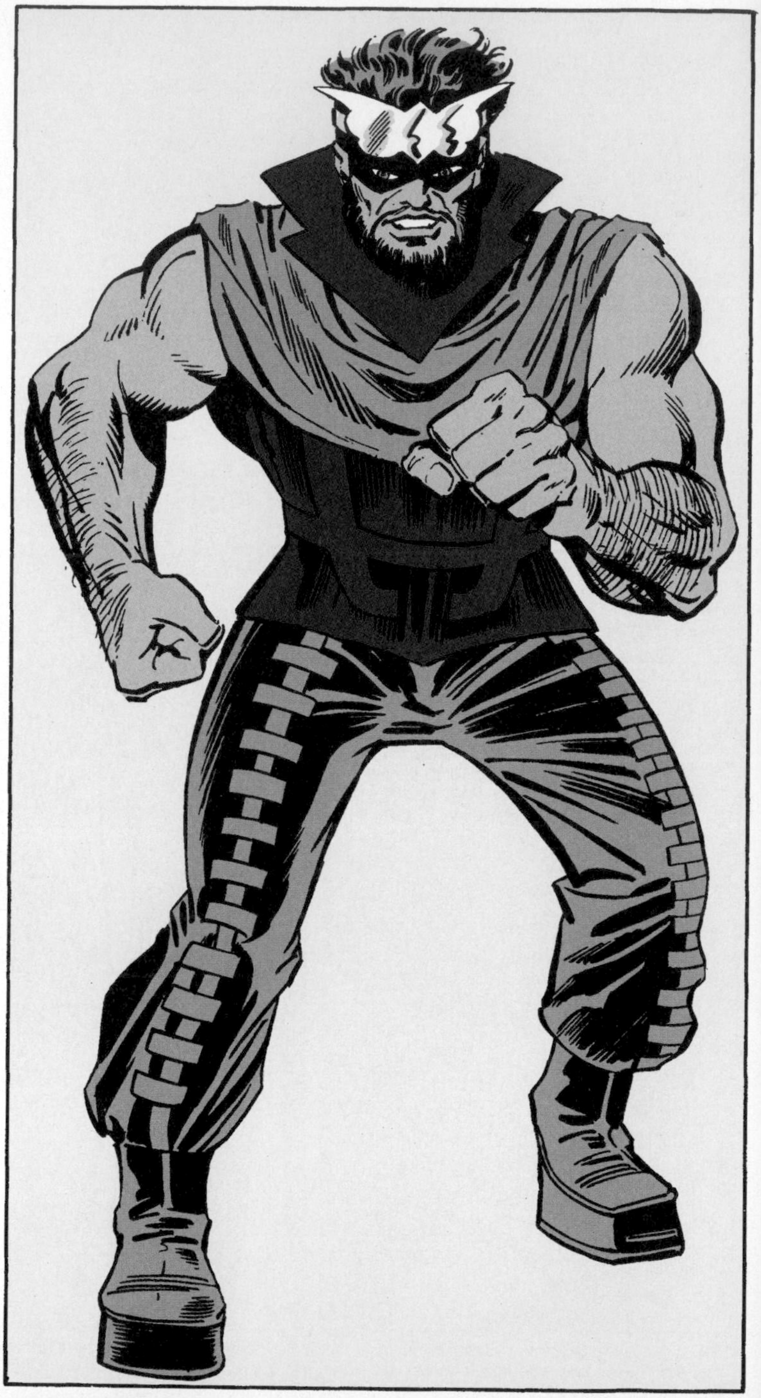

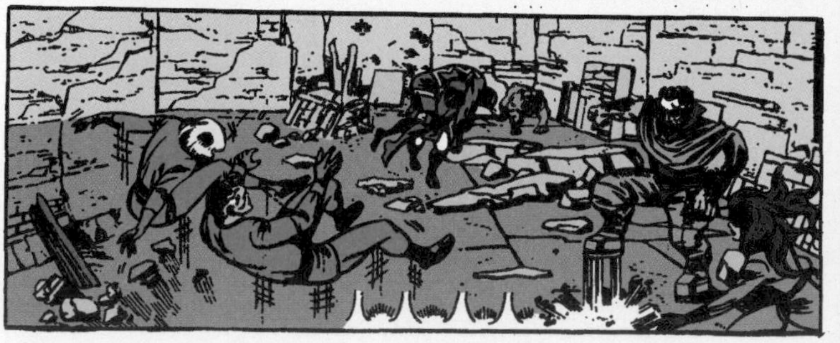

Art by Larry Lieber & Josef Rubinstein

mutation, Gorgon's legs are able to generate vibration on a molecular level in such a way that can develop an intense pulse of kinetic energy. By stomping his hoof to the ground, Gorgon is able to release this kinetic energy in the form of either a dynamic ground wave through the earth, or a more diffuse, radially propagating concussion wave along the surface of the earth. Gorgon is able to create seismic tremors of up to 7.5 on the Richter scale with a single stamp (even greater, from 8.2 to 9.5, if he happens to be near tectonic plate fault lines). This kinetic energy is only generated by an act of will; it does not spontaneously occur every time he takes a step. Gorgon can control the relative intensity of the tremor at will. It takes him no more than a few hundredths of a second to generate sufficient energy to create any size effect up to his maximum capability. He is able to generate and expend his seismic force-waves for several hours of near-constant use before fatigue significantly affects his performance. Gorgon can release the kinetic energy through his hooves without stamping them, but the act of stamping serves as a focusing aid for its release. Once Gorgon generates the energy, he must release it within 4.5 seconds before it spontaneously discharges. He cannot dissipate the energy once it is generated without releasing it.

Abilities: Like all Inhumans, Gorgon is physically superior to normal human beings due to generations of eugenics. Attributes in which Inhumans excel over humans include reaction time, stamina, strength, resistance to injury, and speed. Humans are superior to Inhumans, however, in immunity to disease. ■

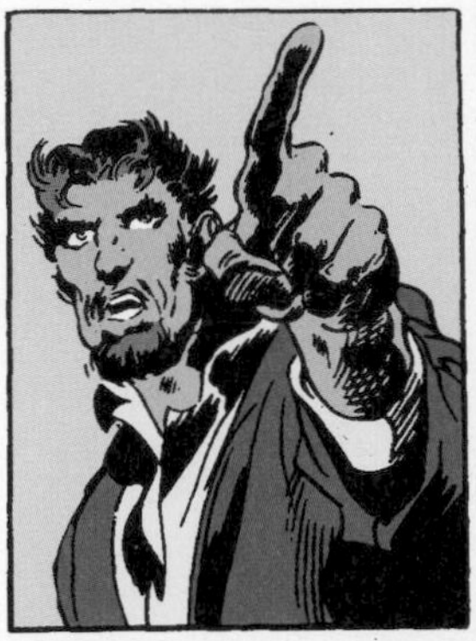

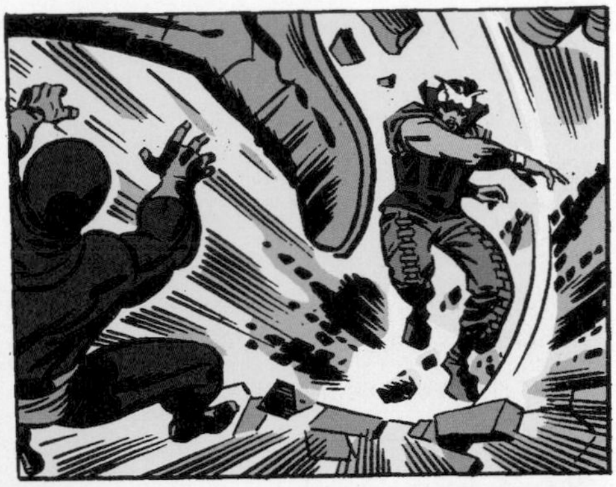

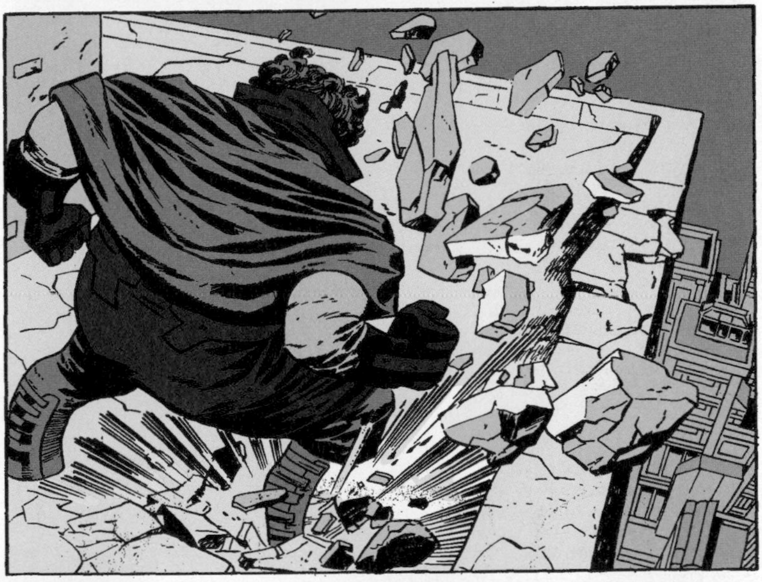

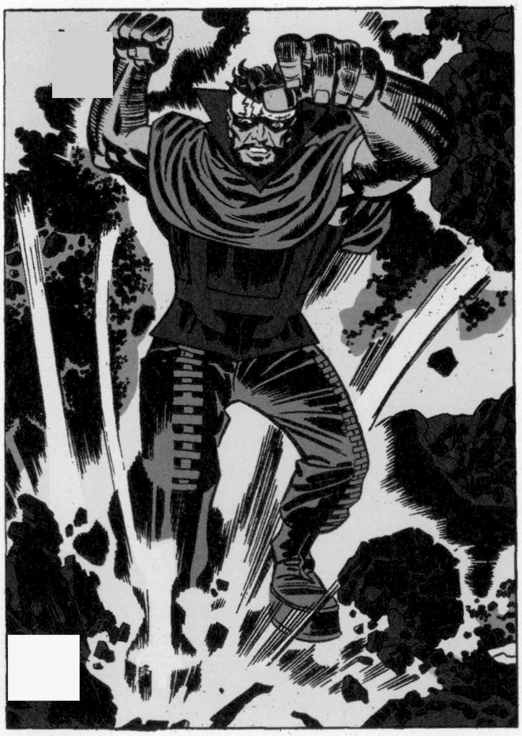

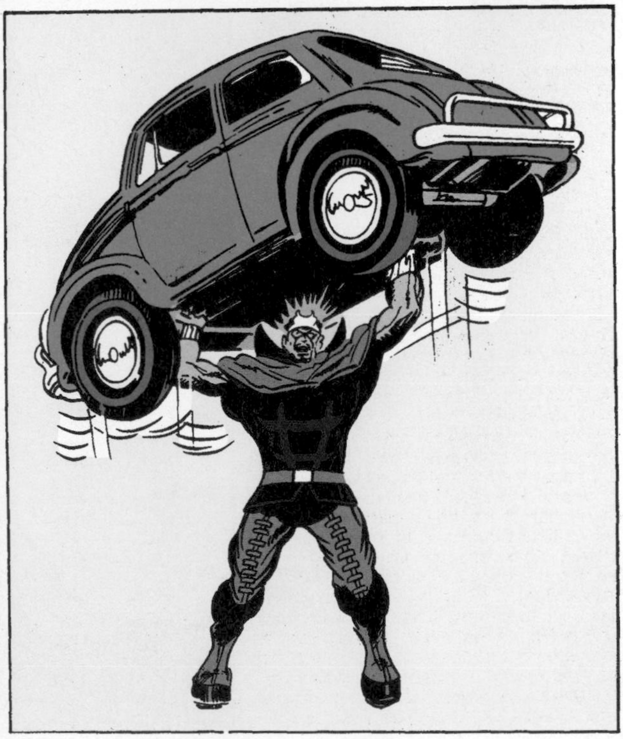

KARNAK

Real Name: Unrevealed
Occupation: Priest/philosopher
Identity: Secret. His existence is not known to the general public of Earth.
Legal status: Citizen of Attilan
Former aliases: The Shatterer
Place of birth: None
Marital status: Single
Known relatives: Mander (father), Azur (mother, deceased), Triton (brother), Black Bolt, Maximus, Crystal, Medusa (cousins)
Group affiliation: Royal Family of the Inhumans
Base of operations: Attilan, Blue Area, the Moon
First appearance: FANTASTIC FOUR #45
History: Karnak was the second son of an Inhuman priest / philosopher named Mander and an ocean biologist named Azur (see *Inhumans*). Having sent their first son Triton into the Terrigen Mist when he was an infant, Mander and Azur decided to raise their second child without Terrigen mutation. Karnak was enrolled in his father's religious seminary in the Tower of Wisdom where he trained in various physical and mental disciplines until he was eighteen years old. Karnak's mother died in a mysterious undersea mishap. Karnak's father is still a teacher at the seminary.
Height: 5′ 7″
Weight: 150 lbs
Eyes: Blue
Hair: Black
Unusual features: Karnak has an unnaturally large cranium in proportion to his body size.
Strength level: Karnak possesses a degree of superhuman strength, derived from his eugenically superior Inhuman heritage and his intensive regimen of regular exercise. Karnak can lift (press) about 1 ton.
Known superhuman powers: Besides strength, Karnak possesses certain physical skills superior to those of human athletes. His Inhuman metabolism affords him slightly greater reaction time, endurance, and speed than the human race's most perfect physical specimen, Captain America (see *Captain America*).

Karnak has physically conditioned his body and mind to their peak levels of efficiency. He has voluntary control over most of his body's autonomic functions: breathing, heartbeat, bleeding, reaction to pain, rate of healing, etc. He is extremely lithe and flexible, able to expand and contract his muscles and contort his body into seemingly painful positions. He has toughened all the striking surfaces of his body in general and his hands in particular, so that they are covered with dense callus. Karnak is capable of shattering wood, cinderblock, and even mild steel.

Through mental discipline, Karnak has gained the extrasensory ability to perceive the stress points, fracture planes, or weaknesses, in all objects or persons around him. By striking or applying pressure at these points, he can split or shatter objects made of seemingly invincible substances or render insensate beings of far greater strength than he. This mental discipline is virtually effortless, and Karnak can attain this state of awareness for extended periods of time.

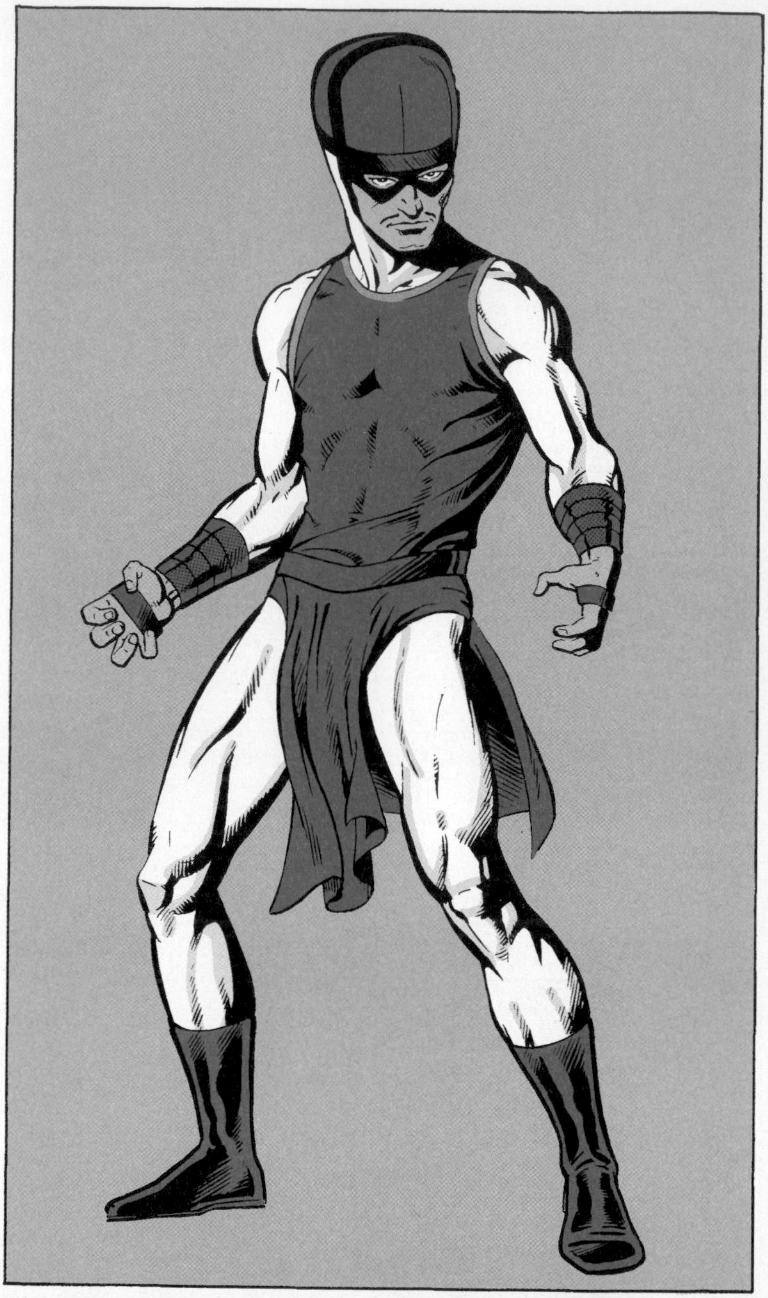

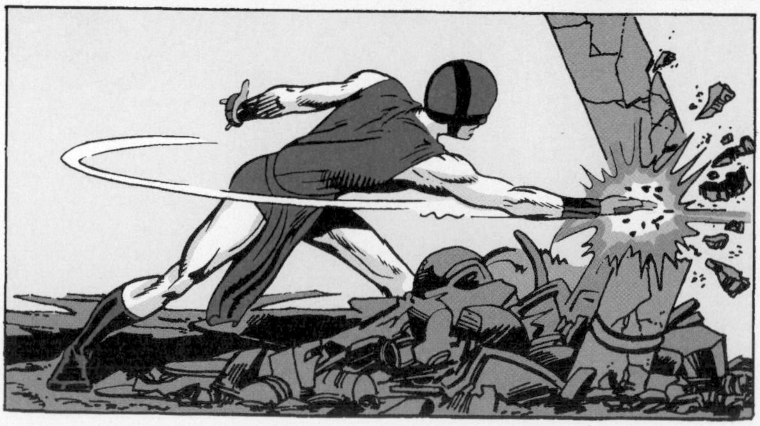

Art by Sandy Plunkett & Josef Rubinstein

LOCKJAW

Real Name: Unrevealed
Occupation: Companion to the Royal Family of the Inhumans
Identity: Lockjaw's existence is known to the Inhumans but not to the general populace of Earth.
Legal status: Citizen of Attilan
Former aliases: None
Place of birth: Island of Attilan, Atlantic Ocean
Marital status: Inapplicable
Known relatives: None
Group affiliation: Companion to the Royal Family of the Inhumans
Base of operations: Attilan, Blue Area, the Moon
First appearance: FANTASTIC FOUR #45
History: Almost nothing has been revealed about Lockjaw's early history. However, it is now known that Lockjaw is not truly a gigantic dog, as he appears to be, but one of the Inhumans themselves, and that he possesses human-level intelligence. Lockjaw can even speak, although with great difficulty. Apparently Lockjaw originally had a humanoid form until, as a child, he was placed within the mutagenic terrigen mists as other Inhumans are. The Inhumans derive their superhuman powers from the effects of the Terrigen mists (see *Inhumans*). It is now known that his exposure to Terrigen gave Lockjaw his canine form, as well as

presumably, his teleportational powers. Apparently it has also given him certain canine instincts and behavioral tendencies (such as urges to chase animals).
Height: 5′ (at shoulder)
Length: 6′ 8″ (from muzzle to hock)
Weight: 1,240 lbs.
Eyes: Brown
Fur: Brown
Unusual features: Lockjaw has a small two-pronged antenna upon his forehead.
Strength level: Lockjaw possesses great physical strength simply from size alone. Due to his canine physiology he is limited to what he can pick up by its shape, that is, whether he can hold it with his mouth. His mouth, however, is unusually large, as is his head, which is about 40 inches from flews to dome. His jaw strength is such that he once clamped onto the Thing's hand and the Thing was apparently unable to free it (see *Thing*). Lockjaw possesses sufficient strength to support 3,600 pounds on his back and still be able to walk, as well as the power and physical toughness to dig through ferro-concrete with his paws.
Known superhuman powers: Lockjaw's major power is the ability to teleport himself and up to about one ton of additional mass (including up to a dozen people, if their combined weight does not exceed that limit), across space and even to other dimensions.

In order for Lockjaw to teleport another person or object with him, the person or object must stand within a radius of about 14 feet from Lockjaw's body, and preferably be in contact with him. Lockjaw is capable of teleporting himself as little as 10 feet or as far as 240,000 miles (the distance from the Earth to the Moon at its apogee) from his original spot. It is not yet known whether he can teleport himself farther than that. The process of teleportation appears to be psionic in nature and is accompanied by a visible discharge of energy from his antenna. The precise method by which his brain taps the associated psionic energies and harnesses them for use is not known. Lockjaw requires no recovery time after utilizing his teleportation power.

The means by which Lockjaw can determine distances and spatial relationships between points of departure and arrival, including interdimensional ones, is as yet unknown. Presumably it is associated with or augmented by the use of psionic energies.

Lockjaw also possesses a sense of smell so keen that he can track or locate a scent across dimensional space. Since odors cannot physically travel across dimensions, this ability of Lockjaw's appears to be at least in part an extrasensory (psionic) one, the precise nature of which is as yet unknown. ∎

Art by Bob Budiansky & Josef Rubinstein

MAXIMUS

Real name: Unrevealed
Occupation: None
Identity: Secret
Legal status: Citizen of Attilan
Other current aliases: Maximus the Mad
Place of birth: Island of Attilan, Atlantic Ocean
Marital status: Single
Known relatives: Agon (father, deceased), Rynda (mother, deceased), Black Bolt (brother), Gorgon, Triton, Karnak, Medusa, Crystal (cousins)
Group affiliation: Royal Family of the Inhumans, leader of "Evil Inhumans," ally of Shatterstar
Base of operations: Attilan, Blue Area, Earth's Moon
First appearance: FANTASTIC FOUR #47
History: Maximus, an Inhuman, was the second son of two of Attilan's top geneticists, Agon, the head of the ruling Council of Geneticists, and Rynda, director of the Prenatal Care Center. Subjected to the DNA-altering Terrigen Mist when he was an infant, Maximus peculiarly showed no outward sign of any mutagenic change. As he matured, he hid his developing psionic powers from the community but was less successful at disguising his antisocial tendencies. When he was about sixteen, his elder brother Black Bolt was released from the protective chamber in which he had been confined since birth due to the destructive nature of his Terrigen mutation (see *Black Bolt*). One of Maximus's first responses to his brother's freedom was an unsuccessful attempt to make him release his power and thus lose his freedom. A month later, Black Bolt witnessed Maximus making a treacherous pact with an emissary of the Kree, the alien race responsible for genetically accelerating the Inhumans eons before (see *Kree*). In an attempt to stop the fleeing emissary so that he could be questioned by the ruling council, Black Bolt used his forbidden power of the quasi-sonic scream and blasted the alien ship out of the sky. When the ship crashed to earth, it landed on the parliament building, killing several key members of the Genetics Council, including the boys' parents. The reverberations of Black Bolt's voice also affected Maximus, who was standing nearby, addling his sanity and suppressing his nascent mental powers. When Black Bolt assumed the throne shortly thereafter, Maximus vowed to oppose his brother and eventually usurp his rule.

Maximus staged his first successful coup a few years later. By performing an illegal experiment on the Alpha Primitives, the subhuman worker clones that once served the Inhumans, Maximus created the Trikon, three bodiless energy beings of great destructive power (see *Alpha Primitives*). While the Trikon wreaked havoc in Attilan, Maximus was able to drive the Royal Family of the Inhumans out of the city in search of the amnesiac Medusa (see *Medusa*). In the several year interval before Black Bolt and his cousins located her in America, Maximus ruled Attilan in Black Bolt's stead. Feeling secure in his position, Maximus bade his servant, the Seeker, to locate the Royal Family and bring them back to Attilan. Immediately upon doing so, Black Bolt seized the crown back, to Maximus's dismay. Maximus, hoping to win back the public's affection, activated the Atmo-Gun device he had been working on, a machine he believed would kill the human race and leave all other living beings intact. Maximus miscalculated, however, and the device had no effect. Out of

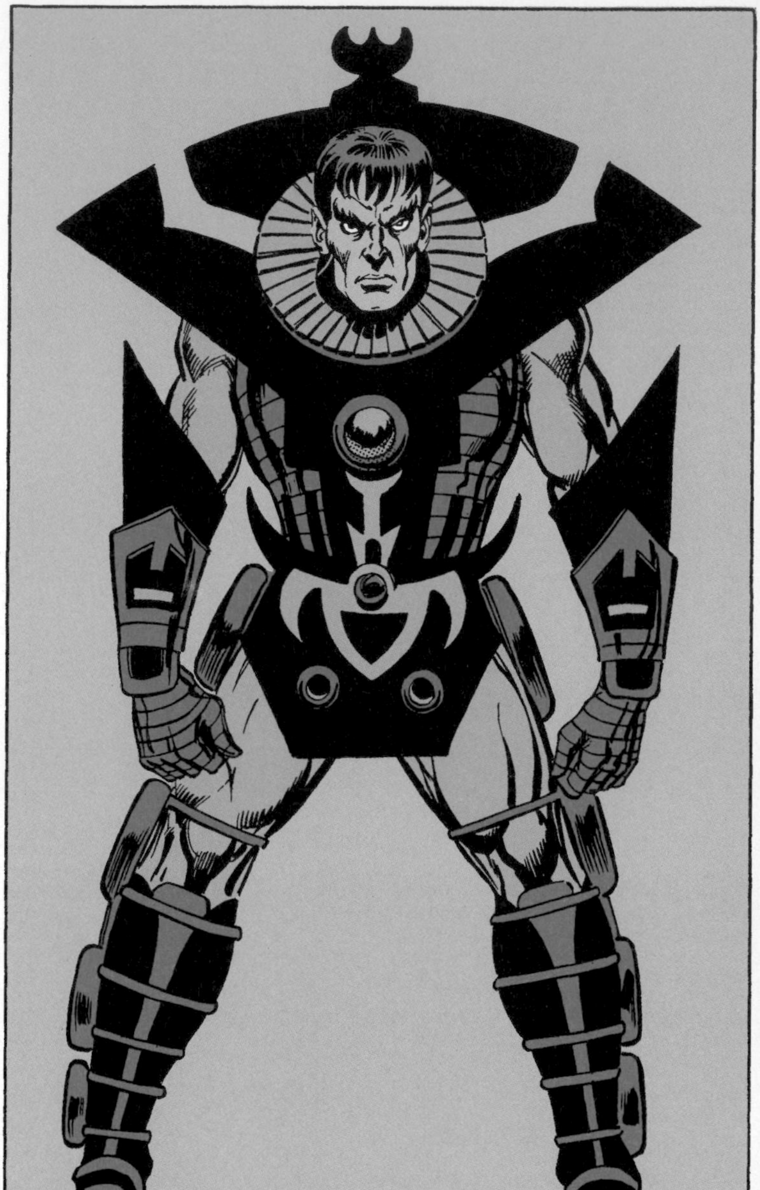

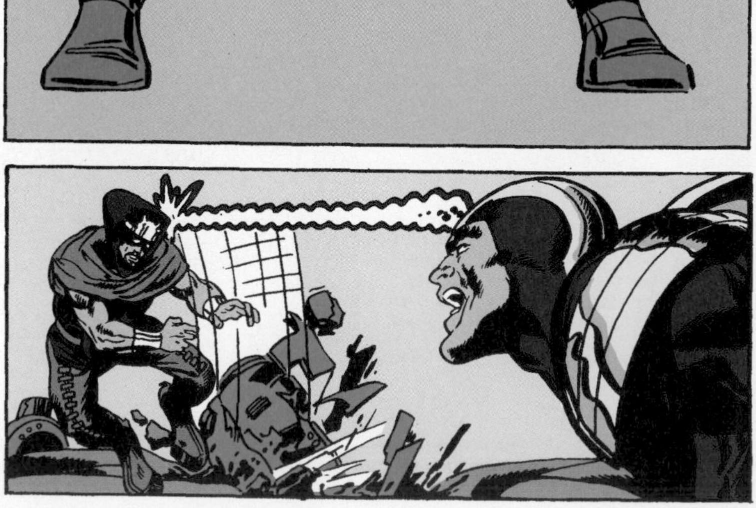

Art by Tom Palmer & Josef Rubinstein

spite, Maximus used the device to erect a "negative zone" (not to be confused with the anti-matter dimension of that name,) a dark force sphere around Attilan, imprisoning the entire race inside. Black Bolt liberated his people by using his quasi-sonic voice to destroy the barrier, at the price of devastating Attilan's ancient architecture.

Maximus then allied himself with six Inhuman criminals, sentenced for their treachery and subversive acts. Freeing Falcona, Aireo, Stallior, Nebulo, Leonus, and Timberius from their place of imprisonment with the Hulk's aid, Maximus then tricked the Hulk into breaching the protective barrier guarding a forbidden chemical substance created by the Inhuman scientist Romnar centuries previous (see *Hulk*). This substance had certain highly unstable energy-absorbing capacities and Maximus intended to use it to usurp the throne again. Black Bolt overpowered him before he could do so.

Maximus succeeded in bringing about his second coup some months later. Drugging the Royal Family with will-deadening "hypno-potions," Maximus wrested the crown from Black Bolt and had the Royal Family imprisoned. Before he could activate his Hypno-Gun which he believed would make all mankind surrender to his will, the Royal Family escaped and subdued him. Maximus's first coup had lasted several years; his second one several days. Escaping Attilan with his band of renegades in a rocket, Maximus landed in the South American country of Costa Salvador, and attempted to build a will-deadening device similar to his Hypno-Gun. His plans were opposed by the Hulk and the United States Army, however, and he and his allies were forced to flee again.

Returning to Attilan, Maximus was welcomed back by his brother Black Bolt who preferred Maximus to be somewhere he could be watched. Black Bolt detected that Maximus's psionic powers, suppressed since he was an adolescent, were beginning to return. Offering no explanation, Black Bolt had Maximus placed in a suspended animation capsule, inside which he could not use his powers. Black Bolt's cousin Gorgon, however, objected to Black Bolt's inhumane treatment of Maximus and freed him. Maximus immediately used his mental powers to subjugate the minds of the Inhuman populace and to give his brother Black Bolt amnesia. Maximus then restored the dark force barrier around Attilan and began negotiations with the alien Kree to sell certain Inhumans to the Kree to be used as soldiers. Eventually Black Bolt's memory returned, and alongside the Avenger, he returned to Attilan and once again destroyed the barrer (see *Avengers*). The Avengers drove the Kree agent away before he could accomplish his mission and Black Bolt liberated the enslaved Inhumans. Maximus's third takeover of Attilan lasted several weeks.

With his mental powers traumatically submerged, Maximus escaped strict punishment for his treachery by feigning insanity. He then began work on his next project to usurp the throne, the construction of the android Omega, whose power source was supposedly the collective guilt evinced by the Inhuman populace over their treatment of the subhuman Alpha Primitives. The Fantastic Four helped the Royal Family thwart the construct, and the damage it caused was slight (see *Fantastic Four*). Maximus staged his fourth successful coup a short time later when the Royal Family had briefly left Attilan

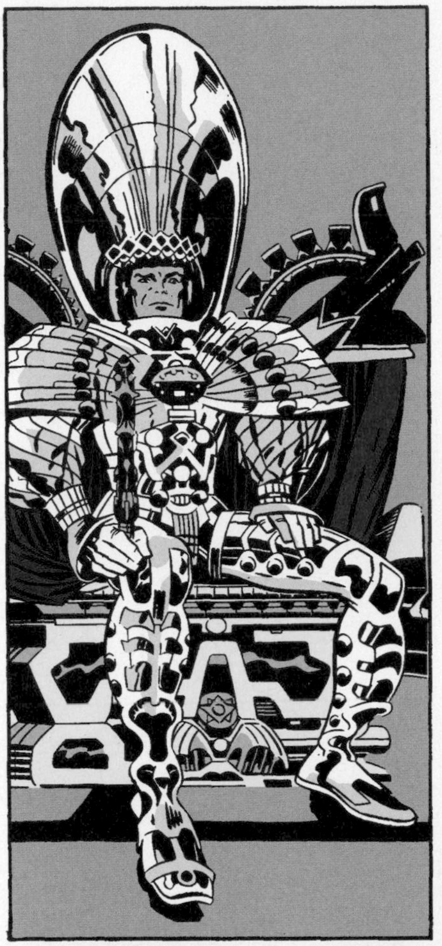

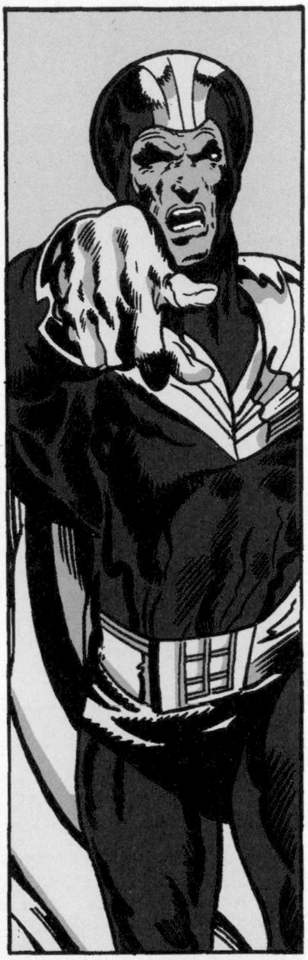

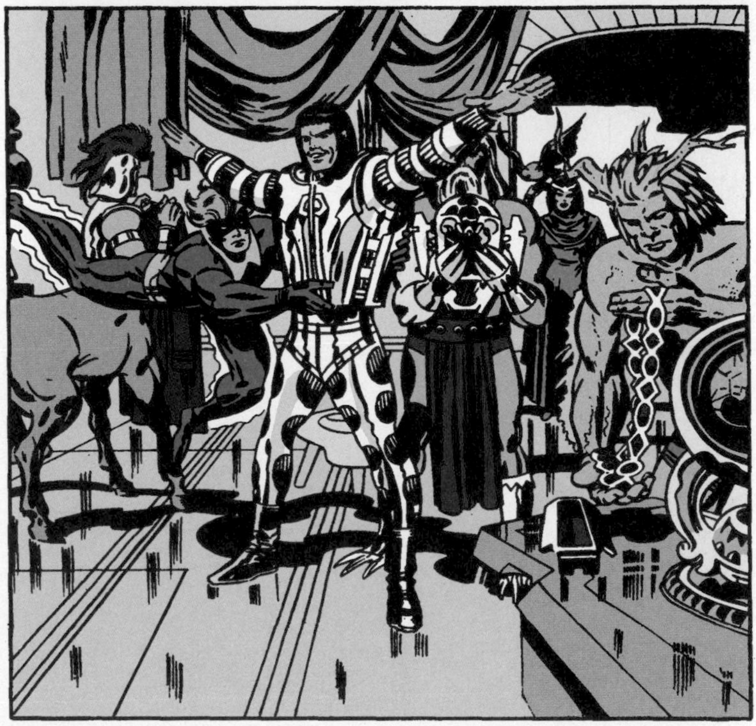

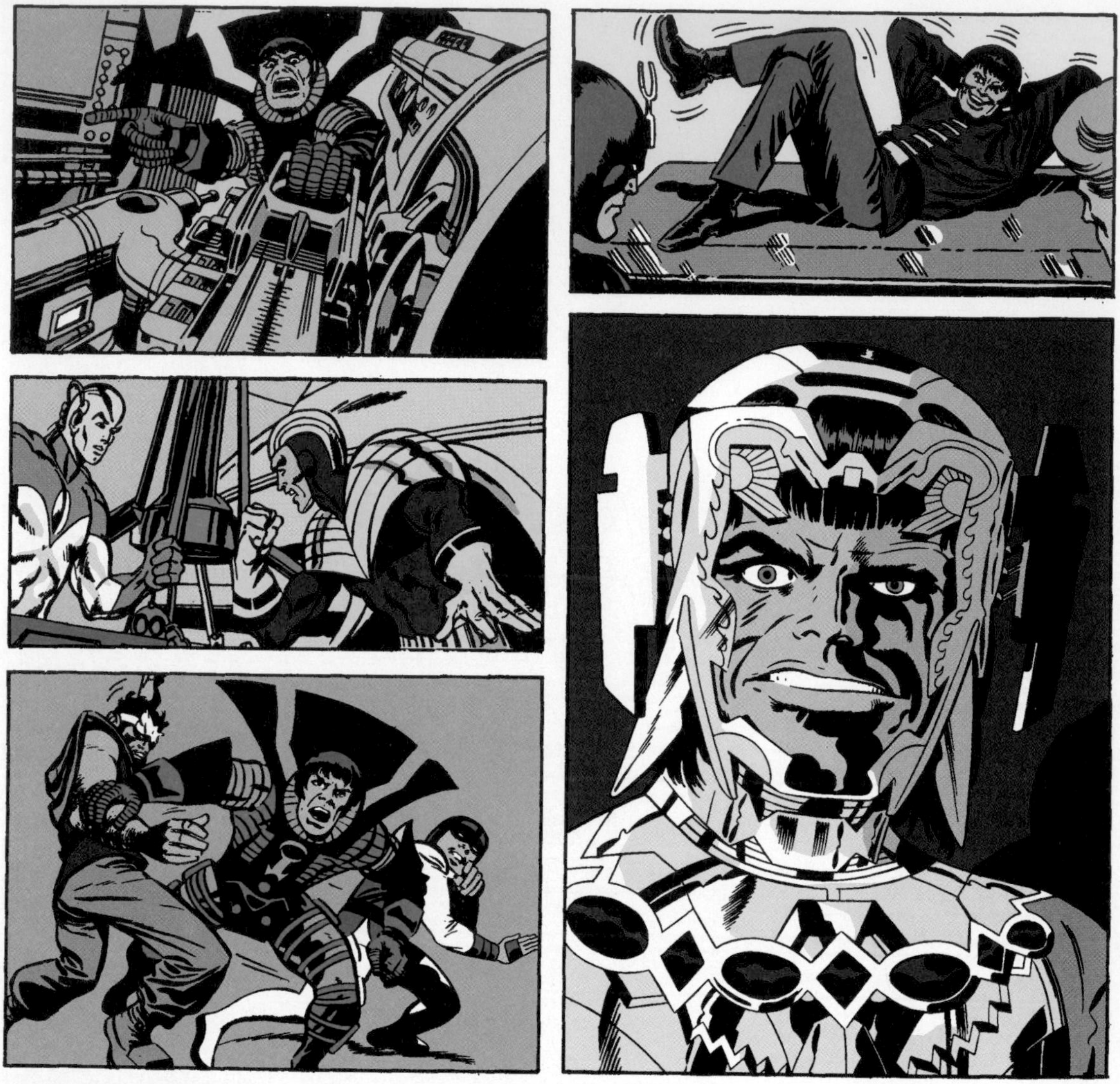

on business. Taking Crystal and her husband Quicksilver captive, Maximus forced Black Bolt to give him the crown in order to spare their lives. Black Bolt did so, and allowed himself to be placed in captivity. Maximus had reestablished contact with the Kree and had negotiated a deal where the Kree would take all of the Inhumans with extraordinary abilities, leaving him the other half of the population to rule. Triton and Karnak managed to rescue most of Maximus's captives and outwit the Kree agent Shatterstar (see *Appendix: Shatterstar*). Unaware of the victory, Black Bolt let loose with his quasi-sonic scream in agony, once again leveling the city. Angered by what had happened, Black Bolt struck Maximus for the first time and had him imprisoned.

Maximus then allied himself with the Enclave, a band of human scientists who managed to capture Medusa (see *Enclave*). The Enclave wanted to conquer Attilan and dispatched an aerial strike force. When the Enclave threatened to execute Medusa, however, Maximus turned on them out of unrequited passion for his brother's betrothed. A weapon Maximus was manning overloaded, leaving Maximus in a death-like coma. Black Bolt had his brother's body placed in a special crypt, and when Attilan was transported from the earth to the moon, Maximus accompanied it. On the moon, Maximus's mind made contact with an alien power crystal located there, and it reawakened his dormant mental powers. When Black Bolt next came to pay his respects to his brother, Maximus was able to use his power to affect a transfer of consciousness between them. For several months Maximus ruled Attilan in Black Bolt's body as Black Bolt lay imprisoned in a tube. Reestablishing contact with the Enclave, Maximus helped them implement meteoroid launchers with which they intended to bombard Earth. With the aid of the Avengers, Maximus's switch was discovered, and the Enclave's schemes were foiled. Maximus was forced to return to his rightful body and was once again placed in solitary confinement. Maximus is currently plotting his sixth takeover of Attilan.

Height: 5′ 11″
Weight: 180 lbs.
Eyes: Blue
Hair: Black
Strength level: Maximus possesses the normal strength of an Inhuman male of his age, height, and build who engages in minimal regular exercise.

Known superhuman powers: Maximus possesses the ability to override the thought processes of other brains around him, although the potency of this power varies greatly over time. At its peak, Maximus can overtake the minds of others. While he is capable of numbing the minds of as many people as there are within a 20-foot radius of him, he can only direct one sort of behavior at a time. He can impose a certain behavior on either a single individual or as many people as are in his radius. Maximus is especially good at controlling the actions of the limitedly intelligent Alpha Primitives worker class. Maximus's power can even cause short-term amnesia if he overpowers a mind with sufficient force. He can blank people's minds or control their actions for as long as he so concentrates: they revert to normal as soon as he stops.

Abilities: Maximus is an inventor of genius level intellect. Despite his mild insanity, he retains an excellent theoretical and practical knowledge of mechanics, physic, and biology. He is particularly gifted at fashioning elaborate machines out of common, simple materials. ■

MEDUSA

Real Name: Medusalith Amaquelin
Occupation: Royal interpreter
Identity: Medusa does not use a dual identity. She is unknown by the general public of Earth to be an Inhuman.
Legal status: Citizen of Attilan
Former aliases: Madame Medusa
Place of birth: Island of Attilan, Atlantic Ocean
Marital status: Married
Known relatives: Quelin (father), Ambur (mother), Crystal (sister), Karnak, Gorgon, Triton (second cousins), Black Bolt (husband), Luna (niece), Pietro Maximoff (brother-in-law)
Group affiliation: Royal Family of the Inhumans, former member of the Frightful Four and Fantastic Four
Base of operations: Attilan, Blue Area, Earth's Moon
First appearance: FANTASTIC FOUR #36
History: Medusa was the first of two children born to the Inhuman nutritionists Quelin and Ambur (see *Inhumans*). Her father Quelin was the brother of Rynda, wife of Agon, king of the Inhumans, and as such she has been considered part of the Royal Family. Medusa's parents elected to expose her to the mutagenic Terrigen Mist when she was an infant, and the process endowed her with hair that she could animate like added appendages. While still in adolescence she began to make frequent visits to the isolation cell of her second cousin, Black Bolt, and learned to communicate with him in a special sign language (see *Black Bolt*). Medusa and Black Bolt developed a special bond between them that blossomed into love when Black Bolt was first allowed out of his cell at the age of eighteen.

In the aftermath of the first coming of the Trikon, Medusa left the Inhumans' Great Refuge (see *Appendix: Trikon*). Afflicted with amnesia sustained in an aircrash, the Inhuman wandered Europe, committing petty thefts to get food to survive. Her animated hair soon brought her unwanted attention and eventually the American criminal called the Wizard heard rumors of her (see *Wizard*). Locating Medusa in Paris, the Wizard brought her to America and enlisted her in the Frightful Four, a band of criminals he had organized. Medusa went along with the criminal activities of the Frightful Four since she felt grateful to the Wizard for her rescue and had nothing better to do. The Frightful Four battled the Fantastic Four, and all but Medusa were captured. Medusa's public exploits enabled Black Bolt and the other members of the Royal Family, who had been exiled from the Great Refuge by Black Bolt's mad brother Maximus, to locate her (see *Maximus*). Seeing them again restored her memory, and they were all taken back to the Great Refuge by the Seeker, an agent of Maximus (see *Appendix: Seeker*).

When Black Bolt regained the throne, Medusa renewed her betrothal to him and served as his royal interpreter. She has remained at his side as his constant companion for most of the time since, seeing the Inhumans through one of their most tumultuous periods in history. Although Medusa has taken various short journeys from the Inhumans' base Attilan without Black Bolt (once where she engaged Spider-Man in battle, another time to thwart the reunion of the Frightful Four), she has only left his side for a period of months twice. The first time she joined the Fantastic Four to take the Invisible Girl's place on the team during her estrangement from her husband (see *Fantastic Four, Invisible Woman*). The second time, she was taken captive by the criminal Enclave, who sought to conquer Attilan (see *Enclave*).

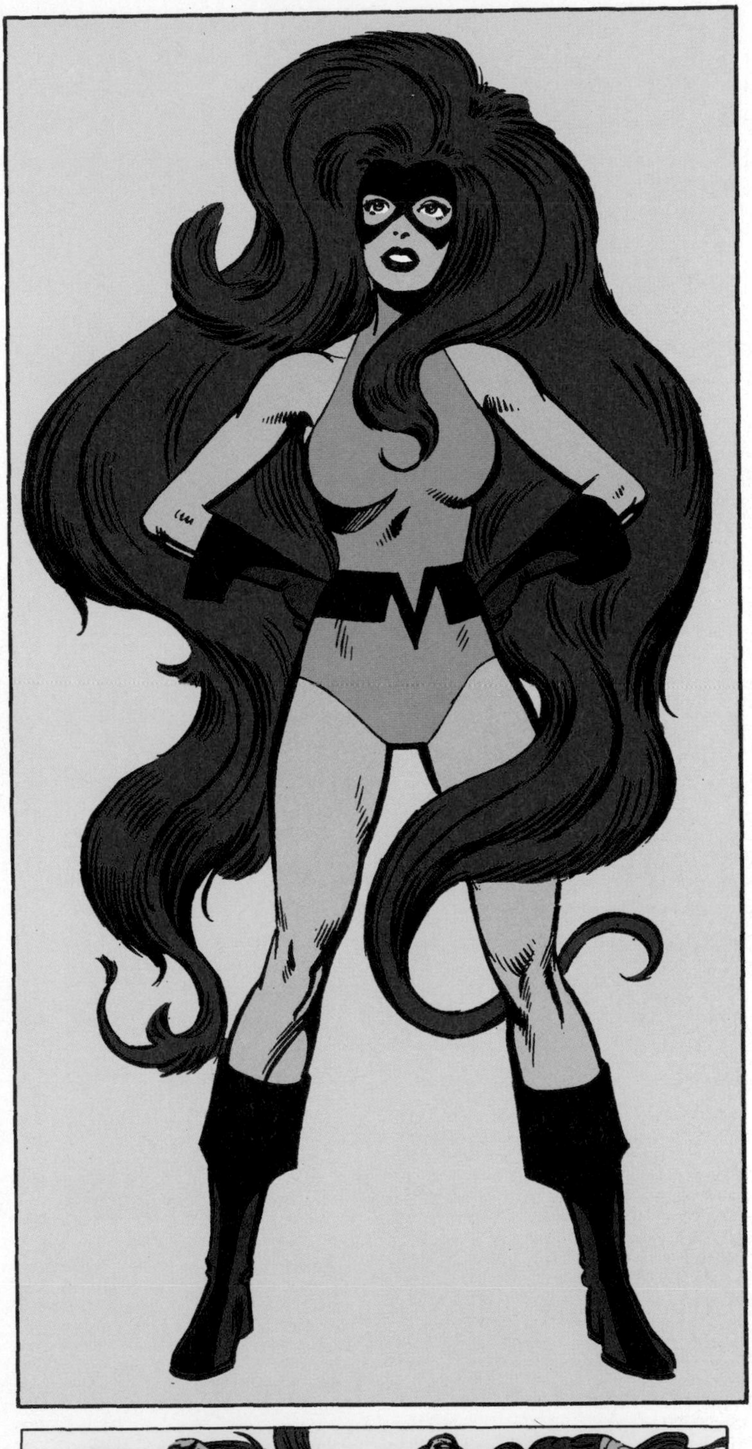

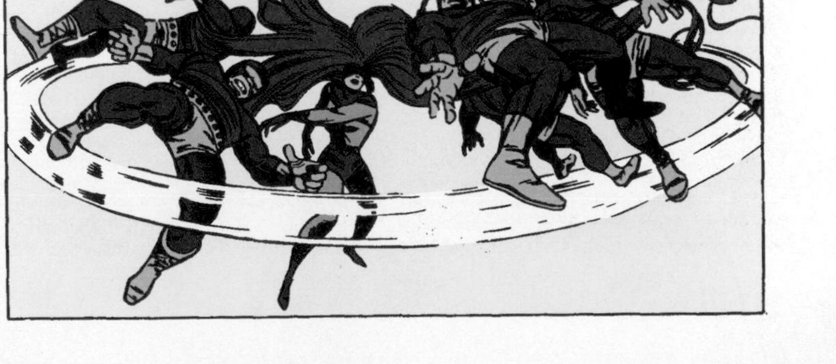

Art by John Byrne & Josef Rubinstein

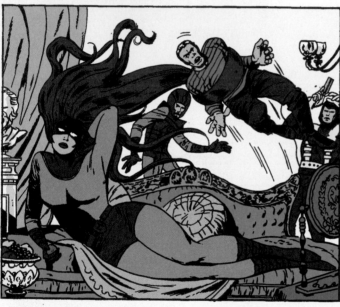

Medusa has recently wed Black Bolt, thus becoming the queen of the Inhumans, after the customary several year royal engagement period was over. She and Black Bolt are expecting a child.

Height: 5′ 11″
Weight: 130 lbs
Eyes: Green
Hair: Red

Strength level: Medusa possesses the normal strength of a female Inhuman of her age, height, and weight who engages in moderate regular exercise. Due to generations of eugenics, Inhumans are superior to humans in strength, reaction time, stamina, resistance to injury, and speed.

Known superhuman powers: Medusa possesses a long, thick head of hair, every strand of which has greater tensile strength, modulus of elasticity, and shear resistance than an iron wire of the same thickness (average hair diameter: .045 inches), as well as the psychokinetic ability to animate her hair

for a number of feats. Her hair, approximately 6 feet in length while relaxed, can elongate to almost twice its normal length with only about a 25% loss of overall tensile strength. One strand of hair, 2-feet long, can support 6.4 pounds, a fist-sized lock of hair can support about 750 pounds and her whole head of hair can lift about 3,200 pounds (1.6 tons). A portion of her hair must be used to anchor the rest at these greater weights, so that more than her scalp/skull is used as a brace.

Medusa can control the movement of her hair as if it were countless thin appendages growing from her head. A psionic field permeates her mutagenically altered hair-cells, causing mutual attraction across the gaps between strands. These relatively small forces operate in conjunction to develop larger forces. Through concentration, she can psionically move her hair in any manner imaginable. She can snap the length of it through the air like a whip (the tip of which

moves faster than the speed of sound), or rotate it in a fan-like manner. She can bind persons or objects with it as if it were rope or use it to lift objects which weigh more than she could lift with her arms. (Her scalp, skull, and neck do not support the weight of an object that she lifts: it is held aloft by the psionic force coursing through the hair.) Medusa can also perform delicate manipulations with her hair such as lock-picking or threading a needle, and such complex acts of coordination as typing or shuffling a deck of cards. Although she has no nerve endings in her hair, she can "feel" sensations on all parts of her hair by a form of mental feedback from her psionic field.

As yet Medusa has not manifested her psychokinetic powers in any way except the animation of her own hair. Whether she has the potential to control other fibrous substances other than her own hair (as can the mutant Gypsy Moth) has not yet been determined (see *Gypsy Moth*). ∎

TRITON

Real name: Unrevealed
Occupation: Scout
Identity: Secret
Legal status: Citizen of Attilan
Former aliases: None
Place of birth: Island of Attilan, Atlantic Ocean
Marital status: Single
Known relatives: Mander (father), Azur (mother), Karnak (brother), Gorgon, Black Bolt, Maximus, Medusa, Crystal (cousins)
Group affiliation: Royal Family of the Inhumans
Base of operations: Attilan, Blue Area, the Moon
First appearance: FANTASTIC FOUR #45

History: Triton is the eldest of two sons born to the Inhuman priest/philosopher named Mander and his wife Azur (see *Inhumans*). Triton was placed in the mutagenic Terrigen Mist when he reached one year of age, and emerged with a number of aquatic mutations. No longer able to breathe air, the young Triton was raised in a specially designed alcove on the shore of the island of Attilan. Triton's mother, a biologist, undertook the study of ocean biology in order to help understand and care for her son. Eventually cumbersome breathing apparatus was designed to enable Triton to survive out of water for extended periods of time. (This apparatus was refined and miniaturized by Maximus some years later. See *Maximus*.) Triton's mother Azur died in an undersea mishap when he was fourteen. At the age of eighteen, Triton became an undersea scout for the Inhumans, keeping watch over human oceangoing traffic in the vicinity. When Triton was captured by sailors, Black Bolt decided that Attilan was in danger of human discovery (see *Attilan, Black Bolt*). Attilan was subsequently moved twice, first to the Himalayas, then to the moon, neither site being close to water. Triton now occupies his time exploring the ancient subterranean water tunnels beneath the moon's Blue City. He occasionally teleports to Earth by means of Lockjaw's power, to swim the oceans and renew old friendships such as that with Prince Namor the Sub-Mariner (see *Lockjaw, Sub-Mariner*).
Height: 6' 1"
Weight: 210 lbs.
Eyes: Green
Hair: None

Unusual features: Triton has scaly, greenish skin over his entire body, webbed feet, a small dorsal fin running from his forehead to the base of his skull and along the length of his spine, and two small fins extending from his temples. Triton has two thin membrane stalks where his eyebrows would be.
Strength level: Triton possesses superhuman strength enabling him to lift (press) approximately 2 tons on land.
Known superhuman powers: Triton possesses a number of superhuman abilities derived from his Terrigen-mutated form. He has a superhumanly strong physiology enabling him to withstand the great water pressure changes that occur beneath the sea. His blood circulation enables him to withstand freezing water temperatures. His vision is more sensitive to the green portion of the visible spectrum, enabling him to see in relatively dark ocean depths. His musculature is adapted for efficient swimming. He can swim at a maximum speed of about 46 knots (40 miles per hour) for several hours before tiring.

As a water-breather, Triton has a number of gills hidden by scales along his throat. These gills enable him to extract sufficient oxygen from ambient water to allow him to function normally while underwater. Triton can live underwater indefinitely. He cannot survive out of water for more than five minutes without special devices before asphixiating. His body is also very susceptible to dehydration.
Paraphernalia: Triton often employs a water circulation system to enable him to function outside water for extended periods of time. The system consists of lengths of plastic tubing running along his torso and limbs which constantly exude a mist of water. Two tiny tubes connect directly to the gills in his throat. In his wrist and ankle gauntlets is a 4-quart supply of water, which is constantly re-oxygenated by means of a selective molecular filter (which allows oxygen molecules to enter the system and respiration waste molecules to exit). The amount of water in the system is continually replenished by a miniaturized moisture condenser located at the rear of Triton's belt. The water is circulated through the tubing by a body-heat powered electric micro-demand pump located next to the selective molecular filter.

■

Art by Mike Zeck & Josef Rubinstein

INHUMANS

The Inhumans are a race of beings who diverged from mainstream humanity twenty-five thousand years ago as a result of genetic experimentation on primitive man performed by the alien Kree (see *Kree*). The Kree had been frequent visitors to Earth's solar system, ever since the alien Skrulls deposited a handful of Kree scientists on Earth's moon in a contest to determine whether to award the Kree the secrets of Skrullian technology (see *Skrulls*). The Kree scientists built the Blue City on the moon, and after seizing certain technologies from the Skrulls, left robotic Sentries on Earth, the moon, and Uranus (see *Sentries*). Millennia after the vastly powerful alien Celestials had performed experiments on primitive man to create the subspecies of humanity called the Eternals, the Eternals engaged in civil war (see *Celestials, Eternals*). The leaders of the vanquished side were exiled into space and happened upon the Kree weapons depot on Uranus. The exiled Eternals fought and destroyed the Kree Sentry posted there, which activated a transgalactic alarm. Believing the destruction to be the handiwork of their enemies the Skrulls, a Kree armada investigated the incident only to discover the Eternals as the culprits. A vivisection of one of the Eternals revealed to the Kree that he was a highly evolved human being. The Kree scientists then petitioned their rulers to be allowed to perform their own experiments on human stock in order to create a race of superhuman warriors to serve the Kree. Returning to Earth, the scientists eventually succeeded in fashioning a small tribe of highly genetically advanced human beings. However, the Kree abandoned their plan to make immediate use of the fledgling race, for reasons as yet undiscovered. This race of beings would someday be known as the Inhumans.

After the Kree left them, the Inhumans wandered the Eurasian continent until they decided to settle upon a tiny island in the Northern Atlantic which they named Attilan (see *Attilan*). There they began to develop technology and culture at an even faster rate than their more powerful predecessors, the Eternals. Chief among their scientific disciplines was genetics, and the Inhumans set up a government based on genocracy, rule by the genetically fittest. Some four thousand years later, mainstream humanity built its first great civilization on the island continent of Atlantis (see *Atlantis*). The Inhumans made every effort to remain isolated from the expanding Atlantean empire, but there must have been some interaction between the peoples to judge by the etymological similarity between the words Atlantis and Attilan. How the Inhumans managed to remain isolated from the Atlanteans is not yet known. Presumably the Inhumans used their superior technology to resist attempts at assimilation. When the continent of Atlantis underwent geothermic upheaval and sank beneath the sea, Attilan somehow protected itself from the cataclysm, again possibly using technology.

Sometime within the Inhumans' first millennium of existence, the Inhuman geneticist Randac isolated a chemical catalyst for human mutation, a substance he called Terrigen. Believing the substance to be the key to making great genetic advances within a single generation's time, Randac subjected himself to total immersion in the Terrigen Mist and emerged with mental-manipulative powers rivalling those of the Eternals. Elected ruler because of his genetic superiority, Randac unselfishly instituted a program by which all Inhumans could undergo Terrigen treatment if they desired. The

program was halted when about half of the Terrigen subjects developed radically nonhuman mutations. It was thereafter decided that individuals would only undergo treatment after being thoroughly genetically tested, but the damage to the gene pool was already done.

Centuries later, an Inhuman leader named Gral, tired of the discrimination against the non-human-looking minority, instituted a reign of terror in which the entire population of Attilan was involuntarily subjected to the mutagenic Terrigen Mist. The Mist transformed over three quarters of the population into non-humanoid types, altering their genetic destinies for untold generations. Successive exposure to the Terrigen only furthered the extent of the mutation. For years, the Inhumans were segregated into Mutation Camps, forced to live only among their own basic phenotypes. Finally, Gral was deposed, and an Inhuman named Auran taught his fellows how to accept the wonderful diversities of their people in peace. This era came to an end about 2,500 years ago, when a contingent of winged Inhumans built their own city suspended high above Attilan. Antagonism between the sky- and ground-dwellers eventually led to the secession of the sky-city from Attilan proper. The small colony of winged Inhumans existed in relative peace until the early part of the Twentieth Century when the race was inadvertently destroyed by a human being they called Red Raven (see *Appendix: Red Raven*).

Over the millennia, Inhuman geneticists have tried to stabilize the diversity of their genetic heritage. Unlike Earth's other genetically variant race, the Deviants, whose offspring tend to inherit none of their parents' genetic traits, Inhuman infants tend to resemble their parents (see *Deviants*). Thus if an Inhuman with amphibian characteristics mated with an Inhuman with avian characteristics, their offspring would have a combination of these traits. This, however, seldom occurs since until recent times, marriages have been arranged by the government to eugenically further the race. At present, rigorous eugenic control has succeeded in restoring about a quarter of the Mutation Camp victims' descendants to human-looking normalcy. Slightly less than half of the present population of Attilan has a visible non-humanoid mutation.

About four thousand years ago, an Inhuman named Avadar convinced the Council of Genetics to lift their ban on cloning experimentation so that he could genetically design a sub-human drone capable of performing all of the menial labors necessary to society. The Council agreed, and Avadar produced a line of worker-clones called the Alpha Primitives (see *Alpha Primitives*). It has only been in recent times that the practice of cloning new slave laborers has ceased.

Since the time of Randac, the government of the Inhumans has consisted of the twelve-member Genetic Council, which is the major legislative, judicial, and executive body. Each Council member belongs to a different family or House, and is elected to membership by the other members of the Council. Membership in the Genetics Council is for life (unless the member commits a crime against the state and is expelled). Consequently membership changes in the Council only when there is a vacancy due to death. The Council elects one of its members as both head of the Council and ruler (or "king") of the Inhumans. This ruler customarily reigns from election to his or her death (again barring dishonorable removal). It takes all eleven other members of the Genetics Council to remove a ruler

from the throne. Kingship then does not follow a strict patriarchal or matriarchal progression, although popular rulers are often succeeded by their sons or daughters. The designation "Royal Family" is a ceremonial one that is passed on from House to House with successive kings.

About 110 years ago, an Inhuman named Agon was elected to the Genetics Council, and subsequently to rulership over the Inhumans. Agon proved to be one of the most popular rulers since Auran. A skilled geneticist, Agon made significant advances in the prediction of Terrigen effects on the Inhuman gene, and convinced his wife Rynda to subject herself to the Terrigen Mist while pregnant. Their son Blackagar (popularly called Black Bolt), became the most powerful Inhuman in the race's history, surpassing the powers of Randac himself (see *Black Bolt*). Agon and Rynda persuaded their brothers and sisters to also subject their children to the mist *in utero*, and each of their offspring was born with a different superhuman ability or mutation. Agon was a decisive ruler, and when he caught a Council member named Phaeder experimenting with clones, he persuaded the Council to have him expelled. Phaeder protested that it was anti-scientific to restrict cloning to the perpetuation of the Alpha Primitives, but Agon prevailed. Faking his own suicide with a clone of himself, Phaeder left Attilan and eventually bore a son to an as yet unknown woman. The son was named Maelstrom, and later became a dangerous enemy of Attilan as well as a purveyor of Attilan's most guarded secret, Terrigen (see *Maelstrom*). About ninety years into Agon's reign, the Kree finally renewed their interest in recruiting the Inhumans for their war effort. Agon's second son, the sinister Maximus, entered into secret negotiations with emissaries of the Kree (see *Maximus*). When Maximus' brother, Black Bolt discovered the treacherous liaison, he used his quasi-sonic powers to blast the Kree spy-ship out of the sky. The damaged ship fell to the Earth, crashing into the laboratory where Agon and Rynda were working. They were killed instantly. Because Agon was such a popular leader, Black Bolt was elected to the Genetics Council to succeed him, and despite his silent protests was soon crowned the new ruler of Attilan.

Black Bolt's rule has been the most tumultuous in the Inhumans' history. Within a year after ascending the throne, Black Bolt was faced with the probable discovery of Attilan by the outside world. To solve this problem, Black Bolt scouted out a new location for the island and found one in the remote Himalayan Mountains of Tibet. While searching for the new site, Black Bolt encountered Ikaris of the Eternals (see *Ikaris*). The Eternals helped excavate the pit that would be Attilan's new foundation. Black Bolt then returned to Attilan and manufactured anti-gravity generators based on those that kept the floating city aloft millennia before. After digging out the base of the island and mounting the anti-gravity generators underneath, the entire island was moved from the mid-Atlantic to the Himalayas. Shortly thereafter, Black Bolt's kingship was challenged by his brother Maximus. With the aid of three transformed Alpha Primitives called the Trikon, Maximus sparked Attilan's first civil war in millennia, a war that succeeded in driving Black Bolt from the throne and into forced exile. For almost a decade, Black Bolt and his loyal cousins wandered Asia, Europe, and finally America. When they finally returned to Attilan, Black Bolt wrested the crown once more from Maximus. Maximus tried to regain the crown from Black Bolt on subsequent occasions, but was never as successful as he had been in his initial attempt. On the second of these attempts,

Maximus manacled Black Bolt and deprived him of food or water for close to a week, while forcing half the Inhuman populace to board an ark to deliver them to the Kree. In this abject state, Black Bolt misjudged his power and in an attempt to destroy the ark, leveled the entire city of Attilan. It was later rebuilt with a totally different style of architecture.

Black Bolt was also obliged to relocate the Inhumans' home for the second time in less than half a century. The debilitating effects of Earth's pollution caused a great plague to sweep through Attilan, and in order to save his people, Black Bolt once again used the anti-gravity generators to move the entire island. This time Attilan was moved off Earth entirely, to the Blue City on the moon. Ironically, the Blue City is a product of the Kree, even as are the Inhumans themselves. The Blue City retains a germ-free oxygen-rich atmosphere, and the anti-gravity generators have been adjusted to create a normal Earth-like gravity beneath Attilan. Although certain radar systems, satellites, and intelligence agencies detected Attilan's exodus, the general public of Earth was unaware of the event. The general public is aware of the existence of the Inhuman race, although few human beings outside the Fantastic Four and Avengers have ever been to Attilan.

At present there are about 1,230 living Inhumans, all of whom dwell in Attilan. By stringent governmental restriction, the Inhumans practice zero population growth, allowing couples to bear a maximum of two offspring. The government also has strict laws regulating Terrigen Mist exposure. Couples must undergo strict genetic testing before their offspring are permitted to be exposed to the Mist. Exposure of infants *in utero* is only permitted if the mother has not already been previously exposed to the Terrigen Mist. If the genetic screening determines a low risk factor, a couple may elect to subject their child to the Mist between one and six years of age. If an individual did not become exposed to the Mist when a child, he or she has the right to choose to take the treatment when he or she reaches 31, the legal age of consent. Recent statistics show that less than half the children born are Terrigenated and only about one tenth of the non-exposed adults choose to undergo the process at 31. At present only about half of the Inhuman population possesses obvious non-human characteristics either through heredity or Terrigen mutation.

Inhumans speak their own language, Tilan, but in recent years, many have elected to learn such human languages as English, Russian, and Chinese. The Inhumans have various trade guilds managing the various disciplines necessary to maintain society. Almost three-fourths of all Inhumans elect to go into their parents' professions. Food is cultivated in hydroponic gardens beneath the city. The chief pursuit of the people is science, but they also have various artists' guilds, including a theatrical company which provide circus-like entertainments as well as a cycle of plays based on famous incidents in Inhuman history. The major religion of the Inhumans involves ancestor-worship and there is a guild of priests and priestesses who administer the faith. Attilan has traditionally had a small police force and perimeter patrol, which, under Black Bolt's rule, has expanded into a small militia of about 50 specially-trained soldiers. Since Attilan has never been at war with any other country, the militia is customarily used as an internal peace keeping force. Attilan has one prison and the king of Attilan serves as its sole judge. Despite the diversity of its citizenry, Inhuman society remains relatively stable, homogenous, and austere.

First appearance: FANTASTIC FOUR #45. ∎

SEEKER

Real Name: Unrevealed
Occupation: Royal ambassador, agent
Legal status: Citizen of Attilan with no criminal record
Identity: No dual identity; existence not known to the general public of Earth
Place of birth: Attilan, Atlantic Ocean
Marital status: Married
Known relatives: None
Height: 6′
Weight: 210 lbs.
Eyes: Brown
Hair: Black
History: The Seeker was appointed by Maximus, then-ruler of Attilan, to find and retrieve the exiled Royal Family so that Maximus could wed Medusa and keep the others under observation.
Strength level: Normal Inhuman non-athlete
Known superhuman powers: None
Weapons: The Seeker employs advanced technology such as the distorter gun.
First appearance: FANTASTIC FOUR #46

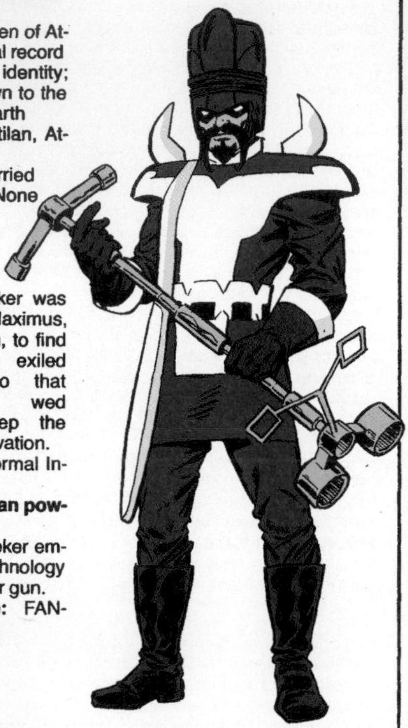

AIREO

Real Name: Unrevealed
Occupation: Former perimeter patrolman, now renegade
Legal status: Citizen of Attilan with record of treason
Identity: No dual identity; existence not known to the general public of Earth
Place of birth: Attilan, Atlantic Ocean
Marital status: Single
Known relatives: None
Height: 5′ 9″
Weight: 110 lbs.
Eyes: Blue
Hair: Reddish blond
History: Aireo underwent Terrigenation soon after birth to gain his superhuman power. He supported Maximus in his first successful takeover of Attilan, as well as his raid on Romnar's hold.
Strength level: Normal Inhuman non-athlete
Known superhuman powers: Aireo can become lighter than air and thus fly at will.
First appearance: FANTASTIC FOUR #47

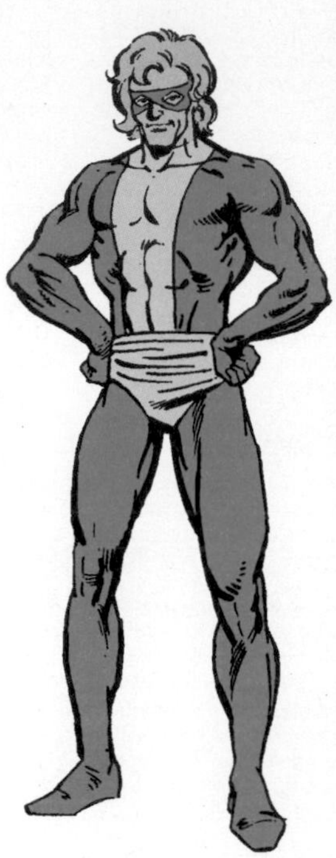

FALCONA

Real Name: Unrevealed
Occupation: Former game keeper, now renegade
Legal status: Citizen of Attilan with record of treason
Identity: No dual identity; existence not known to the general public of Earth
Place of birth: Attilan, Atlantic Ocean
Marital status: Single
Known relatives: None
Height: 5′ 10″
Weight: 135 lbs.
Eyes: Blue
Hair: Black
History: Falcona acquired her affinity for wild birds from undergoing Terrigenation as an infant. She supported Maximus's military takeover.
Strength level: Normal Inhuman non-athlete
Known superhuman powers: Falcona can mentally control all birds of prey, especially falcons.
First appearance: INCREDIBLE HULK ANNUAL #1

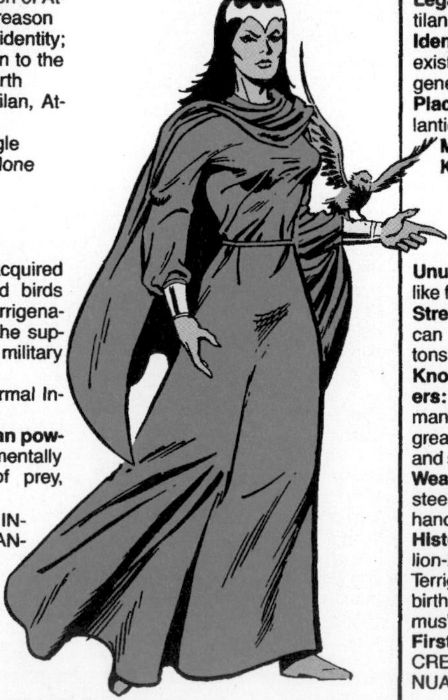

LEONUS

Real Name: Unrevealed
Occupation: Former guardsman, now renegade
Legal status: Citizen of Attilan with record of treason
Identity: No dual identity; existence not known to the general public of Earth
Place of birth: Attilan, Atlantic Ocean
Marital status: Single
Known relatives: None
Height: 6′ 4″
Weight: 230 lbs.
Eyes: Brown
Hair: Blond
Unusual features: Lion-like face, hands and feet
Strength level: Leonus can lift (press) about 10 tons.
Known superhuman powers: Besides his superhuman strength, Leonus has great endurance, agility, and speed.
Weapons: Leonus wears steel-like claws on his hands and feet.
History: Leonus gained lion-like attributes upon his Terrigenation soon after birth. He supported Maximus's military takeover.
First appearance: INCREDIBLE HULK ANNUAL #1

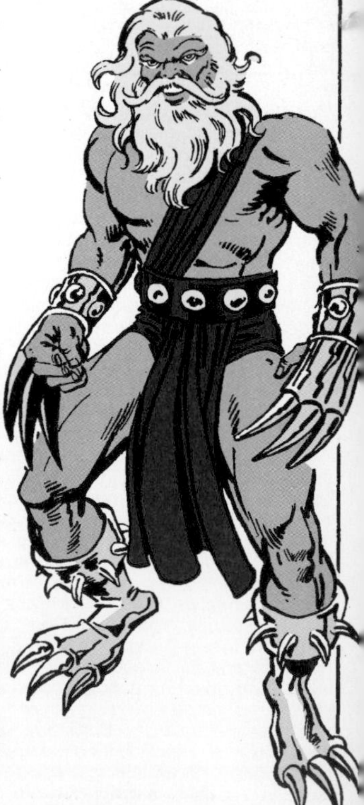

Art by Bob Budiansky & Josef Rubinstein

STALLIOR

Real Name: Unrevealed
Occupation: Former guardsman, now renegade
Legal status: Citizen of Attilan with record of treason
Identity: No dual identity; existence not known to the general public of Earth
Place of birth: Attilan, Atlantic Ocean
Marital status: Single
Known relatives: Chiron (brother)
Height: 7' 1"
Weight: 425 lbs.
Eyes: Brown
Hair: Black
Unusual features: Part human, part horse body (centaur)

History: Stallior's family all has centaurian bodies due to the hereditary transfer of Terrigenated attributes from ten generations. He supported Maximus's military takeover.
Strength level: Normal Inhuman athlete
Known superhuman powers: Stallior has great speed and endurance, and can use his hooves for fighting.
Weapons: Stallior often uses a ball and chain.
First appearance: INCREDIBLE HULK ANNUAL #1

TIMBERIUS

Real Name: Unrevealed
Occupation: Former gardener, now renegade
Legal status: Citizen of Attilan with record of treason
Identity: No dual identity; existence not known to the general public of Earth
Place of birth: Attilan, Atlantic Ocean
Marital status: Single
Known relatives: None
Height: 6' 1"
Weight: 210 lbs.
Eyes: Brown
Hair: None
Unusual features: His skin resembles the bark of a tree
History: Timberius's adaptation was the result of an authorized experiment utilizing plant DNA and Terrigen. He supported Maximus's military takeover.
Strength level: Normal Inhuman athlete
Known superhuman powers: Timberius can cause rapid, wild growth in all plants by touching them.
First appearance: INCREDIBLE HULK ANNUAL #1

LUNA

Real Name: Luna Maximoff
Occupation: Unemployed minor
Legal status: Citizen of Attilan with no criminal record
Identity: No dual identity; existence not known to the general public of Earth
Place of birth: Attilan, the Moon
Marital status: Single
Known relatives: Pietro Maximoff (Quicksilver, father), Crystal (mother), Medusa (aunt), Black Bolt (uncle), Magneto (grandfather)
Height: 1' 11"
Weight: 15 lbs.
Eyes: Blue
Hair: Blonde
History: Luna is the first known offspring of an Inhuman and a human mutant. She displayed no superhuman attributes at birth, and her father had to be persuaded not to Terrigenate her.
Strength level: Normal Inhuman for her age
Known superhuman powers: None
First appearance: FANTASTIC FOUR #240

AGON
Father of Black Bolt (deceased)
First appeared in THOR #148

RYNDA
Mother of Black Bolt (deceased)
First appeared in THOR #148

MAKOTH
Colleague of Randac (deceased)
First appeared in THOR #146

RANDAC
Discoverer of Terrigen (deceased)
First appeared in THOR #147

PHAEDER
Exiled rival of Agon (deceased)
First appeared in TWO-IN-ONE #71

ASMODEUS
Winged guardsman
First appeared in FANTASTIC
FOUR #117

KALIBAN
Guardsman
First appeared in FANTASTIC
FOUR #117

CHIRON
Centaur guardsman
First appeared in FANTASTIC
FOUR #129

FLAIDERMAUS
Flying guardsman
First appeared in FANTASTIC
FOUR #129

AVIUS
Winged guardsman
First appeared in FANTASTIC
FOUR #129

PINYON
Flying guardsman
First appeared in FANTASTIC
FOUR #129

PISKAS
Fish-like citizen
First appeared in FANTASTIC
FOUR #131

DOMINUS
First appeared in FANTASTIC
FOUR #131

GLYTRA
Winged citizen
First appeared in FANTASTIC
FOUR #240

MARAK
Physician
First appeared in FANTASTIC
FOUR #240

NADAR
Scientist
First appeared in TWO-IN-ONE #71

BUDAN
Technician
First appeared in TWO-IN-ONE #71

THRAXTON
Would-be conqueror
First appeared in FF ANNUAL #12

NEBULO
Semi-intangible malcontent
First appeared in HULK ANNUAL #1

ROMNAR
Chemist (deceased)
First appeared in HULK ANNUAL #1

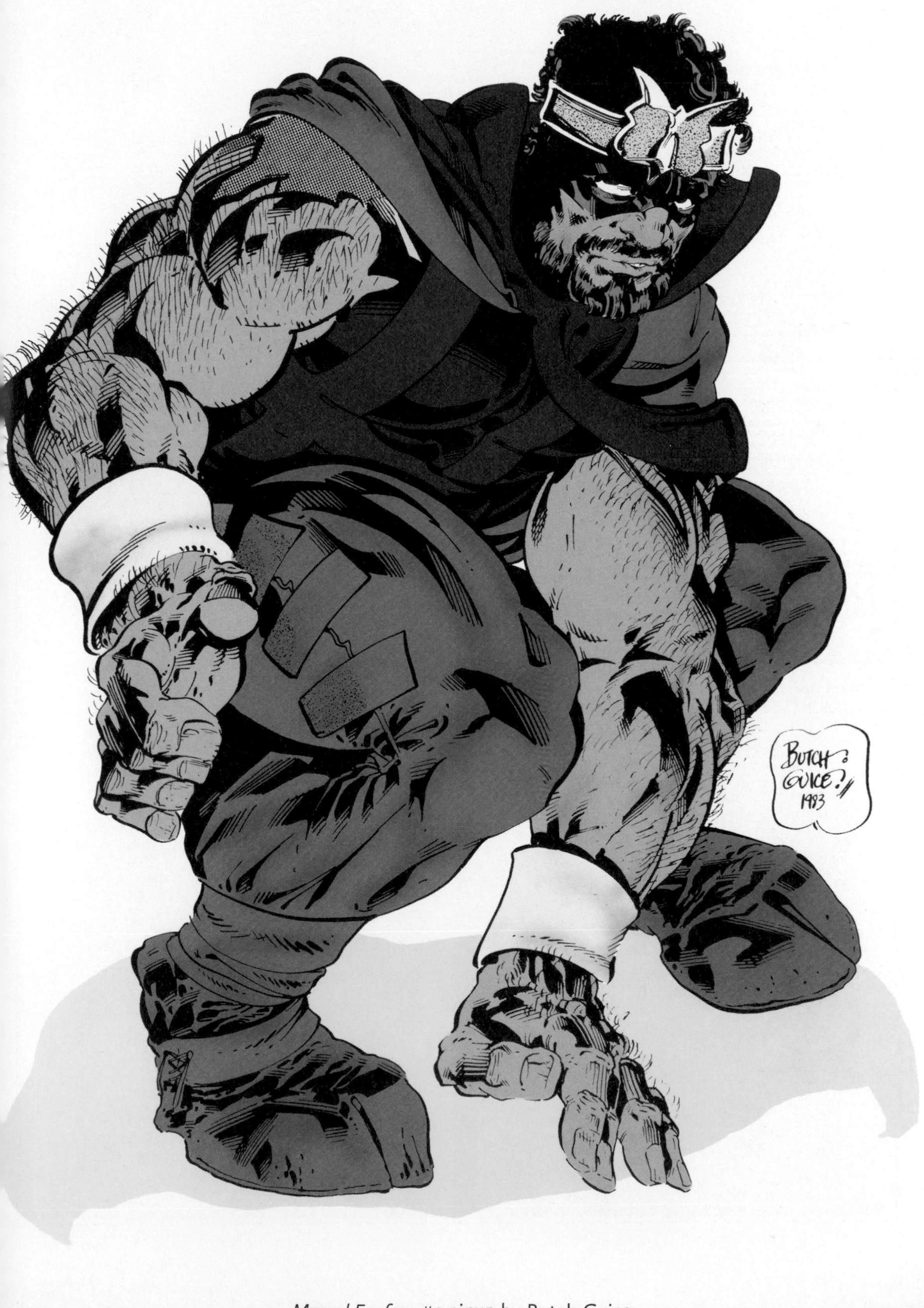
BUTCH GUICE 1983

Marvel Fanfare #9 pinup by Butch Guice

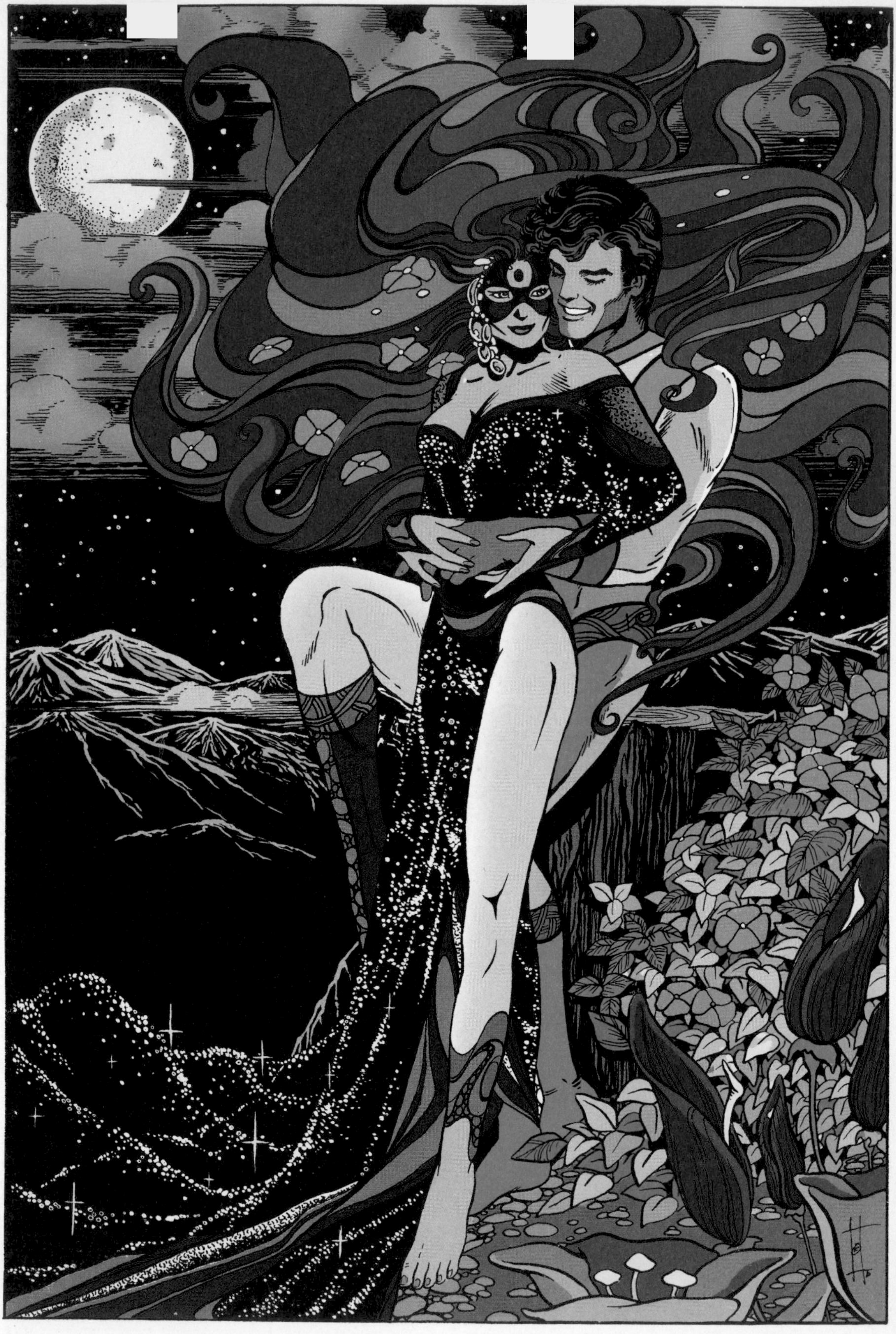

Marvel Fanfare #38 pinup by Colleen Doran & Petra Scotese